SANTA FE, TAOS & ALBUQUERQUE

ZORA O'NEILL

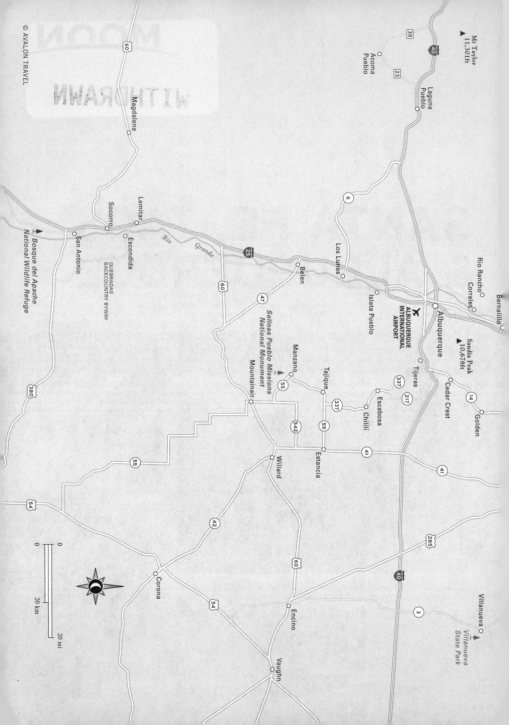

Mt Taylor
11,301ft

38

40

Acoma
Pueblo

23

Laguna
Pueblo

6

Rio Rancho
Corrales

Bernalillo

Sandia Peak
10,678ft

ALBUQUERQUE
INTERNATIONAL
AIRPORT

Albuquerque

Tijeras

337

217

Cedar Crest

14

Golden

Los Lunas

Isleta Pueblo

Manzano

55

Tajique

337

Escabosa

Chilili

55

41

41

285

40

3

Villanueva

Villanueva
State Park

Magdalena

Socorro

Lemitar

Rio Grande

25

Belen

47

60

Salinas Pueblo Missions
National Monument

Mountainair

542

Estancia

Willard

55

Encino

60

54

Vaughn

Corona

42

San Antonio

Escondida

QUEBRADAS
BACKCOUNTRY BYWAY

Bosque del Apache
National Wildlife Refuge

380

54

60

0

20 km

0

20 mi

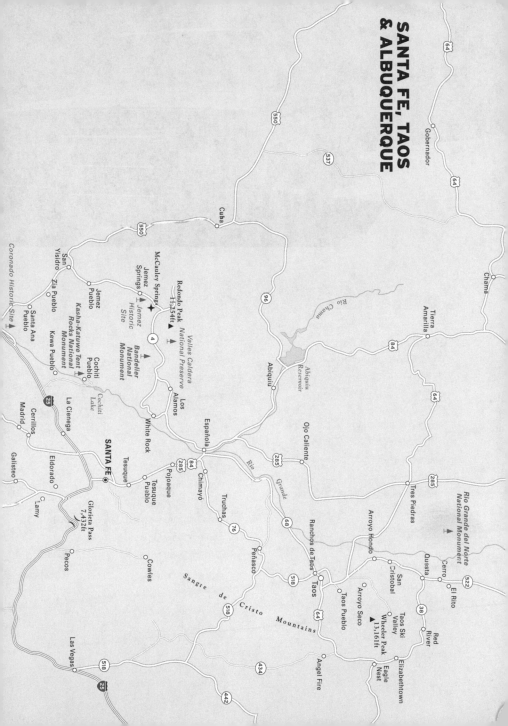

Contents

DISCOVER
Santa Fe, Taos & Albuquerque

When I tell people I grew up in Albuquerque, I often get a blank stare, and sometimes a Bugs Bunny joke. "That's New Mexico, right?" some say cautiously. "I've never met anyone from there." Yes, it's *New* Mexico, it's part of the United States, and for some reason, we don't get out much.

Maybe we're lazy from a lack of oxygen— Albuquerque is 5,352 feet above sea level, and Wheeler Peak, which overshadows Taos, hits 13,161 feet. More likely, it's because New Mexico, and particularly the stretch between Albuquerque and Taos, is so astonishingly beautiful: red sandstone canyons, pine-studded mountain ranges, dramatic gorges. Why go anywhere else, when you can smell lilacs in spring, ozone after summer thunderstorms, spicy roasting green chile, and fragrant piñon crackling in fireplaces? Why stray, when coyotes yelp in the night, western tanagers warble in the trees, and the drums boom at pueblo ceremonies? Why move an inch, when you live under this singular sky: by day, a cloudless, turquoise dome; by night, a velvet backdrop clotted with stars.

I strayed, but I feel fortunate to have this place to return to. It may not be another country, but it is another world. Nicknamed the Land of Enchantment,

---

Clockwise from top left: chile and boot decoration; Santuario de Guadalupe in Santa Fe; skull decor; luminarias in Santa Fe; fresh green chile; winter near Taos

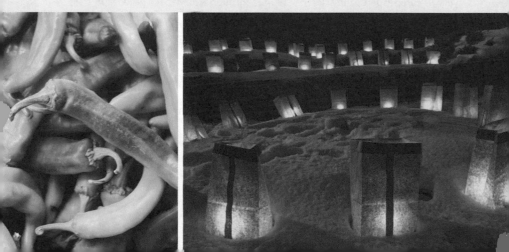

New Mexico may as well be Wonderland. Sixteenth-century Spanish is spoken in tiny mountain towns north of Santa Fe, while in Albuquerque, people fight to preserve Route 66 motor courts built in the 1950s. Santa Fe is a faux-adobe utopia where the economy magically thrives on art and politics, and the hippie homesteaders of Taos aim to get off the grid—the same way the neighboring pueblo has been, for hundreds of years.

Visitors might need time to adjust—to the altitude, certainly, and maybe also to the laid-back attitude. But there's a point of entry for everyone. Outdoor adventurers can hike for an hour or a week, along mountainsides thick with yellow-leafed aspens, and skiers can plunge through armpit-deep powder at Taos Ski Valley, one of the country's most thrilling downhill runs. Culture mavens thrive in Santa Fe, with its world-class contemporary art scene and an eclectic calendar of international film and music. History buffs can climb to ancient cave dwellings, wander among crumbling Franciscan mission churches, or ogle vintage neon signs in Albuquerque.

At the end of the day, you can always pull yourself back into the present with a cold margarita and cuisine with a hot-chile kick—but that's no guarantee you'll shake off northern New Mexico's spell.

Clockwise from top left: truck near Elizabethtown; Rio Grande Gorge near Taos; wild iris in the Enchanted Circle; Christ in the Desert Monastery

Planning Your Trip

Where to Go

Santa Fe

A network of little streets and thick-walled adobe homes, New Mexico's picturesque capital has a human scale and a golden glow. **Museums** are a major draw—for state history, folk art, and more—as are the scores of **galleries** lining Canyon Road. Great **hiking** trails are just a few minutes' drive—or head farther, to the cliff dwellings at **Bandelier National Monument;** to **Abiquiu,** where the scenery inspired painter Georgia O'Keeffe; or to **Los Alamos,** birthplace of the A-bomb.

Taos

A small town of about 6,000, Taos is home to **artists,** trust-fund **hippies, spiritual seekers,** and ski bums—in addition to the Spanish and American Indian families who've called the place home for centuries. There's some sightseeing, at the ancient **Taos Pueblo,** an iconic church, a handful of small museums, and **Taos Ski Valley,** a pilgrimage site for many. But its atmosphere, cultivated in mellow coffee shops and **hidden hot springs,** is the real attraction. Make a day drive around the **Enchanted Circle,** a loop of two-lane roads through high valleys.

Albuquerque

A modern Western city, and the state's biggest, Albuquerque sprawls at the base of the **Sandia Mountains.** It's proud of its Route 66 vintage style, but it's also preserving **farmland** along the **Rio Grande** and redesigning itself as a green burg. To the west, **Acoma Pueblo** sits atop a monolithic mesa, while the wetlands of the **Bosque del Apache National Wildlife Refuge** to the south attract thousands of birds. Head north to Santa Fe through the ghost towns of the **Turquoise Trail** or to the red rocks of the **Jemez Mountains.**

Dramatic cliffs edge the highway north of Abiquiu.

hot-air ballooning over Albuquerque

If You Have . . .

- **Three days:** Pick one city to explore.

- **Five days:** Visit Santa Fe, with a night in Taos; or do Albuquerque, with a night in Santa Fe.

- **One week:** From Santa Fe, add a day in Abiquiu and Bandelier; from Albuquerque, visit Acoma.

- **Two weeks:** Do it all, including the Jemez Mountains and the Bosque.

red rocks on the Jemez Mountain

When to Go

With 300 days of sunshine annually, New Mexico is ready for visitors anytime. **High season** for tourism is mid-May to mid-September, but the early summer can be hot, windy, and dry, with a risk of forest fires. The weather is far more pleasant from **July** on, when the day's heat is usually tamed with a strong, brief rainstorm in the afternoon, and the desert turns green. **Summer** is the only time to hike at higher elevations, as many trails are still snow-covered as late as May. If you want to go **rafting**, plan on late May and early June, when the snowmelt makes the rivers run high and wild. **Winter** sees a surge of visitors heading straight to the ski trails, and traditional celebrations preceding Christmas are wonderful; many sights are closed or have limited hours, however.

The **shoulder seasons** have their own appeal and can be cheaper, particularly in **April**, when ski season has wound down, and in **November**, when it hasn't gotten started. But note that **Taos Pueblo closes** to visitors for about 10 weeks between February and April. And **spring** weather is risky, with chances of snowfall or ceaseless hot winds—and lots of mud. In the **fall**, the crowds disperse, leaving crisp temperatures and generally clear skies through late October—great **hiking** weather, especially among the aspen trees, which turn a brilliant yellow.

If you're planning a visit between Christmas and New Year's, during Santa Fe's summer art markets, or for the October balloon fest in Albuquerque, **book a hotel at least six months in advance.**

autumn in Santa Fe

spring in Santa Fe

New Mexico is a just-show-up kind of place, but a few special elements require some forethought.

- **Ceremonial dances:** Attending a ceremonial dance is worth planning a trip around. They occur several times a year at every pueblo, on village feast days, Catholic holidays, and around seasonal turning points. Check the schedules for Taos Pueblo (page 119), as well as pueblos around Santa Fe (page 72) and Albuquerque (page 164) in advance.

- **Georgia O'Keeffe Home:** The house in Abiquiu is open to guided tours mid-March through November; book at least a month in advance (page 82).

- **Santa Fe Opera:** Online ticket sales start in October for the July and August summer season; book in the winter for the best seat selection (page 46).

- **Santa Fe Indian Market** (August), **Spanish Market** (July), and **Christmas:** Book Santa Fe hotels six to eight months ahead.

Christmas in Santa Fe

basket dancers at Ohkay Owingeh

The Best of Santa Fe, Taos & Albuquerque

While you could conceivably explore Santa Fe, Taos, and Albuquerque for several weeks, seeking out ever more obscure hiking trails and sweeping vistas, six days gives just enough time to appreciate the distinct character of each community.

Day 1

Arrive at Albuquerque's Sunport airport; transfer directly to **Santa Fe.** If you want old-school style, stay at La Fonda—it's that much easier to get to bed after dinner at The Shed nearby and a margarita in the hotel lobby bar.

Day 2

Start with a breakfast burrito at Tia Sophia's, then stroll around the plaza. Depending on your interests, visit the history museum at the **Palace of the Governors** or the **New Mexico Museum of Art.** Pop in to see the free art collection at the **State Capitol,** then cruise the galleries on **Canyon Road,** finishing up with drinks and tapas, and maybe even dancing at El Farol.

Day 3

Get an early start to **Bandelier National Monument,** followed by a late lunch at JoAnn's Ranch O Casados in Española. In late afternoon, return to Santa Fe to stroll around the **Railyard district,** followed by a happy-hour margarita at Cowgirl BBQ. Have dinner at Joseph's or La Boca.

Day 4

Drive to **Taos** via the low road, detouring to the pilgrimage site of **Chimayó.** Stop for lunch at Zuly's in Dixon. In Taos, head straight to **Taos Pueblo.** Admire the sunset at the **Rio Grande Gorge,** then head to the Adobe Bar at the Taos Inn for a margarita and head up the road for dinner at The Love Apple or Orlando's.

Day 5

In the morning, have breakfast at Gutiz or Michael's Kitchen, and, on your way out of town, stop by **San Francisco de Asis Church.** Drive back to **Albuquerque** via the high road

Taos Pueblo

Canyon Road is lined with galleries.

past Truchas and Las Trampas, then along the **Turquoise Trail**, stopping for lunch in **Madrid** and at **Tinkertown Museum.** In Albuquerque, take a sunset ride up the **Sandia Peak Tramway.** Enjoy dinner and drinks downtown.

Day 6

Have a big breakfast at The Frontier and, if time allows, stroll around **Nob Hill** before catching your plane out of the Albuquerque airport.

Pedernal Peak, seen from Ghost Ranch

Santa Fe and Taos have long histories of fostering creative output, much of it inspired by the surrounding landscape. Tour northern New Mexico with a creative eye, and soon you'll be recognizing locations from paintings and maybe find yourself ready to buy ... or to dive into some work of your own.

TAOS

Taos is the best place to see where and how artists lived: At the **Mabel Dodge Luhan House** (page 106), now an inn, Mabel's own bed is still in place in her sunlit room with views of Taos Mountain. Elsewhere in town, the **E. L. Blumenschein Home** (page 103) and **Taos Art Museum at Fechin House** (page 105) both show how artists adapted their residences to their personal styles.

Perhaps the most illuminating spot is Dorothy Brett's miniscule cabin at the **D. H. Lawrence Ranch** (page 138), barely big enough for a bed and a woodstove. Across the yard, in front of Lawrence's only slightly larger home, is the towering pine depicted in Georgia O'Keeffe's *The Lawrence Tree*. Get her perspective, and the curving lines of the painting come into focus: "There was a long weathered carpenter's bench under the tall tree in front of the little old house that Lawrence had lived in there. I often lay on that bench looking up into the tree...past the trunk and up into the branches. It was particularly fine at night with the stars above the tree."

SANTA FE

Art lovers need not spend all their time in museums (though there are some great ones). It can be just as rewarding to visit studios, talk with artists, and see how objects are made. Drive the **High Road to Taos** (page 87) to see woodworkers' studios and weavers' workshops.

Northwest of Santa Fe lies Abiquiu, turf that painter Georgia O'Keeffe called her own, even if she had only a small house in town and a studio at **Ghost Ranch** (page 84). But everything under the sway of flat-topped Pedernal Peak, so often depicted in her work, was grist for her creativity.

Just north of Santa Fe, **Shidoni** and **Tesuque Glassworks** (page 49) sit side by side—the former is a bronze foundry, with demonstrations on weekends, and the latter has an open glassblowing studio where you'll usually find some craftspeople at work. It's remarkable to see such heavy technology creating what are often very delicate pieces. If you're truly inspired, check out the listings with **Santa Fe Creative Tourism** (www.santafecreativetourism.org).

Tinkertown Museum

Weekend Getaways

Just an hour from the Albuquerque airport, Santa Fe lends itself perfectly to a romantic weekend. Settle in at one of the many remarkable hotels and make reservations at a couple of the city's best restaurants (those mentioned here are just a few possibilities). With planning, you could also spend an evening at the Santa Fe Opera in the summer. Isolated, countercultural Taos is worth the extra 90-minute drive if you're really looking to get off the map and off the grid, while Albuquerque offers a fun and funky city break, along with great outdoor activities.

Santa Fe

DAY 1

Fly in to Albuquerque. Head to Santa Fe via the scenic **Turquoise Trail** and check in to your hotel: The Inn of the Five Graces is an exotic, utterly luxurious hideaway, or hole up in the Hacienda wing of the Hotel Santa Fe. If it's summertime, head to **Canyon Road** for the gallery crawl, which gets started around 5pm. In winter,

have a cocktail at Secreto Lounge, then walk over to dinner at Joseph's.

DAY 2

Pick up breakfast at the French Pastry Shop, then spend the morning sightseeing at **New Mexico Museum of Art** and the **Georgia O'Keeffe Museum.** In the afternoon, soak in a private hot tub at **Ten Thousand Waves**, finishing with a massage and then dinner at the spa's restaurant, Izanami. If you're up for more, hit the late-night movie at **Jean Cocteau Cinema.**

DAY 3

Take an early-morning hike on the **Dale Ball Trails** or a less strenuous stroll around the **Santa Fe Canyon Preserve.** Treat yourself to brunch at Harry's Roadhouse or Café Fina, a little south of town, for high-end diner-style goodies and one last great view, then drive back down I-25 to catch your flight out.

San Francisco de Asis Church

Taos

DAY 1

Fly in to Albuquerque. Head to Taos via I-25 and the **low road.** Pick a prime plaza-view room at La Fonda de Taos or luxuriate in a suite at Palacio de Marquesa. Stroll the **plaza** and visit the **E. L. Blumenschein Home** and the galleries on Ledoux Street. Have a gourmet burger for dinner at The Burger Stand, then check out the Alley Cantina.

DAY 2

Visit **Taos Pueblo** in the morning. In the afternoon, tour the **Taos Art Museum** and the **Millicent Rogers Museum.** If you'd rather hike, head for the West Rim Trail along the **Rio Grande Gorge**—it's fairly level, so you shouldn't have too much trouble, despite the elevation. Be dazzled by dinner at El Meze.

DAY 3

Get up early for a dip in **Blackrock Springs.** Drop by **San Francisco de Asis Church** later in the morning, then prep yourself for the drive back south with breakfast at Old Martina's Hall. Head out along the **high road** to Santa Fe and then I-25 to the airport, which takes about four hours without much dawdling; a straight shot back down the low road will shave about 40 minutes off the trip.

Albuquerque

DAY 1

Arrive at Albuquerque airport and transfer to your hotel: try Los Poblanos Historic Inn or another rural-feeling inn in the North Valley, or the Hotel Andaluz downtown if you want to be in the middle of the action. Stroll around downtown and peek in the **KiMo Theatre,** then have sunset drinks at the Apothecary Lounge, followed by dinner down the street at Farina Pizzeria.

DAY 2

If you're feeling ambitious, get an early start to drive straight west to **Acoma Pueblo,** which takes about an hour and a half. On your way back to Albuquerque, stop on the **West Mesa** to clamber up the dormant volcanoes and then drive around the base to see **Petroglyph National Monument.** Or stay in the city and spend the morning at the **Indian Pueblo Cultural Center,** followed by late lunch at Mary & Tito's. Spend the evening in **Nob Hill** or downtown.

DAY 3

Get up early (again) for a **hot-air balloon ride,** overlooking the city from the mesas to the mountains. Head to Barelas Coffee House or The Grove for a late breakfast, then tour **Old Town** or the **National Hispanic Cultural Center** before catching your flight home.

Greater World Earthship Development

Fringy, countercultural, freakish, or just plain quirky—whatever you want to call the offbeat side of northern New Mexico, there sure is a lot of it.

- **Madrid** (page 189) A ghost town made good, Madrid's do-what-you-like spirit has taken over an entire community in the past few decades, inspiring art galleries and assorted odd projects such as the *Nude Geezers* fundraising calendar—no wonder the locals call themselves "Madroids."

- **Greater World Earthship Development** (page 112) All the houses here are off the power grid. But what's most remarkable about these homes is their curvy design, with walls built into hills, around glass bottles, and into whimsical waves.

- **Dar al Islam** (page 82) This retreat was partially built by an Egyptian master of earthen architecture—his adobe work looks both at home and exotic in the hills near Abiquiu.

- **KiMo Theatre** (page 151) An excellent example of "Pueblo Deco" is Albuquerque's contribution to bizarre architecture.

- **Bart Prince House** (page 154) The home and studio work of this local architect resembles a spaceship.

- **Tinkertown Museum** (page 188) This place is a folk-art treasure and genuine roadside attraction, involving hundreds of whittled models, circus dioramas, and plenty more—a treasure trove for kids and adults alike.

Madroids get festive at their Fourth of July parade.

American Indian Heritage

The culture that developed before the Spanish conquest in the 16th century is visible in the pueblos (both ruined and inhabited) and in excellent museums that hold some of the region's finest works. Even if you're visiting only one city on your trip, there's a lot of Native history to see in and around each place—but definitely try to schedule a visit around a dance ceremony, as this will give you the most memorable impression of the living culture.

If you're serious about buying art and jewelry, you could time your visit with the Santa Fe Indian Market in August, which showcases more than 1,200 Native American artisans. Otherwise, be sure to visit the gift shops at the Museum of Contemporary Native Arts in Santa Fe or the Indian Pueblo Cultural Center in Albuquerque to get an idea of prices and quality; you can also buy directly from craftspeople at the pueblos.

Albuquerque

Start with a visit to the **Indian Pueblo Cultural Center,** with its excellent museum and café. Then head to the edge of town: to the West Mesa, where **Petroglyph National Monument** has trails past hundreds of ancient rock carvings, and to Bernalillo, north of the city, where you can climb down into a ceremonial kiva at **Coronado State Monument.**

Mesa-top **Acoma Pueblo** is well worth the drive west of the city—along with Taos Pueblo, it's the most scenic (and oldest) in New Mexico. You can break up the trip with a stop at **Laguna Pueblo** to see its mission church. South and east through the Manzano Mountains are the **Salinas Pueblo Missions,** ruined villages that didn't survive the Spanish conquest. North of the city, the **Jemez Mountain Trail** runs through **Jemez Pueblo**—the red-rock scenery is beautiful, and don't miss the fry bread from the vendors set up in front of the Walatowa Visitor Center.

Rest up from your road trips at the Hyatt Regency Tamaya resort, owned by Santa Ana Pueblo, or Casita Chamisa in Albuquerque's North Valley, which has a small ruin on its grounds, excavated by the owner.

a young participant at the Taos Powwow

Regional Identity

The "tricultural" image of New Mexico is changing, as historians show contributions of other groups over time.

New Mexicans have particular ways of identifying themselves and the elements of the state's unique cultural mix. The people who have lived in the highlands and along the Rio Grande for millennia usually refer to themselves as "Indians," or "American Indians" in formal situations; or they will call themselves by their pueblo's specific name—Jemez or Santa Clara, for instance. The term "Native American" appears occasionally, but most New Mexican Indians see it as just another inaccurate label.

Those who trace their roots to the conquistadors call themselves "Spanish" or "Hispano." The latter is not to be confused with "Hispanic," which refers to Spanish speakers regardless of background. "Hispano" is also distinct from "Mexican" and "Latino."

The third category is the catchall term "Anglo," which really just means "none of the above"—whether you're white, Asian, or even African American, you could be considered Anglo, a relative latecomer to the state of New Mexico.

Santa Fe

On Museum Hill, the **Wheelwright Museum of the American Indian** and the **Museum of Indian Arts & Culture** are two fascinating exhibitions of arts and crafts. Then see what current work is on display at the **Museum of Contemporary Native Arts,** perhaps picking up some craftwork at the gift shop or from the vendors at the **Palace of the Governors.** Even Hotel Santa Fe, co-owned by Picurís Pueblo, showcases tribal art.

The pueblos north of the city offer more in the way of casinos than they do in traditional sightseeing, but the **Poeh Museum** at Pojoaque is worth a stop, and collectors will want to make the drive to **San Ildefonso Pueblo** for its stunning black-on-black pottery. Finally, visit the **Puyé Cliff Dwellings** or **Bandelier National Monument** to see the homes inhabited by the ancestors of today's Pueblo people.

Taos

Head straight to **Taos Pueblo**—one of the most beautiful spots in the state, the organic adobe structures seemingly untouched by time (only *seemingly*—in fact, they get a fresh coat of mud nearly every year). Have a meal at **Tiwa Kitchen,** or at least sample the fry bread and chokecherry syrup. Also don't miss the excellent weaving and pottery collections at the **Millicent Rogers Museum.**

Not Just Hot Tamales

Given the region's distinctive cuisine—from only-in-New-Mexico hot chile to gourmet creativity—it would be easy to plan a vacation entirely around eating.

BEST TRADITIONAL NEW MEXICAN

"Red or green?" is the official state question, the dilemma diners face when they order anything that can be drowned in an earthy red-chile sauce or a chunky, vegetal green one.

posole at San Felipe Restaurant

- **Tia Sophia's:** History was made in this old-school spot near the Santa Fe Plaza: It's allegedly where the breakfast burrito was invented (page 60).

- **Orlando's:** The Taos favorite is known for its green-chile sauce, deceptively smooth and velvety, considering the heat it packs (page 129).

- **Mary & Tito's Café:** This family restaurant was named a James Beard American Classic in 2010, thanks to its *carne adovada* (page 179).

- **San Felipe Restaurant:** In the category of restaurants in a gas station, this one's a winner: enchilada platters plus pueblo favorites like blue-corn mush (page 197).

BEST GREEN-CHILE CHEESEBURGERS

This greasy treat is so genius, it has been immortalized in the official New Mexico Green Chile Cheeseburger Trail (www.newmexico.org). A few GCCB options:

- **Santa Fe Bite:** This casual restaurant grinds its own meat and shapes the enormous patties by hand (page 60).

- **The Frontier:** With a pot of green-chile stew at the condiment counter, you can ladle on as much heat as you want (page 178).

Mesas and Mountaintops

Not only is New Mexico's mountain scenery stunning, but the population is sparse, so it's very easy to get out of town and have the natural splendor all to yourself. This route, which takes nine days, caters to hikers who want to spend as much time as possible outside of the cities. When you arrive in New Mexico and see the scenery, it's tempting to put on your boots and head straight out, but unless you're coming from a comparable elevation, stick to clambering in foothills and scenic drives for the first couple of days. Drink plenty of liquids, and head to bed early.

If you'd prefer not to do the overnight backpacking trip suggested below, leave Taos a day earlier and take a day hike in Bandelier National

- **Shake Foundation:** This burger stand does local lamb or beef, with jack cheese and chile on a buttered bun (page 62).

- **Blake's Lotaburger:** A New Mexico chain, always reliable—keep an eye out for the icon of the man in the red-white-and-blue top hat.

BEST LOCAL AND ORGANIC

New Mexico's extreme climate makes farming difficult—so the foodie set treasures locally grown produce.

- **Café Pasqual's:** At this Santa Fe legend, open since 1979, Chef Katharine Kagel went organic before organic was cool (page 61).

- **Joseph's:** Chef Joseph Wrede, formerly a Taos icon, moved to Santa Fe to teach this glitzy town what New Mexican *terroir* really is—and even elevates the GCCB (page 63).

A GCCB is a thing of beauty.

- **Vinaigrette:** This "salad bistro" in Santa Fe grows its own greens on a nearby farm and can vouch for every other ingredient on its menu (page 175).

- **The Love Apple:** A chalkboard displays the sources of the ingredients at this candlelit bistro: Tucumcari cheese, Pecos beef, and more (page 128).

- **Los Poblanos:** Guests at this historic farm inn in Los Ranchos de Albuquerque enjoy fresh eggs for breakfast and sublime salads and charcuterie at dinner (page 173).

- **Jennifer James 101:** Minimalist chef James composes a short daily menu from local produce, and weekly "community tables" show off seasonal treats (page 180).

Monument instead, staying the night in nearby Los Alamos. In the morning, you can have a longer day at Valles Caldera. As for timing, don't try this itinerary any earlier than **mid-May**; even then you will still encounter snowpack at higher elevations. If you're especially interested in rafting, go in the early part of the summer, when the river is fullest. Visiting in the fall may be colder, but the glowing yellow aspen groves that stud the mountains are a major attraction.

Day 1

Arrive at Albuquerque's Sunport; pick up your rental car and head north to your hotel in **Santa Fe.** If you arrive on an early flight, take a detour to **Kasha-Katuwe Tent Rocks National**

Monument for an easy hourlong hike—but don't push yourself too hard.

Day 2

Rent a bike and get oriented downtown, then head down the **Santa Fe Rail Trail** to Lamy or cruise around **La Tierra Trails** in the rolling hills west of the city. Return to Santa Fe for a hearty barbecue dinner at Cowgirl BBQ.

Day 3

Take your pick of several hikes in the Santa Fe area: The **Rio en Medio** trail north of Tesuque is a good one, or make the trek along **Aspen Vista** if the leaves are turning. At night, relax in the hot tubs at **Ten Thousand Waves**, then have a late dinner at Izanami.

Day 4

Drive to **Taos** via the **high road,** spending the afternoon around town or on a short hike in **Hondo Canyon** near Taos Ski Valley (grab a coffee and a sandwich at the Taos Cow in Arroyo Seco when you head up this way). At night, meet other outdoorsy types at Eske's Brew Pub. Bunk at the Taos Inn.

Day 5

Start out early toward **Red River** to make an overnight hike up the back of **Wheeler Peak,** the highest point in the state.

Day 6

Hike back down the mountain and head back to **Taos.** Around sunset, relax in **Blackrock Springs.** Spend the night in Taos.

Day 7

Hike or mountain bike along the **South Boundary Trail,** or go rafting through the white water in the **Taos Box.** Spend the night in Taos.

Day 8

Drive back south via the **low road** and take a guided hike in **Valles Caldera National Preserve;** stay the night in **Jemez Springs,** where you can soak tired muscles in the healing waters.

Day 9

Return to Albuquerque via the **Jemez Mountain Trail.** Grab a last bite of green-chile stew at The Frontier if you have time before your flight.

wind-whittled peaks at Kasha-Katuwe Tent Rocks National Monument

Santa Fe

Look for ★ to find recommended sights, activities, dining, and lodging.

Highlights

★ **Ghost Ranch**

Española

Los Alamos

Santuario de Chimayó

Bandelier National Monument

New Mexico Museum of Art

La Fonda—

Santa Fe

Canyon Road Galleries

Museum of International Folk Art

© AVALON TRAVEL

0   10 mi

0   10 km

★ **New Mexico Museum of Art:** See the state's long history of creative output, all in one place (page 31).

★ **La Fonda:** The Santa Fe Trail trade route ended on the doorstep of this hotel, which has witnessed the city's fluctuating fortunes—and harbored its assorted characters—for centuries (page 31).

★ **Canyon Road Galleries:** This winding street is the heart of Santa Fe's art scene—and its social life—when it's packed with potential collectors and party hoppers on summer Friday nights (page 37).

★ **Museum of International Folk Art:** In the main exhibition hall, all the world's crafts, from Appalachian quilts to Zulu masks, are jumbled together in an inspiring display of human creativity (page 40).

★ **Bandelier National Monument:** The hidden valley of Frijoles Canyon was home to the ancestors of today's Pueblo people, in an elaborate city complex with cliff-side cave apartments (page 76).

★ **Ghost Ranch:** The spread where Georgia O'Keeffe kept a house has dramatic cliffs and wind-blown pinnacles. Check out the dinosaur museum and hike to Chimney Rock for a view across Abiquiu (page 84).

★ **Santuario de Chimayó:** Faith is palpable in this village church north of Santa Fe, known as "the Lourdes of America," thanks to the healing powers attributed to the holy dirt found here (page 88).

One of Santa Fe's several monikers is "Fanta Se," a play on the name that suggests the city's disconnection from reality.

And indeed, this small cluster of mud-colored buildings in the mountains of northern New Mexico does seem to subsist on dreams alone, as this city of 68,000 has a larger proportion of writers, artists, and performers than any other community in the United States. In the local Yellow Pages, "Art galleries" take up five pages, and "Artists" have their own heading. In all, nearly half the city is employed in the larger arts industry. (Cynics would lump the state legislature, which convenes in the capitol here, into this category as well.)

The city fabric itself is a by-product of this creativity—many of the "adobe" buildings in the distinctive downtown area are in fact plaster and stucco, built in the early 20th century to satisfy an official vision of what Santa Fe ought to look like to appeal to tourists. And the mix of old-guard Spanish, Pueblo Indians, groovy Anglos, and international jet-setters of all stripes has even developed a soft but distinct accent—a vaguely continental intonation, with a vocabulary drawn from the 1960s counterculture and alternative healing.

What keeps Santa Fe grounded, to use the local lingo, is its location, tucked in the foothills of the Sangre de Cristos. The wilderness is never far, even if you're just admiring the forest view from your massage table at a Japanese-style spa or dining at an elegant restaurant on lamb that grazed in high meadows. You can be out of town at a trailhead in 15 minutes, skiing down a precipitous slope in 30, or wandering among the hills you've seen in Georgia O'Keeffe's paintings of Abiquiu in 60. East of the city is the Pecos Wilderness Area, a couple of hundred thousand acres studded with summits such as Santa Fe Baldy and Truchas Peak.

Santa Fe's history, too, gives it strong roots. It's the second-oldest city in the United States (after St. Augustine, Florida), and it's surrounded by pueblos that have been inhabited since well before the Spanish arrived, alongside remnants of older settlements, such as the cliff dwellings in Bandelier National

Previous: chili peppers; turquoise jewelry. **Above:** red chile ristras.

Santa Fe

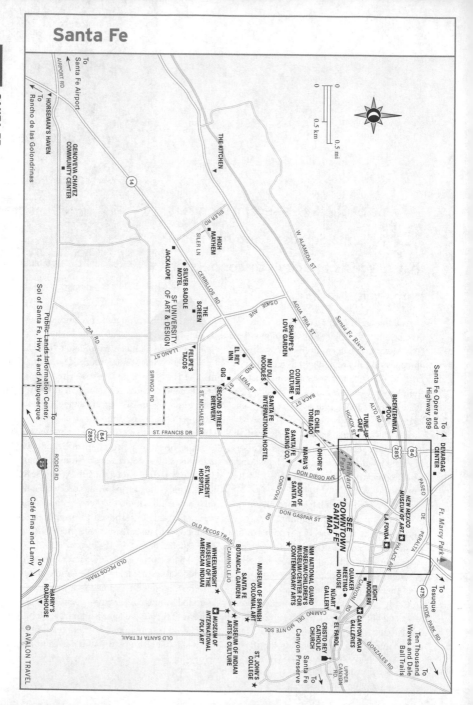

0 0.5 mi
0 0.5 km

To Santa Fe Airport / AIRPORT RD
To Santa Fe Airport
To Rancho de las Golondrinas

HORSEMAN'S HAVEN

GENOVEVA CHAVEZ
COMMUNITY CENTER

Public Lands Information Center,
Sol of Santa Fe, Hwy 14 and Albuquerque

To

THE KITCHEN

SILER RD

HIGH MAYHEM

SILER LN

JACKALOPE

SILVER SADDLE MOTEL

THE SCREEN

SF UNIVERSITY OF ART & DESIGN

CERRILLOS RD

2A RD

LLANO ST

SIRINGO RD

ST. MICHAEL'S DR

ST. FRANCIS DR

84
285

RODEO RD

25

To Café Fina and Lamy

HARRY'S ROADHOUSE

OLD PECOS TRAIL

OLD SANTA FE TRAIL

© AVALON TRAVEL

W ALAMEDA ST

Santa Fe River

AGUA FRIA ST

OSAGE AVE

SHARPE'S LOVE GARDEN

MU DU NOODLES

EL REY INN

FELIPE'S TACOS

GIG

2ND ST

LENA ST

SECOND STREET BREWERY

COUNTER CULTURE

SANTA FE INTERNATIONAL HOSTEL

BACA ST

SANTA FE BAKING CO.

EL CHILE TOREADO

MARIA'S

OHORI'S

DON DIEGO AVE

CORDOVA

BODY OF SANTA FE

DON GASPAR ST

ST VINCENT HOSPITAL

OLD PECOS TRAIL

CAMINO LEJO

WHEELWRIGHT MUSEUM OF THE AMERICAN INDIAN

BOTANICAL GARDEN

SANTA FE COLONIAL ART

MUSEUM OF SPANISH COLONIAL ART

MUSEUM OF INDIAN ARTS & CULTURE

MUSEUM OF INTERNATIONAL FOLK ART

ST. JOHN'S COLLEGE

NM NATIONAL GUARD MUSEUM/CHILDREN'S MUSEUM/CENTER FOR CONTEMPORARY ARTS

QUAKER MEETING HOUSE

NÜART GALLERY

CRISTO REY CATHOLIC CHURCH

EL FAROL

CANYON ROAD GALLERIES

EIGHT MODERN

CAMINO DEL MONTE SOL

Santa Fe Canyon Preserve

To Santa Fe Canyon Rd

UPPER CANYON RD

Santa Fe Opera and Highway 599

BICENTENNIAL POOL

ALTO RD

HICKOX ST

TUNE-UP CAFÉ

84
285

To DEVARGAS CENTER

PASEO DE PERALTA

NEW MEXICO MUSEUM OF ART

LA FONDA

PALACE AVE

Ft. Marcy Park

Railyard Park

"SEE DOWNTOWN SANTA FE" MAP

CANYON RD

475

HYDE PARK RD

GONZALES RD

To Tesuque

To Ten Thousand Waves and Dale Ball Trails

14

285

84

Monument. As the capital of the Spanish territory of Nuevo México, Santa Fe was a far-flung outpost, a gateway to the wilder, emptier lands to the north. And it still is, with two scenic routes running north to Taos: The high road winds along mountain ridges, while the low road follows the Rio Grande.

PLANNING YOUR TIME

Santa Fe is an ideal destination for a **three-day weekend**. Add another day or two to take a hike outside of town or make the drive to Taos, Los Alamos, or Abiquiu. **Summer** is ultra-high season, especially for Spanish Market and Indian Market, in July and August respectively. This is also when the gallery scene is in full swing; plan to be in the city on a Friday night, when Canyon Road galleries have their convivial openings.

In **fall**, the city is much calmer and offers beautiful hiking, because the hills are greener and in October, dense groves of aspen trees on the Sangre de Cristo Mountains turn bright yellow. As in the rest of New Mexico, **spring** and early summer can be hot and windy, but the city is still pleasant, as lilacs bloom in May, tumbling over adobe walls and filling the air with scent. **Winter** is cold and occasionally snowy, but clear. Late December in Santa Fe is a special time, as houses are decked with paper-bag lanterns (*farolitos*), and bonfires light Canyon Road on Christmas Eve. After this, in January and February, hotel prices can drop dramatically, as the few tourists in town are here only to ski.

HISTORY

Around 1609, La Villa Real de la Santa Fé (The Royal City of the Holy Faith) was built as the capital of Spain's northernmost territory in the New World. The Camino Real, the route that connected the outpost with Mexico, ended in the newly built plaza. Mexico's independence from Spain in 1821 marked a shift in the city's fortunes, as the new government opened up its northernmost territory to outside trade, via the Santa Fe Trail, from Missouri.

When the railroad arrived nearby in 1880, it spurred what's still Santa Fe's lifeblood: tourism. Loads of curious Easterners, undeterred by the spur line up from the depot at Lamy, flocked in. In 1912, a council of city planners decided to promote Santa Fe as a tourist destination and preserve its distinctive architecture. By 1917, the Museum of Fine Arts (now the New Mexico Museum of Art) had opened, and the first Indian Market was held in 1922, in response to the trend of Anglos collecting local craft work.

A new element was added to Santa Fe's mix in 1943, when the building at 109 East Palace Avenue became the "front office" and only known address for Los Alamos, where the country's greatest scientists were developing the atomic bomb under a cloud of confidentiality. But the rational scientists left little mark. Right-brain thinking has continued to flourish, and the city is a modern, creative version of its old self, a meeting place where international art dealers swap goods and ideas.

ORIENTATION

Santa Fe is a small town. Most of the major sights are within walking distance from the central plaza; generally, you'll find yourself within the oval formed by **Paseo de Peralta,** a main road that almost completely circles the central district. On its southwest side it connects with **Cerrillos Road,** a main avenue lined with motel courts, shopping plazas, and chain restaurants. Compared with the central historic district, it's unsightly, but there are some great local places to eat along this way, as well as the few inexpensive hotels in town.

Sights

DOWNTOWN

Santa Fe Plaza

When Santa Fe was established in 1610, its layout was based on Spanish laws governing town planning in the colonies—hence the central plaza fronted by the Casas Reales (Palace of the Governors) on its north side. The **Santa Fe Plaza** is still the city's social hub, and the blocks surrounding it are rich with history. In the center of the plaza is the **Soldiers' Monument,** now also a monument to how history gets rewritten. On the original panel, dedicated in 1867 to those who died in "battles with [...] Indians in the territory of New Mexico," the word "savage" was excised in the 1970s, following a debate about the word. One activist took it upon himself to chisel out the word himself, even as some Pueblo leaders thought the word should stand, on the logic that it could accurately describe the way in which Native people fought the Spanish at the time. Another, later panel has been modified too, as "rebel," referring to Southern forces in the Civil War, has been cut away. And then next to it all is yet another plaque, apologizing for the whole mess.

New Mexico History Museum and Palace of the Governors

Opened in 2009, the **New Mexico History Museum** (113 Lincoln Ave., 505/476-5200, www.nmhistorymuseum.org, 10am-5pm daily June-Sept., 10am-5pm Tues.-Sun. Oct.-May, $9) was intended to give a little breathing room for a collection that had been in storage for decades. Oddly, though, it feels like very few actual objects are on display. The exhibits give a good basic overview, though if you're already familiar with the state's storied past, you might not find much new here.

Your ticket also admits you to the adjacent **Palace of the Governors,** the former seat of Santa Fe's government, and a generally more interesting display. Built 1610-1612, it's one of the oldest government buildings in the United States, giving it plenty of time to accumulate stories. De Vargas fought the Indian rebels here room by room when he retook the city in 1693, ill-fated Mexican governor Albino Pérez was beheaded in his office in 1837, and Governor Lew Wallace penned *Ben Hur* here in the late 1870s. The exhibits here showcase some of the most beautiful items in the state's collection: trinkets and photos from the 19th century, as well as the beautiful 18th-century Segesser hide paintings, two wall-size panels of buffalo skin. These works, along with the room they're in (trimmed with 1909 murals of the Puyé cliffs) are worth the price of admission. In a couple of the restored furnished rooms, you can compare the living conditions of the Mexican leadership circa 1845 to the relative comfort the U.S. governor enjoyed in 1893.

New Mexico Culture Pass

A **museum pass** ($25) good for 12 months grants onetime access to all of the state-run museums and historic sites. This includes four Santa Fe institutions—the New Mexico Museum of Art, the New Mexico History Museum, the Museum of Indian Arts & Culture, and the Museum of International Folk Art—as well as two in Albuquerque (the National Hispanic Cultural Center and the natural history museum), and the Coronado and Jemez historic sites. It also covers attractions farther afield, in Las Cruces, Alamogordo, and more—great if you're a state resident or you're already planning a longer return visit within the year.

collection starts with Gerald Cassidy's oil painting *Cui Bono?*, on display since the museum's opening in 1917 and still relevant, as it questions the benefits of pueblo tourism. Look out for an excellent collection of Awa Tsireh's meticulous watercolors of ceremonial dances at San Ildefonso Pueblo, alongside works by other local American Indian artists.

On your way out, don't miss the adjacent St. Francis Auditorium, where three artists adorned the walls with art nouveau murals depicting the life of Santa Fe's patron saint. It's rare to see a secular style usually reserved for languorous ladies in flowing togas used to render such scenes as the apotheosis of Saint Francis and Santa Clara's renunciation, and the effect is beautiful.

As at the history museum, Friday evenings (5pm-8pm) are **free admission** in summer; from November to April, only the first Friday of the month is free. Free docent-led **tours** around the museum run daily at 10:30am and 2pm. The museum also runs art-themed **walking tours** ($10) around the city center at 10am Mondays; June through August, they also run Fridays at 10am.

New Mexico Museum of Art

The museum has **free admission** every Friday (5pm-8pm) May through October, and the first Friday of the month in winter. **Walking tours** depart from the blue gate on the Lincoln Avenue side of the New Mexico History Museum at 10:15am (Mon.-Sat. mid-Apr.-mid-Oct., $10), covering all the plaza-area highlights in about two hours.

★ New Mexico Museum of Art

Famed as much for its building as for the art it contains, the **New Mexico Museum of Art** (107 W. Palace Ave., 505/476-5072, www.nmartmuseum.org, 10am-5pm daily May-Oct., 10am-5pm Tues.-Sun. Nov.-Apr., $9) is dedicated to work by New Mexican artists. Built in 1917, it is a beautiful example of Pueblo Revival architecture, originally designed as the New Mexico pavilion for a world expo in San Diego two years prior. The curvaceous stucco-clad building combines elements from the most iconic pueblo mission churches—the bell towers, for instance, mimic those found at San Felipe. Inside, the

★ La Fonda

La Fonda (100 E. San Francisco St., 505/982-5511, www.lafondasantafe.com), at the corner of San Francisco Street and Old Santa Fe Trail, has been offering respite to travelers in some form or another since 1607, and it still hums with history—even though the stacked Pueblo Revival place you see today dates from 1920. "The Inn at the End of the Trail" boomed in the early years of the trade route across the West, and also in the later gold-digging era, with a casino and saloon. It hosted the victory ball following General Kearny's takeover of New Mexico in the Mexican-American War. During the Civil War it housed Confederate general H. H. Sibley. Lynchings and shootings took place in the lobby. In the 1920s, it got a bit safer for the average tourist, as it joined the chain of Harvey Houses along the country's railways, and the architect Mary Jane Colter (best known for designing the hotels at the

Downtown Santa Fe

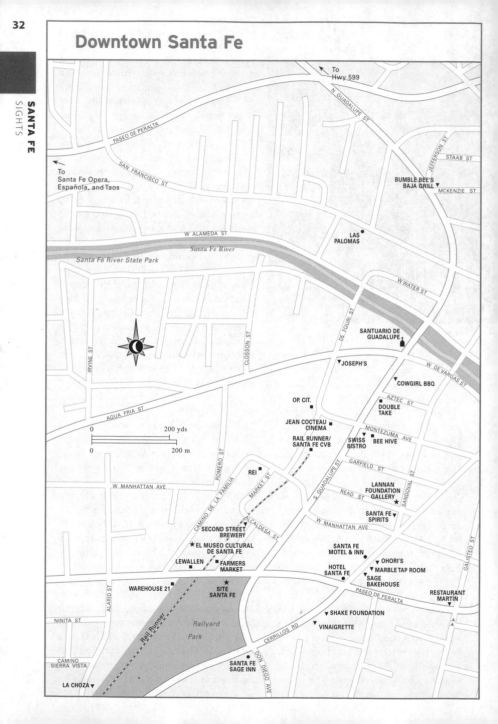

To
Hwy 599

N GUADALUPE ST

PASEO DE PERALTA

JEFFERSON ST

STAAB ST

SAN FRANCISCO ST

To
Santa Fe Opera,
Española, and Taos

BUMBLE BEE'S
BAJA GRILL ▼

MCKENZIE ST

W ALAMEDA ST

LAS
PALOMAS

Santa Fe River

W WATER ST

Santa Fe River State Park

DE FOURI ST

SANTUARIO DE
GUADALUPE

W DE VARGAS ST

CLOSSON ST

▼ JOSEPH'S

▼ COWGIRL BBQ

OP. CIT. ■

AZTEC ST

■ DOUBLE
TAKE

IRVINE ST

AGUA FRIA ST

JEAN COCTEAU ■
CINEMA

MONTEZUMA AVE

RAIL RUNNER/
SANTA FE CVB

SWISS ■ BEE HIVE
BISTRO

0   200 yds

0   200 m

GARFIELD ST

ROMERO ST

REI ■

MARKET ST

S GUADALUPE ST

READ ST

LANNAN
FOUNDATION
GALLERY ★

SANDOVAL ST

W MANHATTAN AVE

CAMINO DE LA FAMILIA

ALCALDESA ST

SANTA FE ▼
SPIRITS

W MANHATTAN AVE

SECOND STREET
BREWERY

★ EL MUSEO CULTURAL
DE SANTA FE

LEWALLEN ■ ■ FARMERS
MARKET

SANTA FE
MOTEL & INN

HOTEL
SANTA FE

▼ OHORI'S

▼ MARBLE TAP ROOM

SAGE
BAKEHOUSE

GALISTEO ST

ALARID ST

WAREHOUSE 21 ■

★ SITE
SANTA FE

PASEO DE PERALTA

RESTAURANT
MARTÍN ▼

NINITA ST

CERRILLOS RD

Railyard
Park

Rail Runner

▼ SHAKE FOUNDATION

VINAIGRETTE ▼

DON DIEGO AVE

CAMINO
SIERRA VISTA

SANTA FE
SAGE INN ●

LA CHOZA ▼

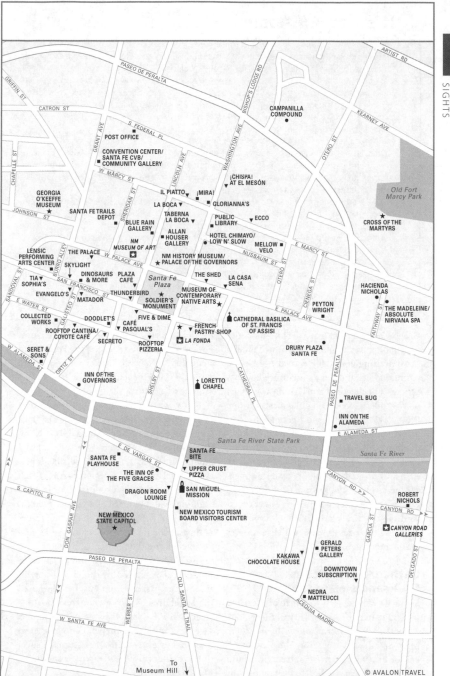

ARTIST RD
PASEO DE PERALTA
GRIFFIN ST
CATRON ST
S FEDERAL PL
BISHOPS LODGE RD
CAMPANILLA COMPOUND
KEARNEY AVE
OTERO ST
POST OFFICE
GRANT AVE
CHAPELLE ST
CONVENTION CENTER/ SANTA FE CVB/ COMMUNITY GALLERY
LINCOLN AVE
WASHINGTON ST
W MARCY ST
Old Fort Marcy Park
GEORGIA O'KEEFFE MUSEUM
¡CHISPA! AT EL MESÓN
IL PIATTO
¡MIRA!
GLORIANNA'S
JOHNSON ST
SANTA FE TRAILS DEPOT
LA BOCA
SHERIDAN ST
TABERNA LA BOCA
PUBLIC LIBRARY
ECCO
CROSS OF THE MARTYRS
BLUE RAIN GALLERY
ALLAN HOUSER GALLERY
HOTEL CHIMAYO/ LOW N' SLOW
MELLOW VELO
E MARCY ST
LENSIC PERFORMING ARTS CENTER
THE PALACE
NM MUSEUM OF ART
W PALACE AVE
NM HISTORY MUSEUM/ PALACE OF THE GOVERNORS
NUSBAUM ST
OTERO ST
BURRO ALLEY
SKYLIGHT
DINOSAURS & MORE
PLAZA CAFÉ
THE SHED
LA CASA SENA
HACIENDA NICHOLAS
TIA SOPHIA'S
SAN FRANCISCO ST
Santa Fe Plaza
CIENEGA ST
FATHWAY ST
SANDOVAL ST
EVANGELO'S
THUNDERBIRD
MATADOR
MUSEUM OF CONTEMPORARY NATIVE ARTS
PEYTON WRIGHT
THE MADELEINE/ ABSOLUTE NIRVANA SPA
E WATER ST
SOLDIER'S MONUMENT
E PALACE AVE
COLLECTED WORKS
GALISTEO ST
DOODLET'S
FIVE & DIME
CATHEDRAL BASILICA OF ST. FRANCIS OF ASSISI
CAFÉ PASQUAL'S
FRENCH PASTRY SHOP
ROOFTOP CANTINA/ COYOTE CAFÉ
SECRETO
LA FONDA
DRURY PLAZA SANTA FE
SERET & SONS
ROOFTOP PIZZERIA
ORTIZ ST
W ALAMEDA ST
INN OF THE GOVERNORS
SHELBY ST
LORETTO CHAPEL
CATHEDRAL PL
PASEO DE PERALTA
TRAVEL BUG
INN ON THE ALAMEDA
E ALAMEDA ST
Santa Fe River State Park
Santa Fe River
E DE VARGAS ST
SANTA FE PLAYHOUSE
SANTA FE BITE
UPPER CRUST PIZZA
CANYON RD
S CAPITOL ST
THE INN OF THE FIVE GRACES
SAN MIGUEL MISSION
ROBERT NICHOLS
DRAGON ROOM LOUNGE
CANYON RD
DON GASPAR AVE
NEW MEXICO STATE CAPITOL
NEW MEXICO TOURISM BOARD VISITORS CENTER
GARCIA ST
CANYON ROAD GALLERIES
PASEO DE PERALTA
GERALD PETERS GALLERY
DELGADO ST
KAKAWA CHOCOLATE HOUSE
DOWNTOWN SUBSCRIPTION
WEBBER ST
OLD SANTA FE TRAIL
NEDRA MATTEUCCI
ACEQUIA MADRE
W SANTA FE AVE
To Museum Hill
© AVALON TRAVEL

It's Not *All* Adobe

Santa Fe's distinctive look is the product of stringent building codes that define and maintain "old Santa Fe style," from the thickness of walls (at least eight inches) to the shade of stucco finish, in only "brown, tan, or local earth tones." But look closely, and you'll see some variations. **Colonial** is the term applied to adobe (or adobe-look) buildings, usually one story, with their typical rounded edges and flat roofs supported by vigas, the long crossbeams made of single tree trunks. The style was developed by the Spanish colonists in the 16th, 17th, and 18th centuries, based on their previous experience with adobe architecture and forms they saw in the pueblos.

In the 19th century, when New Mexico became a U.S. territory and the railroad could carry new building materials, timber-frame houses came into fashion. These so-called **territorial** buildings were often two stories tall, with balconies, and trimmed with brick cornices and Greek revival details, such as fluted wood columns and pediments above windows. The Catron Building, on the northeast corner of the plaza, is a fine example.

But the tide turned again in the early part of the 20th century, when the **Pueblo Revival** style brought the Spanish colonial look back in vogue. Architects like John Gaw Meem and Isaac Rapp admired the mission churches and pueblos for their clean-lined minimalism. Because they used frame construction, Pueblo Revival buildings could be taller: Rapp's New Mexico Museum of Art towers on the northwest corner of the plaza, and Meem's additions to La Fonda make it five stories. The trend coincided with an aggressive tourism campaign and the development of a comprehensive look for the city, and in the process many territorial houses were simply covered over in a thick layer of faux-adobe plaster. The result is not precisely historic, but the city planners achieved their goal: Santa Fe looks like no other city in the United States.

Grand Canyon) redesigned the interior. Since the 1960s, it has been a family-owned hotel.

Something about the waxed tile floors, painted glass, and heavy furniture conveys the pleasant clamor of hotel life the way many more modern lobbies do not. Guests pick up their keys at an old wood reception desk, drop their letters in an Indian-drum-turned-mailbox, and chat with the concierge below a poster for Harvey's Indian Detour car trips. Also look around—including up on the mezzanine level—at the great art collection. La Plazuela restaurant, in the sunny center courtyard, is a beautiful place to rest (with good posole), and the bar is timeless, with live country music many nights.

Cathedral Basilica of St. Francis of Assisi

Santa Fe's showpiece **Cathedral Basilica of St. Francis of Assisi** (131 Cathedral Pl., 505/982-5619, www.cbsfa.org, 9:30am-4:30pm Mon.-Sat., free), visible from the plaza at the end of East San Francisco Street, was built over some 15 years in the late 19th century, by the domineering Bishop Jean-Baptiste Lamy. For more than three decades, the Frenchman struggled to "elevate" the city to European standards, and his folly is exemplified in this grandiose cathedral.

Lamy was shocked by the locals' religious practices, as the cult of the Virgin of Guadalupe was already well established, and the Penitente brotherhood was performing public self-flagellation. He also disliked their aesthetics. How could a person possibly reach heaven while praying on a dirt floor inside a building made of mud? Lamy took one look at the tiny adobe church dedicated to St. Francis of Assisi, which had stood for 170 years, and decided he could do better. Construction on his Romanesque revival St. Francis Cathedral began in 1869, under the direction of architects and craftsmen from Europe. They used the old church as a frame for the new stone structure, then demolished all of the adobe, save for a small side chapel. Lamy ran short of cash, however—hence the stumpy aspect of the cathedral's facade, which should be topped with spires.

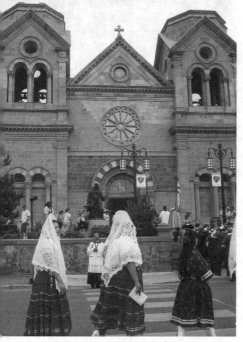

Cathedral Basilica of St. Francis of Assisi

depicting the history of Catholicism in New Mexico. One plaque shows the Italian stone-workers constructing the cathedral, and another shows families fleeing from attack in 1680—a rare depiction of the Pueblo Revolt that's sympathetic to the Spanish.

Museum of Contemporary Native Arts

Set in the city's former post office, the **Museum of Contemporary Native Arts** (108 Cathedral Pl., 505/983-8900, www.iaia. edu, 10am-5pm Mon. and Wed.-Sat., noon-5pm Sun., $10) is the showcase for students, professors, and alumni of the prestigious Institute of American Indian Arts. The space is relatively small, and the shows can be hit or miss—and if it's the latter, the ticket can seem a bit pricey. If your time is limited, the Museum of Indian Arts & Culture is a better bet. But the gift shop stocks items with a good blend of modern and traditional styles.

Loretto Chapel

Initiated by Bishop Lamy in 1873, the **Loretto Chapel** (207 Old Santa Fe Tr., 505/982-0092, 9am-5pm Mon.-Sat., 10:30am-5pm Sun., $3) was the first Gothic structure built west of the Mississippi. It's a beautiful interior with a great story to match, although the recording broadcast inside (the place was de-sanctified in 1971) explaining all this is slightly maddening, on endless loop.

The chapel's decorative elements reflect Lamy's fondness for all things European: the stations of the cross rendered by Italian masons, the harmonium and stained-glass windows imported from France. Even the stone from which it was built was hauled at great expense from quarries 200 miles south.

What really draws the eye is the elegant spiral staircase leading to the choir loft. Made entirely of wood, it makes two complete turns without a central support pole. It was built in 1878 by a mysterious carpenter who appeared seemingly at the spiritual behest of the resident Sisters of Loretto. The carpenter toiled in silence for six months, the story goes, then

Inside is all Gothic-inspired light and space and glowing stained-glass windows, with a gilt altar screen installed in 1987, for the centennial of the building's dedication. It features primarily New World saints, such as Kateri Tekakwitha, a 17th-century Mohawk woman beatified in 1980 and canonized in 2012 (her statue also stands outside the cathedral). She is depicted with a turtle, representing her membership in the Turtle Clan.

The salvaged adobe chapel remains off to the left of the altar. It is dedicated to the figure of La Conquistadora, a statue brought to Santa Fe from Mexico in 1625, carried away by the retreating Spanish during the Pueblo Revolt, then proudly reinstated in 1693 and honored ever since. She glows in her shimmering robes, under a heavy viga ceiling—all of which probably makes Lamy shudder in his crypt in front of the main altar (he died in 1888).

On your way out, check the great cast-bronze doors—they're usually propped open, so you'll have to peer behind to see the images disappeared, without taking any payment. He was never heard from again—though some historians claim to have tracked him down to Las Cruces, where he met his end in a bar fight.

San Miguel Mission

The **San Miguel Mission** (401 Old Santa Fe Tr., 505/983-3974, 9am-5pm Mon.-Sat., 10am-4pm Sun., $1, free silent worship 5pm-7pm Thurs.) is a sturdy adobe building where Mass is still said in Latin at noon on Sunday. It is the oldest church structure in the United States, and it's set in Barrio de Analco, the city's oldest residential neighborhood, at the head of De Vargas, the oldest street. The church was built starting in 1610, then partially reconstructed a century later, after it was set aflame in the Pueblo Revolt. Its stone buttresses are the product of a desperate attempt to shore up the sagging walls in the late 19th century.

The interior is snug and whitewashed, with an altar screen that was restored in 1955 after having been covered over in house paint for decades. The late-18th-century work is attributed to the anonymous Laguna Santero, a Mexican artist who earned his name from the intricately carved and painted screen at the Laguna Pueblo church, near Albuquerque. The screen functions as an enormous picture frame, with both oil paintings and *bultos* (painted wood statues of saints) inserted in the openings. In front of the altar, cutouts in the floor reveal the building's original foundations.

The old church bell, set at the back of the church, is said to have been cast in Spain in 1356. It was brought to the New World and installed at San Miguel in the early 19th century, and it hums beautifully even when tapped.

New Mexico State Capitol

A round building with an entrance at each of the cardinal points, the 1966 **New Mexico State Capitol** (491 Old Santa Fe Tr.) mimics the zia sun symbol used on the state flag. In the center of the rotunda is a mosaic

San Miguel Mission

rendition of the state seal: the Mexican brown eagle, grasping a snake and shielded by the American bald eagle. And don't forget to look up at the stained-glass skylight, with its intricate Indian basket-weave pattern.

But the real attraction of the Roundhouse, as the building is commonly known, is its excellent but often overlooked **art collection** (505/986-4589, www.nmcapitolart.org, 8am-5:30pm Mon.-Fri., also Sat. June-Aug., free), with works by the state's best-known creative types, all accessible at no cost. You'll find paintings and photographs in the halls on every floor, in the upstairs balcony area of the senate, and in the fourth-floor Governor's Gallery.

Oh, and the building is used for legislating—though not particularly often (for 30 days, beginning on the third Tuesday in January, in even-numbered years, and 60 days in odd). When house and senate meetings are in session, visitors are welcome to sit in the galleries and watch the proceedings.

Georgia O'Keeffe Museum

Opened in 1997, the **Georgia O'Keeffe Museum** (217 Johnson St., 505/946-1000, www.okeeffemuseum.org, 9am-5pm Sat.-Thurs., 9am-7pm Fri. June-Oct.; 10am-5pm Sat.-Thurs., 10am-7pm Fri. Nov.-May, $12), northwest of the plaza, honors the artist whose name is inextricably bound with New Mexico. The contrary member of the New York avant-garde ("Nothing is less real than realism," she famously said) started making regular visits to the state in the 1920s, then moved to Abiquiu full-time in 1949, a few years after the death of her husband, photographer Alfred Stieglitz.

Many of O'Keeffe's finest works—her signature sensuous, near-abstract flower blossoms, for instance—have already been ensconced in other famous museums, so the collection here can seem a little thin. To get the most out of a visit, join a docent **tour** (10:30am or 2pm daily.) Exhibits draw on the work that she kept, plus ephemera and other work her foundation has amassed since her death in 1986. Often the space is given over to exhibitions on her contemporaries or those whose work she influenced or admired.

Cross of the Martyrs

Sitting at the top of a hill overlooking downtown Santa Fe, the white **Cross of the Martyrs** is a memorial to the Spanish settlers who were killed in the Pueblo Revolt. It's not a strenuous walk, and the bird's-eye view from the hilltop is excellent.

Behind the cross is **Old Fort Marcy Park**, site of the remnants of the first American fort in the Southwest, built in 1846 by General Stephen Kearny and then abandoned in 1894. The path up to the cross begins on Paseo de Peralta just east of Otero Street.

CANYON ROAD

This narrow one-way street southeast of the plaza epitomizes "Santa Fe style," or at least the ritzy, art-centric side of it. The galleries are the main draw, but it's worth heading a bit off the main drag too. There's a city **parking** lot at the east (upper) end of the road. Public **restrooms** (9:30am-5:30pm daily) are near the west end, in the complex at 225 Canyon Road, behind Expressions gallery.

★ Canyon Road Galleries

The intersection of Paseo de Peralta and

New Mexico's State Capitol, also known as the Roundhouse

Canyon Road is ground zero for the city's **art market.** This is the beginning of a half-mile strip that contains more than 80 galleries, and in the summer, Canyon Road is a solid mass of strolling art lovers, aficionados and amateurs alike. It's especially thronged on summer Fridays, when most galleries have an open house or an exhibition opening, from around 5pm until 7pm or 8pm.

Hard to believe, but the street wasn't always chockablock with thousand-dollar canvases. Starting in the 1920s, transplant artists settled on this muddy dirt road, the area gradually came to be associated with creative exploits, and eventually the art market really boomed in the 1980s. Before that, it was farmland, irrigated by the "Mother Ditch," Acequia Madre, which still runs parallel one block to the south.

In addition to the galleries, you'll also pass the mid-19th-century house **El Zaguán,** which contains the offices of the **Historic Santa Fe Foundation** (545 Canyon Rd., 505/983-2567, www.historicsantafe.org, 9am-noon and 1:30pm-5pm Mon.-Fri., free). Named for its long internal hallway (*zaguán*), the building was the home of a local merchant, James L. Johnson, from 1854, and then occupied by several other city bigwigs after he lost his fortune in 1881. Its garden, laid out in the late 19th century, is a lovely place to rest in the summer; it's open on Saturday (9am-5pm) as well.

Up the road, the **Quaker Meeting House** (630 Canyon Rd., 505/983-7241, www.santafe.quaker.org) is the former home of Olive Rush, who painted the Old Santa Fe Trail mural at La Fonda and willed her house to the Quakers after her death.

Camino del Monte Sol

To get some sense of what the neighborhood was like before the gallery era, walk south on **Camino del Monte Sol,** which is still residential—though decidedly tonier now than in centuries past. Turning off Canyon Road, you'll cross Acequia Madre, shaded by cottonwoods and channeling water through the city. Farther up the road, starting at No. 558, is

a clutch of homes first inhabited in the 1920s by Los Cinco Pintores, the band of young realist painters who called themselves the "five little nuts in five mud huts." (Will Shuster is the best known of the five today, in part because he started the Zozobra tradition; Walter Mruk, Fremont Ellis, Joseph Bakos, and Willard Nash were the other four.)

Cut east on Camino Santander, then north on Camino San Acacio and northwest on Camino Don Miguel to find **Johnnie's Cash Store** (420 Camino Don Miguel, 505/982-9506, 8:30am-5pm Mon.-Sat.), a little relic of a corner store complete with a swinging screen door and a steamer full of tamales.

Cristo Rey Catholic Church

Head beyond the shops and through a residential stretch to the far north end of Canyon Road to see John Gaw Meem's enormous **Cristo Rey Catholic Church** (1120 Canyon Rd., 505/983-8528). Built of 180,000 adobe bricks around a steel frame, the church opened in 1940 but looks as if it could be much older. Inside is a dramatic mid-18th-century baroque stone altarpiece, salvaged from La Castrense, the military chapel that used to occupy the south side of the plaza.

GUADALUPE AND THE RAILYARD

This neighborhood southwest of the plaza developed around the depot for the rail spur from the main line at Lamy. Now it's the terminus for the Rail Runner from Albuquerque. The clutch of cafés and shops here are more casual and local, and generally lighter on the adobe look, as **Guadalupe Street** is just outside beyond the reach of the most stringent historic building codes.

South of the train depot is **The Railyard** (www.railyardsantafe.com), a mixed-use district where former warehouses and workshops have been adapted to new business, including a permanent indoor home for the city farmers market. The south side of this area is the green space of **Railyard Park,** nicely landscaped with local grasses and fruit trees.

Santuario de Guadalupe

Built 1776-1796, the **Santuario de Guadalupe** (417 Agua Fria St., 505/983-8868, www.ologsf.com, 9am-noon and 1pm-4pm Mon.-Sat., free) is the oldest shrine to the Virgin of Guadalupe in the United States. The interior is spare, just folding chairs set up on the wood floor, in front of a Mexican baroque oil-on-canvas altar painting from 1783. Mass is still said regularly and a museum in the small anteroom displays relics from earlier incarnations of the building, such as Greek-style columns carved in wood. In winter, the church is closed on Saturdays.

SITE Santa Fe

The boxy, modern exhibition space of **SITE Santa Fe** (1606 Paseo de Peralta, 505/989-1199, www.sitesantafe.org, 10am-5pm Thurs. and Sat., 10am-7pm Fri., noon-5pm Sun., $10) was started in 1995 to bring a biennial contemporary art show to the city. In the years since, the organization has expanded to show edgy art year-round, often installations that take over the whole interior (and sometimes exterior). In July and August, it's also open Wednesdays, and entrance is free on Fridays and on Saturday till noon, when the farmers market is on, kitty-corner across the train tracks.

El Museo Cultural de Santa Fe

Dedicated to Hispanic culture in New Mexico and beyond, **El Museo Cultural de Santa Fe** (555 Camino de la Familia, 505/992-0591, www.elmuseocultural.org, 1pm-5pm Tues.-Sat., donation) is a grassroots effort in a surprisingly massive warehouse space that has room for installations, live theater, and more. It often hosts special events outside of normal museum hours.

Lannan Foundation Gallery

The influential Lannan Foundation, which funds art projects in Marfa, Texas, and an excellent speaker series in Santa Fe among many other creative endeavors, has the **Lannan Foundation Gallery** (309 Read St., 505/954-5149, noon-5pm Sat.-Sun.). In two adjacent houses, it displays selections from the family's ever-expanding trove of contemporary art, usually with an eye toward social justice.

MUSEUM HILL

These museums on the southeast side merit the trip from the plaza area. It's a short drive, or you can take the "M" route bus or the free Santa Fe Pick-Up shuttle, optionally strolling back downhill to the center, about 30 minutes' walk.

Museum of Spanish Colonial Art

The museum of the **Spanish Colonial Arts Society** (750 Camino Lejo, 505/982-2226, www.spanishcolonial.org, 10am-5pm daily June-Aug., 10am-5pm Tues.-Sun. Sept.-May, $5) exhibits a strong collection of folk art and historical objects dating from the earliest Spanish contact. One-of-a-kind treasures—such as the only signed *retablo* by the 19th-century *santero* Rafael Aragón—are shown alongside more utilitarian items from the colonial past, such as silk mantas, wool rugs, and decorative tin. New work by contemporary artisans is also on display—don't miss Luis Tapia's meta-*bulto, The Folk-Art Collectors*.

Museum of Indian Arts & Culture

The excellent **Museum of Indian Arts & Culture** (710 Camino Lejo, 505/476-1250, www.miaclab.org, 10am-5pm daily May-Oct., 10am-5pm Tues.-Sun. Nov.-April, $9) is devoted to Native American culture from across the country. The cornerstone exhibit *Here, Now and Always* traces the New Mexican Indians from their ancestors on the mesas and plains up to their present-day efforts at preserving their culture. It displays inventive spaces (looking into a HUD-house kitchen on the rez, or sitting at desks in a public schoolroom), sound clips, and stories. Another wing is devoted to contemporary art, while the halls of craft work display gorgeous beaded

the Museum of Indian Arts & Culture on Museum Hill

moccasins, elaborate headdresses, and more. The gift shop has beautiful jewelry and other tidbits from local artisans.

★ Museum of International Folk Art

A marvelous hodgepodge, the **Museum of International Folk Art** (708 Camino Lejo, 505/476-1200, www.internationalfolkart. org, 10am-5pm daily May-Oct., 10am-5pm Tues.-Sun. Nov.-Apr., $9) is one of Santa Fe's biggest treats—if you can handle visual overload. In the main exhibition space, some 10,000 folk-art pieces from more than 100 countries are on permanent display, hung on walls, set in cases, even dangling from the ceiling, juxtaposed to show off similar themes, colors, and materials. The approach initially seems jumbled but in fact underscores the universality of certain concepts and preoccupations.

A separate wing is dedicated to northern New Mexican Hispano crafts (a good complement to the Museum of Spanish Colonial Art) and a lab area where you can see how pieces are preserved. Temporary exhibits take up the rest of the space, usually with colorful interactive shows. Don't skip the gift shop, which stocks some smaller versions of the items in the galleries.

Wheelwright Museum of the American Indian

In the early 1920s, Mary Cabot Wheelwright, an adventurous East Coast heiress, made her way to New Mexico, where she met a Navajo medicine man named Hastiin Klah. Together they devised the **Wheelwright Museum of the American Indian** (704 Camino Lejo, 505/982-4636, www.wheelwright.org, 10am-5pm daily, free), which opened in 1937 as the House of Navajo Religion. The mission has since incorporated all Native American cultures, with exhibits of new work by individual artists rotating every few months. The building is modeled after a traditional Navajo hogan, with huge timbers supporting the eight-sided structure. The basement gift shop is a re-creation of a 19th-century trading post, which would feel like a tourist trap if it weren't for the authentically creaky wood floors and the beautiful antique jewelry on display. A new wing, scheduled to open in 2015, will house displays of southwestern jewelry.

Santa Fe Botanical Garden

Opened in 2013, the 12-acre **Santa Fe Botanical Garden** (715 Camino Lejo, 505/471-9103, www.santafebotanicalgarden.com, 9am-5pm daily Apr.-Oct., 11am-3pm Tues.-Sun. Nov.-Mar., $7) is still growing, and until all three of its planned areas are open and flourishing (by 2016, probably), only really curious gardeners are likely to consider it worth the price of admission. The plantings emphasize drought-tolerant plants, and an orchard has peach, apple, and cherry trees, while a dry garden thrives with zero irrigation. To get the most out of it, take a guided tour at 10am or 2pm.

The gardens also maintain a wetland preserve near Rancho de las Golondrinas, just outside of the city, with free walking tours (by appointment) on weekends, May through October.

SANTA FE METRO AREA

New Mexico National Guard Museum

One of three small museums in a single complex a bit out of the center, the **New Mexico National Guard Museum** (1050 Old Pecos Tr., 505/474-1670, www.bataanmuseum.com, 10am-4pm Tues.-Fri., free) began as a homegrown memorial for soldiers in the Bataan Death March of World War II. It was a particular tragedy in New Mexico because most of the state's national guard, drafted as the 200th Coast Artillery, was among the more than 70,000 U.S. and Filipino soldiers subject to torture, malnourishment, random execution, and three years' imprisonment. Of the 1,800 who started in the regiment, fewer than 900 came home, and a full third of those men died in the first year back. The troops' experience is recalled with newspaper clippings, maps, and testimonials. The museum also contains Civil War memorabilia and exhibits on Native American contributions in U.S. wars, such as the Choctaw and Navajo code talkers.

Santa Fe Children's Museum

Kids can have tons of hands-on fun at the Santa Fe Children's Museum (1050 Old Pecos Tr., 505/989-8359, 10am-6pm Tues.-Wed., Fri.-Sat., 10am-6:30pm Thurs., noon-5pm Sun., www.santafechildrensmuseum.org, $7.50). Fitting for New Mexico, pint-size looms give kids a chance to learn to weave. And then there are the globally appealing bits: a giant soap-bubble pool, face painting, fun-house mirrors, and a dazzling collection of bugs. On Thursdays after 4pm, admission is free.

Center for Contemporary Arts

Behind the Children's Museum, the long-established **Center for Contemporary Arts** (1050 Old Pecos Tr., 505/982-1338, www.ccasantafe.org, noon-5pm Thurs.-Sun., free) has been mounting multimedia art shows and screening films since 1979. (An early James Turrell Skyspace is on the grounds here; unfortunately, it is now in disrepair and not open to visitors, though the center aspires to restore it.) It's a nice alternative to the slicker gallery spaces and usually a good spot to check the pulse of younger resident artists.

Sharpe's Love Garden

Take a break from the gallery scene with a stop at **Sharpe's Love Garden** (Agua Fria St. at Velarde St.), a yard-art party to which, it seems, a plaster-cast Virgin of Guadalupe invited all her ornamental friends, both religious and secular. It's the work of residents Helen and Charles Sharpe, and it's decades in the making.

Rancho de las Golondrinas

About a 15-minute drive southeast, **Rancho de las Golondrinas** (334 Los Pinos Rd., 505/471-2261, www.golondrinas.org, 10am-4pm Wed.-Sun. June-Sept., $6), the "Ranch of the Swallows," is Santa Fe's equivalent of Colonial Williamsburg, a 200-acre museum where staff members in period costumes demonstrate crafts and other aspects of early New Mexican history. The core of it is a restored

Sharpe's Love Garden, a bit of roadside folk art

Spanish colonial *paraje,* a way station on the Camino Real, and outbuildings contain a blacksmith shop, a schoolhouse, mills, and even a rebuilt Penitente *morada* (the docent who works here is a Penitente himself and may sing some of the group's hymns).

The ranch hosts big to-dos—a sheep-shearing fair in early June and a frontier-themed horse show in August, among other things. It's a good idea to pack your own picnic; there's a basic café at the ranch, but it's open only on weekends. Allow a few hours to see the whole place. In April, May, and October, the museum is open on weekdays for guided tours by appointment; call 505/473-4169 to make arrangements. In these shoulder months, the ranch is also occasionally open for special theme weekends.

Rancho de las Golondrinas

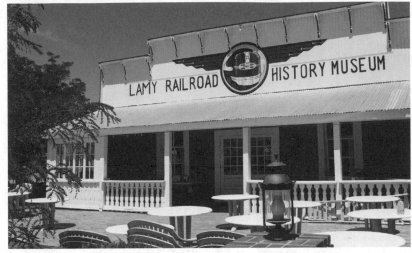

Train buffs can revisit railroad history in Lamy.

Lamy

Probably worth the drive only if you're a rail fan, this village is little more than a depot, though it is a mighty fine place to step off Amtrak's *Southwest Chief.* Across the road, the **Lamy Railroad & History Museum** (151 Old Lamy Tr., 505/466-1650, www.lamymuseum.org, noon-4pm Sat.) is a sprawling Old West saloon and dining room that doubles as a treasure trove of old railroading days; there's even a model train set. The place has a spotty record of opening, so call ahead if you plan to make the trip. (On the other hand, it may also be operating as a full restaurant.)

Take Old Las Vegas Highway (or I-25) southeast out of Santa Fe; six miles out of town, turn south on U.S. 285. After six miles, turn left for the last bumpy mile to Lamy.

Entertainment and Events

NIGHTLIFE

With balmy summer evenings and a populace that always seems to be able to knock off work a little early, Santa Fe typically favors happy hour over late-night carousing.

Bars and Clubs

The lobby watering hole at La Fonda hotel, **La Fiesta Lounge** (100 E. San Francisco St., 505/982-5511, 11am-11pm Sun.-Thurs., 11am-11:30pm Fri.-Sat.), has likely been the setting for thousands of local legends, true or not. Nowadays, it's a bit tamer, but it still has a fine, old-fashioned feel, with portraits of rodeo queens on the wall and live local country acts on the small corner stage.

Another longtime city haunt, the **Dragon Room Lounge** (406 Old Santa Fe Tr., 505/983-7712, 4pm-midnight Tues.-Sun.) is so dim you might not notice at first the huge tree growing up from the left side of the bar. Guys in cowboy hats chat with mountain bikers and dressed-up cocktail drinkers. There's live music Tuesday, Thursday, and Saturday.

Stalwart **Maria's** (555 W. Cordova Rd., 505/983-7929, 11am-10pm daily) may have cut back on the tequila in the margaritas, but considering how staggeringly strong they were before, that might be a good thing. The drinks are still impeccably balanced, made with fresh lime, and available with nearly any brand of tequila you can imagine.

The bar in the Hotel Chimayó, **Low n' Slow** (125 Washington Ave., 505/988-4900, 2pm-10pm Mon.-Thurs., noon-11pm Fri.-Sun.), is worth a mention for its theme alone: As a tribute to cool car culture, it's decked out with cool upholstery and hubcap chandeliers. The lowrider theme continues in cocktails named after car details. Tuesday is trivia night.

If you're hankering for the grungier side of Santa Fe, head to **Evangelo's** (200 W. San Francisco St., 505/982-9014, 11am-1am daily), where soul and blues bands take the small stage at the back; when there's no band, there's room at the pool tables, plus a crew of crusty characters. Its basement space, **The Underground,** hosts all kinds of bands. On the opposite corner, those who descend the stairs to the basement-level **Matador** (116 W. San Francisco St., entrance on Galisteo St., no phone) will find a good cross-section of Santa Fe's younger artists, among other renowned drinkers. If there's not a live band, there's punk rock on the stereo to match the concert posters on the walls.

Breweries

Local operation **Second Street Brewery** has two locations: its original place that gave it its name (1814 2nd St., 505/982-3030, 11am-10pm Mon.-Thurs., 11am-11pm Fri.-Sat., noon-9pm Sun.) and a newer, more central branch in the Railyard (1607 Paseo de Peralta, 505/989-3278), with the same hours. Either way, they usually have half a dozen varieties of their own beer on tap, in a chummy, semi-industrial atmosphere, sometimes backed up by a band. Happy hour is 4pm-6:30pm daily.

An Albuquerque import, **Marble Tap Room** (505 Cerrillos Rd., 505/983-6259, 2pm-11pm Mon.-Thurs., noon-11pm Fri.-Sun.) brings all the popular beers from down south, served up to a mostly local crowd of drinkers. At press time, it served only beer, but plans were in process to move to a larger space in the same complex and serve food.

Cocktail Lounges

The average Santa Fe bar doesn't do much beyond margaritas. **Secreto** (210 Don Gaspar Ave., 505/983-5700, noon-midnight Mon.-Sat., noon-10pm Sun.) is one lounge that is up on the cutting edge of cocktail culture. Its "garden to glass" menu uses only fresh herbs

Open-Air Bars

Get to the **Bell Tower Bar** (100 E. San Francisco St., 505/982-5511, 11am-sunset Apr.-Oct.) early if you can, as this spot on the rooftop at La Fonda fills up fast. It's usually packed with tourists, but the view—from the fifth floor, the highest in the center of town—is inspiring.

If there's no room at La Fonda, the next best spot is **Thunderbird** (50 Lincoln Ave., 505/490-6550, 11:30am-midnight daily), which has a second-floor porch with views onto the plaza. At happy hour, margaritas are $5; it starts early (4pm-6pm), but kicks in again after 10pm.

Hidden away inside a block near the plaza, **Taberna La Boca** (125 Lincoln Ave., 505/988-7102, 11:30am-2pm and 5pm-11pm daily) has a nice patio with a chummy scene starting at happy hour (5pm-7pm). At that time, wine or sherry can be had from $3 a glass, and traditional tapas start at $2.

Over on Canyon Road, **El Farol** (808 Canyon Rd., 505/983-9912, 11am-11pm Sun.-Thurs., 11am-midnight Fri.-Sat.) is a perennial favorite. A bar since 1835, it's the gallery owners' clubhouse, and exuberant dancing occasionally breaks out on the tiny dance floor. There's a long front deck, and a nice back patio too. Happy hour is 3pm-6pm.

The mellow patio scene at **Cowgirl BBQ** (319 S. Guadalupe St., 505/982-2565, 11:30am-midnight Mon.-Thurs., 11am-1am Fri.-Sat., 11am-11:30pm Sun.) gets started early, with happy hour kicking off at 3pm and lasting till 6pm, with two-for-one apps and $4 margaritas. It's good later, too, with live music many nights.

Lensic Performing Arts Center

music five nights a week, with a particularly devoted crew of regulars on Tuesday, for tango night. You can order traditional tapas, or bigger dishes from El Mesón's excellent dinner menu at the bar, or just join in the dancing on the small wood floor.

Trading on its history as a onetime bordello, **The Palace** (142 W. Palace Ave., 505/428-0690, 11am-1am Tues.-Sat., 4pm-11:30pm Sun.) is a half-classy, half-rowdy joint done up in red wallpaper. Happy hour is 4:30pm-6:30pm, with Italian "tapas" and $5 margaritas, but later in the night, the scene is given over to rock bands, karaoke (on Wed.), and, on the last Wednesday of the month, the long-running "trash disco" dance party. Food is served till 1am.

Opened in summer 2014, **Skylight** (139 W. San Francisco St., 505/982-0775, www.skylightsantafe.com, 4pm-2am Mon.-Sat., 4pm-midnight Sun.) became the latest attempt at a late-night dance and live-music venue—the sort of social outlet many in the city crave. This space, run by well-known local DJs, has music every night, including touring bands, and a kitchen to provide munchies for those up past the city's usual bedtime.

Also check the schedule at **Sol of Santa Fe** (37 Fire Pl., www.solofsantafe.com), the performance space next to the Santa Fe Brewing Co., to see if any touring bands are dropping by.

and other seasonal ingredients (plus bitters from local crafters The Bitter End) in such drinks as the Local Beet, a gin-and-tonic turned vivid pink with earthy beet syrup. Of course, it still does a margarita or two: Its Agave Way is a pseudo-margarita that's spicy and sweet with red grapes. Happy hour (4pm-7pm daily) is worth planning around, as it knocks the price down to $7 or so, and you can sit out in the loggia of the Hotel St. Francis and watch the passing parade.

Boozehounds will also want to drop by the tasting room of **Santa Fe Spirits** (308 Read St., 505/780-5906, 3pm-8:30pm Mon.-Sat.), a relaxed place to sample all the local distiller's products. Order a full flight, or enjoy a showcase drink like the Whiskeyrita, which features the distiller's un-aged Silver Coyote whiskey, or a simple gin-and-tonic with its aromatic, sage-infused gin.

Live Music

¡Chispa! at El Mesón (213 Washington St., 505/983-6756, 5pm-11pm Tues.-Sat.) has live

THE ARTS
Performing Arts

Set in a 1931 Moorish curlicue palace, the **Lensic Performing Arts Center** (211 W. San Francisco St., 505/988-1234, www.lensic.com) is Santa Fe's best stage downtown, with 820 seats and an eclectic schedule. The six-week-long summer **Santa Fe Chamber Music Festival** (www.sfcmf.org) holds events here, as well as at the St. Francis Cathedral, with performances nearly every day in July and August. The chamber orchestra **Santa Fe Pro Musica** (505/988-4640, www.santafepromusica.com) also performs at the Lensic, fall through spring, as well as in Loretto Chapel and other intimate venues.

If you think opera is all about tuxes, plush seats, and too-long arias, give the **Santa Fe Opera** (U.S. 84/285, 505/986-5900, www.santafeopera.org) a chance. Half the fun is arriving early to "tailgate" in the parking lot, which involves gourmet goodies, lots of champagne, and time to mill around and check out other attendees' bolo ties. And then there's the show itself, featuring the country's best singers, who treat this as their "summer camp" in July and August. The elegant 2,000-plus-seat open amphitheater is beautiful at sunset; pack blankets to ward off the chill later. If you have kids to entertain, time your visit for bargain-priced "family nights" or a special dress rehearsal with extra info to introduce young ones to the art form.

For other eclectic music, check the schedules at **Gig** (1808 2nd St., www.gigsantafe.com), where singer-songwriters and other acoustic acts take the stage, and **High Mayhem** (2811 Siler Ln., www.highmayhem.org), a raw avant-garde music space that hosts all-ages rock shows, experimental jazz, and lots more.

If it's live theater you want, visit the historic **Santa Fe Playhouse** (142 E. De Vargas St., 505/988-4262, www.santafeplayhouse.org), which occupies a small adobe in Santa Fe's oldest neighborhood. Built in 1922, it's the oldest continuously running theater in the West. It stages a selection of melodrama, folk plays, and work by local playwrights. Tickets are seldom more than $20.

Cinema

The delightful little **Jean Cocteau Cinema** (418 Montezuma Ave., 505/466-5528, www.jeancocteaucinema.com, $10) was shuttered for several years before resident author George R. R. Martin (now known to the TV-watching world as the man behind *Game of Thrones*) bought the place in 2013 and revamped it. Now the 120-seat theater is back to showing the eclectic art-house offerings, to an enthusiastic local audience; on weekends, there's usually a retro late show at 11pm.

Santa Fe University of Art and Design also has an excellent theater, **The Screen** (1600 St. Michaels Dr., 505/473-6494, www.thescreensf.com). The curator brings in excellent first-run art films along with repertory gems. Additionally, the **CCA Cinematheque** (1050 Old Pecos Tr., 505/982-1338, www.ccasantafe.org) has a film program with an emphasis on international titles, and a multiplex, the **Violet Crown** (an Austin, Texas, company), with an artsy bent, was under construction in Railyard Park as this book was going to press. For pure mainstream hits, the **United Artists DeVargas Mall** (562 N. Guadalupe St., 505/988-1110) is the closest to downtown.

Lectures

The **Lannan Foundation Lecture Series** (www.lannan.org) is run by a Santa Fe-based organization funding international writers and socially active artists. The program brings major writers and intellectuals (Noam Chomsky, Karen Russell, and Ta-Nehisi Coates) to the Lensic for interviews and conversation. Events usually sell out quickly—check the schedule a couple of months before your visit.

The **Southwest Seminars Series** (www.southwestseminars.org) runs weekly year-round. Speakers are anthropologists, archaeologists, and other researchers with a special interest in the history and people of the region. Talks take place nearly every Monday (50 weeks a year) at 6pm at the Hotel Santa Fe (1501 Paseo de Peralta).

FESTIVALS AND EVENTS

Santa Fe's summer is packed. In mid-July, the **International Folk Art Market** (505/992-7600, www.folkartalliance.org) showcases traditional crafts from all over the globe, often from the artists in person. It's set up on Museum Hill, so the center of the city is not disrupted. On Sunday, tickets are cheaper and vendors are ready to make deals.

In late July, **Spanish Market** (505/982-2226, www.spanishcolonial.org) takes over the plaza with traditional New Mexican

The International Folk Art Market takes place in July.

centered on the plaza, with some 1,200 Native American artisans selling jewelry, pottery, weaving, and more. Alongside, the upstart **Indigenous Fine Art Market** (www.indigefam.org), based at Railyard Park, emphasizes more contemporary work. It's all a bit of a frenzy, but festive, due to free music and dance performances in the week leading up to the market itself.

After all the frenzy of summer tourism, locals celebrate the arrival of fall with the weeklong **Fiesta de Santa Fe** (505/204-1598, www.santafefiesta.org), which has been celebrated in some form since 1712. It begins with a reenactment of De Vargas's *entrada* into the city, then a whole slew of balls and parades, including the Historical/Hysterical Parade and a children's pet parade—eccentric Santa Fe at its finest. The kickoff event is usually the **Burning of Zozobra** (855/ZOZ-OBRA, www.burnzozobra.com), a neo-pagan bonfire; the schedule has fluctuated a bit, but most recently, it was on the Friday before Labor Day. Some downtown businesses close for some Fiestas, particularly on Zozobra day.

In late September, foodies flock to the city for the **Santa Fe Wine and Chile Festival** (505/438-8060, www.santafewineandchile. org), five days of tastings and special dinners at various venues around town.

woodwork (especially santos), weaving, and furniture.

Finally, the city's biggest annual event is in late August, when 100,000 visitors come for **Santa Fe Indian Market** (505/983-5220, www.swaia.org). Like Spanish Market, it's

Shopping

Even people who clutch their purse strings tight may be a little undone by the treasures for sale in Santa Fe. The rational approach would be to consider the most expensive shops more as free museums. (The cheapest, on the other hand, are stocked with made-in-China junk and eternally on the brink of "going out of business" and should be avoided.) Downtown around the plaza are souvenir shops and a few influential galleries. On Canyon Road cluster art dealers of all stripes. South Guadalupe Street and surrounding blocks have more funky and fun

boutiques. If you buy too much to carry, **Pak Mail** (369 Montezuma Ave., 505/989-7380) can ship your treasures home safely; it even offers free pickup from hotels.

ART GALLERIES

With seemingly every other storefront downtown occupied by a gallery, Santa Fe's art scene can be overwhelming. The densest concentration of work is on Canyon Road, though it can seem a bit crowded with Southwestern kitsch. These are some of the biggest names, plus some of the more affordable galleries.

The Burning of Zozobra

Every fall a raucous chant fills the air in Santa Fe's Fort Marcy Park: "Burn him! Burn him! Burn him!" It's not a witch hunt, but the ritual torching of Zozobra, a 50-foot-tall marionette with long, grasping arms, glowering eyes, and a moaning voice. Old Man Gloom, as he's also known, represents the accumulated sorrows of the populace, as in the weeks before the event, he's stuffed with divorce papers, pictures of ex-girlfriends, hospital gowns, and other anxiety-inducing scraps. Setting this aflame purges these troubles and allows for a fresh start.

Old Man Gloom on the brink of burning

This Santa Fe tradition sounds like a medieval rite, but it dates only from the 1920s, when artist Will Shuster—a bit of a local legend who's also credited with inventing piñon-juniper incense and starting the tradition of citywide bonfires on Christmas Eve—wanted to lighten up the heavily Catholic Fiesta de Santa Fe. Shuster, who had moved to Santa Fe in 1920 to treat his tuberculosis, was inspired by the Mummers Parade from his native Philadelphia, as well as the Yaqui Indians in Tucson, Arizona, who burn Judas in effigy in the week before Easter. A 1926 *Santa Fe New Mexican* article describes the spectacle Shuster developed, with the help of the Kiwanis Club:

> Zozobra ... stood in ghastly silence illuminated by weird green fires. While the band played a funeral march, a group of Kiwanians in black robes and hoods stole around the figure.... [Then] red fires blazed at the foot ... and leaped into a column of many colored flames.... And throwing off their black robes the spectators emerged in gala costume, joining an invading army of bright-hued harlequins with torches in a dance around the fires as the band struck up "La Cucaracha."

Shuster oversaw Zozobra nearly every year until 1964. In the late 1930s, Errol Flynn, in town with Olivia de Havilland and Ronald Reagan to film *The Santa Fe Trail,* set Zozobra aflame. A few years later, during World War II, the puppet was dubbed Hirohitlomus. In 1950, Zozobra appeared on the New Mexico state float in the Rose Bowl parade and won the national trophy.

Although Zozobra (aka O.M.G.) has a Twitter account these days and accepts worries-to-burn online, the spectacle is roughly unchanged, with dozens of white-clad children playing "glooms," followed by a "fire dancer" who taunts Zozo until he bursts into flame; fireworks cap it off. It's a fine sight, and a great cross-section of Santa Feans attend. But anyone leery of crowds may prefer to watch from outside the perimeter of the ball field.

Summer hours are given here; in the winter, most galleries are closed at least Monday and Tuesday.

Definitely in the museum-quality category is **Peyton Wright** (237 E. Palace Ave., 505/989-9888, 9:30am-5pm Mon.-Sat.), a large house where one-off shows deal in modern American masters (need a Marsden Hartley for your foyer?) as well as old-world treasures that look as if they've been culled from a czar's forgotten vault. For quite the opposite feel, lighten up at **Chuck Jones Studio Gallery** (135 W. Palace Ave., 505/983-5999), where you can see original cels and sketches from early Disney films as well as more recent animated hits such as SpongeBob SquarePants and The Simpsons. Or you can just chill out and watch the good stuff on TV.

Local Artists

At the top end of Canyon Road, **Red Dot Gallery** (826 Canyon Rd., 505/820-7338, 10am-5pm Thurs.-Sun.) is the exhibition space for Santa Fe Community College students and alumni, a nice antidote to the high-toned vibe on the rest of the street. In the convention center, the **Community Gallery** (201 W. Marcy St., 505/955-6705, 10am-5pm Tues.-Fri., 9:30am-4pm Sat.) is run by the Santa Fe Arts Commission and always has a wide mix of work on display.

Contemporary

Santa Fe's contemporary scene has cooled a bit since its boom in the 2000s. But granddaddy **LewAllen** (1613 Paseo de Peralta, 505/988-3250, 10am-6pm Mon.-Fri., 10am-5pm Sat.) has survived and is one of the anchors in the Railyard, with a vast industrial space, fittingly across the street from the SITE Santa Fe museum.

Off Canyon Road, **Eight Modern** (231 Delgado St., 505/995-0231, 9:30am-5:30pm Mon.-Sat., 11am-4pm Sun.) focuses on colorful, abstract, and pop art. Nearby, **Nüart Gallery** (670 Canyon Rd., 505/988-3888, 10am-5pm daily) showcases Latin American magical realism.

Native American and Southwestern

Near Canyon Road, **Gerald Peters Gallery** (1011 Paseo de Peralta, 505/954-5700, 10am-5pm Mon.-Sat.) and **Nedra Matteucci Galleries** (1075 Paseo de Peralta, 505/982-4631, 9am-5pm Mon.-Sat.) are the biggies when it comes to Taos Society of Artists and other Western art, though both have contemporary artists too. Even if nothing inside hits the spot, the one-acre sculpture garden and ponds in back of Nedra Matteucci are a treat. Smaller **Robert Nichols Gallery** (419 Canyon Rd., 505/982-2145, 10am-5pm Mon.-Sat., 11am-5pm Sun.) specializes in Native American pottery, including some with often funny, boundary-pushing sensibilities.

Near the plaza, **Blue Rain Gallery** (130 Lincoln Ave., 505/954-9902, 10am-6pm Mon.-Sat.) showcases work from many pueblo residents, such as Tammy Garcia's modern takes on traditional Santa Clara pottery forms—she sometimes renders bowls in blown glass or applies the geometric decoration to jewelry. Across the street, **Allan Houser Gallery** (125 Lincoln Ave., 505/982-4705, 10am-5pm Mon.-Sat.) showcases the work of the Southwest's best-known Native sculptor; it also maintains a sculpture garden outside the city, with visits by appointment.

Sculpture

North of Santa Fe in the village of Tesuque, the bronze foundry **Shidoni** (1508 Bishops Lodge Rd., 505/988-8001, 9am-5pm Mon.-Sat.) has two large gardens full of metalwork sculpture, open from sunrise to sunset every day. If you want to see the foundry, show up at noon on a weekday ($3, for a self-guided tour) or any time between noon and 5pm on Saturday ($5, to see the bronze pouring). Immediately adjacent, **Tesuque Glassworks** (1510 Bishops Lodge Rd., 505/988-2165, 9am-5pm daily) functions as a co-op with a whole range of glass artists using the furnace and displaying their work. To get to Tesuque, head north out of Santa Fe on Washington Avenue, which becomes Bishops Lodge Road; Shidoni will be on the left side.

CLOTHING AND JEWELRY

¡Mira! (101 W. Marcy St., 505/988-3585, 10:30am-5:30pm Mon.-Sat., noon-5pm Sun.) has a hip mix of clothes and housewares, with T-shirts by local designers ("Fanta Se" in the old Santa Fe Railroad logo, say) as well as cool imports from places like Ghana. Just down the block, **Glorianna's** (55 W. Marcy St., 505/982-0353, 10am-4:30pm Mon.-Tues. and Thurs.-Sat., often closed for lunch 1pm-2pm) is a treasure trove of beads, packed to bursting with veritable eggs of raw turquoise, trays of glittering Czech glass, and ropes of African trade beads.

The city's best consignment shop is **Double Take** (321 S. Guadalupe St., 505/989-8886, 10am-6pm Mon.-Sat.), a sprawling two-story space with an excellent selection of boots, as well as cool clothing, rodeo-themed 1950s sofas, Fiestaware, and plenty more.

Another good secondhand outlet is **Ooh La La!** (518 Old Santa Fe Tr., 505/820-6433, 10:30am-5:30pm Mon.-Sat., noon-4pm Sun.), where the city's clotheshorses offload their impulse-buy Armani and Chloé. The shop is a little cramped, but racks are well organized by size and color.

Anyone who wears glasses should stop at **Ojo Optique** (125 Lincoln Ave., 505/988-4444, 10am-7pm Mon.-Sat., noon-5pm Sun.), which specializes in frames from boutique eyewear designers, working independent of the giant conglomerates that control most of the industry.

GIFT AND HOME

The owner of **Seret & Sons** (224 Galisteo St., 505/988-9151, 9am-5:30pm Mon.-Fri., 9am-6pm Sat., 9:30am-5pm Sun.) is a Santa Fe icon who deals in finely woven rugs, antique doors, and life-size wooden elephants from his cavernous warehouse just south of the plaza.

For funky folk art that won't break the bank, head for the equally gigantic **Jackalope** (2820 Cerrillos Rd., 505/471-8539, 9am-6pm Mon.-Sat., 10am-6pm Sun.), where seemingly acres are given over to mosaic-topped tables, wooden chickens, Mexican pottery vases, and inexpensive souvenirs. Sharing the space is a community of prairie dogs—good distraction for children while adults cruise the breakables.

OPEN-AIR MARKETS

One of the most familiar sights of Santa Fe is the portal of the **Palace of the Governors,** where American Indian vendors from all over New Mexico spread out their wares as they've been doing since the 1930s. More than 500 vendors are licensed to sell here after going through a strict application process that evaluates their technical skills. Every morning the 69 spots, each 12 bricks wide, are doled out by lottery. Expect anything from silver bracelets to pottery to *heishi* (shell bead) necklaces to freshly harvested piñon nuts. It's a great opportunity to buy direct from a skilled artisan and learn about the work that went into a piece.

As much a quirky fashion show and social scene as a shopping event, the **Santa Fe Flea** (505/982-2671, www.santafetraditionalflea. com) convenes vintage aficionados, fine artists, crafty folks, and "tailgate traders" of miscellaneous oddities. From late May through mid-October, it takes place at the Santa Fe Downs (27475 West Frontage Rd., just off Hwy. 599, north of I-25, 8am-3pm Fri.-Sun.). In winter, many of the vendors move indoors to **El Museo Cultural** (555 Camino de la Familia, 8am-3pm Sat.-Sun. late Nov.-Apr.) at the Railyard complex.

The **Pueblo of Tesuque Flea Market** (15 Flea Market Rd., 505/670-2599, www.tesuque-fleamarket.com, 9am-4pm Fri.-Sun., Mar.-Dec.) mixes local artists with traders from Africa, Guatemala, and elsewhere, and there are usually some good snacks (if not always amazing bargains) to be had. Take Exit 171 (Flea Market Rd.) off U.S. 84/285, just north of the Santa Fe Opera.

In the Santa Fe Farmers Market Pavilion, the **Railyard Artisan Market** (1607 Paseo de Peralta, www.artmarketsantafe.com, 10am-4pm) runs every Sunday. The selection is better in the shoulder seasons, when fewer competing craft fairs siphon off vendors.

SWEET TREATS

Todos Santos (125 E. Palace Ave., 505/982-3855, 10am-5pm Mon.-Sat.) adds the sweet smell of chocolate to the air in Sena Plaza. The closet-size shop has the perfect (if short-lived) Santa Fe souvenir: *milagros,* the traditional Mexican Catholic prayer charms shaped like body parts, rendered in Valrhona chocolate

Todos Santos deals in creative candies.

and covered in a delicate layer of gold or silver leaf. If you prefer nuts and chews, head to longtime candy vendor **Señor Murphy** (100 E. San Francisco St., 505/982-0461, 10am-5:30pm daily) for some "caramales" (chewy balls of caramel and piñon nuts wrapped up in little corn husks) and other New Mexico-inspired sweets.

Sports and Recreation

It's no accident *Outside* magazine has its offices here. After work and on weekends, Santa Feans leave the town to the tourists and scatter into the surrounding mountains on foot or bike. You'll find something to do all four seasons, though hikes above the foothills shouldn't be attempted till mid-May at least (and not until you're acclimated to the altitude). If you're in town in the fall, don't miss the leaves turning on the aspens, usually in mid-October (for a great, low-effort view, ride the lift at the ski basin). The access route for activities in the Sangre de Cristos is Highway 475—it starts out from the north side of Santa Fe as Artists Road, then the name changes to Hyde Park Road, and farther north it's Ski Basin Road.

Information and Guides

Just off Highway 14, immediately south of I-25, the **Public Lands Information Center** (301 Dinosaur Tr., 505/954-2002, www.publiclands.org, 8am-4:30pm Mon.-Sat.) is the best starting point for any planning. The staff will also know the latest status on areas affected by wildfires or floods. **Outspire!** (505/660-0394, www.outspire.com) runs guided full- and half-day outings—hiking in summer, snowshoeing in winter. For gear, check **REI** (500 Market St., 505/982-3557) in the Railyard district.

BIKING

Mountain bikers have fantastic outlets very close to Santa Fe, while those who prefer the

Santa Fe for Kids

In addition to the **Santa Fe Children's Museum** (1050 Old Pecos Tr., 505/989-8359, 10am-6pm Tues.-Wed., Fri.-Sat., 10am-6:30pm Thurs., noon-5pm Sun., www.santafechildrensmuseum.org, $7.50), the following are fun options, all open 10am-5pm Monday-Saturday, except where noted.

- **Bee Hive** (328 Montezuma Ave., 505/780-8051, also open noon-4pm Sun.) A lovingly curated kids' bookstore, often with story time on Saturdays.

- **Dinosaurs & More** (137 W. San Francisco St., 505/988-3299, also open Sun.) The owner can tell a story about nearly every meteorite, fossil, and geode in the place.

- **Doodlet's** (120 Don Gaspar St., 505/983-3771) Open since 1955, this corner shop is filled with bits and bobs for kids and adults, from toy accordions to kitchen tchotchkes.

- **Harrell House of Natural Oddities** (DeVargas Center, 177-B Paseo de Peralta, 505/695-8569, 10am-7pm Mon.-Fri., 10am-6pm Sat., noon-5pm Sun., $5) An amazing live collection of spiders, snakes, lizards, and more. Kids can pet giant millipedes and fuzzy tarantulas.

- **Moon Rabbit Toys** (112 W. San Francisco St., 505/982-9373, also open noon-4pm Sun.) Worth seeking out inside the Plaza Mercado, for its house-designed strategy games.

- **Toyopolis** (150 Washington Ave., 505/988-5422) The closest toy store to the plaza, for emergency distraction.

- **Warehouse 21** (1614 Paseo de Peralta, 505/989-4423, www.warehouse21.org) This teen arts center hosts a range of workshops, performances, and more.

open road will love the challenges in the winding highways through the mountains north of the city. **Rob & Charlie's** (1632 St. Michaels Dr., 505/471-9119, 9:30am-6pm Mon.-Sat., noon-5pm Sun. in summer) is a reliable shop. For **bike rental**, see **Mellow Velo** (132 E. Marcy St., 505/995-8356, 9am-6pm Mon.-Fri., 9am-5pm Sat., 9am-3pm Sun., from $20/day), just off the plaza.

Mountain Biking

The **Dale Ball Trails** are 22 miles of singletrack routes for both hikers and mountain bikers, winding through stands of piñon and juniper in the foothills. Two trailheads give access to the North, Central, and South Sections of the trail. From the northern trailhead, on Sierra del Norte (immediately off Highway 475 after mile marker 3), the North Section trails vary a bit in elevation, but the Central Section (south from the parking area) is more fun because it's a longer chunk of trails. The southern trailhead, on Cerro Gordo just north of its intersection with Canyon Road, gives access to the Central Section and the South Section, which is for advanced riders only. Note that the trail that starts at the southern trailhead lot, part of the Santa Fe Canyon Preserve, is for foot traffic only—ride your bike one-tenth of a mile down Cerro Gordo to the start of the Dale Ball system.

A local classic, the **Santa Fe Rail Trail** is a paved path starting in Railyard Park, then turns to dirt outside the city limits. Revamped and smoothed out a bit in 2012, the trail is a pleasant, relatively easy route along the railroad tracks to Lamy. The trail is about 12.5 miles one-way; except for a grade near I-25, it's fairly level.

In the rolling hills west of the city, **La Tierra Trails** are for biking, hiking, and horseback riding—though it's the two-wheel crew who makes the most use of them, especially after work, when the day is cooler (there's not much shade out here). There are three trailheads, all interconnected by various loops. Look for the turn west (not at a light) off Highway 599, the bypass road around the city.

The most popular mountain trail is **Winsor Trail** (no. 254), covering a great range of scenery and terrain. It's a long, slow slog up, rewarded by a downhill joyride on the return. There are few deadly steep ascents, so it's tiring but not impossible, and you'll rarely have to hike-a-bike. The main trail begins near Tesuque: Take Washington Avenue north out of the center of Santa Fe, continuing as it becomes Bishops Lodge Road (Highway 590). After not quite four miles, turn right onto County Road 72-A, also signed as Big Tesuque Canyon. There are two small pull-out areas for parallel parking, and the trail starts about one-tenth of a mile up the road from the second parking area—the first half mile is through private land. It's not cheating too badly to shorten the uphill leg by starting at Chamisa Trail, six miles up Highway 475 (Hyde Park Road), which connects with Winsor after 2.5 miles—but you'll need to arrange a pickup at the bottom.

Road Biking

Make sure you're acclimated to the altitude before you set out on any lengthy trip—the best tour, along the high road to Taos, will take you through some of the area's highest elevations. Starting in Chimayó shaves some not-so-scenic miles off the ride and gives you a reasonable 45-mile jaunt to Taos. The annual **Santa Fe Century** (www.santafecentury.com) takes place every May, running a 104-mile loop south down the Turquoise Trail and back north via the old farm towns in the Galisteo Basin, southeast of Santa Fe.

FISHING

Trout teem in the Rio Chama, northwest of Santa Fe. Visit the fly shop **The Reel Life** (526 N. Guadalupe St., 505/995-8114, 8am-7pm Mon.-Fri., 8am-6pm Sat., 8am-5pm Sun.), in DeVargas Center, where you can also arrange a day trip to nearby waters ($295 for two).

GOLF

Marty Sanchez Links de Santa Fe (205 Caja del Rio Rd., 505/955-4400, www.

linksdesanta fe.com) is a "water-aware" course that uses indigenous grasses and other plants to minimize water use. It offers great views of the mountains as you tour the 18 holes designed by Baxter Spann; there's also "The Great 28," an additional par-3 nine-holer that's exceptionally challenging. With five sets of tees, the course is good for both beginners and experts. Greens fees start at $21 for nine holes, and there are discounts after 2pm.

HIKING

Hikers can enjoy these dedicated trails, in addition to the multiuse trails for bicyclists.

Santa Fe Canyon Preserve

For an easy saunter in town, head for this 190-acre patch of the foothills managed by the **Nature Conservancy** (505/988-3867). The area is open only to people on foot—no mountain bikes and no pets. The preserve covers the canyon formed by the now-diverted Santa Fe River. An easy interpretive loop trail leads around the area for 1.5 miles, passing the remnants of the dam and winding through dense stands of cottonwoods and willows. The trailhead is on Cerro Gordo Road just north of its intersection with Upper Canyon Road.

Atalaya Mountain

One of the easiest-to-reach trails in the Santa Fe area (you can take the M city bus to the trailhead on the campus of St. John's College) is also one of the more challenging. The hike heads up to a **9,121-foot peak,** starting out as a gentle stroll along the city's edge, then becoming increasingly steep, for a round-trip of approximately seven miles. Allow about four hours for the full up-and-back.

Randall Davey Audubon Center

Birders of course will want to start a hike here, but even general visitors will be intrigued by the house of artist **Randall Davey** (1800 Upper Canyon Rd., 505/983-4609, 8am-4pm Mon.-Sat., $2) and two very pretty trails that lead into the forest and canyons behind. The

Fall in Northern New Mexico

With its evergreens and scrub trees, New Mexico doesn't seem a likely spot for a vivid display of fall colors. But the deciduous trees that flourish here—aspen, maple, cottonwood—are wild pockets of color against the rocky landscape, often bright gold against red rocks. You don't have to drive far to see the colors, which are usually at their peak in mid-October.

From Albuquerque, head to the east face of the **Sandia Mountains** and up the road to the peak, stopping off at Cienega Picnic Area and Las Huertas Picnic Area, about midway up the mountain. Or head southeast to the Manzano Mountains, where **Fourth of July Canyon**, where maple leaves turn shades of pink and crimson, is a beautiful color show. The area around Jemez is especially nice, with the cottonwoods contrasting with red canyon walls, though when you get close to Valles Caldera National Preserve, you hit wildfire damage.

Closer to Santa Fe, just drive up **Highway 475** (the road to the ski basin), where pullouts are positioned for the best vistas of the many colorful aspen stands. Abiquiu's dramatic rock formations are also a good backdrop for cottonwoods.

From Taos, the entire **Enchanted Circle** drive passes through various patches of color.

---

beautifully painted back rooms of the house are open for a guided **tour** ($5) at 2pm every Friday, and a free guided bird walk departs from the parking lot at 8am every Saturday.

Aspen Vista

The most popular trail in the Sangre de Cristos is probably **Aspen Vista.** But don't be put off by the prospect of crowds, as the promised views of golden aspen groves are indeed spectacular—in the densest spots, when the sun is shining through the leaves, the air itself feels yellow. Even though it's at a high elevation, it's an easy hike, on a service road with a gradual slope. The full length is 11.5 miles, but it's the first 2.5 miles that are the most aspen-intense. A little under 4 miles in, you get a great view of Santa Fe below; this makes a good turnaround point for a two-hour hike. Look for the parking area on the right of Ski Basin Road (Hwy. 475), just under 13 miles up the road from town.

Raven's Ridge

This is another local favorite, though not too heavily traveled, with great views of Santa Fe Baldy (elev. 12,622 feet)—while you're busy slogging up and over several peaks yourself. The trail starts at the Winsor trailhead (no. 254) in the Santa Fe ski area parking lot, but when you reach the wilderness boundary fence, the **Raven's Ridge Trail** heads to the right along the outside of the fence. The trail shows up on only one local map (Drake Mountain Maps' *Map of the Mountains of Santa Fe*), but it's easy to follow once you're up there. When in doubt, just head uphill: You'll bag Deception, Lake, and Tesuque peaks in a total of seven miles and with a top elevation of 12,409 feet, returning to the ski area parking lot by walking down along the Tesuque chairlift. But this final stretch isn't particularly scenic, so you may want to take in only one or two of the peaks (Lake Peak, the second you reach, is the highest) and then retrace your steps.

Rio en Medio

You can lose the crowds just by heading a little farther from town: **Rio en Medio Trail** (no. 163) begins north of Tesuque and leads along a clear stream to a series of waterfalls and then up some rather strenuous switchbacks to a large meadow that's filled with wildflowers in springtime. From the trailhead to the first cascade is 1.7 miles. The meadow is at the 3.5-mile mark, where you'll probably want to turn around, for a hike that will take a total of four or five hours.

To reach the trailhead, drive north out of

Santa Fe on Washington Avenue, which becomes Bishops Lodge Road (Highway 590). Drive straight through the village of Tesuque and then turn right in less than a mile onto Highway 592, following signs for the village of Rio en Medio. In the village, which you reach after 6.5 miles, the road turns into County Road 78-D, a very unpromising-looking dirt track that winds through front yards for 0.8 mile before ending in a small parking area. A forest road carries on from there for a short stretch, and then the trail proper heads off to the right and down along a stream.

ROCK CLIMBING

To polish your skills or get tips on nearby routes, talk to the experts at **Santa Fe Climbing Center** (825 Early St., 505/986-8944, www.climbsantafe.com, 3pm-9pm Mon. and Wed., 9am-9pm Tues. and Thurs.-Fri, noon-8pm Sat., 10am-6pm Sun.). You can play around on the walls at the gym ($14 for a day pass) or sign up for a guided group trip to a nearby climbing site (starting at $90 for half a day).

Ten Thousand Waves brings Japan to Santa Fe.

SPAS

★ **Ten Thousand Waves** (3451 Hyde Park Rd., 505/982-9304, www.tenthousandwaves. com, 9am-10:30pm Wed.-Mon., noon-10:30pm Tues. July-Oct.) is such a Santa Fe institution that it could just as well be listed under the city's major attractions. This traditional Japanese-style bathhouse just outside of town has two big communal pools and seven smaller private ones tucked among the trees so as to optimize the views of the mountains all around; many have adjoining cold plunges and saunas. The place also offers full day-spa services, with intense massages and luxe facials and body scrubs. Prices are relatively reasonable, starting at $24 for unlimited time in the public baths and $112 for one-hour massages. In the winter (Nov.-June), the baths open at 10:30am (at 2pm Tues.) and close earlier on weeknights.

In town, **Absolute Nirvana Spa** (106 Faithway St., 505/983-7942, www.absolute-nirvana.com, 10am-6pm Sun.-Thurs., 10am-8pm Fri.-Sat.) offers Balinese treatments and massages. Afterward, you can relax in the gardens with a cup of tea and some organic sweets from the adjacent tearoom.

Very highly rated by locals, **Body of Santa Fe** (333 W. Cordova Rd., 505/986-0362, www. bodyofsantafe.com, 9am-9pm daily) is praised for its affordable treatments (massages from $80/hour) and relaxed atmosphere. There's a nice café on-site too.

SPECTATOR SPORTS

The **Santa Fe Fuego** (www.santafefuego. com), a baseball team that puts the minor in minor league, plays at Fort Marcy Park, just north of the plaza area, mid-May through July. It's part of the incredibly scrappy Pecos League (www.pecosleague.com), established in 2011 and fielding nine teams from around New Mexico, Arizona, west Texas, and Colorado.

SPORTS FACILITIES

For bargain yoga classes, swimming in a 25-yard indoor pool, and other activities close to the plaza, stop in at the **Fort Marcy Recreation Complex** (490 Bishops Lodge

Rd., 505/955-2500, www.santafenm.gov, 6am-8:30pm Mon.-Fri., 9am-4pm Sat., $4).

Genoveva Chavez Community Center (3221 Rodeo Rd., 505/955-4000, www.chavez-center.com, 5:30am-9:45pm Mon.-Thurs., 5:30am-7:45pm Fri., 8am-7:45pm Sat., 9am-5:45pm Sun., $5) is the city's biggest recreational facility. It has a large swimming pool with a slide and a separate lap pool (both are indoors); basketball and racquetball courts; a gym; and a year-round ice rink.

The city's only outdoor pool is **Bicentennial Pool** (1121 Alto St., 505/955-4778, $3), open from late May through early September.

WINTER SPORTS

Sixteen miles northeast of town in the Santa Fe National Forest, **Ski Santa Fe** (Hwy. 475, 505/982-4429, www.skisantafe.com, $70 full-day lift ticket) is a well-used day area with 77 fairly challenging trails. A major selling point: virtually no lift lines.

Exclusively for cross-country skiers, the groomed **Norski Trail** starts about a quarter of a mile before the Ski Santa Fe parking lot, off the west side of the road. The standard route is about 2.5 miles, winding through the trees and along a ridgeline, and you can shorten or lengthen the tour by taking various loops and shortcuts, as long as you follow the directional arrows counterclockwise.

Just seven miles out of town along the road to the ski area, **Hyde Memorial State Park** (Hwy. 475, 505/983-7175, www.nmparks.com) has an ice rink, a couple of nicely maintained sledding runs, and some shorter cross-country ski routes.

For gear, **Cottam's Ski Shop** (740 Hwy. 475, 505/982-0495) is the biggest rental operation in the area, handily located on the way to Aspen Vista.

Accommodations

Santa Fe offers some great places to stay, but none are cheap. Prices quoted for the bigger hotels are standard rack rates; chances are, you'll find substantially lower ones by calling or booking online, at least at the higher-end properties. Prices spike in July and August, often up to holiday rates. If you're coming for Indian Market or Christmas, try to book at least eight months in advance. On the other hand, despite ski season, rates are often quite low in early December, January, and February.

UNDER $100

As hostels go, **Santa Fe International Hostel** (1412 Cerrillos Rd., 505/988-1153, www.hostelsantafe.com) is not the worst, but neither is it one of the more inspiring—unless you clamp on your rose-colored glasses and view it as an old-school hippie project (it *is* run as a nonprofit). The dorms ($20 pp) and private rooms ($25 s, $35 d) are dim, and cleanliness can be spotty, as you're relying on the previous guests' efforts, as part of the required daily chores. The kitchen has free food, but you have to pay for Internet access ($2/day), and everything is cash only.

For camping, the closest tent sites to the center are at **Hyde Memorial State Park** (Hwy. 475, 505/983-7175, www.nmparks.com), about four miles northwest of the city, with both primitive ($8) and developed sites with electricity ($14). The commercial **Rancheros de Santa Fe** (736 Old Las Vegas Hwy., 505/466-3482, www.rancheros.com, Mar.-Oct.), a 20-minute drive east of the plaza, is an option, but it's geared mainly to RVs; the tent sites ($25) are packed together and not very shady. A little farther along, the **KOA** (934 Old Las Vegas Hwy., 505/466-1419, www.santafekoa.com) has some shadier tent sites ($25), good laundry facilities, and a game room.

Possibly the best lodging deal in Santa Fe, the **Quaker Meeting House** (630 Canyon

Rd., 505/983-7241, www.santa-fe.quaker.org, $45 s, $55 d) rents a guest casita with a kitchenette. It's a small space, and it's a three-night minimum, but the location on Canyon Road can't be beat. Payment is cash only.

Wedged in among the chain hotels on Cerrillos, the self-described "kitschy" ★ **Silver Saddle Motel** (2810 Cerrillos Rd., 505/471-7663, www.santafesilversaddlemotel. com, $62 s, $67 d) plays up the retro charm. Cozy rooms may be pretty basic and have cinder-block walls, but they're decked out with Western accoutrements and kept clean—and the price, which includes breakfast, can't be beat. A handful of later-built rooms have some extra square footage.

$100-150

The bones of ★ **Santa Fe Sage Inn** (725 Cerrillos Rd., 505/982-5952, www.santafesageinn.com, $115 d) are a standard highway motel, but the superclean rooms are done in sharp, modern red and black, with Southwestern rugs hung on the walls. Little touches such as free Wi-Fi, plush beds, and an above-average breakfast (fresh bagels, fruit, yogurt, and more) make this an excellent deal. The place even has a swimming pool. It's still walking distance to the center, and it's right across the street from the Railyard Park and the farmers market.

Despite its location on uncharming Cerrillos Road, about two miles from the plaza, **El Rey Inn** (1862 Cerrillos Rd., 505/982-1931, www.elreyinnsantafe.com, $105 s, $140 d) counts as one of the more charming hotels in Santa Fe. Built in 1935, it has been meticulously kept up and adjusted for modern standards of comfort, with beautiful gardens, a hot tub, a big swimming pool, and a fireside open-air Jacuzzi. The 86 rooms, spread over 4.5 acres, vary considerably in style (and in price), from the oldest section with snug adobe walls and heavy viga ceilings to airier rooms with balconies. Rooms at the back of the property, away from traffic noise, are preferable.

Santa Fe Motel & Inn (510 Cerrillos Rd., 505/982-1039, www.santafemotel.com, $149 d) is an excellent budget option close to the center, with rooms done up in simple, bright decor that avoids motel sameness despite the generic motor-court layout. A few kitchenettes are available, along with some more private casitas with fireplaces. Lots of nice touches—such as bread from the Sage Bakehouse across the street along with the full breakfast—give the place a homey feel without the tight quarters of a typical bed-and-breakfast.

$150-200

In a handy location west of the plaza, **Las Palomas** (460 W. San Francisco St., 505/982-5560, www.laspalomas.com, $153 d) is good to know about for last-minute booking. A cluster of four separate complexes, it usually has room when smaller B&Bs are full, and online booking discounts can be generous. But room layouts vary significantly, and some casitas have bedrooms facing parking lots, which feels no better than a motel. Call to book, if you can.

East of the plaza, twin bed-and-breakfasts under the same ownership offer two kinds of style: The rooms at **Hacienda Nicholas** (320 E. Marcy St., 505/986-1431, www.haciendanicholas.com, $165 d) have a tasteful Southwest flavor, decorated with a few cowboy trappings and Gustave Baumann prints; most rooms have fireplaces. Across the street, **The Madeleine** (106 Faithway St., 505/982-3465, www.madeleineinn.com, $165 d) is set in a wood Victorian, but the lace curtains are offset with rich Balinese fabrics. In both places, breakfast is a continental spread, but that doesn't mean you'll go away hungry—the banana bread is fantastic.

Hotel Chimayó (125 Washington Ave., 505/988-4900, www.hotelchimayo.com, $169 d), offers good value very close to the plaza, though not everyone will like its folky style, done up with wooden crosses and striped rugs from its namesake village. Upstairs rooms have private balconies, and some suites have fireplaces.

Majority-owned by Picurís Pueblo, **Hotel Santa Fe** (1501 Paseo de Peralta,

Hotel Chimayó

800/825-9876, www.hotelsantafe.com, $169 d) is both a successful business experiment and a very nice hotel, with one of the few large outdoor pools in town, set against the neo-pueblo hotel walls. The standard rooms are a bit small—the real value is in the luxe **Hacienda** wing, where the huge rooms with fireplaces and butler service can be as low as $199 online—a steal compared with other high-end places in town.

Hotel Santa Fe

The 100-room **Inn of the Governors** (101 W. Alameda St., 505/982-4333, www.in-nofthegovernors.com, $189 d) doesn't look like much on the outside, but inside it has a personable only-in-Santa-Fe feel, starting with the afternoon "tea and sherry hour," when guests are plied with free drinks and *bizcochitos*. Its unique profit-sharing system may account for the exceptionally nice staff. Other perks: Breakfast is generous, parking is free (unheard-of elsewhere downtown), and there's even a tiny pool. Rooms in the Governors Wing are quietest.

$200-250

Opened in 2014, **Drury Plaza Santa Fe** (228 E. Palace Ave., 505/424-2175, www.

druryplazasantafe.com, $210 d) has a somewhat corporate feel, but it occupies a big historic hospital complex behind the St. Francis Cathedral—a very convenient location, at a pretty good price for amenities like a rooftop pool, full breakfast, and free drinks in the afternoon. Rooms are a little small but very comfortably furnished.

Inn on the Alameda (303 E. Alameda St., 505/984-2121, www.innonthealameda. com, $229 d) is a good option for people who want adobe style *and* space, and its location near Canyon Road is handy for gallery-hoppers. The big rooms have triple-sheeted beds, wireless Internet access, and overstuffed armchairs that are only lightly dusted with Southwestern flair; most also have a patio or balcony. Gas fireplaces are usually an additional $20. The continental breakfast spread is generous, and there's a wine-and-cheese hour every afternoon.

A rental condo is a great option if you have a family or group, and those at **Campanilla Compound** (334 Otero St., 800/828-9700, www.campanillacompound.com, $235) are especially nice, with whitewashed walls, fireplaces, and Mexican-tiled kitchens. Each unit has plenty of space inside and out, with a private patio or porch, and, thanks to the location on a hill, some have excellent views of the city and the sunset. There's a two-night minimum.

The iconic, family-owned ★ **La Fonda** (100 E. San Francisco St., 505/982-5511, www. lafondasantafe.com, $229 s, $249 d) underwent a major renovation in 2013, which lightened up its guest rooms considerably. They feel slightly more generic and modern as a result, though many do have original folk art, and a few have *latilla* ceilings and kiva fireplaces—along with all the necessary luxuries, such as pillow-top beds. You can soak up most of the place's atmosphere in the public areas, of course, but the location couldn't be better. It helps to have flexible dates—in periods of high demand, the rates can spike to exorbitant levels.

A wonderfully restful spot is **Houses of the Moon** (3451 Hyde Park Rd., 505/992-5003, www.tenthousandwaves.com, $239 d), the guest cottages at Ten Thousand Waves spa. Some have more of a local feel, with viga ceilings and kiva fireplaces, while others are straight from Japan, both samurai era and contemporary anime. Some larger suites have kitchens. Rates include a suitably organic granola breakfast as well as free access to the communal and women's tubs.

OVER $250

Special occasion? The Relais & Chateaux property **The Inn of the Five Graces** (150 E. De Vargas St., 505/992-0957, www.fivegraces.com, $450 per suite) can transport you to exotic lands—for at least slightly less than a plane ticket. Outside, it looks like a typical historic Southwestern lodge, a collection of interconnected adobe casitas on Santa Fe's oldest street. But inside, the 24 sumptuous suites are done in the style of an opium dream: antique Turkish kilims, heavy wood doors, and mosaics—all courtesy of the boho-style dealers Seret & Sons. Rates include full breakfast, delivered to your room if you like.

Food

Dining is one of Santa Fe's great pleasures. For a relatively tiny population, it offers a dazzling range of restaurants. Sure, you can get a cheese-smothered, crazy-hot plate of green-chile-and-chicken enchiladas, but most locals eat more globally than that. "Santa Fe cuisine" cheerfully incorporates Asian, Southwestern, and Mediterranean flavors, with an emphasis on organic and holistic.

DOWNTOWN

The ring formed by Alameda Street and Paseo de Peralta contains some classic Santa Fe spots, plus a few hidden treats. On the

Santa Fe's Finest Dining

In Santa Fe, there is a certain category of restaurant that one reader of this guide dubbed "Vegas-style"—that is, a place where the blingier your bolo tie or cowboy boots, the better. They're not totally superficial—in fact, **Coyote Café** (132 W. Water St., 505/983-1615, 5:30pm-9pm Sun.-Thurs., 5:30pm-10pm Fri.-Sat., $40) at least deserves a spot in the history books for having pioneered haute Southwestern cuisine in the late 1980s, under Chef Mark Miller. Today that restaurant is owned by the same team as **Geronimo** (724 Canyon Rd., 505/982-1500, 5:45pm-9pm daily, $42), and both have opted for more generic fine dining with the occasional local nod—chile-rubbed pork chops, haute green-chile mac-and-cheese, etc. **La Casa Sena** (125 E. Palace Ave., 505/988-9232, 11am-9pm Mon.-Wed., 11am-10pm Thurs.-Sat., $30) and **The Compound** (653 Canyon Rd., 505/982-4353, 11:30am-2:30pm and 5pm-9pm Mon.-Sat. and 5:30pm-9pm Sun., $38) run in the same vein, though both have notably, beautiful settings.

They're all acceptable in terms of food, but certainly not great value, and you'll be dining, for the most part, alongside other visitors, not locals. The best way to see the scene without emptying your wallet is at their bars. The Coyote Café has its lively **Rooftop Cantina** (505/983-1615, 11:30am-11pm daily, Apr.-Oct.), and the snug bar at Geronimo is a good place to put your feet up after a Canyon Road cruise. La Casa Sena is set in a truly dreamy garden courtyard. Order a cocktail and an appetizer, or perhaps lunch, and enjoy the eye candy.

plaza itself, the carnitas cart and the fajitas cart are classics too—and the Chicago hot dog stand, when it's set up, gets strong votes for authenticity.

Cafés

Ecco (105 E. Marcy St., 505/986-9778, 7am-9pm Mon.-Thurs., 7am-10pm Fri., 8am-10pm Sat., 8am-7pm Sun.) is packed with coffee junkies and Wi-Fi fanatics in the mornings; later, people come in for panini (at the counter next door) and gelato.

The **French Pastry Shop** (100 E. San Francisco St., 505/983-6697, 6:30am-5pm daily, $7) has been doling out sweet crepes, buttery pastries, croques monsieurs, and chewy baguette sandwiches for more than 40 years. Early mornings attract a fascinating crew of Santa Fe regulars.

★ **Tia Sophia's** (210 W. San Francisco St., 505/983-9880, 7am-2pm Mon.-Sat., 8am-1pm Sun., $8) is one of the last places in the plaza area that feels untouched by time and tourists, serving old-time New Mexican plates to a slew of regulars without a touch of fusion—so authentic, in fact, the kitchen claims to have invented the breakfast burrito decades back.

Plaza Café (54 Lincoln Ave., 505/982-1664,

7am-9pm daily, $11) may look shiny and new, but it's a city institution where residents roll in to read the paper and load up on coffee and great renditions of New Mexican and American diner favorites. This is no greasy spoon, though—the granola is house-made, the posole is perfectly toothsome, and the piñon blue-corn pancakes are fluffy and fresh.

For a very casual lunch, stop in at the **Five & Dime General Store** (58 E. San Francisco St., 505/992-1800, 8:30am-10pm Mon.-Sat., 9am-9pm Sun., $5), on the south side of the plaza. In this former Woolworth's where, allegedly, the Frito pie was invented (Frito-Lay historians beg to differ), the knickknack shop has maintained its lunch counter and still serves the deadly combo of corn chips, homemade red chile, onions, and shredded cheese, all composed directly in the Fritos bag. Eat in, or, better, lounge on the plaza grass—and don't forget the napkins.

Longtime burger connoisseurs may remember Bobcat Bite, just outside of the city. It closed in 2013, and ★ **Santa Fe Bite** (311 Old Santa Fe Tr., 505/982-0544, 11am-9pm Tues.-Fri., 8am-9pm Sat., 8am-8pm Sun., $12) is the new and even better incarnation, close to the plaza, in much more comfortable digs.

The same 10-ounce burgers, from beef ground fresh every day, on a home-baked bun, are the stars. But there's plenty more, including tacos, big salads, and, on Fridays, fish-and-chips. Wash it down with a cold Mexican Coke.

Fresh and Local

Open since the late 1970s, ★ **Café Pasqual's** (121 Don Gaspar St., 505/983-9340, 8am-3pm and 5:30pm-9:30pm daily, $28) has defined its own culinary category, relying almost entirely on organic ingredients. Its breakfasts are legendary, but the food is delicious any time of day. Just brace yourself for the inevitable line, as the brightly painted dining room seats only 50 people, and loyal fans number in the thousands. Expect nearly anything on the menu: smoked-trout hash or Yucatán-style *huevos motuleños* for breakfast; for dinner, mole enchiladas or Vietnamese squid salad.

Italian

Rooftop Pizzeria (60 E. San Francisco St., 505/984-0008, 11am-10pm Sun.-Thurs., 11am-11pm Fri.-Sat., $15) is a good place to enjoy a view along with your meal, on a long balcony overlooking Water Street (enter on the plaza side of the shopping complex and head upstairs). You have the option of a crust with a hint of blue-corn meal, and toppings range from plain old onions to duck and crab, and they come in combinations like the BLT (the lettuce is added after the pie comes out of the oven, luckily). It also has a good selection of wines by the glass. Winter closing time is an hour earlier.

Off the plaza, next to Mission San Miguel, **Upper Crust Pizza** (329 Old Santa Fe Tr., 505/982-0000, 11am-10pm daily, $12) has a pleasantly rustic atmosphere, with a nice creaky front porch, often with a live country crooner. It does regular, whole-wheat, or gluten-free crust. Hot deli sandwiches and big superfresh salads round out the menu.

Locals head to amber-lit **Il Piatto** (95 W. Marcy St., 505/984-1091, 11:30am-10:30pm Mon.-Sat., 4:30pm-10:30pm Sun., $22) for casual Italian and a neighborly welcome from the staff, who seem to be on a first-name basis with everyone in the place. Hearty pastas like pappardelle with duck are served in generous portions—a half order will more than satisfy lighter eaters. This is a great place to take a breather from enchiladas and burritos, without breaking the bank. Its bar offers a pleasant later happy hour, 9pm-10:30pm every night.

Mexican

The specialty at **Bumble Bee's Baja Grill** (301 Jefferson St., 505/820-2862, 11am-8:30pm Sun.-Thurs., 11am-9pm Fri.-Sat., $5) is Baja-style shrimp tacos, garnished with shredded cabbage and a creamy sauce, plus a spritz of lime and your choice of house-made salsas. Lamb tacos are also delicious, as are the fried-fresh tortilla chips and that Tijuana classic, Caesar salad.

New Mexican

The Shed (113½ E. Palace Ave., 505/982-9030, 11am-2:30pm and 5:30pm-9pm daily, $17) has been serving up platters of enchiladas since 1953—bizarrely, with a side of garlic bread. But that's just part of the tradition at this colorful, comfortable, marginally fancy place that's as popular with tourists as it is with die-hard residents. There are perfectly decent distractions like lemon-garlic shrimp and fish tacos on the menu, but it's the red chile you should focus on.

Spanish

Cozy creative-tapas joint **La Boca** (72 W. Marcy St., 505/982-3433, 11:30am-10pm daily, little plates $7-14) starts from Spain, then pulls in other Mediterranean influences: a salad spiked with apricots and figs, Moroccan *merguez*, and more. The little plates can add up fast, unless you're there 3pm-5pm weekdays, when there's a selection for half price. Reserve, ideally, and go early if you're sensitive to noise.

If you prefer a more traditional approach to Spanish food, head for the offshoot **Taberna La Boca** (125 Lincoln Ave., 505/988-7102, 11:30am-2pm and 5pm-11pm daily, $12), around the corner, tucked in the middle of the block. The atmosphere is a bit more casual here, with music in the evenings, and paella is a deal on Tuesdays, when a three-course meal is $20, as are select bottles of wine.

GUADALUPE AND THE RAILYARD

An easy walk from the plaza, these few square blocks hold some of the better, quirkier dining options in town.

American

All things Texan are the specialty at **Cowgirl BBQ** (319 S. Guadalupe St., 505/982-2565, 11:30am-10:30pm Sun.-Wed., 11:30am-4pm Thurs., 11:30am-11pm Fri., 11am-11pm Sat., $15)—but it has been a Santa Fe fixture for so long that it doesn't seem like "foreign" food. It's a kitsch-filled spot that's as friendly to kids as it is to margarita-guzzling, barbecue-rib-gnawing adults. Non-meat-eaters won't feel left out: An ooey-gooey butternut squash casserole comes with a salad on the side. Both carnivores and veggies can agree on the pineapple upside-down cake and the ice-cream "baked potato."

Beloved local chef Chris Knox, formerly of the great restaurant Aqua Santa, went casual with **Shake Foundation** (631 Cerrillos Rd., 505/988-8992, 11am-6pm daily, $6), a casual outdoor burger joint that's so good people flock to it even in winter. The dainty burgers (you might want a double) are good, vouched-for beef or lamb, served on lavishly buttered buns, and piñon nuts are an optional topping for the Taos Cow ice cream. Even the Caesar salad is ingenious: a veritable bouquet of whole romaine leaves, to dip and dunk in a creamy dressing.

Cafés

Make room in your morning for an almond croissant from ★ **Sage Bakehouse** (535 Cerrillos Rd., 505/820-7243, 7:30am-2:30pm Mon.-Sat., $4). Washed down with a mug of coffee, these butter-soaked pastries will have you set for hours. Before you leave, pick up some sandwiches for later—classic combos

The party gets started early at Cowgirl BBQ.

like smoked turkey and cheddar on the bakery's excellent crust. And maybe a pecan-raisin wreath. And a cookie too.

A few steps away is **Ohori's Coffee, Tea & Chocolate** (505 Cerrillos Rd., 505/988-9692, 7:30am-6pm Mon.-Fri., 8am-6pm Sat., 9am-2pm Sun.), Santa Fe's small-batch coffee epicures. Its dark-as-night brew makes Starbucks seem weak. There's a second shop just out of the center at 1098 South St. Francis Drive.

Fresh and Local

If you're on green-chile-and-cheese overload, head to ★ **Vinaigrette** (709 Don Cubero Alley, 505/820-9205, 11am-9pm Mon.-Sat., $14) and dig into a big pile of fresh greens. The so-called salad bistro uses largely organic ingredients from its farm in Nambé, in imaginative combos, like a highbrow taco salad with chorizo and honey-lime dressing. The setting is pure homey Santa Fe, with tea towels for napkins, iced tea served in canning jars, and local art on the whitewashed walls. There's a pretty patio too. Heading north on

Cerrillos Road, turn off just after La Unica Cleaners.

Just outside the Paseo de Peralta loop, the **Tune-Up Café** (1115 Hickox St., 505/983-7060, 7am-10pm Mon.-Fri., 8am-10pm Sat.-Sun., $9) is a homey one-room joint that locals love, whether for fish tacos or a suitably Santa Fe-ish brown-rice-and-nut burger. The Salvadoran *pupusas* are tasty.

Swiss Bistro & Bakery (401 S. Guadalupe St., 505/988-1111, 7am-3pm Mon.-Wed., 7am-9pm Thurs.-Sun., $11) has a delectable selection of pastries, and, thanks to the owner's interest in vegetable gardening, beautiful heirloom varieties of tomatoes and other rare produce make their way into typical Euro delights like quiche, crepes, and schnitzel.

The popular **Santa Fe Farmers Market** (1607 Paseo de Peralta, 505/983-4098, www.santafefarmersmarket.com, 8am-1pm Tues., 7am-noon Sat., Sat. only Dec.-Apr.) is a great place to pick up fresh treats as well as souvenir chile *ristras*. It's in a market hall in the Railyard complex, off Paseo de Peralta near Guadalupe Street.

New Mexican

The under-the-radar cousin of The Shed, **La Choza** (905 Alarid St., 505/982-0909, 11am-2:30pm and 5pm-9pm Mon.-Sat., $16) has a similar creative New Mexican menu but can be more of a local hangout—though it has become better known now that the rail yard has been developed around it. This also makes it a handy destination if you're coming to Santa Fe on the train—just walk back down the tracks a few minutes.

Fine Dining

Whether you want hearty bar food or an ethereal creation that will take your taste buds in new directions, Chef Joseph Wrede, formerly of the great Joseph's Table in Taos, delivers. His lovely, candlelit space, ★ **Joseph's** (428 Agua Fria St., 505/982-1272, www.josephsofsantafe.com, 4:30pm-10pm Sun.-Thurs., 4:30pm-11pm Fri.-Sat., $28), is this author's favorite restaurant in Santa Fe. Wrede worships fresh produce, and his best dishes are vegetable-centric, though not necessarily vegetarian. But he's also into local meats, so carnivores will find hearty elk steaks and a seemingly simple lamb patty that may be the state's best green-chile cheeseburger. Book ahead if you can, or try for a seat at the bar. And whatever happens, don't miss the duck-fat ice cream.

Restaurant Martín (526 Galisteo St., 505/820-0919, 11:30am-2pm and

asparagus harvest at the farmers market

5:30pm-10pm Tues.-Fri. and Sun., 5:30pm-10pm Sat., $34) is run by longtime local hero Chef Martín Rios. His "progressive American" food can be more style than substance, especially for full-price dinners, but it's a good place for a grown-up lunch—smooth service and a mix of full plates as well as a big burger on a cornmeal bun ($14).

CANYON ROAD

Gallery hopping can make you hungry—but there are only a handful of places to eat on Canyon Road, and most are more dedicated to getting caffeine into your system.

Cafés

For morning brew, jog off the strip to **Downtown Subscription** (376 Garcia St., 505/983-3085, 7am-6pm daily), an airy coffee shop that stocks perhaps a million magazines. Chocolate freaks should go a little farther to ★ **Kakawa Chocolate House** (1050 E. Paseo de Peralta, 505/982-0388, 10am-6pm Mon.-Sat., noon-6pm Sun., $4), opposite the Gerald Peters Gallery. It specializes in historically accurate hot chocolate, based on Mesoamerican and medieval European recipes, and you can also get regular coffee drinks, truffles, and pastries here. It's in a tiny adobe house—after one drink, you'll be bouncing off the walls.

For a mellower high, head to the top end of Canyon Road and **The Teahouse** (821 Canyon Rd., 505/992-0972, 9am-9pm daily, $12), where some 13 pages of the menu are devoted to teas, plus organic vittles such as kale salad with sunflower-seed dressing, and a deliciously hearty bowl of oats, rice, and wheat berries for breakfast. The service could be euphemistically described as "very Santa Fe" (i.e., spacey), but the food is good, and it's a great place to put your feet up after a long art crawl.

Spanish

The lively evening spot is stalwart **El Farol** (808 Canyon Rd., 505/983-9912, 11am-10pm Sun.-Thurs., 11am-11pm Fri.-Sat., $8). It's very popular as a bar, but its outside seating, under a creaky wooden portal and on a back patio, is an appealing place for a big stuffed sandwich (tuna and egg with arugula, say) or garlicky Spanish snacks.

CERRILLOS ROAD

This commercial strip isn't Santa Fe's most scenic zone, but you'll find some great culinary gems out this way.

African

Just next to the Hobby Lobby in a strip mall, ★ **Jambo** (2010 Cerrillos Rd., 505/473-1269, 11am-9pm Mon.-Sat., $11) has a menu of spicy, earthy food that's well priced and almost always satisfying. The menu features primarily Indian-inflected dishes from East Africa—lentil stew spiked with chile and softened with coconut, for instance—as well as Caribbean and Moroccan stews.

Asian

A little oasis of Asian-inflected organic food in a chain-restaurant part of town, **Mu Du Noodles** (1494 Cerrillos Rd., 505/983-1411, 5:30pm-9pm Tues.-Sat., $18) cuts the strip-mall glare with warm-hued walls and bamboo screens. The menu ranges from Central Asia to Japan, offering lamb pot stickers, coconutty and spicy Malaysian *laksa,* and Indian yellow curry along the way. Reviving citrusade with ginger is delicious hot or cold, or you can order beer or wine. It's open Mondays in summer.

Cafés

Community activists need caffeine too—and they head to the **Santa Fe Baking Co.** (504 W. Cordova Rd., 505/988-4292, 6am-8pm Mon.-Sat., 6am-6pm Sun., $9) to get it. The scene is talkative (local radio station KSFR broadcasts a live show from here weekday mornings), and vegetarians will find a lot to eat—but so will fans of gut-busters such as chile dogs. Breakfast is served all day.

Counter Culture (930 Baca St., 505/995-1105, 8am-3pm Sun.-Mon., 8am-9pm

Tues.-Sat., $12) is generally a locals-only scene, well liked for its range of food (green chile, Vietnamese sandwiches, cinnamon buns), its casual-industrial vibe, and its outdoor space where kids can run around.

Mexican

Great things come out of the modest truck called **El Chile Toreado** (W. Cordova Rd., 505/800-0033, 8:15am-3pm Mon.-Fri., 8:15am-2pm Sat., $7), parked on Cordova Road, just east of Cerrillos. Its green salsa is a near-mystical cilantro experience, and its carnitas may be the best in town. It also serves excellent breakfast burritos—get one with Mexican chorizo.

New Mexican

Green chile has been getting milder over the years—but not at ★ **Horseman's Haven** (4354 Cerrillos Rd., 505/471-5420, 8am-8pm Mon.-Sat., 8:30am-2pm Sun., $8), which claims to serve the hottest green chile in Santa Fe. It picks and mixes chile varieties to offer a couple of consistent grades. Like all good chile purveyors, it's in an unassuming box of a building next to a gas station, and it takes cash only.

Long notorious for its dazzling list of margaritas, ★ **Maria's** (555 W. Cordova Rd., 505/983-7929, 11am-10pm daily, $10) is well worth settling into for a meal of hearty New Mexican classics, starting with a genuinely hot table salsa and chips. Both red and green are solid here, and the tamales are exceptionally rich and creamy (even the vegetarian ones!).

SANTA FE METRO AREA
American

Out on Old Las Vegas Highway, the frontage road for I-25, **Harry's Roadhouse** (96 Old Las Vegas Hwy., 505/989-4629, 7am-9:30pm daily, $11) is a good destination, or an easy place to pop off the freeway (at the Old Santa Fe Trail exit). The patio has a great view across the flatlands, there's a full bar, and the diner-style menu includes cold meat-loaf sandwiches, catfish po'boys, lamb stew, and an awe-inspiring breakfast burrito. Oh, and pie: Chocolate mousse, lemon meringue, and coconut cream pies could be crowding the pastry case at any given time.

Asian

The restaurant at Ten Thousand Waves, **Izanami** (3451 Hyde Park Rd., 505/428-6390, 11am-10pm daily, small plates $5-14), melds old Japan and new, without feeling like a theme restaurant. On the menu, there's pickled burdock root and sticky sweet potatoes, as well as wagyu-beef burgers and tempura-fried artichokes, served in small plates to share. The dining room has a rustic mountain-lodge feel, with an optional shoes-off tatami-mat seating area. Throw in a vast sake menu and surprisingly reasonable prices, and it's one of Santa Fe's coolest places to eat, whether you make the drive up for dinner or just wander over after your bath.

Fresh and Local

At exit 290 off I-25, **Café Fina** (624 Old Las Vegas Hwy., 505/466-3886, 7am-3pm Mon.-Fri., 8am-3pm Sat.-Sun., $9) is a casual order-at-the-counter place, with a short but flavor-packed menu (ricotta pancakes, Reuben sandwiches) from mostly organic ingredients. The view from the hill here is lovely.

On the grounds of the Plants of the Southwest nursery, **The Kitchen** (3095 Agua Fria St., 505/438-8888, 11am-2pm daily May-Nov., $9) is the ultimate grassroots café: one woman cooking a single vegetarian lunch each day. Wholesome home cooking, with a European bent.

The all-vegetarian **Tree House** (163 Paseo de Peralta, 505/474-5543, 9am-6pm Mon., 8am-6pm Tues.-Sat., $10) is somewhat incongruously set in the DeVargas Center mall, but its food, from the nut-and-rice-stuffed "birdhouse burger" to cherry pie, conjures a wholesome, hippie-ish A-frame in the woods. (Gluten-free baked goods are available too.)

Mexican

In a strip mall off St. Michaels Drive,

Felipe's Tacos (1711-A Llano St., 505/473-9397, 9am-5:30pm Mon.-Fri., 9am-3pm Sat., $6) makes soft tacos just like you get south of the border: steaming corn tortillas wrapped around grilled chicken or steak, or the chile-soaked pork *al pastor,* and then topped with radish slices, salsa, and lime. Bigger appetites will want a hefty burrito. There are lots of vegetarian combos as well, plus fresh limeade to drink.

Outside Santa Fe

Less than an hour's drive from Santa Fe, you can visit the vast mountain wilderness of Pecos, six-century-old ruins of Ancestral Puebloan culture at Bandelier, and the 20th-century atomic developments in Los Alamos, home of the Manhattan Project. Abiquiu, best known as Georgia O'Keeffe country, is a landscape of rich red rocks along the tree-lined Rio Chama. The most popular outing from Santa Fe is to Taos, but even that presents several possibilities. The main options are the low road along the Rio Grande or the high road that passes through tiny mountain villages. You can also take a more roundabout route through Ojo Caliente, a village built around hot springs.

PECOS

Santa Fe backs up against the 223,000 acres of the Pecos Wilderness, the second-largest nature reserve in New Mexico (after the Gila, in the southwest). The mountain streams seethe with trout, and elk ramble through emerald-green meadows. The core of the wilderness is still recovering from the 2011 Pacheco Fire, but day visitors will still find plenty to enjoy. The gateway to the wilderness area is the former logging town of Pecos, where mountain men rub shoulders with alternative healers and monks; south of town are the ruins of Pecos Pueblo, the regional power before the Spanish arrived.

On the drive out on I-25, near exit 295, you pass the site of the westernmost Civil War battle in the United States, the **Battle of Glorieta Pass.** It raged March 26-28, 1862, part of a Confederate plan to invade the West with a force of Texans—a plan that was foiled in this decisive rout. The fight is reenacted here annually, and the property owner maintains a makeshift memorial and exhibit on the side of the highway.

Pecos National Historical Park

When the Spanish made first contact with local people in 1540, Pecos was the largest pueblo in the region, population 2,000, in four- and five-story stone buildings sealed with mud. In **Pecos National Historical Park** (Hwy. 63, 505/757-7241, www.nps.gov/peco, 8am-6pm daily June-Aug., 8am-5pm Sept.-May, $3), the ruins of this complex community are accessible to visitors via a 1.5-mile paved interpretive trail that winds through the remnants of the Pecos Pueblo walls, a couple of restored kivas, and, most striking, the shell of a Franciscan mission. A free **guided walking tour** around the site runs daily at 10am in summer. Additional **van tours** ($2) cover different aspects of local history; check the website for schedules. In winter, the visitors center closes at 4:30pm.

On a ridge looking out on the plains to the northeast and the mountains behind, the park provides a beautiful view today; around 1100, when the area was being settled with the first villages, it also provided a livelihood. The ridge was part of a natural trade path between the Rio Grande farmers and the buffalo hunters of the Great Plains. Both groups met in Pecos, itself an agricultural community, to barter. What began as a series of small villages consolidated in the 14th century into a city, with a layout so orderly it appears to have been centrally planned, and by 1450,

Outside Santa Fe

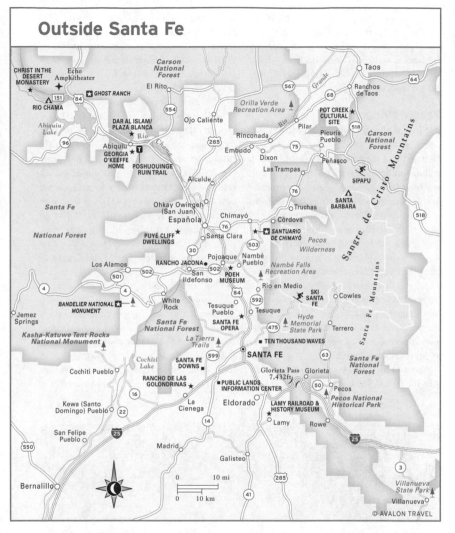

CHRIST IN THE DESERT MONASTERY
Echo Amphitheater
Carson National Forest
El Rito
GHOST RANCH
RIO CHAMA
Abiquiu Lake
DAR AL ISLAM/ PLAZA BLANCA
Ojo Caliente
Orilla Verde Recreation Area
Abiquiu
Rio
GEORGIA O'KEEFFE HOME
POSHUOUINGE RUIN TRAIL
Alcalde
Rinconada
Embudo
Dixon
Las Trampas
Pilar
Picuris Pueblo
Peñasco
Taos
Ranchos de Taos
POT CREEK CULTURAL SITE
Carson National Forest
SIPAPU
Santa Fe
National Forest
Ohkay Owingeh (San Juan)
Española
PUYÉ CLIFF DWELLINGS
Santa Clara
Chimayó
Córdova
SANTUARIO DE CHIMAYÓ
Truchas
SANTA BARBARA
Pecos Wilderness
Sangre de Cristo Mountains
Los Alamos
RANCHO JACONA
San Ildefonso
POEH MUSEUM
Pojoaque
Nambé Pueblo
Nambé Falls Recreation Area
Rio en Medio
SKI SANTA FE
Cowles
BANDELIER NATIONAL MONUMENT
White Rock
Tesuque Pueblo
Jemez Springs
Kasha-Katuwe Tent Rocks National Monument
SANTA FE OPERA
Tesuque
Hyde Memorial State Park
Terrero
Santa Fe National Forest
La Tierra Trails
TEN THOUSAND WAVES
Santa Fe Mountains
Cochiti Lake
SANTA FE DOWNS
SANTA FE
Glorieta Pass 7,432ft
Glorieta
Santa Fe National Forest
Cochiti Pueblo
RANCHO DE LAS GOLONDRINAS
PUBLIC LANDS INFORMATION CENTER
Eldorado
Pecos
Pecos National Historical Park
Kewa (Santo Domingo) Pueblo
La Cienega
LAMY RAILROAD & HISTORY MUSEUM
Lamy
Rowe
San Felipe Pueblo
Madrid
Galisteo
Bernalillo
Villanueva State Park
Villanueva

0   10 mi
0   10 km

© AVALON TRAVEL

the fortress of Pecos was the major economic power in the area.

Perhaps it was the city's trading culture and relative worldliness that made the Pecos Indians welcome Francisco Vásquez de Coronado and his men in 1540 with music and dancing rather than bows and arrows. Nearly 60 years later, Don Juan de Oñate visited the area and ordered a mission church built—a giant structure with six bell towers and buttresses 22 feet thick in some spots.

The building was destroyed during the Pueblo Revolt, however, and the Pecos people dug a kiva smack in the middle of the ruined convent area—symbolic architecture, to say the least.

But the Spanish returned, and they were even welcomed and aided at Pecos. When they built a new church in the early 1700s, it was noticeably smaller, maybe as a form of compromise. But even as a hybrid Pueblo-Spanish culture developed, the Indian population was falling victim to disease and drought. When the Santa Fe Trail opened up in 1821, Pecos was all but empty, and in 1838, the last city dwellers marched to live with fellow Towa speakers at Jemez Pueblo, 80 miles west; their descendants still live there today.

Pecos Wilderness

Stop in at the **Pecos Wilderness ranger station** (Hwy. 63, 505/757-6121, 8am-4:30pm Mon.-Fri.) on the south end of Pecos town to get maps and information on trail conditions, as well as the eight developed campgrounds. At this high elevation, summer temperatures are rarely above 75°F and can dip below freezing at night, so pack accordingly.

Highway 63 is the main access route into the wilderness, running north out of town along the Pecos River. If you've forgotten anything, you can probably get it at the **Terrero general store** (1911 Hwy. 63, 505/757-6193, 8am-6pm daily in summer), about 13 miles along the two-lane road. The road then narrows and steadily rises, passing fishing access points and campgrounds.

About a mile after Mora campground is the turn for Forest Road 223, a very rough road (ideally, for high-clearance cars only, or proceed very slowly) that leads 4.5 miles up to Iron Gate Campground and **Hamilton Mesa Trail** (no. 249), a fairly level 3.8-mile hike to a wide-open meadow—look for strawberries among the wildflowers.

At Cowles Ponds, a developed fishing area where a mining camp once stood, you can turn left on Windsor Road to follow a paved one-lane road 1.5 miles to Panchuela campground, the start of **Cave Creek Trail** (no. 288). It's an easy 3.6-mile out-and-back that follows a small waterway up to some caves that have been carved out of the white limestone by the stream's flow. If you go past the caves, up a steep hillside, you reach an area burned in the 2013 Jaroso Fire; this is not recommended, due to the danger of falling trees.

Continuing straight past Cowles on Highway 63 brings you in about three more miles to Jack's Creek campground and **Jack's Creek Trail** (no. 257), a short out-and-back. Turn back at the junction with Dockweiler Trail (no. 259), about four miles in, to avoid the burned area. All trails in this area require a $2 trailhead parking fee; additional fees

Pecos National Historical Park

apply for camping or picnicking, depending on the spot.

Accommodations and Food

For staying the night, the **Benedictine Monastery** (Hwy. 63, 505/757-6600, www. pecosmonastery.org, $75 s) maintains simple rooms with beautiful views; the rate is a suggested donation and includes meals. Several mountain lodges deeper in the forest, such as **Los Pinos Ranch** (505/757-6213, www. lospinosranch.com, $145 pp), are typically open summers only and offer multiday packages with all meals and a variety of outdoor activities.

At the main crossroads in Pecos, where Highway 50 meets Highway 63, **Frankie's at the Casanova** (12 Main St., 505/757-3322, 8am-2pm daily, 5:30pm-8:30pm Fri.-Sat., $9) is the town social center, set in an old adobe dance hall. The food isn't always a hit, but it's worth a stop just to see the murals over the bar.

THE PUEBLOS

Between Santa Fe and Taos lie seven pueblos, each on a separate patch of reservation land. Unlike scenic Taos Pueblo, these are not notable for their ancient architecture but unremarkable modern housing. Moreover, some are closed to outsiders all or part of the year.

With the exception of the cliff dwellings at Santa Clara and shopping for pots at San Ildefonso, none of these pueblos merit a visit on an average day—but do make the trip on feast days or for other ceremonial dances if you can.

Tesuque and Pojoaque

Just north of Santa Fe, the highway overpasses are decorated with the original Tewa names of the pueblos. Tesuque (Te Tesugeh Owingeh, "village of the cottonwood trees") is marked by **Camel Rock,** a piece of sandstone on the west side of the highway that has eroded to resemble a creature that looks right at home in this rocky desert.

Farther north, Pojoaque manages the **Poeh Museum** (78 Cities of Gold Rd., 505/455-5041, 10am-4pm Mon.-Sat., www.poehcenter. org, free), in a striking old-style adobe building just off the highway. It shows (and sells) local artwork, as well as a permanent installation relating to the Pojoaque people's path (*poeh*) through history.

Just north of the Cities of Gold Casino is a tasting room for New Mexico's largest craft distillery, **Don Quixote Distillery** (U.S. 84/285, www.dqdistillery.com, noon-6pm daily). You can sample the husband-and-wife team's blue-corn-based vodka and gin flavored with locally foraged juniper berries

A Little Farther: Villanueva

From exit 323 off I-25, 14 miles past Pecos, Highway 3 is a beautiful drive south. The two-lane road runs through a narrow valley with rich red earth cut into small farm plots. Villages such as Ribera and El Pueblo were founded in the late 18th century. The excellent **La Risa Café** (Hwy. 3, 575/421-3883, 11am-8pm Thurs.-Sat., 8am-6pm Sun., $9) is a popular stop for locals and day-trippers to enjoy spicy New Mexican food and astounding slices of pie. Nearby is **Arrow's Ridge B&B** (County Rd. B40, 575/421-1444, www.arrows-ridge.com), also known for its excellent food and occasional group dinners. Farther along is the tiny, family-run **Madison Winery** (Hwy. 3, 575/421-8028, 10am-5pm Sat., noon-5pm Sun. in summer, other times by appointment), between El Pueblo and Sena. The small but beautiful **Villanueva State Park** (575/421-2957, www.nmparks.com, $5/car) occupies a bend in the Pecos River against 400-foot-tall sandstone cliffs. It's rarely crowded—you'll probably have the 2.5-mile Canyon Trail to yourself and the choice of **campsites** (from $8). Spring comes early, filling trails with wildflowers by late April; fall is a burst of red scrub oak and yellow cottonwood leaves, in sharp contrast to the evergreens.

Tribal Economies in the Gaming Age

North of Santa Fe on U.S. 84/285, Cities of Gold Casino looms beside the road, a sight that would have dazzled any conquistador in search of El Dorado. It was the first of the pueblo casinos, and a much-debated project within the community of **Pojoaque** before it opened in the 1990s. Casinos were effectively permitted by the federal Indian Gaming Regulatory Act in 1988 and then legalized in New Mexico in 1994.

The main argument in Pojoaque for getting into the industry was a need for cash and jobs in communities that had virtually no industry. At the time, up to 72 percent of pueblo residents were jobless, and the average income in many communities was less than $10,000 per year—almost inconceivably below national standards. Now, Pojoaque boasts close to zero unemployment as well as attractive apartment housing and a beautifully appointed museum funded by casino profits (including the Buffalo Thunder Resort, opened in 2008), and many other nearby Rio Grande-area pueblos have followed with their own projects.

Remoter pueblos have taken different strategies. Small and somewhat conservative Picurís voted against its own gambling palace; the elders did eventually agree to co-owning the Hotel Santa Fe, a venture initiated by a few Anglo entrepreneurs who aimed to capitalize on a unique relationship with a pueblo. Jemez Pueblo attempted to open a casino in southern New Mexico, far from its own land, but its application was denied at the federal level in 2011.

Puebloans and Anglos alike complain about the aesthetics of the gaudy, brightly lit casinos, and others worry about the apparent loss of tradition that goes along with courting lowest-common-denominator tourism. But for many pueblo people who, previously, had been considered to be not much more than a scenic backdrop in New Mexico—a mute patch of "local color"—there's no incongruity at all. As George Rivera, the governor of Pojoaque, has put it, "You don't have to be poor to have your culture."

Camel Rock is a landmark north of Santa Fe.

and other botanicals. They also make intense vanilla extract, bitters, and port wine based on New Mexican monks' 16th-century recipe. If you're interested in the manufacturing, visit their place in White Rock. It's on the west side of the highway, just north of the exit for Highway 502; coming from the south, you'll have to double back at the next light.

San Ildefonso

Best known for its black-on-black pottery (first by María Martinez and her husband, Julian, and now from a number of skilled potters), the pueblo of San Ildefonso is off Highway 502, on the way to Los Alamos. Of all the pueblos just north of Santa Fe, it's probably the most scenic, with even its newer houses done in faux-adobe style, and the main plaza shaded by giant old cottonwoods. You must first register at the **visitors center** (off Hwy. 502, 505/455-3549, 8am-5pm Mon.-Fri., $10/car), then proceed on foot. There is a very small **museum** (8am-4:30pm daily), which is really just an excuse to walk across the village. The only other attractions are pottery shops—which are interesting even if you're not in the market, as it's a chance to peek inside people's homes, and chat a bit.

Santa Clara

On the land of Santa Clara (Kha P'o, or Shining Water), on Highway 30 south of Española, are the beautiful **Puyé Cliff Dwellings** (888/320-5008), which were occupied until the early 1600s. They're accessible only by guided tour, and a slightly expensive one at that: $20 for a one-hour walk either along the cliff side or the mesa top, or $35 for both. But tour leaders come from the pueblo and connect the ancient ruins with current culture in an intimate and fascinating way. At the base of the cliffs is a stone building from the Fred Harvey Indian Detour days of the early 1900s, when carloads of intrepid visitors would trundle off the train and out to these exotic sights; it now houses a small museum. The Puyé Cliffs Welcome Center—better recognized as a gas station on Highway

30—marks the turn to the cliffs; you can buy your tickets here (preferred, so they know you're coming) or up the road at the site. **Tours** run on the hour 9am-5pm daily April through September; the rest of the year, tours run 10am-4pm.

Getting There

From downtown Santa Fe, northbound Guadalupe Street turns into U.S. 84/285, which runs north through Tesuque in 5 miles and Pojoaque in 15 miles. Though this stretch of casinos and tax-free cigarette shops isn't particularly scenic, don't be tempted to race through it—the area is a major speed trap.

To reach San Ildefonso, turn off U.S. 84/285 in Pojoaque at the exit for Highway 502 to Los Alamos; the turn for the pueblo is about 6 miles ahead on the right. From San Ildefonso, you can continue to Santa Clara by turning north on Highway 30; the cliff dwellings are 7 miles ahead on the left. The slightly more direct route to Santa Clara is via Española, following signs for Highway 30; the total drive from the edge of Santa Fe is about 23 miles.

LOS ALAMOS

Unlike so many other sights in New Mexico, which are rooted in centuries of history, Los Alamos, home of the atomic bomb, is a product of the modern age. You may only spend a few hours here, visiting the museum and admiring the view from this high plateau, but you'll still sense a different atmosphere from anywhere else in New Mexico. If you can, visit on a weekday, as more businesses are open; weekends are quite sleepy in this town that draws specialized commuters from around the state.

During World War II, an elite, rugged boys' school was requisitioned by the army to become the top-secret base for development of the nuclear bomb, home for a time to J. Robert Oppenheimer, Richard Feynman, Niels Bohr, and other science luminaries. The Manhattan Project and its aftermath, the Cold War arms race, led to the establishment of Los Alamos National Lab (LANL). Only in 1957 did the

Ceremonial Dances

This is an approximate schedule for dances at pueblos in the Santa Fe area. Pueblo feast days are always on the same date every year, but seasonal dances (especially Easter and other spring rituals) can vary. Confirm details and start times—usually afternoon, but sometimes following an evening or midnight Mass—with the **Indian Pueblo Cultural Center** (505/843-7270, www.indianpueblo.org) before setting out.

- **January 1** - Ohkay Owingeh (San Juan): cloud or basket dance

- **January 6** - Picurís: various dances; Nambé: buffalo, deer, and antelope dances

- **January 22** - San Ildefonso: vespers and firelight procession at 6pm

- **January 23** - San Ildefonso: Feast of San Ildefonso, with buffalo and deer dances

- **January 25** - Picurís: Feast of San Pablo

- **February 2** - Picurís: various dances for Candlemas (Día de la Candelaria)

- **Easter** - Nambé: bow dance; San Ildefonso: various dances

- **June 13** - Ohkay Owingeh (San Juan), Santa Clara, and Picurís: Feast of San Antonio

- **June 24** - Ohkay Owingeh (San Juan): Feast of San Juan Bautista

- **July 4** - Nambé: celebration at the waterfall

- **August 9-10** - Picurís: Feast of San Lorenzo

- **August 12** - Santa Clara: Feast of Santa Clara

- **September 8** - San Ildefonso: corn dance

- **October 4** - Nambé: Feast of San Francisco de Asís

- **November 12** - Tesuque: Feast of San Diego

- **December 12** - Pojoaque: Feast of Nuestra Señora de Guadalupe

- **December 24** - Picurís and Ohkay Owingeh (San Juan): torchlight procession at sundown, followed by Los Matachines; Tesuque and Nambé: various dances, beginning after midnight Mass

- **December 25** - San Ildefonso, Ohkay Owingeh (San Juan), Picurís, and Tesuque: various dances

- **December 26** - Ohkay Owingeh (San Juan): turtle dance

- **December 28** - Picurís and Santa Clara: children's dances to celebrate Holy Innocents Day

onetime military base become an actual public town; it's now home to about 18,000 people (if you count the "suburb" of White Rock, just down the hill on Highway 4). The highway up the mountainside is wider than it used to be, but the winding ascent to the mesa of "Lost Almost"—as the first scientists dubbed their officially nonexistent camp—still carries an air of the clandestine. The town has a jarring newness about it, with street names like Bikini

Atoll Road, and it's only emphasized by the dramatic landscape surrounding it.

The town is spread over three long mesas that extend like fingers from the mountain behind. Highway 502 arrives in the middle mesa, depositing you on Central Avenue and the main downtown area. The north mesa is mostly residential, while the south mesa is occupied by the labs and two routes running back down the mountain and connecting with Highway 4.

Los Alamos

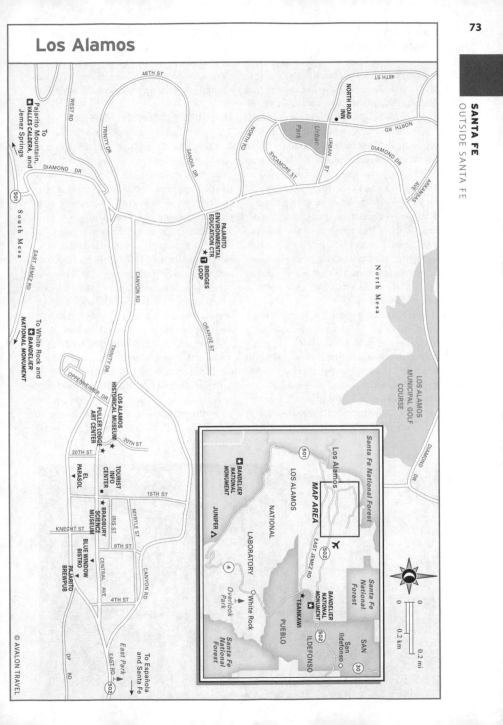

© AVALON TRAVEL

48TH ST
48TH ST
NORTH ROAD INN
NORTH RD
WEST RD
Urban Park
URBAN ST
DIAMOND DR
To Pajarito Mountain, VALLES CALDERA, and Jemez Springs
TRINITY DR
SANDIA DR
NORTH RD
SYCAMORE ST
ARKANSAS AVE
DIAMOND DR
501
DIAMOND DR
South Mesa
EAST JEMEZ RD
PAJARITO ENVIRONMENTAL EDUCATION CTR
BRIDGES LOOP
North Mesa
To White Rock and BANDELIER NATIONAL MONUMENT
CANYON RD
ORANGE ST
LOS ALAMOS MUNICIPAL GOLF COURSE
DIAMOND DR
TRINITY DR
OPPENHEIMER DR
LOS ALAMOS HISTORICAL MUSEUM
FULLER LODGE ART CENTER
20TH ST
20TH ST
TOURIST INFO CENTER
EL PARASOL
15TH ST
MYRTLE ST
BRADBURY SCIENCE MUSEUM
IRIS ST
9TH ST
KNECHT ST
BLUE WINDOW BISTRO
PAJARITO BREWPUB
CENTRAL AVE
CANYON RD
4TH ST
DP RD
East Park
EAST RD
502
To Española and Santa Fe

BANDELIER NATIONAL MONUMENT
501
LOS ALAMOS
Santa Fe National Forest
Los Alamos
MAP AREA
JUNIPER
LOS ALAMOS NATIONAL LABORATORY
EAST JEMEZ RD
502
Santa Fe National Forest
4
Overlook Park
White Rock
TSANKAWI
BANDELIER NATIONAL MONUMENT
502
ILDEFONSO
SAN ILDEFONSO PUEBLO
San Ildefonso
30
Santa Fe National Forest

0   0.2 km
0   0.2 mi

Los Alamos Historical Museum

Even a manufactured town like Los Alamos has a history. See what the area was like pre-Manhattan Project at the fascinating **Los Alamos Historical Museum** (1050 Bathtub Row, 505/662-4493, www.losalamoshistory.org, 9:30am-4:30pm Mon.-Fri., 11am-4pm Sat.-Sun., free) set in an old building of the Los Alamos Ranch School, the boys' camp that got the boot when the army moved in. The exhibits cover everything from relics of the early Tewa-speaking people up to juicy details on the social intrigue during the development of "the gadget," as the A-bomb was known. Volunteer docents lead two-hour **walking tours** ($10, 11am Mon., Fri., and Sat.) from the museum from late May till early October; if you miss this, pick up a brochure for a self-guided walk.

In front of the museum is **Fuller Lodge Art Center** (2132 Central Ave., 505/662-1635, 10am-4pm Mon.-Sat., free), originally the Ranch School's dining room and kitchen. It usually has a community art exhibit downstairs, plus a room upstairs restored to the era when schoolteachers bunked here. The architect John Gaw Meem built the structure in 1928, handpicking more than 700 pine poles to form the walls, and designing the cowboy-silhouette light fixtures in the main hall.

The museum is just west of the main street, Central Avenue—you'll see Fuller Lodge on Central, with the museum set back behind it.

Bradbury Science Museum

Set up by Los Alamos National Lab, the **Bradbury Science Museum** (1350 Central Ave., 505/667-4444, www.lanl.gov/museum, 10am-5pm Tues.-Sat., 1pm-5pm Sun.-Mon., free) on the miracles of atomic energy has the feel of a very high-grade science fair, with plenty of buttons to push and gadgets to play with. There's also an air of a convention sales booth—the museum's mission is definitely to sell the public on LANL's work and nuclear technology in general, though a public forum corner gives space to opposing views. More interesting are the relics of the early nuclear age: Fat Man and Little Boy casings, gadgetry from the Nevada Test Site, and the like.

Atomic City Van Tours (505/662-3965, www.buffalotoursla.com, 1:30pm daily, Mar.-Oct., $15) leave from the parking lot in front of the museum. The 1.5-hour tour is a good way to see more of the town, which is otherwise a bit difficult to navigate, and learn some of the history. Call ahead to reserve. If you can't

Fuller Lodge Art Center in Los Alamos

make the set tour time, you can download a short self-guided tour from the website; this route takes the free city bus to the main part of LANL, pointing out town landmarks along the way.

Recreation

The mountain behind Los Alamos is recovering from the 2011 Las Conchas Fire, but the canyons below Los Alamos were untouched, and offer good hiking. They are crisscrossed with a network of county-maintained hiking trails, easily accessible from the town's main roads. Pick up a map and get recommendations from the visitors center, or start at the **Pajarito Environmental Education Center** (3540 Orange St., 505/662-0460, www.pajaritoeec.org, noon-4pm Tues.-Fri., 10am-1pm Sat.); the **Bridges Loop** trail that starts here takes about 45 minutes.

The most dramatic views in the area are in White Rock, where the **White Rock Rim Trail** runs three miles along the cliff edge—you'll have suburban tract homes to your back and a dizzying canyon out in front of you. Even if you don't much feel like a hike, stop by where the walk starts in Overlook Park, just for the view; follow signs from Highway 4 at the first stoplight in town. You can also take a strenuous hike into the gorge along the **Red Dot Trail,** which passes a few petroglyphs on its way down to the Rio Grande; follow signs from Highway 4 for Overlook Park, at the back end of a subdivision.

Thanks to the canyon walls, White Rock is also popular with **rock climbers,** who most frequently head to **The Overlook,** a 65-foot basalt wall below Overlook Park. The **Los Alamos Mountaineers** (www.lamountaineers.org) maintain a good website with detailed route guides and information on smaller area walls.

A bit of a locals' secret, **Pajarito Mountain** (505/662-5725, www.skipajarito.com, 9am-4pm Fri.-Sun. and holidays) offers good skiing and snowboarding for relatively cheap ($49/full day), with five lifts giving access to bunny slopes as well as double-black-diamond trails. The area is just a few miles northeast of Los Alamos, off Highway 501.

Accommodations

The few hotels in Los Alamos cater primarily to visiting engineers, though it's a handy place to bunk if you want to get an early start at Bandelier. The chain hotels are functional, and one smaller B&B is a nice alternative. A converted apartment complex in a

the view from Overlook Park in White Rock

quiet residential area, **North Road Inn** (2127 North Rd., 505/662-3678, www.northroadinn. com, $79 s, $92 d) has large rooms (some are suites with kitchenettes); upper-level rooms are a bit more private.

Food

Los Alamos is not exactly bursting with restaurants, and many are open weekdays only. For lunch, the branch of the Española taco specialists **El Parasol** (1903 Central Ave., 505/661-0303, 7am-7pm Mon.-Fri., 8am-3pm Sat., 9am-2pm Sun., $6) is reliable and well priced.

Blue Window Bistro (813 Central Ave., 505/662-6305, 11am-2:30pm and 5pm-8:30pm Mon.-Fri., 5pm-9pm Sat., $18) is the fanciest restaurant in town, which in Los Alamos still doesn't mean too fancy. It's a colorful, bustling place with a bit of outdoor seating. Food is typical fresh American: huge salads and hot sandwiches for lunch, creative pasta and steaks in the evening. If you're headed back down the hill for the night, it's not worth staying for dinner, but if you're here overnight, it's your best option.

Kitty-corner across the parking lot, **Pajarito Brewpub** (614 Trinity Dr., 505/662-8877, 11am-11pm Sun.-Wed., 11am-1am Thurs.-Sat.) is the liveliest (er, maybe only) bar in town, but the food is pricey.

Starbucks on Central Avenue is notable just for the deeply scientific conversations on which you can eavesdrop.

Information

Stop at the **tourist info center** (109 Central Park Sq., 505/662-8105, www.visitlosalamos. org, 9am-5pm Mon.-Fri., 9am-4pm Sat., 10am-3pm Sun.) for maps and advice on hikes. There's a bigger office office in **White Rock** (115 Hwy 4, 505/672-3183, 8am-6pm daily), en route to Bandelier.

Getting There

Los Alamos is 36 miles (45 minutes by car) from downtown Santa Fe, via U.S. 84/285 north to Highway 502 west. From Española,

a cliff dwelling at Bandelier National Monument

it's 20 miles (30 minutes) west on Highway 30 to Highway 502.

New Mexico Airlines (888/564-6119, www.flynma.com) makes the 20-minute flight to Los Alamos airport (LAM, www.flylosalamos.com) from Albuquerque, on three flights daily. The airport is on Highway 502 at the east edge of town.

★ BANDELIER NATIONAL MONUMENT

One of New Mexico's most atmospheric ancient sites, **Bandelier National Monument** (www.nps.gov/band, $12/car) comprises 23,000 acres of wilderness, including the remarkable Frijoles Canyon, lined on either side with cave "apartments," while the remnants of a massive settlement from the 16th century occupy the valley floor.

The place gets so busy in summer that from Memorial Day through October, the park is accessible only by shuttle bus from the visitors center in White Rock. The best way to avoid crowds is to arrive early on a weekday, if possible. Another approach is to join a torch-lit, silent **night walk** ($6) into Frijoles Canyon; they're typically on Friday nights, but call the visitors center or check online for the schedule.

In the park, another **visitors center** (505/672-3861, 9am-4:30pm daily) has a museum and the usual array of maps and guides. If you're interested in wildflowers, pick up a Falls Trail guide (even though this trail is unfortunately closed due to floods in 2013), as it has good illustrations of what grows in the area. Rangers run free **guided walks** around the main loop a few times a day, or you can pick up the trail guide for $1.

Main Loop Trail and Alcove House Trail

A paved walkway leads out the back of the visitors center into Frijoles Canyon, passing the ruins of the major settlements—or at least the ones that have been thoroughly excavated. You first reach **Tyuonyi** (chew-ON-yee), a circle of buildings that was settled for about 200 years, beginning in the 1300s. Built of bricks cut from tuff (the volcanic rock that makes up most of the area) and adobe plaster, some of the 250 rooms at one time stood several stories tall.

The trail then goes up next to the cliffs, dotted with small caves dug out of the soft stone, and to **Long House,** the remnants of a strip of condo-style buildings tucked into the rock wall. Paintings and carvings decorate the cliff face above. If you're here near sunset, keep an eye on the **bat cave** near the end of the strip, home to thousands of the animals.

Continue another half mile to the **Alcove House,** accessible by 140 feet of ladders. It's well worth the climb up, if you can handle heights—though at the time of research, floods had required rerouting of the trail, making it a bit trickier. Also, the kiva at the center of the cliff house was closed for restoration.

Frey Trail

The 1.5-mile **Frey Trail** used to be the main access route to Frijoles Canyon, before

the access road was built by the Civilian Conservation Corps in the 1930s. Descending from **Juniper Campground** (just off Highway 4 northwest of the park access road), it's a nice approach to the area, with great views over Tyuonyi, and a general sense of what it must have been like to "discover" the canyon. The trail has no shade, however, so it's best hiked early in the day. The shuttle bus can drop you at the trailhead, so you can hike down, then ride back to the depot.

Tsankawi

Well before you reach the main entrance to Bandelier, you pass **Tsankawi** on the east side of Highway 4. (This area is accessible by car year-round.) Unique pottery excavated in this separate section, disconnected from the main park, suggests that it was inhabited by a different people from those who settled in Frijoles Canyon, and some sort of natural border seems to have formed here, despite a shared cliff-dwelling culture: Today the pueblos immediately north of the Bandelier area speak Tewa, while those to the south speak Keresan. A 1.5-mile loop, with ladders to climb along the way, leads past unexcavated ruins, cave houses, and even a few petroglyphs.

Camping

Juniper Campground ($12), just inside the park's northern border, is usually open year-round, with 94 sites. There are no hookups or showers. No reservations are taken, but it's usually not full. The scenery up on the plateau is a bit bleak, due to the 2011 fire, but you will get an early start on the day if you overnight here.

Getting There

Bandelier is 45 miles (one hour) from downtown Santa Fe, via U.S. 84/285 north to Highway 502 and Highway 4 west. From Jemez Springs, it's 41 miles (one hour) via Highway 4 east.

From June through October (9am-5pm), access to the park is via **shuttle bus** only. The service departs from the **White Rock** visitors center (Hwy. 4) every 20 or 30 minutes; the last bus to Bandelier leaves at 4:30pm. (Because the park is open dawn till dusk, you can enter by car early or late in the day.)

White Rock is a 40-minute drive from Santa Fe via U.S. 84/285 north to Highway 502 and Highway 4 west. From Jemez Springs, it's about an hour drive via Highway 4 north and east (but you'll have to drive past the Bandelier entrance, and double back in the shuttle bus). The bus also stops at the Frey Trail trailhead en route to the main park.

ESPAÑOLA

Midway between Santa Fe and Taos, Española lacks the glamour or scenery of its neighbors. The relatively modern town of 10,000 is fairly rough around the edges, but if you're driving through at mealtime, it's a great place to stop for some authentic local food. And although it doesn't have much in the way of its own sights (except for the occasional excellent lowrider), it is at a convenient crossroads and has a couple of good-value hotels.

Española architecture

Sights

No, you haven't made a wrong turn—you're still in Española. The **Chimayó Trading Post** (110 Sandia Dr., 505/753-9414, 10am-4pm Wed.-Sat.), on the west side of the main highway, relocated here in the 1930s, after several decades at its original location in Chimayó. Now it's a listed landmark, as one of the last remaining historic trading posts, and it has everything you'd expect: creaky wood floors, dim lighting, and a jumbled stock of treasures that includes of course Chimayó rugs, as well as Nepalese silver jewelry; cuttin candleholders, made locally; skeins of handmade wool yarn; postcards; and even free coffee. The remaining elderly owner (one of a pair of airline employees, back in the real jet-set age) is no longer seriously replenishing his stock, but there are still some nifty finds. Hours can be a bit erratic.

Española's tiny museum, **Bond House** (706 Bond St., 505/747-8535, 1pm-3:30pm Mon.-Wed., noon-4pm Thurs.-Fri., free),

devotes half its space to artwork and the other small room to various historic artifacts. Down the hill, past the replica Alhambra fountain, is the **Misión Museum,** another replica, of the town's original mission church, furnished with traditional craft work from around the valley. It is open sporadically—ask at the Bond House if no one is around.

Santa Cruz de la Cañada Church

Midway through Española, take a right turn at Highway 76 to reach the village of Santa Cruz, established in 1695. The sizable **Santa Cruz de la Cañada Church** (varied hours, free) that's here now (turn left at the traffic light after one mile) dates from 1733, and its altar screen is another colorful work attributed to the Laguna Santero, who also painted the reredos at San Miguel Mission in Santa Fe and the church at Laguna Pueblo. It is dated 1795 but was completely painted over—with the same images—in the mid-19th century, presenting a particular challenge to preservationists, who

Española

To Embudo and Taos

To Ojo Caliente and Abiquiu

68

Río Grande

FAIRVIEW   LN

84
285

JOANN'S
RANCH O
CASADOS

N RIVERSIDE DR

MCCURDY RD

TORTAS
RAINBOW

PASEO DE OÑATE

SANTA
CLARAN

EL PARASOL

SPRUCE
ST

INN AT
THE DELTA

16

To Santa Cruz
Church   CHIMAYÓ
and Truchas

BOND ST

MISIÓN
MUSEUM

CHIMAYÓ
TRADING POST

BOND
HOUSE

PASEO DE OÑATE
LA COCINA

SAINTS &
SINNERS

SANTA CLARA BRIDGE RD

S RIVERSIDE DR

30

0   0.5 mi

84

285

To Puyé Cliff Dwellings,
Rancho Jacona
and Los Alamos

0   0.5 km

To Santa Fe

© AVALON TRAVEL

cleaned and restored the piece in 1995. Each panel presents a different combination of the original artist's work and the fresh paint applied half a century later.

Accommodations

Española is not a common overnight stop, but it has some hotels that are so nice, you might rethink your itinerary. They can be especially handy after a night at the Santa Fe Opera, when all the traffic toward Santa Fe is backed up—but the road north is wide open. The ★ **Inn at the Delta** (243 Paseo de Oñate, 505/753-9466, www.innatthedelta.biz, $120 s, $160 d) is a beautiful rambling adobe complex built by a long-established local family. The positively palatial rooms are decorated with locally made furniture, and each has a fireplace, a porch, and a jet tub. Rates include breakfast.

A project of the local pueblo, the **Santa Claran** (460 N. Riverside Dr., 877/505-4949, www.santaclaran.com, $85 d) also has spacious rooms, tastefully done in subdued grays and browns. Perks include fridges and laundry machines, but Internet is wired only in rooms; there's wireless access in the lobby.

South of town, on the road to Los Alamos, ★ **Rancho Jacona** (277 County Rd. 84, 505/455-7948, www.ranchojacona.com, $170 d) is a working farm dotted with 11 casitas, each with a kitchen and space for three

Chimayó Trading Post in Española

Española Yogis

Around Española, you'll notice a high proportion of Anglos clad in white kurtas and tightly wrapped turbans—these are members of the Sikh Dharma community in **Sombrillo**, just east of Española. The group is an unlikely product of the commune era, one of the oldest and largest ashrams established by Sikh Dharma's leader, Harbhajan Singh Yogi, later known as Yogi Bhajan.

The India-born yogi came to New Mexico in 1969 to teach kundalini yoga to the hippie masses. Twinkly-eyed and white-bearded, he had a knack for inspiring his followers not only to make their bodies strong ("healthy, happy, holy" are the tenets of his teaching, a New Age-inflected version of orthodox Sikhism), but to build up their bank accounts as well. In particular, he focused on "turning chicks into eagles"—his phrase for teaching women financial empowerment—and he encouraged all of his students to start businesses.

The first Sikh Dharma-owned enterprise was Yogi Tea, followed by Golden Temple Foods, and then—in a departure from hippie stereotypes—Sun and Son Computers and Akal Security. The security firm was founded in Española in 1980 by a would-be police officer, turned down for jobs because of his beard and turban. "Start a company, and the police will work for you," Bhajan counseled his student. Akal is now a major security provider in the United States, with its guards at nearly every federal courthouse.

Based on these contributions to the state economy, as well as directly to the Democratic and Republican parties, Yogi Bhajan became influential in New Mexico politics. Prominent lawmakers attended his birthday every year, and when he died in 2004, at age 75, then-governor Bill Richardson delivered the keynote speech at his funeral.

Although the Sikhs might look out of place to visitors, locals don't give them a second glance. The best evidence of their integration? The all-veggie "Khalsa Special" burrito at El Parasol takeout stand—a savvy business move that Yogi Bhajan himself surely admired.

to eight people. You'll likely get some fresh chicken eggs for breakfast, and kids can frolic in the pool. There's a three-night minimum.

Food

Thirsty? Look out for **Saints & Sinners** (503 S. Riverside Dr., 505/753-2757), a long-established package liquor store where you can also crack open a beer. It stocks an excellent selection of tequilas, and the neon sign should get landmark status (yes, they sell souvenir T-shirts). Cash only.

For a quick bite, stop at **El Parasol** (603 Santa Cruz Rd., 505/753-8852, 7am-9pm Mon.-Sat., $5), a takeout stand with picnic tables under cottonwood trees and a Spanglish menu ("pollo with guacamole taco"). Another option: the big Mexican-style sandwiches at **Tortas Rainbow** (745 N. Riverside Dr., 505/747-1791, 9am-8pm daily, $6). It's in a strip mall and can be easy to miss—look for (ironically) the Subway.

For a sit-down breakfast or lunch,

diner-style **JoAnn's Ranch O Casados** (938 N. Riverside Dr., 505/753-1334, 7am-9pm Mon.-Sat., 7am-4pm Sun., $10) does all-day breakfast, plus very good and inexpensive enchiladas, fajitas, and more. The red chile is rich and mellow, and you can get half orders of many dishes.

Open for dinner as well, long-established **La Cocina** (415 S. Santa Clara Bridge Rd., 505/753-3016, 7am-8:30pm Mon.-Sat., 7am-8pm Sun., $12) does all the New Mexican classics, including burritos made with local lamb.

Getting There

Española is about a 45-minute drive from central Santa Fe via U.S. 84/285 north. Leaving Española, take Highway 68 (also called Riverside Drive) north from here to Taos (45 miles), or cross over the Rio Grande and continue on U.S. 84 to Abiquiu (22 miles) or U.S. 285 to Ojo Caliente (25 miles). From an intersection in the middle of Española, Highway 76 leads east to Chimayó (8 miles), then to shower; $209 d, full bath) are no great value (although rates do include access to the springs). But camping ($20) is an option, and the bathroom facilities were upgraded in 2014. If you do want to stay overnight, **The Inn at Ojo** (505/583-9131, www.ojocaliente.com, $130 s), just down the road, is better value.

Just behind the springs, **Posi Trail** leads into public land; the area is especially popular with mountain bikers. The resort office has trail maps. If you happen to have forgotten your swimsuit, **Cornelia's** thrift and gift shop, on U.S. 285 north of the turn to the springs, usually has a stock of cheap ones that could work in a pinch.

Getting There

Ojo Caliente is 50 miles from downtown Santa Fe, about an hour's drive north on U.S. 84/285, then U.S. 285 east where it splits, north of Española. From Española, allow 30 minutes' driving time. From Abiquiu, avoid backtracking by going through El Rito; take Highway 554 north to Highway 111 north, coming out on U.S. 285 a few miles north of Ojo Caliente. This route takes about 45 minutes.

From Ojo Caliente, you can continue 41 miles to Taos (about a one-hour drive). Follow U.S. 285 north for 10 miles, then turn right (east) on Highway 567. In nine miles, Highway 567 ends at a T junction; turn left (north) on Taos County Road and continue about eight miles. You will meet U.S. 64 about one mile west of the Rio Grande Gorge; Taos is to the right (east).

ABIQUIU

Northwest of Española, along U.S. 84, the valley formed by the Rio Chama is one of the most striking landscapes in northern New Mexico. Lush greenery on the riverbanks clashes with bright red mud; roaming sheep and cattle graze by the roadside. The striated hills represent dramatic geological shifts, from purple stone formed in the dinosaur era 200 million years ago to red clay formed by forests, then gypsum from sand dunes, then a layer of lava only eight million years old.

the porch at the historic Ojo Caliente Mineral Springs resort

Truchas and the other high-road towns on the way to Taos. From the old main plaza on the west side of the Rio Grande, Highway 30 is the back road to Los Alamos (20 miles).

OJO CALIENTE

Twenty-six miles north of Española on U.S. 285, **Ojo Caliente Mineral Springs** (505/583-2233, www.ojospa.com, 8am-10pm daily) is effectively the center of a tiny settlement that built up around the hot springs here. Established in 1916, it's now a somewhat posh resort. The various paved pools ($18 Mon.-Thurs., $28 Fri.-Sun., $14/$24 after 6pm) have different mineral contents, and there's a mud area with rich local clay, as well as private soaking tubs and a full spa. It's a pretty little place, set up against sandstone bluffs, but not necessarily worth the drive specifically from Santa Fe, unless you've tired of Ten Thousand Waves, or you prefer mineral waters; in any case, try to go on a weekday, as it gets busy on weekends.

The hotel rooms at the resort ($169 d, no

Far more recently, Abiquiu became inextricably linked with the artist Georgia O'Keeffe, who made the place her home for more than 40 years, entranced by the glowing light and dramatic skyline.

Although Abiquiu often refers to the whole river valley, the unofficial town center is **Bode's** (21196 U.S. 84, 505/685-4422, 6:30am-7pm Mon.-Thurs., 6:30am-8pm Fri., 7am-8pm Sat., 7am-7pm Sun.), pronounced BO-deez. This long-established general store also has gas, pastries and green-chile cheeseburgers (11:30am-3pm daily), fishing licenses and tackle, and local crafts. In winter, it closes earlier on weekends.

Up the hill opposite Bode's is the actual **village of Abiquiu**, established in 1754 by *genízaros* (Hispanicized Indians) through a land grant from the Spanish Crown. O'Keeffe's house forms one side of the old plaza; on the other is the Santo Tomás de Abiquiu Church, built in the 1930s after the community opted for the legal status of village rather than pueblo. Past O'Keeffe's house is the village *morada,* dramatically set on a hilltop. You're not really welcome to poke around, however—the village maintains a privacy policy similar to those of the pueblos. So it's best to visit on a guided tour of the house.

Poshuouinge Ruin Trail

About two miles south of Abiquiu proper, on the west side of the road, the 0.5-mile **Poshuouinge Ruin Trail** leads to an ancestral Tewa site, literally the "village above the muddy river," inhabited only between 1420 and 1500—why it was abandoned is unclear. The village contained about 137 rooms, as well as surrounding field grids, though there's not much to see today (thorough excavations took place in 1919, and it has been left to melt away since then). Nonetheless, it's a good place to get out and stretch your legs and take in the view from the hilltop.

Georgia O'Keeffe Home

The artist's main residence, where she lived 1949-1984, fronts the small plaza in the village center of Abiquiu. The **Georgia O'Keeffe Home** (505/685-4539, www.okeeffemuseum. org) is open for hourlong guided tours mid-March-November. The price, even for the basic tour, can seem a bit steep, but for fans of modernism of any kind, it's a beautiful place to see. The rambling adobe, parts of which were built in the 18th century, is a great reflection of O'Keeffe's aesthetic, which fused the starkness of modernism with an organic sensuality. If you're on a budget, console yourself with the fact that in many ways the surrounding landscape reflects O'Keeffe's work as much as her home does—and be sure to stop at Ghost Ranch, for more (and cheaper) info on the painter.

The schedule varies by month, but there are five **tours** ($35) daily on Tuesday, Thursday, and Friday. From June through October, tours are also scheduled on Wednesdays and Saturdays ($45). Longer, special tours with Judy Lopez ($65), who worked with O'Keeffe for more than a decade, run Thursdays from June to November. A Wednesday-night "behind-the-scenes" tour ($60) includes a visit to O'Keeffe's fallout shelter, among other things. Tours depart from the Abiquiu Inn on U.S. 84; you must make reservations at least a month in advance.

Dar al Islam and Plaza Blanca

In another chapter of New Mexico's long utopian history, a few American converts established **Dar al Islam** (505/685-4515 ext. 21, www.daralislam.org, 10am-4pm Mon.-Fri., free), an intentional religious community, in 1980. It was meant to be a place in which Muslims—some 30 families to start with— could practice their religion in every aspect of life, from education to food. The group established a ranch and built the Abiquiu Inn and a few other local businesses, but the village concept eventually foundered. More recently, Dar al Islam has been reinvented as a retreat center that's open to visitors.

Anyone interested in architecture will want to visit to see Hassan Fathy's adobe mosque, all organic, sinuous lines, and in general, the

Ancient Egypt in Northern New Mexico

"Adobe," the word for the sun-dried mud bricks the Spanish used to build their houses for the first few centuries they lived in New Mexico, is derived from Arabic (*al-tub*), which in turn comes from Coptic, a language with its roots in Pharaonic Egypt. The etymology came full circle in 1980, when an Egyptian architect named Hassan Fathy came to Abiquiu to build an adobe mosque and madrassa, as the cornerstone of **Dar al Islam,** a newly established community of American-born Muslims.

Fathy was a lifelong champion of vernacular architecture, especially of adobe. He drew international interest in the 1940s, when he built the village of New Gourna near Luxor in Egypt. Modernists scoffed at his use of mud brick, but it provided cheap, efficient, even elegant housing, which residents could help construct and, later, make their own repairs to.

By the time the Dar al Islam community hired him in 1980, Fathy was in his 80s, but he nonetheless came to New Mexico to help personally with the mosque construction.

Hassan Fathy's distinctive curves at Dar al Islam

It was his first and only commission in North America, and he was excited to work so near the pueblos, where, he noted, the proportions of the mud bricks were nearly the same as those that make up the Temple of Hatshepsut. He brought with him two Nubian assistants and hired a team of locals to help.

An awkward culture clash ensued. Fathy had been built up as an expert to New Mexican *adoberos,* who resented the deference, especially when he was wrong. In particular, they saw that his construction was not adapted to the cold climate, and he used techniques that could not be applied after he left. The minaret proved too expensive, and a plan to build individual homes in Dar al Islam had to be scrapped because modern building codes required framing in adobe structures.

The innovations Fathy did bring are lovely, though: arched doorways and roofs, and—best of all—the signature adobe domes and barrel vaults that the architect had derived from ancient Nubian temples. The gentle curves of the complex's roofline and its rounded, whitewashed interior spaces echo the nearby Plaza Blanca hills, so the building seems beautifully integrated into its natural surroundings—even though it differs from its Spanish-style adobe neighbors.

view from the hilltop across the Chama River valley is a beautiful one. The head of the center requests that visitors dress modestly (arms, legs, and cleavage covered) and be quiet, so as not to disturb classes or workshops in session. Stop at the office first (back a bit and to the right of the parking area) to introduce yourself.

The community's land, some 8,500 acres, also includes the towering gypsum formations of **Plaza Blanca** (White Place). The eerie space, bleached as bones, was recorded in a series of Georgia O'Keeffe paintings, and it has also been used for numerous movie

shoots. Two main trails lead out from the parking area.

Coming from the south, the community is accessible via Highway 554, which runs east from U.S. 84, just south of Abiquiu (follow signs for El Rito). Immediately after crossing the Chama River, turn left on County Road 0155. Continue 3.2 miles, and turn right through a wooden gate made of telephone poles. Coming from the north on U.S. 84, look for County Road 0155, which is unpaved here, just north of Bode's; the wooden gate will be on the left, 2.3 miles on, shortly after the paving starts. Once through the gate, the road forks after less than a mile: To the left is the entrance to Dar al Islam; to the right, Plaza Blanca.

Abiquiu Lake

An Army Corps of Engineers dam project created the 4,000-acre **Abiquiu Lake** with fingers running into the canyons all around. The view coming in is marred by the power station, but past that the water glimmers at the base of the flat-topped mountain Pedernal ("Flint") Peak, the distinctive silhouette that found its way into so many of O'Keeffe's paintings. ("It's my private mountain," she often said. "God told me if I painted it often enough, I could have it.") The overly paved **campground** (505/685-4433, www.nmparks. com) at the lake is open year-round, but water and electric hookups ($14) are available only in the summer.

★ Ghost Ranch

Ghost Ranch (U.S. 84, 505/685-1000, www. ghostranch.org), a 21,000-acre retreat owned by the Presbyterian Church, is famous for several things: First, Georgia O'Keeffe owned a small parcel of the land and maintained a studio here. Then, in 1947, paleontologists combing the red hills discovered about a thousand

skeletons of the dinosaur *Coelophysis* ("hollow form," for its hollow, birdlike bones), the largest group discovered in the world.

The grounds are open to visitors, to see the **Florence Hawley Ellis Museum of Anthropology** and the **Ruth Hall Museum of Paleontology** (both 9am-5pm Mon.-Sat., $2), which display the local finds, including remnants of the prehistoric Gallina culture from the ridge above the valley and an eight-ton chunk of *Coelophysis*-filled siltstone in the process of being excavated. In summer, both museums are also open 1pm-5pm on Sundays.

You can also **hike** on your own after registering at the reception desk ($3 suggested conservation donation). The best trek, which takes about two hours round-trip, is to **Chimney Rock,** a towering landmark with panoramic views of the entire area. Don't be daunted—the steepest part of the trail is at the start—but do slather on the sunscreen, as there's no shade on this route. **Box Canyon** is an easier, shadier, all-level walk that's about four miles round-trip. **Kitchen Mesa Trail,** which starts at the same point, is much more difficult, requiring some climbing to get up the cliffs at the end (though you could hike the easy first two-thirds, then turn around).

Guided **tours** (various times, $25-35) of

Plaza Blanca near Abiquiu

the ranch grounds run mid-March through November, on various topics, from local archaeology to movie settings. One walking tour visits O'Keeffe's painting spot in the red Chinle hills behind the ranch. **Horseback rides** ($85) are another option, visiting various spots key to O'Keeffe's painting life.

Christ in the Desert Monastery

Thirteen miles up a dirt road, the Benedictine **Christ in the Desert Monastery** (Forest Rd. 151, 575/613-4233, www.christdesert.org, 9:15am-5pm daily) is said to be the remotest monastery in the Western hemisphere. The drive follows the Chama River through a lush valley, ending at a striking modern church designed in 1972 by the woodworker and architect George Nakashima to blend in with the dramatic cliffs behind. Most of the outbuildings are straw-bale construction, running on solar power, and the monks grow much of their food and brew their own Belgian-style beer, Monks Ale (look for it at Bode's in Abiquiu). A gift shop next to the modern church sells various monastery products. The annual hop harvest, in late August, is a convivial event that draws volunteers from all

over. Look for Forest Road 151 off the west side of U.S. 84, north of Ghost Ranch.

If you'd like to hike, **Rim Vista trail** (no. 15) is a good route, climbing up to a mesa in about 2.3 miles one-way, for a view across the valley to Ghost Ranch and the red rocks there. Look for the trailhead less than one mile in on Forest Road 151, off the north side of the road; turn right, then bear right at the fork and park after a quarter mile. The trail is best in spring and fall, as there is not much shade here.

Echo Amphitheater

Echo Amphitheater, a bandshell-shape rock formation, is a natural wonder of acoustics and a great place to let kids run around and yell to their hearts' content. It's four miles north of Ghost Ranch on U.S. 84. There are pleasant picnic areas ($2/car) tucked in the brush.

Accommodations and Food

The **Abiquiu Inn** (21120 U.S. 84, 505/685-4378, www.abiquiuinn.com) functions as the area's visitors center. Lodging ($160 d) consists of some pretty casitas at the back of the property, with great views of the river, and a cluster of motel rooms closer to the front (opt for rooms 2-6, which face away from the

Ghost Ranch, north of Abiquiu

road). Solo travelers should reserve well ahead for "El Vado Económico," a cozy one-bed room ($120). The inn's restaurant, ★ **Café Abiquiu** (7am-9pm daily, $13) is delectable, with fresh ingredients, a nice mix of traditional New Mexican and more creative food, and especially good and creative breakfasts.

You can also stay at **Ghost Ranch** (U.S. 84, 505/685-4333, www.ghostranch.org) when it's not full for retreats, in various room options. The cheapest are cabins with shared bath ($50 s, $90 d, with breakfast), which are an especially good deal for solo travelers. Private-bath rooms ($92 s, $125 d) have fine views over the valley. You can also camp for $19. Rates include breakfast, and day visitors can take simple **meals** (noon-1pm and 5pm-6pm) at the dining hall.

Christ in the Desert Monastery (Forest Rd. 151, 801/545-8567, www.christdesert.org, $70 s, $90 d) offers wonderful accommodations (two-night minimum) for a suggested donation, which includes all meals. At the 11.5-mile mark on the same road, **Rio Chama Campground** is preferable to Abiquiu Lake if you really want to get away from it all.

Getting There

Abiquiu is about 50 miles (one hour) from downtown Santa Fe. From Santa Fe, take U.S. 84/285 north for 26 miles to Española. From Española, continue on U.S. 84 north for 23 miles to Abiquiu. From Abiquiu to Taos, it's about 70 miles, or an hour and a half, via El Rito or Ojo Caliente. Continuing north on U.S. 84, you'll reach the Rio Chama in another 60 miles (one hour).

LOW ROAD TO TAOS

The lush farmland around the Rio Grande is the highlight of this drive north—the valley filled with apple orchards is as green as New Mexico gets. The route begins past the modern town of Española, winding into an ever-narrower canyon and finally emerging at the point where the high plains meet the mountains. This dramatic arrival makes it the better route for heading north to Taos; you can then loop back south via the high road.

Embudo and Dixon

The village of Embudo is really just a bend in the river, where the Chili Line railroad from Denver used to stop (the old station is across the river). But it offers a random roadside attraction in the **Classical Gas Museum** (1819 Hwy. 68, 505/852-2995, free) a front yard filled with old service station accoutrements. If the

the Classical Gas Museum in Embudo

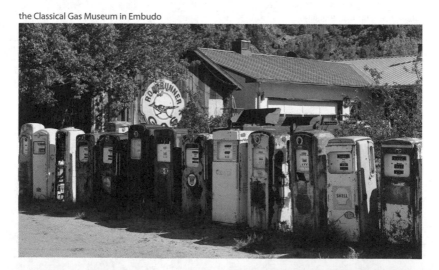

gate is open, the owner is probably home, and you can peek inside to see a beautiful collection of neon signs and restored gas pumps. There's also a good eating option: **Sugar's** (1799 Hwy. 68, 505/852-0604, 11am-6pm Thurs.-Sun., $6), a small roadside trailer that doles out seriously big food, such as barbecue brisket burritos. It's takeout only, but there are a few plastic picnic tables where you can sit down.

If you're into wine, keep an eye out for the various wineries just north of here: **Vivác** (2075 Hwy. 68, 505/579-4441, 10am-6pm Mon.-Sat., 11am-6pm Sun.) is on the main highway and **La Chiripada** (505/579-4437, 10am-6pm Mon.-Sat., noon-6pm Sun.) is down Highway 75 a few miles in the pleasant little town of Dixon, known for its dense concentration of artists, organic farmers, and vintners. The convivial **farmers market** runs on summer and fall Wednesdays (4:30pm-7pm), and in early November, look for the long-running **Dixon Studio Tour** (www.dixonarts.org). A good year-round reason to make the turn is ★ **Zuly's** (234 Hwy. 275, 505/579-4001, 8:30am-3pm Tues.-Thurs., 8:30am-7pm Fri., 9am-7pm Sat., $8), serving strong coffee and classic New Mexican food with a bit of hippie flair; hours cut back slightly in winter.

Pilar

Beginning just south of the village of Pilar and stretching several miles north, **Orilla Verde Recreation Area** ($3/car) is public land along either side of the Rio Grande, used primarily as a put-in or haul-out for rafting, but you can camp on the riverbanks as well. Petaca and Taos Junction have the best sites ($7 per night).

Running about 1.2 miles one-way along the west edge of the river, the **Vista Verde Trail** is an easy walk with great views and a few petroglyphs to spot in a small arroyo about a third of the way out. The trailhead is located on the other side of the river, half a mile up the hill from the Taos Junction Bridge off the dirt road Highway 567 (turn left off the highway in Pilar, then follow signs into Orilla Verde). Stop first on the main highway at the **Rio Grande Gorge Visitors Center** (Hwy. 68, 575/751-4899, 8:30am-4:30pm daily June-Aug., 10am-2pm daily Sept.-May) for maps and other information.

Across the road, **Pilar Yacht Club** (Hwy. 68, 575/758-9072, 8am-6pm daily mid-May-Aug., 9am-2pm daily Apr.-mid-May and Sept.-Oct.) is the center of the action, selling tubes for lazy floats, serving food to hungry river rats, and functioning as an office for a couple of outfitters.

Getting There

This low-road route is more direct than the high road to Taos, and has fewer potential diversions. Driving the 70 miles direct from downtown Santa Fe to Taos (on U.S. 84/285 and Hwy. 68), with no stops, takes about an hour and a half. There are no gas stations between Española and Taos.

HIGH ROAD TO TAOS

Chimayó, Córdova, Truchas, Las Trampas, Peñasco—these are the tiny villages strung, like beads on a necklace, along the winding highway through the mountains to Taos. This is probably the area of New Mexico where Spanish heritage has been least diluted—or at any rate relatively untouched by Anglo influence, for there has been a long history of exchange between the Spanish towns and the adjacent pueblos. The local dialect is distinctive, and residents can claim ancestors who settled the towns in the 18th century. The first families learned to survive in the harsh climate with a 90-day growing season, and much of the technology that worked then continues to work now; electricity was still scarce even in the 1970s, and adobe construction is common.

To casual visitors, these communities, closed off by geography, can seem a little insular, but pop in at the galleries that have sprung up in a couple of the towns, and you'll get a warm welcome. And during the **High Road Art Tour** (www.highroadnewmexico.com), over two weekends in September, modern artists and more traditional craftspeople famed particularly for their wood-carving skills open their home studios.

The route starts on Highway 503, heading east off U.S. 84/285 just north of Pojoaque.

Estrella del Norte Vineyard

Planted just in 2008 on the site of a previously abandoned vineyard, **Estrella del Norte Vineyard** (Hwy. 503, 505/455-2826, www.estrelladelnortevineyard.com, 10am-5pm Mon.-Sat., noon-5pm Sun.) is a pretty, lush spot to stop, whether you're a wine lover or not. It serves its own pinot noir, as well as a few wines from neighboring vineyards, and ciders made from apples from up the road in Dixon. Santa Fe School of Cooking also hosts classes up here.

Nambé Pueblo

A few miles off Highway 503, **Nambé Falls Recreation Area** (505/455-2306, $10/car) is open to the public for swimming and fishing. A rough trail leads to the falls themselves, a double cascade of water from the dam on the river here. It's a nice place to stretch your legs, but its alleged opening hours (7am-7pm daily) are not always adhered to, and you may find it closed.

Incidentally, the Nambé line of high-end housewares has nothing to do with this pueblo of 1,700 people—weaving and micaceous pottery are some of the traditional crafts here. The biggest annual event is Fourth of July, celebrated with dances and a crafts market.

Chimayó

From Nambé Pueblo, Highway 503 continues to a T junction; make a hard left onto Highway 98 to descend into the valley of Chimayó, site of the largest mass pilgrimage in the United States. During Holy Week, some 50,000 people arrive on foot, often bearing large crosses. The destination is a remarkable church.

★ SANTUARIO DE CHIMAYÓ

The pilgrimage tradition began in 1945, as a commemoration of the Bataan Death March, but the **Santuario de Chimayó** (Hwy. 98, 505/351-9961, www.holychimayo.us,

Santuario de Chimayó, "the Lourdes of America"

Walk on, Santo Niño

In northern New Mexico, the figure of Santo Niño de Atocha is a popular one. This image of Jesus comes from a Spanish legend, when the Christians were battling the Moors in the medieval period, around 1300, the Muslims took a number of prisoners after a brutal battle in Atocha, near Madrid, and would not allow the captives' families to visit them. After many desperate prayers on the part of Atocha's Christian women, a mysterious child appeared, carrying food and water, to care for the prisoners. The populace guessed that it must be the child Jesus—thus Santo Niño de Atocha became the patron saint of prisoners, and he is depicted carrying a pail for bread and a gourd for water and wearing a large hat emblazoned with a scallop shell, the symbol of pilgrims.

Santo Niño de Atocha in Chimayó

In **Chimayó** alone, Santo Niño de Atocha is installed in the main church and in a separate 1857 chapel just a block away. He is seen now as a broader intercessor not just for those imprisoned, but also for the chronically ill. New Mexicans have developed a unique folk practice, placing baby shoes at the Santo Niño's feet, on the assumption that his own have worn out while he was walking in the night.

9am-6pm daily May-Sept., 9am-5pm daily Oct.-Apr.) had a reputation as a miraculous spot from its start, in 1814. It began as a small chapel, built at the place where a local farmer, Bernardo Abeyta, is said to have dug up a glowing crucifix; the carved wood figure was placed on the altar. The building later fell into disrepair, but in 1929, the architect John Gaw Meem bought it, restored it, and added its sturdy metal roof; Meem then granted it back to the archdiocese in Santa Fe.

Unlike many of the older churches farther north, which are now open very seldom, Chimayó is an active place of prayer, always busy with tourists as well as visitors seeking solace, with many side chapels and a busy gift shop. (Mass is said weekdays at 11am and on Sunday at 10:30am and noon year-round.) The approach from the parking area passes chain-link fencing into which visitors have woven twigs to form crosses, each set of sticks representing a prayer. Outdoor pews made of split tree trunks accommodate overflow crowds,

and a wheelchair ramp gives easy access to the church.

But the original adobe *santuario* seems untouched by modernity. The front wall of the dim main chapel is filled with an elaborately painted altar screen from the first half of the 19th century, the work of Molleno (nicknamed "the Chile Painter" because forms, especially robes, in his paintings often resemble red and green chiles). The vibrant colors seem to shimmer in the gloom, forming a sort of stage set for Abeyta's crucifix, Nuestro Señor de las Esquípulas, as the centerpiece. Painted on the screen above the crucifix is the symbol of the Franciscans: a cross over which the arms of Christ and Saint Francis meet.

Most pilgrims make their way directly to the small, low-ceiling antechamber that holds *el pocito*, the little hole where the glowing crucifix was allegedly first dug up. From this pit they scoop up a small portion of the exposed red earth, to apply to withered limbs and arthritic joints, or to eat in hopes of curing internal ailments. (The parish refreshes the well each year with new dirt, after it has been blessed by the priests.) The adjacent sacristy displays handwritten testimonials, prayers, and abandoned crutches; the figurine of Santo Niño de Atocha is also said to have been dug out of the holy ground here as well. (Santo Niño de Atocha has a dedicated chapel just down the road—the artwork here is modern, bordering on cutesy, but the back room, filled with baby shoes, is poignant.)

CHIMAYÓ MUSEUM

The only other official sight in the village is the tiny **Chimayó Museum** (Plaza del Cerro, 505/351-0945, www.chimayomuseum.org, 11am-3pm Wed.-Sat., free), set on the old fortified plaza. It functions as a local archive and displays a neat collection of vintage photographs. Look for it behind Ortega's weaving shop.

SHOPPING

Chimayó has also been a weaving center for centuries, commercially known since 1900, when Hispano weavers started selling locally crafted "Indian" blankets to tourists. The two main shops are **Ortega's** (505/351-4215, 9am-5pm Mon.-Sat.), at the intersection of County Road 98 and Highway 76, and **Centinela Traditional Arts** (505/351-2180, 9am-6pm Mon.-Sat., 10am-5pm Sun.), about one mile east on Highway 76. While both are rigorously traditional in techniques, the work at Centinela shows more creative use of color and pattern.

ACCOMMODATIONS

Chimayó makes a good base for exploring north of Santa Fe, as you're away from the unscenic highways south of Española yet still at a convenient crossroads. For old Spanish style, opt for **Rancho de Chimayó** (Hwy. 76, 505/351-2222, www.ranchodechimayo.com, $79 d), an offshoot of the restaurant across the road, just north of the church. The converted hacienda building, with a central courtyard, has seven rooms, some with fireplaces and all with a rustic, low-tech (no TVs or a/c) feel. Or

you can stay with a known wood-carving family, at **El Mesón de la Centinela** (Hwy. 76, 505/351-2280, www.innatchimayo.com, $85 d), which has three homey casitas with patios, all part of a big adobe ranch house. Look for the turn off Highway 76, opposite Centinela Traditional Arts.

For more modern style, **Rancho Manzana** (26 Camino de Mision, 505/351-2227, www.ranchomanzana.com, $75 s, $115 d) has a rustic-chic feel, with excellent breakfasts (the owner also runs cooking classes). En route to Española, **Casa Escondida** (64 County Rd. 100, 505/351-4805, www.casaescondida.com, $115 s, $145 d) is the slickest place in the area, with eight rooms, a big backyard, a hot tub, and a sunny garden.

FOOD

For lunch, head across the parking lot from the Santuario de Chimayó to **Leona's** (505/351-4569, 10am-5pm Fri.-Mon., $3), where you can pick up bulk chile and pistachios as well as delicious tamales and crumbly *bizcochitos*. For a more leisurely sit-down meal, ★ **Rancho de Chimayó** (County Rd. 98, 505/351-4444, www.ranchodechimayo.com, 11:30am-9pm daily May-Oct., 11:30am-9pm Tues.-Sun. Nov.-Apr., $12) offers great local food on a beautiful terrace—or inside the old adobe home by the fireplace in wintertime. Likewise, the menu offers all possible options: posole or rice, whole pintos or refried beans, smooth red sauce (from Chimayó chiles) or chunkier *chile caribe*. The place is also open for breakfast on weekends, 8:30am-10:30am.

Córdova

From Chimayó, turn right (east) on Highway 76 (west takes you to Española), to begin the climb up the Sangre de Cristo Mountains. Near the crest of the hill, about three miles along, a small sign points to Córdova, a village best known for its austere unpainted santos and *bultos* done by masters such as George López and José Dolores López. Another family member, **Sabinita López Ortiz** (9 County Rd. 1317, 505/351-4572, variable hours), sells her work and that of five other generations of wood-carvers. **Castillo Gallery** (County Rd. 1317, 505/351-4067, variable hours) mixes traditional woodwork with more contemporary sculpture.

Truchas

Highway 76 winds along to the little village of Truchas (Trout), founded in 1754 and still not much more than a long row of buildings set into the ridgeline. On the corner where the highway makes a hard left north, is the village *morada,* the meeting place of the local Penitente brotherhood.

Head straight down the smaller road to reach **Nuestra Señora del Rosario de las Truchas Church,** tucked into a small plaza off to the right of the main street. It's open to visitors only June-August—if you do have a chance to look inside the dim, thick-walled mission, you'll see precious examples of local wood carving. Though many of the more delicate ones have been moved to a museum for preservation, those remaining display an essential New Mexican style—the sort of "primitive" thing that Bishop Lamy of Santa Fe hated. They're preserved today because Truchas residents hid them at home during the late 19th century. Santa Lucia, with her eyeballs in her hand, graces the altar, and a finely wrought crucifix hangs to the right, clad in a skirt because the legs have broken off.

Just up the road is **The Cordovas Handweaving Workshop** (32 County Rd. 75, 505/689-1124, 8am-5pm Mon.-Sat.), an unassuming wooden house that echoes with the soft click-clack of a broadloom, as this Hispano family turns out subtly striped rugs in flawless traditional style, as it has done for generations. Prices are quite reasonable.

Las Trampas

Farther north on Highway 76, the village of Las Trampas was settled in 1751, and its showpiece, **San José de Gracia Church** (10am-4pm Sat.-Sun. June-Aug.), was built nine years later. It remains one of the finest examples of New Mexican village church architecture. Its thick adobe walls are balanced by vertical bell towers; inside, the clerestory at the front of the church—a very typical design—lets light in to shine down on the altar, which was carved and painted in the late 1700s. Other paradigmatic elements include the *atrio,* or small plaza between the low adobe boundary wall and the church itself, utilized as a cemetery, and the dark narthex where you enter, confined by the choir loft above, but serving only to emphasize

horses outside Truchas

the sense of light and space created in the rest of the church by the clerestory and the small windows near the viga ceiling.

As you leave the town heading north, look to the right—you'll see a centuries-old acequia that has been channeled through a log flume to cross a small arroyo. Less than a mile north of the village, you pass the turn for El Valle and Forest Road 207, which leads to the **Trampas Lakes** trailhead. This 6.1-mile hike goes through gorgeous alpine scenery—steep rock walls jutting from dense forest, myriad wildflowers, and the two lakes themselves, which are clear and frigid. A spur trail at the last junction leads to Hidden Lake (2 miles round-trip). This route makes a very pleasant overnight trek, giving you time to fish and relax at the end, but with an early start, you could also do the trail as an intense all-day outing.

San José de Gracia Church

Picurís Pueblo

The smallest pueblo in New Mexico, Picurís has only about 300 members. It is also one of the few Rio Grande pueblos that has not built a casino; instead, it capitalizes on its beautiful natural setting, a lush valley where bison roam and aspen leaves rustle. You can picnic here and fish in small but well-stocked Tu-Tah Lake. The **San Lorenzo de Picurís Church** looks old, but it was in fact rebuilt by hand in 1989, following exactly the form of the original 1776 design—the process took eight years. As at Nambé, local traditions have melded with those of the surrounding villages; the Hispano-Indian Matachines dances are well attended on Christmas Eve. Start at the **visitors center** (575/587-1099 or 575/587-1071, 9am-5pm Mon.-Sat.) to pick up maps. The pueblo is a short detour from the high road proper: At the junction with Highway 75, turn west, then follow signs off the main road.

Peñasco

Peñasco is best known to tourists as the home of ★ **Sugar Nymphs Bistro** (15046 Hwy. 75, 575/587-0311, 11:30am-2:30pm Mon.-Wed.., 11:30am-3pm and 5:30pm-8pm

Thurs.-Sat., 11am-2:30pm Sun., $12), a place with "country atmosphere and city cuisine," where you can get treats like grilled lamb, fresh-pressed cider, piñon couscous, and staggering wedges of layer cake. An adjoining **Peñasco Theatre** (www.penascotheatre.org) hosts quirky music and theatrical performances June to September. In winter, restaurant hours are more limited, so call ahead.

This is also the northern gateway to the **Pecos Wilderness Area**—turn on Forest Road 116 to reach Santa Barbara Campground and the Santa Barbara Trail to Truchas Peak, a 23-mile round-trip that requires advance planning. Contact the **Española ranger district office** (1710 N. Riverside Dr., 505/753-7331, 8am-4:30pm Mon.-Fri.) or the one in the town of Pecos for conditions before you hike.

Sipapu

Detouring right (east) along Highway 518, you reach **Sipapu** (Hwy. 518, 800/587-2240, www.sipapunm.com), an unassuming, inexpensive ski resort—really, just a handful of

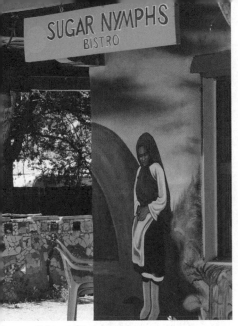
Peñasco's finest dining

Returning to the junction, continue on to Taos via Highway 518, which soon descends into a valley and passes **Pot Creek Cultural Site** (575/587-2255, 9am-4pm Wed.-Sun. July-Aug.), a mildly interesting diversion for its one-mile loop trail through Ancestral Puebloan ruins from around 1100.

You arrive in Taos at its very southern end—really, in Ranchos de Taos, just north of the San Francisco de Asis Church on Highway 68. Turn left to see the church, or turn right to head up to the town plaza and to Taos Pueblo.

Getting There

From downtown Santa Fe, the high road to Taos is about 90 miles. Follow U.S. 84/285 north for 17 miles to Pojoaque. Turn right (east) on Highway 503, following signs for Nambé Pueblo; turn left where signed, onto County Road 98, to Chimayó, then left again on Highway 76. In about 30 miles, make a hard left onto Highway 518, and in 16 miles, you'll arrive in Ranchos de Taos, just north of the church and about 3 miles south of the main Taos plaza. The drive straight through takes a little more than two hours; leave time to dawdle at churches and galleries, take a hike, or have lunch along the way.

cabins (from $69) and campsites ($12) at the base of a 9,255-foot mountain. Cheap lift tickets ($44 full-day) and utter quiet make this a bargain getaway.

Information and Services

TOURIST INFORMATION

The **Santa Fe Convention and Visitors Bureau** (800/777-2489, www.santafe.org) hands out its visitors guide and other brochures from offices at the **convention center** (201 W. Marcy St., 8am-5pm Mon.-Fri.) and at the **Rail Runner depot** (401 S. Guadalupe St., 9am-5pm Mon.-Sat., 10am-2pm Sun.); the depot office is closed on Sundays November-April. The New Mexico Tourism Department runs a **visitors center** (491 Old Santa Fe Tr., 505/827-7336, www.newmexico.org, 8am-5pm Mon.-Fri.) near San Miguel Mission.

For info on the outdoors, head to the Bureau of Land Management's comprehensive **Public Information Access Center** (301 Dinosaur Tr., 505/954-2000, www.publiclands.org, 8am-4:30pm Mon.-Fri.), just off Highway 14 (follow Cerrillos Road until it passes under I-25). You can pick up detailed route descriptions for area day hikes, as well as guidebooks, topo maps, and hunting and fishing licenses.

Books and Maps

Santa Fe has several particularly good bookshops in the center of town. **Travel Bug** (839 Paseo de Peralta, 505/992-0418, 7:30am-5:30pm Mon.-Sat., 11am-4pm Sun.) specializes in maps, travel guides, gear, and free advice. For more general books, **Collected Works** (202 Galisteo St., 505/988-4226, 8am-8pm Mon.-Sat., 8am-6pm Sun.) is the place to go for a trove of local-interest titles. Finally, the eclectic new and secondhand stock at **op.cit.** (500 Montezuma Ave., 505/428-0321, 8am-7pm Mon.-Sat., 8am-6pm Sun.), in Sanbusco Center, is endlessly browsable.

Local Media

The *Santa Fe New Mexican* is Santa Fe's daily paper. On Fridays, it publishes events listings and gallery news in its *Pasatiempo* insert. For left-of-center news and commentary, the *Santa Fe Reporter* is the free weekly rag, available in most coffee shops and cafés.

Radio

KBAC (98.1 FM), better known as Radio Free Santa Fe, is a dynamic community station with eclectic music and talk. Tune in Friday afternoons for news on the gallery scene.

Another public station is **KSFR** (101.1 FM), run by Santa Fe Community College.

SERVICES
Banks
First National Santa Fe (62 Lincoln Ave., 505/992-2000, 8am-5pm Mon.-Fri.) is on the west side of the plaza.

Post Office
Santa Fe's **main post office** (120 S. Federal Pl., 505/988-2239, 8am-5:30pm Mon.-Fri., 9am-4pm Sat.) is conveniently just north of the plaza, near the district courthouse.

Laundry
Most self-service laundries are on or near Cerrillos Road. One of the largest and nicest is **St. Michael's Laundry** (1605 St. Michaels Dr., 505/989-9375, 6am-9pm daily), a couple of blocks east of Cerrillos Road. It also has drop-off service.

Getting There and Around

AIR
Santa Fe Municipal Airport (SAF, 121 Aviation Dr., 505/955-2900), west of the city, receives direct flights from Dallas and Los Angeles with American Eagle, and from Denver with United. Typically, fares are better to the Albuquerque airport (ABQ), an hour's drive away.

    Sandia Shuttle Express (888/775-5696, www.sandiashuttle.com) does hourly pickups from the Albuquerque airport 8:45am-11:45pm and will deliver to any hotel or B&B ($28 one-way).

TRAIN
The **Rail Runner** (866/795-7245, www.riometro.org) goes from Albuquerque to downtown Santa Fe—the final stop is at the rail yard in the Guadalupe district (410 S. Guadalupe St.). The ride takes a little over 90 minutes and costs $9, or $10 for a day pass

(only $9 if you buy it online), and the last train back to Albuquerque leaves at 9pm weekdays, 10:07pm Saturdays, and 8:12pm Sundays.

    Barring a rerouting due to lack of track-maintenance funding, **Amtrak** (800/872-7245, www.amtrak.com) runs the *Southwest Chief* once a day through Lamy, 18 miles south of Santa Fe. It's a dramatic place to step off the train—you'll feel very Wild West, as there's no visible civilization for miles around. Trains arrive from Chicago and Los Angeles in the afternoon, and Amtrak provides a shuttle van to the city.

BUS AND SHUTTLE
Santa Fe Pick-Up (505/231-2573, www.santafenm.gov, free) is a shuttle designed for passengers arriving on the Rail Runner—though any tourist can use it. Its route starts and ends in front of Jean Cocteau Cinema, on Montezuma Avenue just north of the depot,

and it stops at the capitol, the St. Francis Cathedral, four points on Canyon Road, Museum Hill, and a few other tourist-friendly spots around town. It runs every 20 minutes or so, 6:30am-6:30pm Monday to Friday and 7:30am-4:30pm Saturday.

The reasonably useful city bus system, **Santa Fe Trails** (505/955-2001, www.santafenm.gov), can take you to all of the major sights from the handy central depot on Sheridan Street northwest of the plaza. The M route goes to Museum Hill; Route 2 runs along Cerrillos Road. Buses on all routes run only every 30 to 60 minutes. The Museum Hill and Cerrillos Road buses run on Sundays. Fare is $1, or you can buy a day pass for $2, payable on board with exact change.

CAR

Ideally, you would not have a car while in Santa Fe itself. The area around the plaza is a maze of one-way streets, and parking is limited and expensive. **Hertz, Budget, Avis,** and **Thrifty** all have branches on Cerrillos Road.

From Albuquerque to Santa Fe, it's a straight shot north on I-25 for 65 miles; you'll reach Santa Fe in about an hour.

Coming from Taos, allow 1.5-2.5 hours, depending on whether you come on the low road (on Hwy. 68 and U.S. 84/285, via Española), via Ojo Caliente (mostly on U.S. 285), or on the high road (mostly on Hwy. 76, via Truchas).

Taos

A dobe buildings cluster around a plaza. Steep mountains beckon. Art galleries, organic bakeries, and yoga studios proliferate. But the town of Taos is not just a miniature Santa Fe.

It's more isolated, reached by two-lane roads along either the winding mountain-ridge route or the fertile Rio Grande Valley, and it has a rougher, muddier feel. The glory of the landscape, from looming Taos Mountain to the blue mesas dissolving into the flat western horizon, can be breathtaking. The mysticism surrounding Taos Pueblo is intense, as is the often wild creativity of the artists who have lived here. No wonder people flock here on pilgrimages: to the ranch where D. H. Lawrence lived, to the hip-deep powder at Taos Ski Valley, to the San Francisco de Asis Church that Georgia O'Keeffe painted. Then they wind up staying. The person pouring your coffee at the café probably has a variation on this very story.

Taos has long been associated with artists and writers, and even some more recent Hollywood types, but this doesn't translate to wealth and exclusivity. Hispano farmers in Valle Valdez scrape by on acequia-fed farm plots as they have for centuries. The same goes for residents of old Taos Pueblo, the living World Heritage Site that still uses no electricity or running water. Add to that a strong subculture of ski bums, artists, off-the-grid eco-homesteaders, and spiritual seekers, and you have a community that, while not typically prosperous, is more loyal and dedicated to preserving its unique way of life than perhaps any other small town in the western United States.

North and east from Taos, the so-called Enchanted Circle byway loops around Wheeler Peak, the highest mountain in New Mexico at 13,161 feet. Unlike the rest of northern New Mexico, the area was settled primarily by miners and ranchers in the late 19th century. Along the way, you can stop at a mining ghost town, a moving Vietnam veterans' memorial, or a couple of less extreme ski resorts.

Previous: ice cream bus at the Rio Grande Gorge; Taos Mountain. **Above:** snowcapped peaks in Taos

Look for ★ to find recommended sights, activities, dining, and lodging.

Highlights

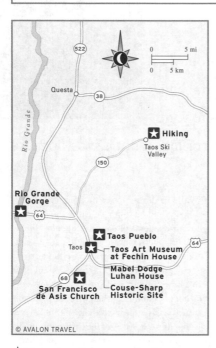

© AVALON TRAVEL

★ **Taos Art Museum at Fechin House:** In the early 1930s, Russian artist Nicolai Fechin designed his home in a fusion of Tartar, Spanish, and American Indian styles. His and other artists' paintings hang inside (page 105).

★ **Mabel Dodge Luhan House:** See where U.S. counterculture thrived in the mid-20th century, as encouraged by the arts doyenne who made Taos her home. Countless writers, painters, and actors visited Mabel here in her idiosyncratic home (page 106).

★ **Couse-Sharp Historic Site:** An illuminating guided tour through an artist's workspace, led by the artist's granddaughter, offers an excellent slice of Taos history (page 107).

★ **San Francisco de Asis Church:** With its massive adobe buttresses and rich earthy glow, this 350-year-old Franciscan mission is one of the most recognizable in the world, thanks to its frequent depiction in paintings and photographs (page 108).

★ **Taos Pueblo:** The stepped adobe buildings at New Mexico's most remarkable pueblo seem to rise organically from the earth. Don't miss the ceremonial dances performed here, about eight times a year (page 109).

★ **Rio Grande Gorge:** Think how dismayed the first homesteaders must have been when they reached "New Mexico's Grand Canyon," an 800-foot-deep channel cut through the rock to the west of Taos. Think how overjoyed today's whitewater rafters are in the spring, when mountain runoff surges through the rift (page 111).

★ **Hiking:** The mountains and mesas around Taos are some of the most stunning places in northern New Mexico to get some fresh air—you can even climb the state's highest peak (page 120).

Taos Area

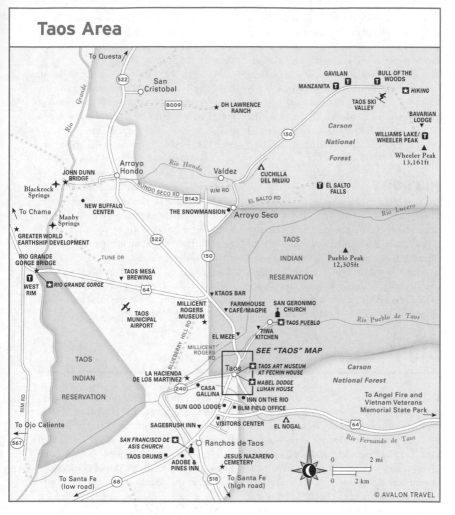

To Questa

522

San Cristobal

B009

DH LAWRENCE RANCH

GAVILAN

MANZANITA

BULL OF THE WOODS

HIKING

TAOS SKI VALLEY

BAVARIAN LODGE

WILLIAMS LAKE/ WHEELER PEAK

Carson

National

Forest

Wheeler Peak 13,161ft

150

Rio Grande

Rio

Arroyo Hondo

JOHN DUNN BRIDGE

Rio Hondo

Valdez

CUCHILLA DEL MEDIO

EL SALTO FALLS

Blackrock Springs

To Chama

Manby Springs

NEW BUFFALO CENTER

HONDO SECO RD

RIM RD

B143

EL SALTO RD

Rio Lucero

THE SNOWMANSION

Arroyo Seco

GREATER WORLD EARTHRDEVELOPMENT

522

TUNE DR

TAOS

RIO GRANDE GORGE BRIDGE

150

INDIAN

Pueblo Peak 12,305ft

WEST RIM

RIO GRANDE GORGE

TAOS MESA BREWING

64

RESERVATION

TAOS MUNICIPAL AIRPORT

MILLICENT ROGERS MUSEUM

KTAOS BAR

FARMHOUSE CAFÉ/MAGPIE

SAN GERONIMO CHURCH

Rio Pueblo de Taos

TAOS PUEBLO

EL MEZE

TIWA KITCHEN

MILLICENT ROGERS RD.

SEE "TAOS" MAP

TAOS

INDIAN

RESERVATION

LA HACIENDA DE LOS MARTINEZ

BLUEBERRY HILL RD

Taos

240

CASA GALLINA

TAOS ART MUSEUM AT FECHIN HOUSE

MABEL DODGE LUHAN HOUSE

Carson

National Forest

To Angel Fire and Vietnam Veterans Memorial State Park

RIM RD

SUN GOD LODGE

INN ON THE RIO

BLM FIELD OFFICE

To Ojo Caliente

567

SAGEBRUSH INN

VISITORS CENTER

EL NOGAL

64

Rio Fernando de Taos

SAN FRANCISCO DE ASIS CHURCH

Ranchos de Taos

TAOS DRUMS

ADOBE & PINES INN

JESUS NAZARENO CEMETERY

0   2 mi

To Santa Fe (low road)

68

518

To Santa Fe (high road)

0   2 km

© AVALON TRAVEL

TAOS

PLANNING YOUR TIME

Taos's busiest tourist season is **summer**, when a day's entertainment can consist of some strolling and museum-going, then settling in to watch the afternoon thunderheads gather and churn, followed by the sun setting under lurid red streaks across the broad western mesas. **Wintertime** also gets busy with skiers between November and April, but as they're all up on the mountain during the day, museums scale back their hours, and residents reclaim the town center, curling up

with books at the many coffee shops. **Taos Pueblo closes to visitors** for up to 10 weeks in February and March. By May, the peaks are relatively clear of snow, and you can hike to high meadows filled with wildflowers. **Fall** is dominated by the smell of wood smoke and the beat of drums, as the pueblo and the rest of the town turn out for the Feast of San Geronimo at the end of September.

From Santa Fe, it's possible to visit Taos as a **day trip**—as plenty of people do in the summertime—but you'll of course get a better sense of the place if you stay overnight. A three- or four-night visit gives you time for an afternoon at Taos Pueblo, a couple of mornings at galleries and museums, a hike or skiing, and a day tour of the Enchanted Circle.

As for the **Enchanted Circle,** the 84-mile loop is typically done as a day trip. By no means attempt to visit Taos *and* do the Enchanted Circle loop in a single day—you'd be terribly rushed, and this is hardly the spirit of Taos.

HISTORY

The first human inhabitants of the area at the base of Taos Mountain were Tiwa-speaking descendants of the Ancestral Puebloans (also called Anasazi) who migrated from the Four Corners area around AD 1000. Taos (how Spaniards heard the Tiwa word for "village") was a thriving village when Spanish explorers, part of Francisco de Coronado's crew, passed through in 1540. By 1615, settlers had arrived.

By the mid-18th century, Taos was the hub of a large trade in beaver pelts, which drew French fur trappers, Mexican traders, and local settlers to swap meets.

But in 1879 the railroad arrived in Raton, bumping Taos from its position as a trading hub. Fortunes turned only in 1898, when Bert Geer Phillips and Ernest Blumenschein, two painters on a jaunt from Denver, "discovered" Taos after their wagon wheel snapped near town. They established the Taos Society of Artists (TSA) in 1915, making names for themselves as painters of the American West and a name for Taos as a destination for creative types. In the 1960s, creativity took a turn to the communal, with groups such as the New Buffalo commune in Arroyo Hondo—an inspiration for Dennis Hopper's film *Easy Rider.* The culture clash at first was fierce, but in the decades since, hippies (and their richer relatives, ski bums) have become part of the town's most basic fabric.

Sights

The area referred to as Taos encompasses a few nearby communities as well. Arriving via the low road, on Highway 68, you pass first through **Ranchos de Taos**; it's connected to Taos Plaza by Paseo del Pueblo Sur, a stretch of chain stores and cheap motels. The intersection with Kit Carson Road (U.S. 64) is the center of town proper (**Taos Plaza** is just west); for **parking,** there's a pay lot at the light, or a free lot a few blocks farther east on Kit Carson.

Heading north past Kit Carson, the road becomes Paseo del Pueblo Norte. It curves west after half a mile, and a smaller road continues north about two miles to **Taos Pueblo.** Paseo del Pueblo Norte carries on through what is technically the separate village of El Prado, then to a four-way intersection that will forever be called "the old blinking light," even though the flashing yellow signal was replaced with a newfangled three-color traffic

light in the 1990s. Here U.S. 64 shoots **west to the Rio Grande,** and Highway 522 leads northwest to the outlying village of **Arroyo Hondo,** then to Questa and the Enchanted Circle. Highway 150 goes north to **Arroyo Seco,** and eventually to **Taos Ski Valley,** at the base of the slopes.

TAOS PLAZA

The central **Taos Plaza,** enclosed by adobe buildings with deep portals, is easy to miss if you just cruise through on the main road—it's just west of the intersection with Kit Carson Road. Once an informal area at the center of a cluster of settlers' homes, the plaza was established around 1615 but destroyed in the Pueblo Revolt of 1680. New homes were built starting in 1710, as defense against Comanche and Jicarilla raiders. But fires repeatedly gutted the block-style buildings, so the structures that edge the plaza all date from around

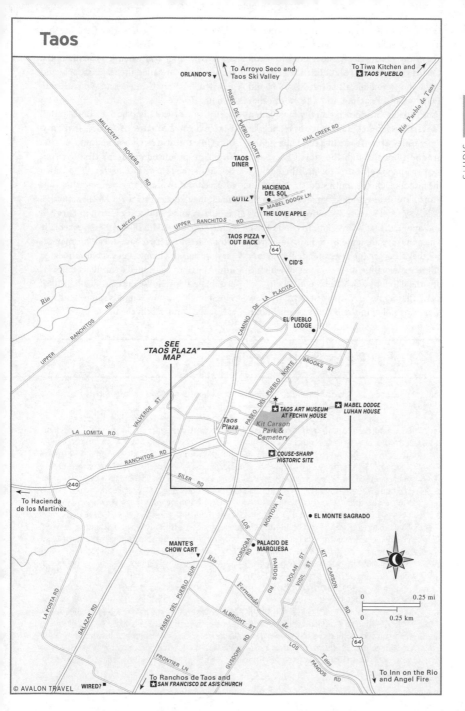

Taos

ORLANDO'S ▼

To Arroyo Seco and
Taos Ski Valley

To Tiwa Kitchen and
⭐ *TAOS PUEBLO*

PASEO DEL PUEBLO NORTE

MILLICENT ROGERS RD

HAIL CREEK RD

Rio Pueblo de Taos

TAOS
DINER ▼

HACIENDA
DEL SOL ●

GUTIZ ▼

MABEL DODGE LN

THE LOVE APPLE

Lucero

UPPER RANCHITOS RD

TAOS PIZZA ▼
OUT BACK

64

▼ CID'S

Rio

RANCHITOS RD

UPPER

CAMINO DE LA PLACITA

EL PUEBLO
LODGE ●

SEE
"TAOS PLAZA"
MAP

BROOKS ST

PASEO DEL PUEBLO NORTE

VALVERDE ST

Taos
Plaza

⭐ TAOS ART MUSEUM
AT FECHIN HOUSE

⭐ MABEL DODGE
LUHAN HOUSE

Kit Carson
Park &
Cemetery

LA LOMITA RD

RANCHITOS RD

⭐ COUSE-SHARP
HISTORIC SITE

SILER RD

240

← To Hacienda
de los Martinez

● EL MONTE SAGRADO

MONTOYA ST

LOS

MANTE'S
CHOW CART ▼

CORDOBA RD

● PALACIO DE
MARQUESA

KIT CARSON RD

Rio

PANDOS RD

DOLAN ST

VIGIL ST

0   0.25 mi

0   0.25 km

LA POSTA RD

SALAZAR RD

PASEO DEL PUEBLO SUR

Fernando

ALBRIGHT ST

de

los

Taos

FRONTIER LN

GUSDORF RD

PANDOS RD

64

© AVALON TRAVEL   WIRED? ■

To Ranchos de Taos and
⭐ SAN FRANCISCO DE ASIS CHURCH

To Inn on the Rio
and Angel Fire ↓

1930—and unfortunately virtually all are now filled with rather cheesy souvenir shops.

On the plaza's north side, the **old Taos County courthouse** contains a series of WPA-sponsored murals painted in 1934 and 1935 by Emil Bisttram and a team of other Taos artists. The door is usually open when the farmers market is on, but not reliably at other times. Still, it's worth a try: Enter on the ground floor through the North Plaza Art Center and go upstairs, toward the back of the building. On the south side, the **Hotel La Fonda de Taos** harbors a small collection of D. H. Lawrence's "erotic" paintings (2pm, 4pm, and 6pm daily, $6 admission, free to guests). The paintings are tame by today's standards, but they flesh out (no pun intended) the story of the writer's time in Taos, some of which is described in his book *Mornings in Mexico*.

In the center is a **monument** to New Mexicans killed in the Bataan Death March of World War II. The U.S. flag flies day and night, a tradition carried on after an incident during the Civil War when Kit Carson and a crew of his men nailed the flag to a pole and guarded it to keep Confederate sympathizers from taking it down.

In front of the historic La Fonda hotel, a large bronze **statue of Padre Antonio Martinez** gestures like a visionary. This local hero produced the area's first newspaper, *El Crepúsculo de la Libertad* (The Dawn of Freedom), which later became the *Taos News*; he also established a co-ed school, a seminary, and a law school. Bishop Lamy in Santa Fe criticized his liberal views, especially after Martinez defied Lamy's call for mandatory tithing, and Lamy later excommunicated him. Martinez continued to minister to locals at a chapel in his house until his death in 1867. The statue's enormous hands suggest his vast talent and influence in the town.

Taos: Fact and Fiction

Just as San Francisco de Asis Church has inspired countless painters and photographers, the people of Taos have found their way into novels and short stories.

One of Taos's more revered figures is **Padre Antonio Martinez,** a popular priest in the mid-1800s who clashed with **Bishop Jean-Baptiste Lamy** in Santa Fe. So some Taos residents aren't fond of Willa Cather's *Death Comes for the Archbishop* (New York: Vintage, 1990), even if it is a classic. The 1927 novel is based on the mission of Lamy, with sympathy for his efforts to straighten out "rogue" Mexican priests like Martinez. The padre gets more balanced coverage in *Lamy of Santa Fe* (Middletown, CT: Wesleyan University Press, 2003), a Pulitzer Prize-winning biography by Paul Horgan.

Famous Western novelist Frank Waters, a Taos resident for almost 50 years, fictionalized **Edith Warner**, a woman who ran a small café frequented by the Los Alamos scientists while they developed the nuclear bomb. *The Woman at Otowi Crossing* (Athens, OH: Swallow Press, 1987) is his portrait of a woman who seeks isolation in the New Mexico wilderness but is drawn back into the world through the largest event of her time. The novel is fairly true to life, but a biography, *The House at Otowi Bridge: The Story of Edith Warner and Los Alamos* (Albuquerque: University of New Mexico Press, 1973), is stricter with the facts. It's by Peggy Pond Church, who lived at Los Alamos for 20 years before the area was taken over by the military.

Another Taos writer, **John Nichols**, earned acclaim for his 1974 comic novel *The Milagro Beanfield War* (New York: Owl Books, 2000), later made into a film by Robert Redford. The war of the title is an escalating squabble in a tiny village over the acequia, the type of irrigation ditch that's still used in Valle Valdez and other agricultural communities in the area. But if you think it takes comic melodrama and a star such as Redford to make irrigation interesting, look into the beautiful and fascinating *Mayordomo: Chronicle of an Acequia in Northern New Mexico* (Albuquerque: University of New Mexico Press, 1993), **Stanley Crawford**'s memoir about his term as "ditch boss" in the valley where he runs his garlic farm.

Taos Plaza

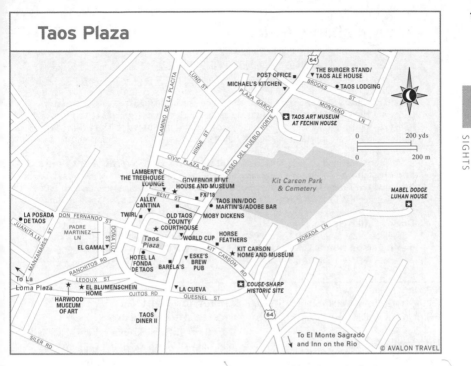

Harwood Museum of Art

The **Harwood Museum of Art** (238 Ledoux St., 575/758-9826, 10am-5pm Mon.-Sat., noon-5pm Sun., closed Mon. Nov.-Mar., $10), set in the sprawling Pueblo Revival-style home of the Harwood patrons, tells the story of Taos's rise as an art colony, beginning with Ernest Blumenschein's fateful wagon accident, which left him and his colleague Bert Phillips stranded in the tiny town in 1898.

Modern Taos painters are represented as well in the temporary exhibit spaces upstairs, and it's interesting to see the same material—the mountain, the pueblo, the river, local residents—depicted in different styles over the decades. Also upstairs is a small but very good assortment of Hispano crafts, including some beautiful 19th-century tinwork and a couple of santos by Patrocinio Barela, the Taos wood-carver who modernized the art in the 1930s. A separate back wing is dedicated to seven ethereal abstractions by painter Agnes Martin.

E. L. Blumenschein Home

Ernest Blumenschein, one of the founding fathers of the Taos Society of Artists, moved into what is now the **E. L. Blumenschein Home** (222 Ledoux St., 575/758-0505, www.taoshistoricmuseums.org, 10am-5pm Mon.-Sat., noon-5pm Sun. Apr.-Oct., 10am-4pm Mon., Tues., and Thurs.-Sat. Nov.-Mar., $8) in 1919 with his wife, Mary Shepherd Greene Blumenschein, also an accomplished artist. The house's decoration largely reflects her taste, from the sturdy wood furnishings in the dining room to the light-filled studio and the cozy wood-paneled library.

Throughout, the walls are hung with sketches and paintings by their contemporaries. Some of the finest are in the back "Green Room," including a beautiful monotype of Taos Mountain by Oscar E. Berninghaus. The main bedroom, entered through a steep arch, is decorated with Mary's lush illustrations for *The Arabian Nights*. Throughout, you can admire the variety of

Taos Walking Tour

The major sights around Taos Plaza are listed in the order of a potential walking tour. Stroll quickly to get oriented, or take your time and visit the museums along the way. Either way, you'll pass a few other historical spots as well.

Starting on **Taos Plaza,** walk out the southwest corner to **Ledoux Street** and the museums (such as the **Harwood Museum of Art**). Make a short jog left (southwest) down Lower Ranchitos Road to **La Loma Plaza.** Return to Ranchitos, and then turn left into **Padre Martinez Lane,** where the influential pastor lived until his death in 1867. At the end of the street, turn right and walk to Camino de la Placita, then turn left.

After a couple of blocks, turn right (east) on **Bent Street,** passing **Governor Bent House and Museum,** home of the first American governor, Charles Bent. At Paseo del Pueblo Norte, turn left and walk to **Taos Art Museum at Fechin House,** at least to admire the structure. Backtrack and enter **Kit Carson Park** to find the **cemetery** where many Taos notables are buried. Cut out the back of the park, past the baseball diamonds to Morada Lane—at the end is the **Mabel Dodge Luhan House.**

Take Morada Lane back to **Kit Carson Road,** passing the **Couse-Sharp Historic Site** and the **Kit Carson Home.** Turn right (west) to get back to Paseo del Pueblo, passing Carson's home on the way. Another right turn gets you to a well-deserved drink at the **Taos Inn.**

---

ceiling styles, from rough-hewn split cedar (*rajas*) to tidy golden aspen boughs (*latillas*).

La Loma Plaza

To see what Taos Plaza looked like before the souvenir-shop economy, stroll down Lower Ranchitos Road and turn on Valdez Road to reach **La Loma Plaza.** The center of a smaller farm settlement in the 1780s, the ring of adobe homes around a central open space is dusty and little changed through the centuries. Exit the plaza by continuing uphill and bearing right—this takes you past La Loma's tiny old chapel and onto paved San Antonio Street, which leads downhill and back to Lower Ranchitos.

Governor Bent House and Museum

This dusty little backroom exhibit space is odd, but well worth a visit if it happens to be open (the posted hours aren't always maintained). The **Governor Bent House and Museum** (117 Bent St., 10am-5pm daily, $3) is the former residence of Charles Bent who, following the onset of the Mexican-American War, was appointed the first governor of the territory of New Mexico in 1846, based on his extensive experience as a Western trader (he and his brother had built Bent's Fort, an important trading center in southern Colorado). But Bent died in 1847, at the hands of an angry mob dissatisfied by the new U.S. government.

Taos Museum Passes

The **Museum Association of Taos** (www.taosmuseums.org) manages five museums in town and offers a nontransferable **Super Ticket** ($25), valid for one year—a good deal if you plan to visit three or more exhibits. You can buy it at any of the participating museums: the Taos Art Museum at Fechin House, the Millicent Rogers Museum, the Harwood Museum of Art, the E. L. Blumenschein Home, and Hacienda de los Martinez.

Alternatively, if you plan to visit just **Hacienda de los Martinez** and the **E. L. Blumenschein Home**, ask about discounted admission to both places for $12 (as opposed to $8 each).

Amid the slightly creepy clutter, which includes a malevolent-looking ceremonial buffalo head, Inuit knives, and photos of Penitente rituals from an old *Harper's* magazine, is the very hole in the very wall that Bent's family quickly dug to escape while Bent tried to reason with the murderous crowd. The back room only gets stranger, with taxidermy, sinister doctor's instruments, and lots of old guns. The place may feel like an antiques store where nothing's for sale, but it still gives a surprisingly good overview of the period.

★ Taos Art Museum at Fechin House

This sunny space, the former home of artist and wood-carver Nicolai Fechin, is a showcase not only for a great collection of paintings, but also for Fechin's lovely woodwork. When the Russian native moved to Taos in 1927, hoping to cure his tuberculosis, he purchased seven acres of land, including the small, two-story **Taos Art Museum** (227 Paseo del Pueblo Norte, 575/758-2690, 10am-5pm Tues.-Sun. May-Oct., till 4pm Nov.-April, $8). He proceeded to hand-carve the lintels, staircases, bedsteads, and more, in a combination of Russian Tartar and local styles. His blending of traditions is flawless and natural—a small altar, also in the dining room, is set with Orthodox icons but could just as easily hold local santos.

The collection of paintings shown here is eclectic: Victor Higgins's 1936 *Indian Nude* recalls Gauguin, while Dorothy Brett's *Rainbow and Indians* from 1942 is more enamored of the powerful landscape. One room is dedicated to Fechin's own portrait work, characterized by broad, dynamic brushstrokes and a canny eye for distinctive facial features. One work is an etching of the same set of haggard, mustachioed twins who are rendered in oil by Ernest Hennings on a canvas hanging at the Harwood Museum. After all the work Fechin did on the house, he stayed in Taos only six years, when his wife divorced him. He moved on to Los Angeles with his daughter, Eya (her sunny study, on the ground floor, contains the child-scale furniture that her father made for her). After her father died in 1955, Eya, by then practicing psychodrama and dance therapy, returned to live in the studio (the back building that also houses the gift shop) and helped establish the main house as a museum.

Kit Carson Park and Cemetery

After seeing where Mabel Dodge Luhan lived,

Nicolai Fechin's hand-built house is home to the Taos Art Museum.

you can also visit her grave, in Taos's oldest cemetery. A shady sprawl of gravestones in a corner of **Kit Carson Park** (on Paseo del Pueblo Norte north of the Taos Inn), the cemetery was established in 1847 to bury the dead from the Taos Rebellion, a melee incited by wealthy Spanish landowners and Catholic priests anxious about their loss of influence under the Americans. Mobs killed New Mexico's first American governor, the veteran merchant Charles Bent, as well as scores of other Anglo landowners in the area. The cemetery earned its current name when the bodies of Carson and his wife were moved here in 1869, according to his will.

Many of Taos's oldest families, particularly the merchants of the late 1800s, are buried here. Mabel had been a very close friend of the trader Ralph Meyers, and they often joked about being buried together. When Mabel died in 1962, a few years after Ralph, writer Frank Waters recalled their wishes and suggested that Meyers's grave be scooted over to make room for Mabel. She was the last person to be buried in the cemetery, in 1962, and her grave is squeezed into the far southwest corner. Other local luminaries at rest here include Padre Antonio Martinez, who stood up to Catholic bishop Lamy, and an Englishman named Arthur Manby, whose grave actually stands outside of the cemetery proper, due to his lifetime of shady business deals, land grabs, and outright swindles perpetrated in town. Manby was found beheaded in his mansion in 1929, and the unsympathetic populace was happy to attribute the death to natural causes.

★ Mabel Dodge Luhan House

Now used as a conference center and B&B, arts patroness **Mabel Dodge Luhan's House** (240 Morada Ln., 575/751-9686, 9am-7pm daily, free) is open to curious visitors as well as overnight guests. Knock at the main building first; the caretaker will give you information for a self-guided tour around the public areas of the house.

Mabel Dodge, a well-off, freethinking

the entrance to the Mabel Dodge Luhan House

woman who had fostered art salons in New York City and Florence, decamped to Taos in 1916, following her third husband. Eventually she got married again, to Taos Pueblo member Tony Luhan, and her name became inextricably linked with Taos's 20th-century history, thanks to all the budding artists and writers she encouraged to visit. D. H. Lawrence dubbed Taos "Mabeltown," and figures as grand and varied as Greta Garbo, Willa Cather, Ansel Adams, Georgia O'Keeffe, Robinson Jeffers, and Carl Jung made the long trek to her home.

Bordering the Taos reservation, the house was built to Luhan's specifications starting in 1918. Unsurprisingly, given her artistic taste, she exercised a firm hand in its design. Alongside a small original structure—a low row of adobe rooms that were already a century old at that point—she added a three-story main building, topped with a huge sunroom open on three sides. This, and the similarly glass-enclosed bathroom on the second floor, scandalized her neighbors, the pueblo residents.

One of them, however, didn't seem to mind: Tony Luhan, the foreman of the construction project, became her next husband. But Mabel's custom love nest brought out some latent prurience even in D. H. Lawrence, who objected to the curtainless bathroom windows; to soothe his sensibilities, if not Mabel's, he painted colorful swirls directly on the glass.

★ Couse-Sharp Historic Site

Tours of the **Couse-Sharp Historic Site** (146 Kit Carson Rd., 575/751-0369, www.couse-sharp.org, May-Oct., donation) are by appointment only, but it is well worth arranging to see the interior of the painter Eanger Irving Couse's home and studio. Couse, a friend of E. L. Blumenschein's, came to Taos in 1902 with his wife, Virginia, and spent the summers here, working as a figurative painter, until he died in 1936.

Not only has the Couse home and garden been meticulously kept up, as has adjacent property owned by friend and fellow painter Joseph Henry Sharp, but the tours are led by Couse's granddaughter and her husband, who have a wealth of stories to share. And not only artists will be intrigued; Couse's son, a mechanical engineer who developed mobile repair vehicles, built a vast machine shop here.

Kit Carson Home and Museum

Old photographs, memorabilia, and assorted trinkets from the frontier era conjure the spirit of the legendary scout at the **Kit Carson Home and Museum** (113 Kit Carson Rd., 575/758-4945, www.kitcarsonhomeandmuseum.com, 10am-5:30pm daily in summer, 11am-4pm daily in winter, $5), where he lived with his third wife, Josefa Jaramillo, from 1843 until they both died in 1868.

The definitive mountain man, Carson was one of many solitary scouts, trackers, and trappers who explored the American West. He was an intrepid adventurer who, after a childhood on the barely settled edge of Missouri, joined a wagon train headed down the Santa Fe Trail; he arrived in Taos in 1826. His talent for tracking, hunting, and translating from Spanish and various Indian languages soon put him in high demand. Whether he was scouting for John C. Frémont as the explorer mapped the trails west to Los Angeles or serving as an officer in the Civil War, or, less heroically, forcing the Navajos on the Long Walk to Fort Sumner, he called Taos home.

a chapel converted into an art studio at the Couse-Sharp Historic Site

Taos Inn

Distinguished by its large glowing thunderbird sign, the oldest neon sign in town, the **Taos Inn** (125 Paseo del Pueblo Norte, 575/758-2233, www.taosinn.com) was as central to previous generations of *Taoseños'* lives as it is now. Granted, today it's the hotel bar that everyone goes to, but starting in the 1890s, it was the home of Dr. T. P. Martin, Taos's first and only county doctor, who had a good reputation for accepting chickens or venison from his poorer patients in lieu of cash. His home looked out on a small plaza and a well—which has since been covered over and made into the hotel lobby.

HACIENDA DE LOS MARTINEZ

The word *hacienda* conjures a sprawling complex and fields, but the reality in 19th-century Taos was quite different, as the carefully restored **Hacienda de los Martinez** (708 Hacienda Rd., off Lower Ranchitos Rd., 575/758-1000, www.taoshistoricmuseums.org, 10am-5pm Mon.-Sat., noon-5pm Sun. April-Oct., 10am-4pm Mon., Tues., and Thurs.-Sat. Nov.-Mar., $8) from 1804 shows. Its builder and owner, Severino Martinez, was a prominent merchant who hosted the Taos trade fairs at the hacienda and eventually became the mayor of Taos in the 1820s. His oldest son was Padre Antonio Martinez, the valley leader who clashed with the French bishop Jean-Baptiste Lamy.

Despite the family's high social standing, life was fairly rugged, cramped, and cold: 21 simple rooms arranged around two courtyards allowed room for sleeping, cooking, and, in the single room with a wood floor, dancing. Some of the spaces have been furnished to reflect their original use; others are dedicated to exhibits, such as a very interesting display on slavery in the area, and an especially creepy wood carving of Doña Sebastiana, Lady Death, with her glittering mica eyes, in the collection of Penitente paraphernalia. During the summer, local craftspeople are on hand to demonstrate weaving, blacksmithing, and the like in the house's workshops; in the fall, the trade fair is reenacted.

★ SAN FRANCISCO DE ASIS CHURCH

Just as photographs of the Great Pyramid of Cheops seldom show the sprawl of modern Cairo crowding up to its base, **San Francisco de Asis Church** (east side of U.S.

Hacienda de los Martinez

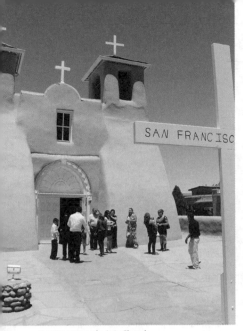

San Francisco de Asis Church

The Shadow of the Cross, an eight-foot-high canvas in which the figure of Christ can be seen to luminesce—allegedly miraculously.

★ TAOS PUEBLO

Even if you've been in New Mexico for a while and think you're inured to adobe, **Taos Pueblo** (575/758-1028, www.taospueblo.com, 8am-4:30pm Mon.-Sat., 8:30am-4:30pm Sun., 8:30am-4pm daily in winter, closed for 10 weeks Feb.-Mar., $16) is an amazing sight. Two clusters of multistory mud-brick buildings make up the core of this village, which claims, along with Acoma Pueblo, to be the oldest continually inhabited community in the United States. The current buildings, annually repaired and recoated with mud, are from the 1200s, though it's possible that all their constituent parts have been fully replaced several times since then.

About 150 people (out of the 1,200 or so total Taos reservation residents) live here year-round. These people, along with the town's designation as a UNESCO World Heritage Site, have kept the place remarkably as it was in the pre-Columbian era, save for the use of adobe bricks (as opposed to clay and stone), which were introduced by the Spanish, as the main structural material. The apartment-like homes, stacked up at various levels and reached by wood ladders, have no electricity or running water, though some use propane gas for heat and light.

As you explore, be careful not to intrude on private space: Enter only buildings that are clearly marked as shops, and stay clear of the ceremonial kiva areas on the east side of each complex. These round structures form the ritual heart of the pueblo, a secret space within an already private culture.

You're welcome to wander around and enter any of the craft shops and galleries that are open—a good opportunity to see inside the earthen structures and to buy some of the distinctive Taos pottery, which is only very lightly decorated but glimmers with mica from the clay of this area. These pots are also renowned for cooking beans.

68 in Ranchos de Taos, 575/758-2754, 9am-4pm daily, Mass 7am, 9:30am, and 11:30am Sun., donation) is depicted in, say, Georgia O'Keeffe's paintings and Ansel Adams's photographs, as a shadow-draped fortress isolated on a hilltop. In fact, the iconic church, completed in the early 19th century as a Franciscan mission, is at the center of a plaza, ringed with buildings.

It's easy to see what has fascinated so many artists: the clean lines, the shadows created by the hulking buttresses, the rich glow of the adobe in the sun. The church is living architecture, as much a part of the earth as something raised above it. As with every traditional adobe structure, it must be refinished every year with a mix of clay, sand, and straw; it is then coated with a fine layer of water and sand, and buffed with sheepskin. This happens over two weeks in June, during which the church is open only at lunchtime and on Sunday.

Inside, the whitewashed walls are covered with *bultos* and *retablos*. In the **parish hall** (9am-3:30pm daily, $3) is the 1896 painting

Dennis Hopper in Taos

In 1968, a Taos Pueblo elder told Dennis Hopper, "The mountain is smiling on you!" No wonder the *Easy Rider* actor and real-life renegade claimed the town as what he called his "heart home." His early years here were wild: He's notorious for having ridden his motorcycle across the roof of the Mabel Dodge Luhan House, which he bought in 1969. Over the decades, he mellowed just a bit, and Taos locals came to think of him as one of their own. In 2009, as part of a 40th-anniversary celebration of the Summer of Love, the Harwood Museum mounted an exhibit of his photography and paintings, along with works by some of his compatriots from that era.

Hopper died not long after, in 2010. His funeral was held at the San Francisco de Asis Church, and attended by fellow 1960s veterans Peter Fonda and Jack Nicholson. Following Pueblo tradition, Hopper was buried in a pine box under a dirt mound, in the nearby **Jesus Nazareno Cemetery.** Fans can pay their respects there. To find it, take Highway 518 south; about a quarter mile along, turn left (east) on Espinoza Road. The cemetery is a short way along, off the left side of the road. From the main gate Hopper's grave is near the back, on the right-hand side.

Visitors to Dennis Hopper's grave leave mementos.

SAN GERONIMO CHURCH

The path from the Taos Pueblo admission gate leads directly to the central plaza, a broad expanse between Red Willow Creek (source of the community's drinking water, flowing from sacred Blue Lake higher in the mountains) and **San Geronimo Church.** The latter, built in 1850, is perhaps the newest structure in the village, a replacement for the first mission the Spanish built, in 1619, using forced Indian labor. The Virgin Mary presides over the room roofed with heavy wood beams; her clothes change with every season, a nod to her dual role as the Earth Mother. (Taking photos is strictly forbidden inside the church at all times and, as at all pueblos, at dances as well.)

The older church, to the north behind the houses, is now a cemetery—fitting, given its tragic destruction. It was first torn down during the Pueblo Revolt of 1680; the Spanish rebuilt it about 20 years later. In 1847 it was again attacked, this time by U.S. troops sent in to quell the rebellion against the new government, in retaliation for the murder of Governor Charles Bent. The counterattack brutally outweighed what had sparked it. More than 100 pueblo residents, including women and children, had taken refuge inside the church when the soldiers bombarded and set fire to it, killing everyone inside and gutting the building. Since then, the bell tower has been restored, but the graves have simply intermingled with the ruined walls and piles of dissolved adobe mud. All of the crosses—from old carved wood to new finished stone—face sacred Taos Mountain.

PUEBLO CRAFTS

You're welcome to wander around and enter any of the craft shops and galleries that are open—a good opportunity to see inside the mud structures and to buy some of the distinctive Taos pottery, which is only very lightly decorated but glimmers with mica from the clay of this area. These pots are also renowned for cooking especially tender beans. On your way out of the pueblo, you may want to stop in at the **Oo-oonah Art Center** (575/779-3486, 1pm-5pm daily Oct.-Apr.), where the gallery displays the work of pueblo children and adults enrolled in its craft classes.

MILLICENT ROGERS MUSEUM

A dashing, thrice-married New York City socialite and designer, Millicent Rogers moved to Taos in 1947 on a tip from a friend, Hollywood actress Janet Gaynor. In the process, she brought Southwestern style to national attention, as she modeled Navajo-style velvet broomstick skirts, concha belts, and pounds of silver-and-turquoise jewelry for photo spreads in *Vogue* and *Harper's Bazaar*. Though she died just six years after she moved to Taos, at the age of 51, she managed to accumulate a fantastic amount of stuff. The **Millicent Rogers Museum** (1504 Millicent Rogers Rd., 575/758-2462, www.millicentrogers.org, 10am-5pm daily Apr.-Oct., 10am-5pm Tues.-Sun. Nov.-Mar., $10) was established by her son, Paul Peralta-Ramos, and is set in the warren of adobe rooms that make up her former home.

The collection reflects her discerning taste, with flawless pieces of pottery, rugs, and jewelry—both local works and her own designs.

Peralta-Ramos also contributed his own collection, including beautiful pieces of Hispano devotional art. Aside from the works' individual beauty, they make an excellent broad introduction to the crafts of the area, from ancient times to modern. But it's not all rooted in local culture: Rogers's goofy illustrations of a fairy tale for her children fill the last room. The gift shop here is particularly thorough and includes beautiful vintage jewelry and very old rugs.

WEST ON U.S. 64
★ Rio Grande Gorge

Heading west on U.S. 64 from the "old blinking light," you pass the Taos airstrip on the left; then, after a few more miles, the ground simply drops away. This is the **Rio Grande Gorge** (also called the Taos Gorge), plunging at its most alarming point 800 feet down into malevolent-looking basalt. The river courses below, but it's not just millions of years of rushing water that have carved out the canyon—seismic activity also caused a rift in the earth's surface. The crack extends north to just beyond the Colorado state line and south almost to Española.

The elegant, unnervingly delicate-looking bridge that spans it was built in 1965 to

The Rio Grande Gorge bridge casts a long shadow.

supplement entrepreneur John Dunn's rickety old toll crossing eight miles north. Critics mocked the newer structure as "the bridge to nowhere" because the highway on the western bank had yet to be built, but the American Institute of Steel Construction granted it the Most Beautiful Steel Bridge award in 1966. At 650 feet above the river, the cantilever truss was a stunning engineering feat; it is still the sixth-highest bridge in the United States. On either side of the bridge is the stretch of white water called the Taos Box, two words that inspire wild tales in any seasoned river-runner. The Class III and IV rapids are considered the best place for rafting in New Mexico.

On the west side of the gorge is a rest area, and the start of the **West Rim Trail,** running south from the parking lot and yielding great views of the bridge to the north.

Greater World Earthship Development

If you brave the slender gorge bridge and continue a mile or so west on U.S. 64, you soon see some whimsically curved and creatively stuccoed houses along the right side of the road. These are Earthships: modular, low-priced homes that function entirely on collected rainwater and wind and solar power. Although they look like fanciful Hobbit homes or Mars colony pods, Earthships are made of rather common stuff: The walls, built into hillsides for efficient heating and cooling, are stacks of used tires packed with rammed earth, while bottles stacked with cement and crushed aluminum cans form front walls and colorful peepholes.

Greater World is the largest of three local all-Earthship subdivisions, and headquarters of the architecture office that developed the design. The **Greater World Earthship Development visitors center** (575/613-4409, www.earthship.com, 9am-6pm daily in summer, 10am-4pm daily in winter, $7) is the most unconventional model home and sales office you'll ever visit. You can take the self-guided tour of a basic Earthship and watch a video about the building process and the

the Greater World Earthship Development

rationale behind the design. If you're hooked, you can of course get details on buying a lot in the development or purchasing the plans to build your own place elsewhere. Or try before you buy: You can stay the night in an Earthship here, starting at $130. Look for the green building on the right 1.8 miles past the bridge.

HIGHWAY 150
Arroyo Seco

Bemoaning the gallerification of downtown Taos? The sheer touristy mayhem? From the "old blinking light," head north on Highway 150 to the village of **Arroyo Seco,** a cluster of buildings at a bend in the road to the ski area, and you'll slip back a couple of decades. Sure, there's some art up here too, but this smaller community, though only a half-hour drive from the Taos Plaza, maintains an even more laid-back and funky attitude than Taos—if such a thing is possible. It has been a retreat for decades: Frank Waters, celebrated author of *The Man Who Killed the Deer* and

bustling "downtown" Arroyo Seco

The Woman at Otowi Crossing, lived here off and on from 1947 until his death in 1995.

"Downtown" Arroyo Seco, all one block of it, has grown up around a bend in the road and **La Santísima Trinidad Church,**

set back from Highway 150 on the left. The church, built in 1834, has adobe walls that are alarmingly eroded in patches, but it sports a cheery red metal roof; the spare traditional interior is decorated with *bultos* and *retablos,* but the doors are often locked. Secular pursuits in this area are better: a fine bar and general store, for instance, and El Salto Falls, up the mountain a bit.

The Rim Road

As Highway 150 continues, the road to the ski area eventually makes a hard right, and the so-called "rim road" heads to the left, along the canyon edge. It gives a great view of **Valle Valdez** below, where tidy farm plots are set along Rio Hondo and the traditional acequia irrigation that has been used here for more than four centuries. In typical modern real-estate distribution, the not-so-well-off native *Taoseños* value their fertile soil, while wealthy arrivistes (Julia Roberts, most famously) have claimed the swoon-inducing views on the rim road, which was developed only in the later part of the 20th century. On the north side of the valley, the ritzy Turley Mill development is built on the site of a still that produced the powerful bootleg hooch known as "Taos lightning" from the 1700s to 1847. (Also glossed

TAOS
SIGHTS

lush farmland in Valle Valdez

A Little Farther: Chama

The Cumbres & Toltec steam train runs north of Chama.

Continuing west on U.S. 64 takes you up and over one of the most dramatic mountain passes in the state, then to U.S. 84 northbound, through the tiny community of Tierra Amarilla, where sheepherding continues as it has for centuries. Close to the Colorado border, in Chama, rail fans can board the **Cumbres & Toltec Scenic Railroad** (888/286-2737, www.cumbrestoltec.com), a steam train that ascends the pass through the Rockies, up to what feels like the very top of the world.

The drive to Chama takes about two hours, and the train leaves at 10am (most of the year), so you'll need to make an early start or stay over the night before. **Chama Station Inn** (423 Terrace Ave., 575/756-2315, www.chamastationinn.com, $85 d) and **The Hotel** (501 S. Terrace Ave., 575/756-2416, www.thehotel.org, $64 d) are good. Stop for coffee in Tierra Amarilla at **Three Ravens Coffeehouse** (15 Hwy. 531, 575/588-9086, 7am-4pm Mon.-Fri.) and to see the great local weaving at **Tierra Wools** (91 Main St., Los Ojos, 575/588-7231, 9am-6pm Mon.-Sat., 11am-4pm Sun. Apr.-Oct., 10am-5pm Mon.-Sat. Nov.-May).

over in the development: The still was burned and its owner and customers killed during the uprising against Governor Bent.) The area is now home to Donald Rumsfeld and other occupants of million-dollar casitas.

Taos Ski Valley

Highway 150 winds relentlessly up through Hondo Canyon, the steep mountain slopes crowded with tall, dense pines that in winter disappear into a wreath of clouds. The road dead-ends at the village of **Taos Ski Valley.** When you get out of the car and take in the vertiginous view up to Kachina Peak (elevation 12,481 feet and often white-capped even in July), you'll see why it inspires legions of reverential skiers every winter, when an average of 305 inches of snow falls on the mountain—almost 10 times the amount they get down in town.

For decades, it was *only* skiers here. Snowboarders were banned, allegedly because the slopes were too steep—more than half the trails are rated expert level, and many of them are left ungroomed. But the mountain was finally opened to all in 2008. It was a major adjustment for TSV's loyal customers, and it leaves just three resorts in the country that don't allow snowboarding (Utah's Deer Valley and Alta, and Mad River Glen in Vermont).

In the summer, there's free music at the resort center on Saturday afternoons, and

Hondo Canyon's many trails make for very good hiking or picnicking. The road is dotted on either side with picnic areas and campgrounds—Cuchilla del Medio is a particularly nice area for a picnic. The **visitors center** (575/776-1413, www.taosskivalley.com) in the ski area parking lot stocks trail descriptions and maps.

Entertainment and Events

Taos is a small town: no glitzy dance clubs, no bars where you're expected to dress up. Nighttime fun is concentrated in a handful of places where, even after a couple of visits, you'll get to know the regulars quickly. The various town-wide celebrations—including music and dancing on the plaza on summer Thursdays—draw a good cross section of the population.

NIGHTLIFE
Bars and Clubs
Starting around 5pm, the **Adobe Bar** (125 Paseo del Pueblo Norte, 575/758-2233), in the lobby of the Taos Inn (look for the neon thunderbird sign), is where you'll run into everyone you've seen over the course of the day, sipping a Cowboy Buddha ($12) or some other specialty margarita—the best in town.

Mellow jazz or acoustic guitar sets the mood from 7pm. To give hotel residents a break, the bar closes at 10pm.

The dance floor at the **Sagebrush Inn** (1508 Paseo del Pueblo Sur, 575/758-2254) gets packed with cowboy-booted couples stepping lively to country cover bands whose members always seem to resemble Kenny Rogers. The scene encompasses all of Taos, from artists to pueblo residents to mountain men with grizzled beards. Booze is a bargain, and the fireplace is big.

Wood-paneled **Eske's Brew Pub** (106 Des Georges Ln., 575/758-1517) is across from the plaza, tucked back from the southeast corner of the intersection of Paseo del Pueblo Sur and Kit Carson Road. With live music on Fridays and Saturdays, it serves its housemade beer to a chummy après-ski crowd.

New Mexico's Communes

Something about New Mexico's vast empty spaces inspires utopian thinking, as if the landscape were a blank slate, a way to start from scratch and do things right. Spanish settlers felt it in the 16th century. Gold miners banked on it in the 1800s. And in the 1960s, freethinkers, free-lovers, and back-to-the-landers fled crowded cities and boring suburbs to start communities such as the Hog Farm and the New Buffalo commune, both near Taos. For a while, New Mexico was the place to be: Dennis Hopper immortalized New Buffalo in his film *Easy Rider*, Janis Joplin chilled out in Truchas, and Ken Kesey drove his bus, *Further*, through the state. At the end of the decade, some 25 communes had been established.

In most of the rest of the United States, these experimental communities and their ideals were just a brief moment of zaniness—their legacy appears to be Hog Farm leader Wavy Gravy's consecration on a Ben & Jerry's label. But in New Mexico, many of the ideals set down by naked organic gardeners and tripping visionaries took root and sprouted in unexpected ways. Yogi Bhajan, a Sikh who taught mass kundalini yoga sessions in New Mexico in 1969, later became a major contributor to the state economy through all the businesses he established. Buddhist stupas dot the Rio Grande Valley, the product of Anglo spiritual seekers working with Tibetan refugees brought to New Mexico by Project Tibet, cofounded by John Allen, who also ran the commune Synergia Ranch near Santa Fe. Allen was also instrumental in building Biosphere 2, the experimental glass dome in the Arizona desert—probably the most utopian vision yet to have sprouted in New Mexico.

Offbeat bands and beers meet at this spot on the mesa.

You're in New Mexico—you should at least *try* the green-chile ale.

Everyone's default late-night spot is **The Alley Cantina** (121 Teresina Ln., 575/758-2121) for another hour or so. This warren of interconnected rooms (one of which is supposedly the oldest in Taos...but don't they all say that?) can be potentially baffling after a few drinks. There's shuffleboard for entertainment if you're not into the ensemble onstage—its name usually ends in "Blues Band"; a cover of $5-7 applies on weekends. The kitchen is open until 11pm.

Cocktail Lounges

A more upscale member of Taos's bar scene is **The Treehouse Lounge** (123 Bent St., 575/758-1009, 5pm-10pm daily), the upper floor of an adobe house downtown. With a full bar and the creative minds running it, the range of cocktails ($10) is highly stimulating. Happy hour is 2:30pm-5:30pm.

Live Music

Is your drinking unsustainable? Fix that at the **KTAOS Bar** (9 Hwy. 150, 575/758-5826 ext. 206, www.ktao.com, 4pm-9pm Sun.-Thurs., 4pm-11pm Fri.-Sat.), the social wing of the local radio station, which happens to be entirely solar-powered. You can peek into the radio studios, or dance on the lawn out back, in front of the large stage that hosts major shows. Happy hour (4pm-6pm) sees drinks as low as $2, and kids are usually welcome, with plenty of room to play.

If your style is cramped by old adobes, head out to **Taos Mesa Brewing** (20 ABC Mesa Rd., 575/758-1900, www.taosmesabrewing.com, noon-late daily), on U.S. 64 opposite the airport, where there's plenty of room to groove. The metal Quonset hut looms like a far-flung Burning Man camp, and the entertainment roster is eclectic, from theremin masters to major global artists performing outside (cover from $5 some nights). The crowd is all of Taos's younger hippies, plus hops aficionados of all stripes. The food ($10) is veg- and beer-friendly.

Finally, check the schedule at **Old Martina's Hall** (4140 Hwy. 68, 575/758-3003, www.oldmartinashall.com) for special events in this renovated old adobe theater. It may not get as wild as back in the days when Dennis Hopper owned the joint, but the new wood dance floor is a treat.

THE ARTS

Given the high concentration of artists of all stripes, it's no surprise that Taos's theater scene is so rich for such a small town. Check at the **Taos Center for the Arts** (133 Paseo del Pueblo Norte, 575/758-2052, www.tcataos. org) to find out what shows may be on; the group also organizes chamber music performances and film screenings.

SMU in Taos (6580 Hwy. 518, 575/758-8322, www.smu.edu/taos) organizes a summer lecture series at its Fort Burgwin campus about seven miles east of Ranchos de Taos. The Tuesday-night gatherings (from 7:30pm, free), from late May through mid-August, bring noted historians, anthropologists, authors, and others with an interest in the Southwest.

The Storyteller (110 Old Talpa Canyon Rd., 575/751-4245, www.storyteller7.com) shows first-run films on seven screens, with an occasional arty option.

FESTIVALS AND EVENTS

July is chockablock: the loopy creativity of the **Arroyo Seco Fourth of July parade**, then, in the second week, the **Taos Pueblo Powwow** (www.taospueblo.com), a major get-together of Pueblo Indians and tribal members from around the country. Try to be there for the Grand Entry, the massive opening procession. The event takes place at the powwow grounds in El Prado near the Overland Sheepskin store. The next weekend, the town turns out for the **Fiestas de Taos** (www.fiestasdetaos.com), a three-day celebration of Santiago de Compostela and Santa Ana, with a parade, food and crafts booths on the plaza, and the crowning of the Fiestas Queen.

For years, KTAO radio station hosted the multiday **Taos Solar Music Festival** (www.solarmusicfest.com) in July as well. The solar-powered event, which drew thousands of happy campers and some excellent performers, went on hiatus for a bit, but, as of press time for this book, was supposed to restart in 2015.

Taos galleries put out their finest at the **Taos Fall Arts Festival** (www.taosfallarts.com), a two-week-long exhibition in late September and early October that shows the works of more than 150 Taos County artists.

Taos's biggest annual festivity (for which many local businesses close) is the **Feast of San Geronimo,** the patron saint assigned to Taos Pueblo by the Spanish when they built their first mission there in 1619. The holiday starts the evening of September 29 with vespers

What to Expect at Pueblo Dances

Visiting a pueblo for a ceremonial dance or feast-day celebration is one of the most memorable parts of a trip to New Mexico. But it's important to remember that a pueblo dance is not at all for the benefit of tourists. It is a ceremony and a religious ritual, not a performance—you are a guest, not an audience.

Keep this in mind as a guide to your own behavior. Applause is not appropriate, nor is conversation during the dance. Queries about the meaning of the dances are generally not appreciated. Never walk in the dance area, and try not to block the view of pueblo residents. The kivas, as holy spaces, are always off-limits to outsiders. During feast days, some pueblo residents may open their doors to visitors, perhaps for a snack or drink—but be considerate of others who may also want to visit, and don't stay too long. Photography is strictly forbidden at dances (sometimes with the exception of Los Matachines, which is not a religious ritual). Don't even think about trying to sneak a shot with your camera phone, as tribal police will be more than happy to confiscate it.

On a practical level, be prepared for a lot of waiting around. Start times are always approximate, and everything depends on when the dancers are done with their kiva rituals. There will usually be a main, seasonal dance—such as the corn dance at the summer solstice—followed by several others. If you go in the winter, dress very warmly, but in layers. Ceremonies often start inside the close-packed, overheated church, and then dances often proceed outside in the cold.

in the pueblo church and continues the next day with footraces and a pole-climbing contest. Hacienda de los Martinez usually reenacts a 19th-century Taos trade fair, with mountain men, music, and artisans' demonstrations.

On the first weekend in October, the **Taos Wool Festival** (www.taoswoolfestival.org) has drawn textile artists as well as breeders since 1983. Admire the traditional Churro sheep or an Angora goat and then pick up a scarf made from its wool.

In winter, the glow of *farolitos* and torch-light on snow produces a magical effect. On the first weekend in December, the **tree-lighting ceremony** on the plaza draws the whole town, and the rest of the season sees numerous celebrations, such as the reenact-ments of the Virgin's search for shelter, called Las Posadas, which take place at Our Lady of Guadalupe Church west of the plaza on the third weekend in December. At the pueblo, vespers is said at San Geronimo Church on Christmas Eve, typically followed by a chil-dren's dance. On Christmas Day, the pueblo hosts either a deer dance or the Spanish Matachines dance.

Shopping

ARTS AND CRAFTS

In the Overland Ranch complex, **Magpie** (1405 Paseo del Pueblo Norte, 781/248-0166, 11am-5pm Tues.-Sat.) promises "wonderful things for your nest." The owner, a Taos native returned from living on the East Coast, has selected a colorful array of handcrafted fur-niture, pottery, handmade jewelry and more, nearly all produced by Taos residents.

Daniel Barela, great-grandson of legendary wood-carver Patrocinio Barela (whose work is on view in the Harwood Museum), can often be found working in **Barela's Traditional Fine Art** (124-A Paseo del Pueblo Sur, 575/779-5720, noon-3pm daily). The raw, ca-sual gallery space houses his and his relatives' hand-carved saint figures, as well as work by several Salazars, another noted woodwork-ing family.

Taos Drums (3956 Hwy. 68, 800/424-3786, 10am-5pm Mon.-Fri., 11:30am-5pm Sun.) is a giant shop and factory dedicated to mak-ing Taos Pueblo-style percussion instruments, from thin hand drums to great booming ones out of hollow logs. Trying out the wares is en-couraged. The shop is located on the west side of the highway five miles south of the plaza.

Taos has long nurtured a strong commu-nity of fiber artists—weavers, knitters, spin-ners of yarn. In the John Dunn Shops just north of the plaza, visit **Mooncat Fiber** (120-B Bent St., 575/758-9341, 10am-6pm daily) for hand-spun yarns and some fin-ished pieces, and **Common Thread** (124-E Bent St., 575/758-8987, 10am-5:30pm daily), which deals in beautiful imported fabrics from India, Guatemala, and more, both in one-off pieces and by the yard. Up in Arroyo Seco, **Weaving Southwest** (487 Hwy. 150, 575/758-0433, 10am-5:30pm Mon.-Sat., 11am-5pm Sun.) stocks raw wool, yarns, and gor-geous finished clothing and rugs as well.

CLOTHING AND JEWELRY

Gussy yourself up in Western trappings from **Horse Feathers** (109-B Kit Carson Rd., 575/758-7457, 10:30am-5:30pm daily), where you can pick up a full cowpoke getup, from ten-gallon hat to jingling spurs. The big money is in the vintage cowboy boots, but you can find less expensive, eclectic gift items, such as giant belt buckles or campfire cook-books from 1900.

GIFT AND HOME

FX/18 (103-C Bent St., 575/758-8590, 11am-6pm Mon.-Sat., noon-5pm Sun.) has a great selection of goodies: groovy housewares, lively kids' stuff, nifty stationery. And the selection

Ceremonial Dances at Taos Pueblo

In addition to the Feast of San Geronimo, ceremonial dances are open to visitors. This is only an approximate schedule—dates can vary from year to year, as can the particular dances. Contact the **pueblo** (505/758-1028, www.taospueblo.com) for times, or check the listings in the *Tempo* section of the paper for that week.

Every night May through October, there are demonstration dances at the **Kachina Lodge** (413 Paseo del Pueblo Norte)—a little touristy, but nice if your trip doesn't coincide with a dance at the pueblo itself.

- **January 1** - Turtle dance

- **January 6** - Deer or buffalo dance

- **May 3** - Feast of Santa Cruz: corn dance

- **June 13** - Feast of San Antonio: corn dance

- **June 24** - Feast of San Juan: corn dance

- **July 25-26** - Feast of Santiago and Santa Ana: corn dances and footraces

- **September 29-30** - Feast of San Geronimo

- **December 24** - Sundown procession and children's dance

- **December 25** - Various dances

of contemporary Southwest-style jewelry is particularly good.

Up Highway 150, **Arroyo Seco Mercantile** (488 Hwy. 150, 575/776-8806, 10am-5:30pm Mon.-Sat., 11am-5pm Sun.) is the town's former general store, now a highly evolved junk shop that has maintained the beautiful old wood-and-glass display cases. Its stock ranges from the practical (books on passive-solar engineering and raising llamas) to the frivolous, with lots of the beautiful, like antique wool blankets.

TOYS

Taos is also home to an exceptionally magical toy store, **Twirl** (225 Camino de la Placita, 575/751-1402, www.twirlhouse.com, 10am-6pm daily). Tucked in a series of low-ceiling adobe rooms, it's crammed with everything from science experiments to wooden trains to fairy costumes. Even the kiva fireplace gets a fantastical 1,001 Nights treatment, and there's a big roster of activities in the huge play space out back.

Sports and Recreation

The wild setting presses in all around Taos, and the mountains loom up behind every town view. Downhill skiing is the main draw in the winter, but you can also try more solitary snowshoeing and Nordic skiing. In summer, peak-baggers will want to strike out for Wheeler, the state's highest, while rafters, rock climbers, and mountain bikers can head the other direction, to the dramatic basalt cliffs of the Rio Grande Gorge. In the water, river-runners challenge the churning rapids of the legendary Taos Box (late May and early June make up the best season for this).

Information

Stop in at the **Carson National Forest**

Supervisor's Office (208 Cruz Alta Rd., 575/758-6200, 8:30am-4:30pm Mon.-Fri.) for booklets on recommended trails and maps. Just down the street, the **Bureau of Land Management Taos Field Office** (226 Cruz Alta Rd., 575/758-8851, 8am-4:30pm Mon.-Fri.) can help with prep for rafting or longer camping trips, with plenty of maps and brochures.

The **Taos Youth and Family Center** (407 Paseo del Cañon, 575/758-4160, 9am-8pm Mon.-Thurs., 9am-7pm Fri.-Sun.) has a big indoor pool, as well as an ice-skating rink. Hours are more limited in fall and winter.

Sudden thunderstorms are common in summer months, as are flash floods and even freak blizzards. Well into May, snow can blanket some of the higher passes, so wherever you go, always carry more warm clothing than you think you'll need. And don't skimp on the sunscreen, even when it's below freezing.

BIKING

Taos has several great trails for mountain biking. A popular ride close to town is **West Rim Trail** along the Rio Grande Gorge, either from the gorge bridge up to John Dunn Bridge, about 15 miles round-trip, or from the gorge bridge south to the Taos Junction Bridge near Pilar, about 18 miles out and back. Either way, you'll have great views and fairly level but rugged terrain. For some downhill action, **Taos Ski Valley** offers mountain biking in summer; the 3.6-mile Berminator route is good for intermediate cyclists.

For road touring, you can make a pleasant 25-mile loop from Taos through Arroyo Hondo and Arroyo Seco. With no steep grades, it's a good way to get adjusted to the altitude. Head north up Paseo del Pueblo Norte, straight through the intersection with Highway 150, then, in Arroyo Hondo, turn right onto County Road B-143. Cross Highway 230, and you arrive in Arroyo Seco behind The Snowmansion. Turn right on Highway 150 to loop back to Taos.

For a longer road challenge, take on the 84-mile Enchanted Circle. Each September,

more than a thousand riders participate in the **Enchanted Circle Century Tour** (800/348-6444, www.redriverenchantedcirclecenturytour.com), sponsored by the Red River Chamber of Commerce. A mountain-biking race takes place the day after.

Gearing Up (129 Paseo del Pueblo Sur, 575/751-0365) rents mountain and hybrid bicycles for $50 per day. If you're bringing your bicycle with you, consider having it shipped here, and they'll reassemble it and have it waiting when you arrive.

★ HIKING

With Taos Mountain and Wheeler Peak in the backyard, you can ramble along winding rivers or haul up 2,000 feet in less than four miles. Be prepared for a cold snap or storm at any time, and don't plan on anything before May—it takes that long for the snow to thaw, though even in high summer, you can still hit some of the white stuff in the alpine meadows. If you prefer some animal companionship (and something to carry your pack) while hiking, contact **Wild Earth Llama Adventures** (800/758-5262, www.llamaadventures.com), which runs day hikes with lunch ($99), as well as multiday treks (from $375). These are just a few suggestions for spots to hike.

Taos Ski Valley

Varied trails lead off Highway 150 en route to Taos Ski Valley. Just before the parking lot for the ski area, **Gavilan Trail** (no. 60) leads off the north side of the road. It's plenty steep but leads to a high mountain meadow. The route is five miles round-trip, or you can connect with other trails once you're up on the rim.

Purists will want to head for **Wheeler Peak Summit Trail** (no. 67), which scales New Mexico's highest mountain in about four miles (one-way). The first two miles of the route are on the relatively easy and popular **Williams Lake Trail** (no. 62), which starts near the end of Twining Road, a narrow dirt road that leads out of the top of the Taos Ski Valley parking lot. (Before starting up Twining Road, stop first at the visitors

Let Wild Earth Llama Adventures carry your pack on a hike.

center in the parking lot, for trail descriptions.) Williams Lake is a nice destination and, after you get past the early rocky stretch, the trail is pleasant hiking. In summer, on the Saturday closest to the full moon, there's a free guided **moonlight hike** to Williams Lake, starting at 7:30pm; check the schedule at www.taosskivalley.com.

If all that sounds too strenuous, you can take the **chairlift** (10am-4:30pm Thurs.-Mon. June-Aug., $15) up to the top of the mountain,

then wander down any of several wide, well-marked trails, all with stunning views.

El Salto Falls

Some theorize that the mysterious "Taos Hum"—the faint, low drone that many in the area claim to hear—emanates from the caves at **El Salto Falls** (575/776-2371, $4), a scenic spot on a patch of private land in Arroyo Seco. Whether or not you solve this sonic mystery, the falls are a great Taos natural landmark,

El Salto Falls

and an easy hike or a challenging one, depending on just how much you'd like to see. Save this hike for dry weather, unless you have a four-wheel drive—the road is rough when muddy or snowy.

In Arroyo Seco, take El Salto Road east (go straight where Highway 150 makes a hard right); after about a mile is a sign on the left asking visitors to pay. Leave cash in the honor box on the porch of the house just off the road, and fill out a waiver and a permit to place on your dashboard. Continue driving another 0.7 mile and bear left; from here, it's 0.9 mile up to a green gate and small parking area. Walk in, following the road as it curves left, then bearing right. This leads in just a few minutes to the lowest, largest cave and the first waterfall—though most of the year, it is often just a trickle. Intrepid hikers can climb up to the right of the cave, to ever smaller falls and notches in the cliff face.

HOT SPRINGS

Two spots along the Rio Grande have natural pools of warm water, by-products of the seismic upsets that formed the gorge. They're popular with locals, and clothing is optional. Don't crowd in if several people are already in the spring, and never leave trash behind.

The easier spot to reach is **Blackrock Springs**, accessible by a 0.25-mile hike. From the intersection with U.S. 64, head north on Highway 522 about six miles to where the road dips; immediately after the bridge, turn left on County Road B-005, which runs along the north side of the small Rio Hondo and past the New Buffalo commune. The road crosses the water, then climbs a hill and descends again, toward the Rio Grande. Cross the old John Dunn Bridge to reach the west side, then turn left and park at the first switchback. Hike down the rocks and downstream to the springs.

Also called Stagecoach Springs, **Manby Springs** are at the edge of the river where the stage road used to meet a bridge and cross to the west side of the gorge. The hike down is on the old road, now quite rocky, and takes about 20 minutes. (In the late afternoon, keep an eye out for bighorn sheep near the trail.) To find the parking area, take U.S. 64 four miles west, just past the airport, and turn right on Tune Drive; follow this to the end, approximately another four miles. The old road is off the southwest side of the parking area.

HUNTING AND FISHING

Taos's mountain streams and lakes teem with fish. The feisty cutthroat trout is indigenous to Valle Vidal, north of Questa, or you can hook plenty of browns in the wild waters of the Rio Grande. Eagle Nest Lake and Cabresto Lake (northeast of Questa) are both stocked every year. If you'd like a guide to show you around, **Cutthroat Fly Fishing** (575/776-5703, www.cutthroatflyfishing.com) and **The Solitary Angler** (866/502-1700, www.thesolitaryangler.com) are two good operators. Stop into the shop at the **Tailwater Gallery** (204-B Paseo del Pueblo Norte) for tackle and info on flows and other conditions.

Elk are the primary target in hunters' rifle scopes, but you can also bag mule deer, bear, and antelope; **High Mountain Outfitters** (575/751-7000, www.huntingnm.com) is one of the most experienced expedition leaders, and it has access to private land for hunting exotics. Visit the website of the New Mexico Department of Game and Fish (www.wildlife.state.nm.us) for details on seasons, permits, and licenses.

RAFTING AND TUBING

The **Taos Box**, the 16-mile stretch of the Rio Grande between the John Dunn Bridge and Pilar, provides perhaps the best rafting in New Mexico, with Class III rapids with ominous names like Boat Reamer and Screaming Left-Hand Turn. The river mellows out a bit south of the Taos Box, then leads into a shorter Class III section called the Racecourse—the most popular run, usually done as a half-day trip.

Beyond this, in the Orilla Verde Recreation Area around Pilar, the water is wide and flat, a place for a relaxing float with kids or other water newbies; you can flop in an inner tube if you really want to chill out. North of the John Dunn Bridge, there's another intermediate run called La Junta that's a half-day trip.

Los Rios River Runners (800/544-1181, www.losriosriverrunners.com) leads trips to all these spots as half-day outings ($54), day trips (from $105), and overnight trips. Another outfitter, **Far-Flung Adventures** (575/758-2628, www.farflung.com), can add on rock climbing and horseback riding. With both organizations, you can choose whether you want a paddleboat—where you're actively (and sometimes strenuously) paddling—or an oar boat, where guides row, and you can sit back. The best season is late May and early June, when the water is high from mountain runoff.

ROCK CLIMBING

From popular sport-climbing spots such as the basalt Dead Cholla Wall in the Rio Grande Gorge to the more traditional routes at Tres Piedras, Taos is a climber's dream. One of the most impressive pitches is at Questa Dome, north of Taos on Highway 378, where the flawless granite on the Questa Direct route is graded 5.10 and 5.11. And you're not limited to the summer, as winter sees some terrific ice climbs at higher elevations. **Taos Mountain Outfitters** (113 N. Plaza, 575/758-9292, 9am-6pm Mon.-Tues., 10am-8pm Wed.-Fri., 8am-8pm Sat., 10am-6pm Sun.) can provide maps, ropes, and more details. For climbing lessons or guided tours, contact **Mountain Skills** (575/776-2222, www.climbtaos.com) in Arroyo Seco.

SPECTATOR SPORTS

The local baseball team, the **Taos Blizzard** (www.taosblizzard.com), faces off against eight other teams in the exceedingly minor Pecos League (www.pecosleague.com) from around New Mexico, Arizona, west Texas, and Colorado. Games in season (mid-May through July) are at 7pm at the Taos High School ball field (134 Cervantes St.).

WINTER SPORTS

Taos Ski Valley (866/968-7386, www.ski-taos.org, $82 full-day lift ticket) is a mecca for downhill skiing. The resort is open from late November through the first weekend in April, with 110 trails served by 15 lifts and snowmaking capacity on all beginner and intermediate areas in dry spells. The dedicated can hike to Kachina Peak, an additional 632 feet past where the lift service ends. The highly regarded Ernie Blake Snowsports School is one of the best places to learn the basics or polish your skills. Novice "yellowbirds" can take one ($115) or two ($180) days of intensive instruction specially geared to new skiers.

For cross-country skiing and snowshoeing, **Enchanted Forest** (575/754-6112, www.enchantedforestxc.com, $18 full-day pass), between Elizabethtown and Red River on the Enchanted Circle loop, offers miles of groomed trails. There are also easy ski access points in the Carson National Forest—at Capulin Campground on U.S. 64, for instance, five miles east of Taos and along **Manzanita Trail** in the Hondo Canyon on the road to the ski valley.

Don't have your own gear? **Cottam's Ski & Outdoor** (207-A Paseo del Pueblo Sur, 575/758-2822, 7am-7pm Mon.-Fri., 7am-8pm Sat.-Sun.) has the biggest stock of rental skis, snowboards, and snowshoes. The shop also sells everything else you'll need to get out and enjoy the snow; there's another location at the ski valley (575/776-8719) and one at Angel Fire (575/377-3700).

Accommodations

Taos hotels can be a bit overpriced, especially at the lower end, where there are few reliable bargains. But because Taos is awash in centuries-old houses, bed-and-breakfasts have thrived. For those skeptical of B&Bs, don't despair: The majority of them have private bathrooms, separate entrances, and not too much country-cute decor. Certainly, just as in Santa Fe, the Southwestern gewgaws can be applied with a heavy hand, but wood-burning fireplaces, well-stocked libraries, hot tubs, and big gardens can make up for that.

For better deals, consider staying outside of Taos proper. Arroyo Seco is about a half-hour drive from the plaza, as is the Earthship subdivision, and rates here and in Ranchos de Taos can be a little lower. In the summer, the lodges near the ski valley cut their prices by almost half—a great deal if you want to spend some time hiking in the canyon and don't mind driving to town for food and entertainment. If you're in town without a car, Taos's Chile Line bus serves a few good budget choices; the line caters to skiers in the winter, with pickups from down on the southern end of town all the way up to the ski valley.

CENTRAL TAOS
Under $100

Not a hotel at all, but simply a clutch of well-maintained one- and two-bedroom private casitas, **Taos Lodging** (109 Brooks St., 575/751-1771, www.taoslodging.com, $75 studio) is in a quiet, convenient block about a 10-minute walk north from the plaza. Here, eight cottages, arranged around a central courtyard, have assorted floor plans, but all have porches, full kitchens, and living rooms, as well as access to a shared outdoor hot tub. The smallest, a 350-square-foot studio, sleeps two comfortably; the largest ($130 for two) sleep up to six. Plus, the same group manages two additional properties nearby, for those who want a larger condo.

Of the various motels on the south side, none are excellent, but **Sun God Lodge** (919 Paseo del Pueblo Sur, 575/758-3162, www.sungodlodge.com, $69 d) is better than most. Maintenance can be spotty, but rooms are set around a big grassy, tree-shaded courtyard and, in back, a small hot tub; there's also a laundry. But note that this can foster a somewhat rowdy atmosphere, especially in ski season or after big summer events.

$100-150

In addition to being a tourist attraction, the ★ **Mabel Dodge Luhan House** (240 Morada Ln., 575/751-9686, www.mabeldodgeluhan.com, $105 d) also functions as a homey bed-and-breakfast. Even the least expensive rooms, in a 1970s outbuilding, feel authentically old and cozy, with wood floors and antique furniture. In the main house, Mabel's original bedroom ($200) is the grandest (you can even sleep in her bed). But for those who don't mind waking at the crack of dawn, the upstairs solarium ($130) is gloriously sunny, with gorgeous views of the mountain. Either way, you'll feel a little like you're bunking in a museum (which means those who want modern amenities like air-conditioning should look elsewhere). Breakfast is a cut above standard B&B fare.

Walking distance from the plaza, ★ **El Pueblo Lodge** (412 Paseo del Pueblo Norte, 575/758-8700, www.elpueblolodge.com, $120 d) is a budget operation with nice perks such as free laundry. Rooms vary from a snug nook in the oldest adobe section to new, slick motel rooms complete with gas fireplaces. Those in the 1960s motel strip are a good combo of atmosphere and amenities. The grounds are pleasant, with a heated outdoor pool, a hot tub, and hammocks slung between the big cottonwoods in the summertime.

$150-200

Inn on the Rio (910 E. Kit Carson Rd., 575/758-7199, www.innontherio.com, $150

d) might be more accurately called Motel on the Creek. But what a motel: Each of the 12 thick-walled rooms has been decorated with rich colors and retro Western details. The vintage wall heaters, still cranking from the old motor-court days, keep the rooms as toasty as a fireplace would. A hot tub between the two wings, plus luxe sheets and locally made bath gels, are nice upgrades. Pair this with longtime resident owners and a great morning meal, and you have all the benefits of a bed-and-breakfast without the feeling that you have to tiptoe in late at night. Rates are lower on weekdays in summer.

La Posada de Taos (309 Juanita Ln., 575/758-8164, www.laposadadetaos.com, $169 d) hits the sweet spot between luxury comforts and casual charm. All the amenities are here, such as wood fireplaces (in five of the six rooms) and whirlpool tubs (in three), but the overall atmosphere is homey and informal, and the decor is distinctly Taos without being heavy-handed, with sparing country touches. The price is right too, coming in on the lower end compared to other places with the same perks. El Solecito, in the older adobe

section with its own back terrace, is a particularly nice room.

Of the two landmark hotels in town, **Hotel La Fonda de Taos** (108 S. Plaza, 575/758-2211, www.lafondataos.com, $179 d) has a few more modern perks, such as gas fireplaces and mostly reliable Internet. Plus, you can feel quite grand opening your balcony doors over the plaza (though you may also be subjected to predawn street-cleaning noise). But the **Historic Taos Inn** (125 Paseo del Pueblo Norte, 575/758-2233, www.taosinn.com, $185 d), established in 1936 in the former home of the town doctor, has a cozier feeling, even if it is slightly overpriced. Rooms in the main building are more historic feeling and cheaper (about $120 in high season); in the courtyard section or other outbuildings, you may get a kiva fireplace.

Everything at **Hacienda del Sol** (109 Mabel Dodge Ln., 575/758-0287, www.taoshaciendadelsol.com, $180 d) is built in relation to Taos Mountain, which looms up in the backyard with no other buildings cluttering the view. With this view, even the smallest of the 11 rooms in the adobe complex feel

One of Taos's better motels also has one of the best signs.

expansive. The style is cozy without being too oppressively Southwestern, and perks like robes, bathtubs, and mini fridges approximate hotel service. The innkeepers are former cruise-ship employees, and they keep this place shipshape as well.

Decorated with an artist's eye, the five guest cottages at **Casa Gallina** (613 Callejon, 575/758-2306, www.casagallina.net, $195 d) showcase beautiful handicrafts from Taos and around the globe. Kitchens can be stocked with occasional goodies from the garden and eggs from resident hens (they're also pressed into service for the fresh and delicious breakfasts). And it doesn't hurt that the meticulous owner also happens to be a massage therapist.

$200-250

The most lavish hotel in town, **El Monte Sagrado** (317 Kit Carson Rd., 575/758-3502, www.elmontesagrado.com, $219) is unfortunately not as well run as it could be, and repeat guests have mentioned maintenance issues. That said, the style of the place is cool, especially in the eclectic Global Suites, and it has a good sustainable infrastructure, with water-reuse systems, solar panels, and more. The least-expensive rooms, the Taos Mountain rooms, are a little generic, with their white-linens-and-dark-wood look, but they carry a reasonable price for entry into the swank grounds, which include a lovely spa.

Over $250

Fully renovated in 2013 (it used to be the Casa de las Chimeneas), **Palacio de Marquesa** (405 Cordoba Rd., 575/758-4777, www.marquesataos.com, $275 d) is run by the excellent Heritage Hotels group. The rooms have an air of what might be called Pueblo Minimalism: heavy beamed ceilings, with white walls, white leather chairs, and marble baths. What might feel too austere is warmed up with kiva fireplaces and radiant floor heating. Spa services and the option of breakfast delivered to your room add to the cocoon-like feel.

ARROYO HONDO
Under $100

A wild card budget option: **New Buffalo Center** (108 Lower Hondo Rd., Arroyo Hondo, 575/776-2015, www.newbuffalocenter.com), which began as a storied commune. It has been spruced up a bit since Dennis Hopper crashed here, and welcomes overnight guests, with space for up to 12 people in five guest rooms. Rates are on a sliding scale.

ARROYO SECO
Under $100

The best lodging bargain in the area is **The Snowmansion** (Hwy. 150, Arroyo Seco, 575/776-8298, www.snowmansion.com). Conveniently set midway to the Taos Ski Valley in bustling "downtown" Arroyo Seco, this cheerful place offers bunks in dorm rooms ($25) and private rooms (from $50). In the summer, you can also camp (from $20) or sleep in a tepee ($55), and nosh on veggies from the hostel garden. But as the name suggests, winter sports fanatics are the main clientele, and if you don't want to be woken by skiers racing for the Chile Line bus outside, opt for an individual cabin with shared bath ($45).

RANCHOS DE TAOS
$100-150

At the south edge of Ranchos de Taos, **Adobe & Pines Inn** (4107 Hwy. 68, 575/751-0947, www.adobepines.com) is built around an 1830s hacienda, shaded by old trees and overlooking a lush garden. Of the eight rooms, six are quite large (from $179), with especially lavish bathrooms. But even the two smallest rooms ($109 and $119) have fireplaces—and everyone gets the exceptionally good breakfasts, with fresh eggs from the on-site chickens.

RIO GRANDE GORGE
$100-150

For an only-in-Taos experience, stay the night in an **Earthship** (U.S. 64, 575/751-0462, www.earthship.com, $130 d). Four of the curvy, off-the-grid homes are available, with room for up to six people in the largest one. Not only does an Earthship feel like a Hobbit house with banana trees (in the south-facing greenhouse areas), but you're out in the larger, all-Earthship subdivision, with great views of the mountain. And yes, you'll have running water, a refrigerator, and all the other comforts. It's a bit of a drive from town (west of the Rio Grande), but it's an only-in-Taos experience.

Food

For a town of its size, Taos has a broad selection of restaurants. But most close relatively early, and many smaller places don't take plastic—so load up on cash and get seated by 8pm at the latest. You'll need reservations only during the holidays, and the whole dining scene is relatively casual. At one of the New Mexican places, be sure to try some posole—it's more common here than in Albuquerque or Santa Fe, often substituted for rice as a side dish alongside pinto beans. Also, the breakfast burrito—a combo of scrambled eggs, green chile, hash browns, and bacon or sausage in a flour tortilla—is commonly wrapped up in foil and served to go, perfect if you want an early start hiking or skiing.

CENTRAL TAOS
Café
The location of **World Cup** (102-A Paseo del Pueblo Norte, 575/737-5299, 7am-7pm daily, $3) on the corner of the plaza makes it a popular pit stop for both tourists and locals—the latter typically of the drumming, dreadlocked variety, lounging on the stoop.

Breakfast and Lunch
Michael's Kitchen (304-C Paseo del Pueblo Norte, 575/758-4178, 7am-2:30pm Mon.-Thurs., 7am-8pm Fri.-Sun., $8) is famous for New Mexican breakfast items like huevos rancheros and blue-corn pancakes with pine nuts, served all day, but everyone will find something they like on the extensive menu at this down-home, wood-paneled family restaurant filled with chatter and the clatter of dishes. "Health Food," for instance, is a double order of chile cheese fries. The front room is devoted to gooey doughnuts, cinnamon rolls, and pie.

Taos Diner (908 Paseo del Pueblo Norte, 575/758-2374, 7am-2:30pm daily, $10) is as straight-ahead as its name. The pleasant surprise: Much of the enchiladas, egg plates, pancakes, and other typical diner fare is prepared with organic ingredients. Plus, the largely local scene provides good background theater to your meal—the servers seem to know everyone. There's a second outpost, **Taos Diner II** (216-B Paseo del Pueblo Sur, 575/751-1989, 7am-3pm daily), just south of the plaza.

World Cup is the place to start the morning.

Euro-Latino might be the best catchall term for the menu at ★ **Gutiz** (812-B Paseo del Pueblo Norte, 575/758-1226, 8am-3pm Tues.-Sun., $10), which borrows from France and Spain and adds a dash of green chile. Start your day with a chocolate croissant or an impressive tower of scrambled eggs and spinach. Lunch sees traditional croques monsieurs or cumin-spiced chicken sandwiches.

Set in bucolic gardens with a view of Taos Mountain, **Farmhouse Café** (1405 Paseo del Pueblo Norte, 575/758-5683, 7am-5pm daily, $12) is a beautiful spot to revive over a hearty salad, a bison burger, or a homemade pastry, including killer gluten-free options like a chocolate-peanut-butter crispy-rice bar. In summer, the café also serves dinner, usually on weekends only. Look for it behind the Overland Sheepskin store.

Just west of the plaza, **El Gamal** (112 Doña Luz St., 575/613-0311, 9am-5pm Mon.-Wed., 9am-9pm Thurs.-Sat., 11am-3pm Sun., $7) brings the best of Israeli street snacks to Taos, with *shakshuka* (spicy scrambled eggs) and bagels for breakfast and falafel and *sabich* (eggplant and egg) sandwiches at lunch, washed down with a fizzy yogurt soda. There's also more standard hippie fare on the menu: homemade granola and the like.

In the Taos Inn, elegant **Doc Martin's** (125 Paseo del Pueblo Norte, 575/758-1977, 11am-10pm Mon.-Fri., 7:30am-2:30pm and 4pm-10pm Sat.-Sun., $10) is fine at dinner, but weekend brunch is when the kitchen really shines—especially on dishes like the Kit Carson (poached eggs on yam biscuits topped with red chile) or blue-corn pancakes with blueberries. The lunch menu is also tasty and doesn't reach the stratospheric prices of dinner.

American
★ **The Burger Stand** (401 Paseo del Pueblo Norte, 575/758-5522, 11am-11pm daily, $9) is an outpost of a Kansas restaurant—but it fits right in in Taos, in large part because it makes not one but two killer veggie burgers—we recommend the one topped with feta cheese, pickled green beans, and rich romesco sauce. (The beef and lamb burgers are great too, and decked out in similarly creative ways.) It doesn't hurt that it's set inside the Taos Ale House, where there's great beer and music—and, best of all, it's open relatively late.

Fresh and Local
★ **The Love Apple** (803 Paseo del Pueblo Norte, 575/751-0050, 5pm-9pm Tues.-Sun.,

The Farmhouse Café is set in a pretty garden.

$20) wears its local, organic credentials on its sleeve, and the food delivers in simple but powerful flavor combinations, such as a quesadilla made sweet with apple and squash, and posole enriched with local lamb and caramelized onions. The atmosphere is like early-days Chez Panisse filtered through a northern New Mexican lens: a thick-walled adobe chapel, with candles glimmering against wine bottles along the walls. In summer, the restaurant is open seven nights a week (plus brunch 10am-2pm Sun.), but it can get hot inside, so go early to snag a patio table.

Italian

Taos Pizza Out Back (712 Paseo del Pueblo Norte, 575/758-3112, 11am-10pm daily, $8) serves up the best pie in town, using mostly local and organic ingredients. A glance at the menu—with items like green chile and black beans, and the popular portobello-gorgonzola combo—often makes first-timers blanch, but after a bite or two they're converts, like everyone else in town. Soups and a good Greek salad are also available, if you want to round out your meal.

Mexican

Tiny ★ **La Cueva** (135 Paseo del Pueblo Sur, 575/758-7001, 10am-9pm daily, $8) looks like a New Mexican restaurant at first glance, as it has all the usual green-chile-smothered dishes. But its owners are from south of the border and round out the menu with fantastically fresh and homemade-tasting dishes like chicken mole enchiladas and an omelet with housemade chorizo, as well as exceptionally savory beans. No alcohol, though.

New Mexican

A small, festively painted place on the north side of town, the family-run **Orlando's** (1114 Don Juan Valdez Ln., 575/751-1450, 10:30am-9pm daily, $10) is invariably the first restaurant named by anyone, local or visitor, when the question of best chile comes up. That said, there are occasional whisperings about inconsistency (heresy!). But Orlando's still generally serves very satisfying, freshly made New Mexican standards, such as green-chile chicken enchiladas. The posole is quite good too—perfectly firm, earthy, and flecked with oregano. It's always busy, but a fire pit outdoors makes the wait more pleasant on cold nights.

On the road to Taos Pueblo, **Tiwa Kitchen** (328 Veterans Hwy., 575/751-1020, 11am-4pm Wed.-Mon., $13) is a friendly,

The Burger Stand doesn't cut corners on veggie burgers.

super-family-run place (your "waitress" might be not much taller than your table) that specializes in Pueblo food. That means all the usual chile-laced goods, plus nice hyper-local touches like fry bread stuffed with buffalo meat or, for dessert, topped with chokecherry syrup from homegrown fruit.

A drive-through never offered something so good: **Mante's Chow Cart** (402 Paseo del Pueblo Sur, 575/758-3632, 7am-9pm Mon.-Thurs. and Sat., 7am-10pm Fri., $7) specializes in breakfast burritos, as well as genius inventions like the Susie, a whole chile relleno wrapped up in a flour tortilla with salsa and guacamole. Perfect road food.

Road-food aficionados will appreciate the old-school atmosphere of **El Taoseño** (819 Paseo del Pueblo Sur, 575/758-4142, 6am-9pm Mon.-Thurs., 6am-10pm Fri.-Sat., 6am-2pm Sun., $8), which has been open since 1983 and looks it. It's not Taos's tastiest New Mexican food, but it is cheap and fast and kid-friendly.

Fine Dining

★ **El Meze** (1017 Paseo del Pueblo Norte, 575/751-3337, 5:30pm-9:30pm Mon.-Sat., $24) just might be Taos's best restaurant, thanks to both its exceptional food and tiny touches such as complimentary mineral water and plush blankets for cool evenings outside. Chef Frederick Muller shows the link between New Mexico, Spain, North Africa, and the Middle East, in dishes that are both brainy and deep-down satisfying. Delectable mountain trout is seasoned with Spanish paprika and served with a lavish herb salad, while fried green olives stuffed with blue cheese are the bar snack to beat in all of New Mexico. The setting is cozy in winter, inside a thick-walled hacienda, and expansive in summer, with a large patio with a view of Taos Mountain.

Open since 1988 but relatively new to this cozy adobe house, **Lambert's** (123 Bent St., 575/758-1009, 11:30am-2:30pm and 5:30pm-9pm Mon.-Sat., $32) is a Taos favorite, where everyone goes for prom, anniversaries, and other landmark events. Its New American menu is a bit staid, but everything is executed perfectly. Get one of the game-meat specials if you can; otherwise, the signature pepper-crusted lamb is fantastic. A full liquor license means good classic cocktails, which you can also enjoy upstairs at the **Treehouse Lounge** (2:30pm-close).

Markets

Planning a picnic? Stop at **Cid's Grocery** (623 Paseo del Pueblo Norte, 575/758-1148, 8am-8pm Mon.-Sat.) for great takeout food, as well as freshly baked bread and a whole range of organic and local goodies, from New Mexican wines to fresh elk steaks.

From mid-May through October, the **Taos Farmers Market** (www.taosfarmersmarket.org, 8am-1pm Sat.) takes place on the plaza. Vendors sell some prepared food and good gifts like local honey, so you won't be left out even if you don't have a kitchen.

RANCHOS DE TAOS

Just off the plaza near the church, **Ranchos Plaza Grill** (6 St. Francis Plaza, 575/758-5788, 11am-3pm and 5pm-8:30pm Tues.-Sat., 11am-3pm Sun., $11) is a casual spot, known for its red *chile caribe,* made from crushed, rather than ground, chiles, for a really rustic effect.

Across the road, the chile at **Old Martina's Hall** (4140 Hwy. 68, 575/758-3003, www.old-martinashall.com, 7am-9:30pm Wed.-Mon., $20) may be dialed down for out-of-state palates, but this somewhat upscale place has other redeeming qualities. The once-derelict adobe theater with a soaring ceiling has been lovingly redone, now hosting special events, and serves the likes of goat-cheese salads, farro risotto, and truffle fries. It's more casual for breakfast and lunch ($10 for sandwiches), and the light is lovely. Check out all the rooms and levels. The building is across the road from the turn to the church.

ARROYO SECO

★ **Abe's Cantina y Cocina** (489 Hwy. 150, 575/776-8516, 7am-5pm Mon.-Fri., 7am-1:30pm Sat., $4), a creaky old all-purpose general store/diner/saloon, has earned fans from all over for its satisfying and cheap breakfast burritos. There's a full menu of tacos and green-chile cheeseburgers, if you care to eat in, and a nice back patio. And don't miss the sweet, flaky empanadas next to the cash register in the store.

For coffee, though, you'll want to go next door to **Taos Cow** (485 Hwy. 150, 575/776-5640, 7am-7pm daily), a chilled-out coffee bar par excellence, with writers scribbling in one corner and flute players jamming in another. But it's the ice cream that has made the Taos Cow name (you'll see it distributed all around town, and elsewhere in New Mexico and Colorado). The most popular flavors are tailored to local tastes: Café Olé contains cinnamon and Mexican chocolate chunks, while Cherry Ristra is vanilla with piñon nuts, dark chocolate, and cherries. Sandwiches ($9) are an option too, if you want real sustenance.

ACEQ (480 Hwy. 150, 575/776-0900, 5pm-close daily, $15) merges green chile with Brooklynesque comfort food, all making the most of local produce and meats. Think "New Mexico poutine" (fries topped with gravy and queso; we'll let it slide that the oozy melted cheese is a Texan import), baby back ribs, and a kale Caesar salad. The brunch menu, with dishes like lamb chilaquiles, gets raves.

TAOS SKI VALLEY

For nourishment by the ski area, fortify yourself with a green-chile cheeseburger or bowl of smoky-hot green-chile stew at the **Stray Dog Cantina** (105 Sutton Pl., Taos Ski Valley, 575/776-2894, 8am-9pm daily, $12), which gets busy after 3pm, when tired skiers come down from a day on the slopes. In the summer, it doesn't open till 11am on weekdays, but it's a nice destination for a drive, as you can sit on the deck and listen to the river flow by.

More adventurous drivers can head for **Bavarian Lodge** (100 Kachina Rd., 575/776-8020, 11:30am-9pm daily in ski season, $15), way up Twining Road near the southeast edge of the ski area and Kachina Lift 4. You'll need four-wheel drive in winter; in summer, the huge front deck is a lovely place to have a beer (served by actual German speakers) in the pines, though note that it's open only around the weekend (11:30am-4:30pm Thurs. and Mon., 11:30am-8:30pm Fri.-Sat.). The menu is typical Wiener schnitzel and spaetzle.

The Enchanted Circle

The loop formed by U.S. 64, Highway 38, and Highway 522 is named for its breathtaking views of the Sangre de Cristo Mountains, including Wheeler Peak. The area is a cultural shift from Taos, much of it settled by Anglo ranchers and prospectors in the late 1800s and currently populated by transplanted flatlander Texans enamored of the massive peaks. The main towns on the route—Angel Fire and Red River—are ski resorts. As the scenery is really the thing, you can drive the 84-mile route in a short day, with time out for a short hike around Red River or a detour along the Wild Rivers scenic byway. If you like country music, you might want to plan on being in Red River for the evening.

Driving counterclockwise around the loop, as described below, gives you the breathtaking descent into the Taos Valley from Questa—but note that your eating options dwindle near the end of the route. Avoid driving the circle on a Sunday, as significantly more attractions and businesses are closed.

To start, head east on Kit Carson Road, which turns into U.S. 64, winding along next to the Taos River and past numerous campgrounds and hiking trails. At Palo Flechado Pass, the road descends into the high Moreno Valley, a gorgeous expanse of green in early spring and a vast tundra in the winter.

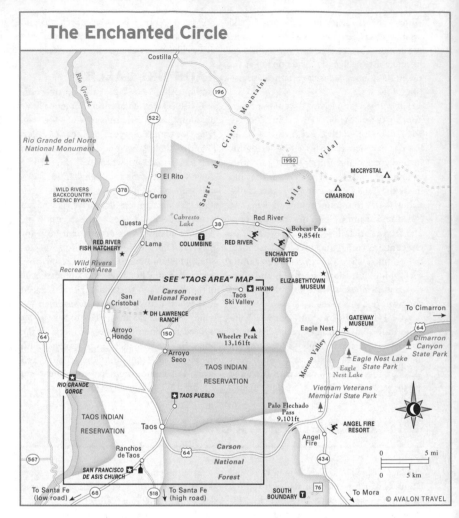

The Enchanted Circle

ANGEL FIRE

A right turn up Highway 434 leads to this tiny ski village, a cluster of timber condos at the base of a 10,600-foot mountain. In comparison with Taos Ski Valley, **Angel Fire Resort** (800/633-7463, www.angelfireresort.com, $66 full-day lift ticket) looks like a molehill, with a vertical drop of 2,077 feet. But it is far friendlier to snowboarders, and it has two freestyle terrain parks. For those with no snow skills at all, the three-lane, 1,000-foot-long tubing hill provides an easy adrenaline rush.

In summer, the resort transforms itself with activities like fishing at **Monte Verde Lake** ($25/person) and an elaborate zipline course ($119), the only one in New Mexico. Off the slopes, **Roadrunner Tours** (Hwy. 434 in town, 575/377-6416, www.rtours.com) does trail rides into the high mountains.

But the main warm-weather diversion is mountain biking, on the mountain itself, and on the storied **South Boundary Trail** (no. 164), which runs from a trailhead off Forest Road 76 south of Angel Fire. The route to Taos is about 5 vertical-seeming miles up and over the pass, then another 22 or so back to El Nogal trailhead on U.S. 64, a couple of miles east of Taos. **Gearing Up** (129 Paseo del Pueblo Sur, 575/751-0365) offers shuttle service, so you can bike one-way.

Food

For lunch, **Hail's Holy Smoked BBQ** (3400 Hwy. 434, 575/377-9938, 11am-7pm Tues.-Thurs., 11am-8pm Fri.-Sat., $12) represents Texan cuisine, with smoked brisket, cowboy beans, and homemade desserts. **Hatcha's Grill** (3453 Hwy. 434, 575/377-7011, 10am-8pm Mon.-Sat., 10am-7pm Sun., $9) represents good home-style New Mexican, with extras like chicken sandwiches to satisfy all tastes. If you happen to be around for dinner, check **The Pub 'n Grub** (52 N. Angel Fire Rd., 575/377-2335, 3pm-8pm daily in winter, 5pm-9pm daily in summer) for fresh, hearty bar food like buffalo burgers; it's closed October and November.

Information

The Angel Fire CVB maintains a **visitors center** (3365 Hwy. 434, 575/377-6555, www. angelfirefun.com, 8am-5pm Mon.-Sat., 9am-3pm Sun.) just south of the T intersection with Angel Fire Road. The **Angel Fire Chamber of Commerce** (3407 Hwy. 434, 575/377-6353, www.angelfirechamber.org, 9am-5pm Mon.-Fri.) has its own office where the lobby is open 24 hours, so you can pick up brochures and maps anytime.

VIETNAM VETERANS MEMORIAL STATE PARK

Back on U.S. 64, a little more than a mile past the turn for Angel Fire, a swooping white structure rises on the hill to your left. This is the **Vietnam Veterans Memorial State Park** (575/377-2293, www.nmparks.com, 9am-5pm daily, chapel open 24 hours), built by Victor "Doc" Westphall as a remembrance for his son David, who was killed in the war. When Westphall commissioned Santa Fe architect Ted Luna to design the graceful white chapel in 1968, it was the first such memorial for the casualties of Vietnam. An adjacent visitors center was built later and now holds a small but moving museum about the conflict and its aftermath. In the garden are a Huey

Vietnam Veterans Memorial State Park

helicopter and the graves of Victor Westphall and his wife, Jeanne.

EAGLE NEST

At the junction of U.S. 64 and Highway 38, **Eagle Nest** is a small strip of wooden buildings, all that's left of what was a jumping gambling town in the 1920s and 1930s, when bars hosted roulette and blackjack, and enterprising businesspeople would roll slot machines out on the boardwalks to entice travelers en route to Raton and the train. The small lake here is the main focus of fun, but there's also good hiking just east in Cimarron Canyon State Park.

Eagle Nest Lake State Park

East of U.S. 64, south of town, **Eagle Nest Lake** was created in 1918 with the construction of a privately financed dam on the Cimarron River. Today it's a state park, stocked with trout, and a popular summertime recreation spot (the Fourth of July fireworks display is legendary). For the marina and **visitors center** (575/377-1594, 8am-4:30pm daily, $5/car day use), look for the turn off U.S. 64 marked by a large RV park sign. Stop here for an exhibit on the dam, as well as camping ($10).

Gateway Museum

The community **Gateway Museum** (U.S. 64, 575/377-5978, www.gatewaymuseum. org, 9:30am-4pm Mon.-Sat., 11am-4pm Sun., donation), at the east edge of Eagle Nest, gives an overview of the good old days and often hosts events, such as a mountain-man rendezvous.

Accommodations and Food

Laguna Vista Lodge (575/377-6522, www. lagunavistalodge.com, $85-125 d) has standard motel rooms connected by a screened porch, as well as cabins and apartments with a view of the lake.

Retro **Kaw-Lija's** (Therma Dr., 575/377-3424, 11am-3pm Wed., 11am-8pm Fri.-Tues., $6) is the most reliable place to eat

The Gateway Museum in Eagle Nest hosts a mountain-man rendezvous.

here, with burgers and the like. Opening hours can be erratic, and it closes in the winter. In the town's oldest hotel, built out of old railroad ties, **Calamity Jane's** (51 Therma Dr., 575/377-9530, 11am-9pm daily, $10) is the town's main restaurant and bar hangout, though the steak-house food is inconsistent.

Information

The **Eagle Nest Chamber of Commerce** (51 Therma Dr., 575/377-2420, www.eaglenestchamber.org, 10am-4pm Tues.-Sat.) has an enthusiastic staff.

ELIZABETHTOWN

Blink and you'll miss it: A small sign on the right side of the road 4.8 miles past Eagle Nest points to a left turn to the former gold-rush site of Elizabethtown, the first incorporated village in New Mexico. When gold was discovered in 1866, it grew to more than 7,000 people, then faded to nothing after a dredge-mining project failed in 1903. It's now a barely

A Little Farther: Cimarron

From Eagle Nest, continuing east on U.S. 64 takes you through **Cimarron Canyon State Park** (575/377-6271, www.nmparks.com, $5/car), known for excellent trout fishing in the Cimarron River, the dramatic granite palisades that form the canyon walls, and a couple of nice hiking spots. Twelve miles east of the canyon, you reach the town of Cimarron, where the **St. James Hotel** (Hwy. 21, 575/376-2664, www.exstjames.com, $100 d) is one of the state's best historic hotels, notorious for gunfights in the years of the Colfax County War and still rich with atmosphere. Lunch is very good at **The Porch** (636 E. 9th St., 575/376-2228, 7:30am-2pm Mon.-Fri., 10am-2pm Sat., 10am-1pm Sun. June-Aug., 10am-2pm Mon.-Fri. Sept.-May, $6).

discernible ghost town, with the paltry stone ruins of the Mutz Hotel, the former center of social activity. The only signs of life are, ironically, in the **cemetery,** which is still used by residents of Colfax County and contains graves dating as far back as 1880. The quirky **Elizabethtown Museum** (575/377-3420, 10am-5pm Mon.-Sat. June-Aug., $2 donation) details Elizabethtown's brief but lively history with items collected from local families' troves, from the gold-rush years and much later (including a few nonworking vintage pinball machines).

RED RIVER

The ski village of Red River is a cluster of tidy rows of wooden buildings, all done up in Old West facades, complete with boardwalks and swinging saloon doors. Like Elizabethtown, this was once a community of wild prospectors, but when mining went bust, the town salvaged itself by renting out abandoned houses to vacationers escaping the summer heat at lower elevations. Just when air-conditioning started to become widespread in the 1950s, the ski area opened, saving the town from a major slump. Red River still thrives, with a year-round population of only about 450. The town hosts a rowdy Memorial Day Motorcycle Rally, as well as a large Fourth of July parade and a Mardi Gras street party; contact the **Red River Chamber of Commerce** (575/754-2366, www.redrivernewmex.com) for more details.

Elizabethtown's liveliest spot

Skiing

Compared with Taos Ski Valley, **Red River Ski & Snowboard Area** (575/754-2223, www.redriverskiarea.com, $67 full-day lift ticket) may be a baby hill, but it's nothing if not convenient: The trails run right into town, so it's walking distance from anywhere to the chairlift. (In summer, the ski slopes are converted into a dry-tubing area, from $15/three runs.)

Cross-country skiers will want to follow Highway 38 east of town, to the **Enchanted Forest** cross-country ski area (575/754-6112, www.enchantedforestxc.com, $18 full-day pass), which has more than 20 miles of groomed trails through the trees and up the mountainside. Nonskiers can rent snowshoes. And, for a special overnight experience, you can trek in to a **yurt** ($50-150, depending on season), nicely appointed with a wood stove. It's available year-round, and snowmobile delivery of your gear is an option in winter.

Hiking

This is the back side of Wheeler Peak, so the ascents are much more gradual, while still yielding dramatic views. Stop in at the **visitors center** (100 E. Main St., 575/754-3030, www.redriver.org, 8am-5pm daily), in the town hall, for area maps and trail guides. The least strenuous hiking option is the **Red River Nature Trail,** which starts in town at Brandenburg Park and runs two miles one-way, with signs identifying plants and geological formations.

West of town, the road leads past a number of trailheads that make for a good amble. **Columbine Trail,** on the left (south) seven miles out (or about four miles east of Questa), starts out easy, crossing Deer Creek, but soon moves to a series of long switchbacks that lead through a large aspen grove, then above the tree line to the ridge, a total of about five miles. As an incentive, wild berry bushes flourish alongside the trail in the late summer. The right side of the road, however, is a little less scenic because a molybdenum mine has stripped a good chunk of the mountain.

Entertainment

Red River has a lively old-time country music scene, heavily influenced by the Texans who have long come here for vacation. "Outlaw country" singer and songwriter Michael Martin Murphey, whose song "The Land of Enchantment" is the official state ballad, has long been an active participant here, and he owns the **Rocking 3M Chuckwagon Amphitheater** (178 Bitter Creek Rd., 575/754-6280), where he also performs regularly in summer. **Bobcat Pass** (1670 Hwy. 38, 575/754-2769, www.bobcatpass.com, 5:30pm Tues., Thurs., and Sat. mid-June-Aug.), which offers horseback riding by day, hosts "cowboy evenings," which include a home-style steak dinner along with a night of singing and picking and a bit of poetry. And in town, you can pretty much always count on music at the aptly named **Lost Love Saloon** (406 E. Main St., 575/754-6280), the bar at Texas Reds.

Food

Red River has the largest selection of lunch options on the Enchanted Circle, but none of them are particularly remarkable. Business turnover can be high here, but at least **Texas Reds** (400 E. Main St., 575/754-2922, 4:30pm-9pm Mon.-Thurs., 11:30am-3pm and 4:30pm-9pm Fri.-Sun., $17) is consistent; it has relocated twice and still packs 'em in for big steaks in a wood-paneled Western-look room, the floors scattered with peanut shells. For Tex-Mex, **Sundance** (401 High St., 575/754-2971, 5pm-9pm Mon.-Wed., 11:30am-2pm and 5pm-9pm Thurs.-Sun., $13) is equally reliable—it's on the street uphill and parallel to the main drag. For smaller meals, **Dairy Bar** (417 E. Main St., 575/754-9969, 11am-9pm daily, $5) does burgers, chile, quesadillas, and of course soft-serve ice cream.

Information

The chamber of commerce staffs a **visitors center** (100 E. Main St., 575/754-3030, 8am-5pm daily) inside the town hall, off the north side of the main drag.

QUESTA

Arriving in Questa, at the junction of Highway 38 and Highway 522, you're back in Spanish New Mexico. The town, which now has a population of about 1,700, was established in 1842 and is still primarily a Hispano farming village, though a few Anglo newcomers have set up art spaces here. **Ocho** (8 Hwy. 38, www.ochozone.org) is one; it hosts community music jams and other events.

Across the road is the **visitors center** (Hwy. 38, 575/613-2852, www.questa-nm.org, 9:30am-5pm Thurs.-Sun. June-Aug.), though it has little to share. The heart of town, a few blocks back, is the 1841 **San Antonio Church,** which has been undergoing a multiyear restoration after a wall collapsed in 2008; volunteers have been gradually rebuilding on nights and weekends.

Unfortunately, the few eating options here can't be recommended with enthusiasm; **Bronson's Burgers** (Hwy. 522, 575/586-1445, 11am-4:30pm Mon.-Sat., $6), in the B&R gas station on the south edge of town, will do. The better strategy is to drive north about five miles to Cerro, where **My Tia's Café** (Hwy. 378, 575/586-2203, 11am-6pm Mon., Thurs., and Fri., 8am-7pm Sat.-Sun., $7) does New Mexican home cooking; it's en route to the Wild Rivers Recreation Area.

Wild Rivers Recreation Area

In 2014, the **Río Grande del Norte National Monument** (575/758-8851, blm.gov/riograndedelnorte) was established, protecting the river all the way from the Colorado border down to Pilar, south of Taos. Perhaps the wildest section of the land is found north of Questa, in the **Wild Rivers Recreation Area,** where the Red River meets the Rio Grande, in two deep canyons. Red-tailed hawks circle over gnarled, centuries-old piñon and juniper trees, and river otters thrive here, after their reintroduction in 2008. Whitewater **rafting** is very popular here in the Class III rapids of the Red River Confluence run; contact an outfitter in Taos.

The access road to the recreation area is three miles north on Highway 522 from the main Questa intersection, then west on Highway 378, which leads through the town of Cerro and to the area's **visitors center** (575/586-1150, 9am-6pm daily June-Aug., $3/car day use).

Steep **hiking** trails lead down into the gorge and along the river, so you can make a full loop, starting down from **La Junta Overlook,** then taking Little Arsenic Trail back up (about 4.5 miles total), or **Big Arsenic Trail** for a longer hike (6 miles). If you'd prefer not to descend (and, necessarily, ascend) the canyon, follow the more level 1.7-mile **Pescado Trail** along the Red River rim and gently down to the Red River Fish Hatchery.

Five developed **campgrounds** (but no RV hookups; $7/car) on the rim can be reached by car, or you can hike in to campsites by the river ($5).

Valle Vidal

Northeast of Questa lies Valle Vidal, a 102,000-acre chunk of the Carson National Forest that straddles some of the highest peaks in the Sangre de Cristo range. The access road, Highway 196, is out of the way north of Questa, off Highway 522, but for those seeking pristine wilderness, Valle Vidal is perhaps the last, best place to get a sense of what New Mexico was like before mining and ranching took off in the 19th century. The area is home to the state's largest elk herd, and its watershed is essential for the rare Rio Grande cutthroat trout. In a 2006 deal, Pennzoil traded the land to the National Forest Service in exchange for tax breaks, after a long grassroots campaign to prohibit mining and drilling.

There are no services in the wilderness, very few trails, and only two formal camping areas with no services but toilets. Coming from Highway 522, you first reach the 35 sites at **Cimarron Campground** ($10), tucked amid trees with many trout-fishing creeks nearby. Eight miles farther is **McCrystal Creek Campground** ($8), set on a flat plain, with a few ponderosas providing shade. For current conditions and advisories (parts of the valley are closed seasonally to protect the elk), contact the **Questa Ranger District office** (575/586-0520), which manages the whole area.

RED RIVER FISH HATCHERY

On Highway 522 heading south from Questa, after 3.5 miles you pass the turn for the **Red River Fish Hatchery**, an operation that produces almost 400,000 trout every year to stock lakes all over northern New Mexico. It's not a thrilling destination, but if the kids are getting antsy in the back seat, stop in at the **visitors center** (9am-5pm daily). There's a free self-guided "tour," which doesn't show you much more than some cryptic tanks behind chain-link fencing. You can feed "trout chow" to the biggest specimens, or (if you have your gear) cast a line at the small pond. The **Pescado Trail**, off the south end of the pond parking lot, leads up to the Wild Rivers Recreation Area.

THE D. H. LAWRENCE RANCH

After Questa, the view opens up as you descend into the valley, with mesas stretching far to the west. Five miles east on a rutted road is the 160-acre **Kiowa Ranch** (10am-4pm Mon., Thurs., and Sat. June-Oct.), where English writer and provocateur D. H. Lawrence lived in 1924 and 1925 with his wife, Frieda, and the painter Dorothy Brett. The ranch was closed to visitors for several years, but reopened in 2014, with a docent on-site to answer questions. Though there's not much to see, it is as good a reason as any to drive up a back road and into the fragrant pine forests. (Don't bother driving up on a closed day—the property is now fully fenced and locked up.)

The 160-acre spread was a gift from Mabel Dodge Luhan—generous, but nonetheless a bare-bones existence, as you can see in the

inside "that outhouse of a shrine" at the D. H. Lawrence Ranch

cabins the artists occupied. Lawrence soon returned to Europe, but Frieda stayed on. Years after the writer died of tuberculosis in France in 1930, Frieda exhumed and cremated his body and brought the ashes to New Mexico. This plan sparked anger among Lawrence's friends, including Mabel, who characterized Frieda's planned site for the ashes as "that outhouse of a shrine." Tales abound about how the ashes never made the trip. Some of the earliest visitors to pay their respects at the ranch include Tennessee Williams and Georgia O'Keeffe, whose painting *The Lawrence Tree* was inspired by the view from the base of a gnarled pine in front of the Lawrences' cabin.

Coming from the north, turn left at the *second* sign for County Road B-009 (the first is in the town of San Cristobal). Coming up from Taos, look for the historic marker on the right side of the road, immediately before the turn.

Information and Services

TOURIST INFORMATION

A few miles south of the plaza, the **Taos Visitors Center** (1139 Paseo del Pueblo Sur, 575/758-3873, www.taos.org, 9am-5pm daily) is helpful, as long as you don't show up right before closing time. Stop here for flyers and maps galore, free coffee, and the very thorough weekly news and events bulletin (also posted online), which includes gallery listings, music, and more.

Books and Maps

Moby Dickens (124-A Bent St., No. 6 Dunn House, 575/758-3050, 10am-5pm Mon.-Wed., 10am-6pm Thurs.-Sat., noon-5pm Sun.) is Taos's best bookstore, well informed on local history and culture and stocking plenty of maps, as well as rare books, a good CD collection, and assorted gifts.

Local Media

The *Taos News* comes out every Thursday; its *Tempo* entertainment section covers music, theater, and film listings. Many hotels offer free copies of *Tempo* to their guests. The *Albuquerque Journal* publishes a special northern edition daily, focused on local issues.

Radio

While you're in town, don't miss tuning in to KTAO (101.9 FM), a local radio station that's all solar-powered. The musical programming is broad, and you're sure to learn interesting tidbits about the community as well.

SERVICES

Banks

US Bank (120 W. Plaza, 575/737 3540, 9am-5pm Mon.-Fri.), just off the southwest corner of the plaza, is the most convenient bank and ATM while on foot. The drive-through service at **Centinel Bank of Taos** (512 Paseo del Pueblo Sur, 575/758-6700, 9am-5pm Mon.-Fri.) is easily accessible from the main drag.

Post Offices

The Taos **post office** (710 Paseo del Pueblo Sur, 575/751-1801, 9am-1pm and 2pm-4:30pm Mon.-Sat.) is on the south side; there's another on the north side (318 Paseo del Pueblo Norte, 575/758-2081, 8:30am-5pm Mon.-Fri.).

Internet

Wired? (705 Felicidad Ln., 575/751-9473, www.wiredcoffeeshop.com, 8am-5pm daily), behind Albertson's off La Posta Road, is a laid-back Internet café and business center with a big garden, good veggie and raw-food meals, and free wireless access for laptops; computer use is $2 for 15 minutes.

Getting There and Around

CAR

From Santa Fe, the drive to Taos takes about 1.5 hours (70 miles) along the direct "low road" through the river valley (via Española, U.S. 84/285 to Hwy. 68). If taking the high road (via Chimayó and Truchas, mostly on Hwy. 76), plan on at least 2 hours for the 80-mile drive.

From Albuquerque, add at least an hour's travel time for the 60-mile drive up I-25 (the most direct route).

Once in Taos, you will need a car to get to outlying sights, but will also have to bear the daily traffic jam on Paseo del Pueblo. There are paid parking lots close to the plaza, and a free one less than a quarter mile down Kit Carson Road. For rental cars, **Enterprise** (1350 Paseo del Pueblo Sur, 575/758-5333, www.enterprise.com, 8am-5pm Mon.-Fri., 9am-noon Sat.) has a convenient office.

BUS AND SHUTTLE

For pickup at the Albuquerque airport, **Twin Hearts Express** (575/751-1201, $50 one-way) runs a shuttle four times a day (11:30am, 1:30pm, 3:30pm, and 5:30pm), with drop-offs at most hotels. Allow at least 2.5 hours for travel time.

From Santa Fe, there's great weekend service from city-sponsored **Taos Express** (575/751-4459, www.taosexpress.com, $10 round-trip), which runs from Taos and back once on Friday afternoon, and again on Saturday and Sunday, completing a loop in the morning and another in the afternoon. The one-way trip takes 1 hour and 50 minutes, and you must reserve a seat in advance.

In Santa Fe, the bus picks up passengers near the Rail Runner main depot (Montezuma at Guadalupe) and at the South Capitol station. In Taos, it drops off at the Loretto parking lot, one block west of the plaza; going back south, it also picks up passengers at the Sagebrush Inn (1508 Paseo del Pueblo Sur). The schedule syncs with the Rail Runner's arrival in Santa Fe (and it can carry bicycles), making it a potentially seamless three-hour trip all the way from Albuquerque. It can also stop at the Santa Fe airport.

Within Taos, the **Chile Line bus** runs north-south from the Ranchos de Taos post office to the Taos Pueblo, approximately every 40 minutes 7:30am-5:30pm Monday-Friday. The fare (exact change only) is $0.50. Mid-December-April, a **ski shuttle** ($1) runs to Taos Ski Valley, with five buses daily making stops at key motels en route to the mountain; not all buses stop at all hotels. Contact the city (575/751-4459, www.taosgov.com) for maps and schedules.

Albuquerque

Look for ★ to find recommended
sights, activities, dining, and lodging.

Highlights

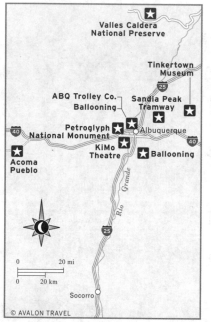

★ **Sandia Peak Tramway:** Zip up the world's longest single-cable tram to the crest of the mountain that looms over the east side of Albuquerque. At the top, you'll get a vertigo-inducing view across the whole metro area and out to the hazy western horizon (page 156).

★ **Petroglyph National Monument:** The city's West Mesa is covered with fine rock carvings made centuries ago by the ancestors of the local Pueblo people. Don't miss the views across the city from the dormant volcanoes that stud the top of the ridge (page 157).

★ **Ballooning:** In the American capital for hot-air balloons, enjoy the silent city on a dawn flight. You'll get a true bird's-eye view, and dip down to skim the Rio Grande (page 167).

★ **Acoma Pueblo:** This windswept village on a mesa west of Albuquerque is one of the oldest communities in the United States. Visit for the views as well as for the delicate black-on-white pottery made only here (page 183).

★ **Tinkertown Museum:** An enthralling collection of one man's lifetime of whittling projects, this folk-art exhibit is inspiring for adults and a delight for kids (page 188).

★ **Valles Caldera National Preserve:** In the crater formed by a collapsed volcano, some 89,000 acres of grassy valleys are set aside for very controlled public access. You must make reservations to hike here, but the reward is beautiful solitude (page 195).

★ **ABQ Trolley Co.:** The best tour in the state is aboard an open-sided, faux-adobe tram-on-wheels, with the lively, knowledgeable owners sharing Albuquerque lore (page 146).

★ **KiMo Theatre:** A fantasia of Southwestern decorative details, this former cinema is one of the few examples of Pueblo Deco style. Restored and run with city money, it's the showpiece of downtown (page 151).

As a tourist destination, Albuquerque has long labored in the shadow of the jet-set arts colonies to the north, but that has slowly started to change as visitors discover a city that's fun, down-to-earth, and affordable.

If Santa Fe is the "City Different" (a moniker *Burqueños* razz for its pretentiousness), then New Mexico's largest city, with a population of 900,000 in the greater metro area, is proudly the "City Indifferent," unconcerned with fads and flawless facades.

The city does have its pockets of historic charm—they're just not visible from the arteries of I-40 and I-25, which intersect in the center in a graceful tangle of turquoise-trimmed bridges. The Duke City was founded three centuries ago, its cumbersome name that of a Spanish nobleman but its character the product of later eras: the post-1880 downtown district; the University of New Mexico campus, built in the early 20th century by John Gaw Meem, the architect who defined Pueblo Revival style; and Route 66, the highway that joined Albuquerque to Chicago and Los Angeles in 1926.

Spread out on either side of the Rio Grande, from volcanic mesas on the west to the foothills of the Sandia Mountains along the east, Albuquerque has accessible hiking and biking trails that run through diverse environments. In the morning, you can stroll under centuries-old cottonwood trees near the wide, muddy river; in the afternoon, you can hike along the edge of a windswept mountain range with views across the vast empty land beyond the city grid. And at the end of the day, you'll see Albuquerque's most remarkable feature, the dramatic light show on the Sandia Mountains—Spanish for "watermelon," for the bright pink hue they turn at sundown.

The city is also an excellent base for exploring the many interesting pueblos and natural attractions nearby, and it's just an hour's drive to Santa Fe, with easy day trips or scenic drives through the mountains in between. To the west is Acoma Pueblo, an ancient settlement perched atop a mesa. To the southeast is a series of ruined pueblos, last inhabited during the early years of the Conquest, linked by a

---

Previous: Madrid; I-40 and I-25 intersect in Albuquerque. **Above:** A hot-air balloon above the West Mesa.

Albuquerque

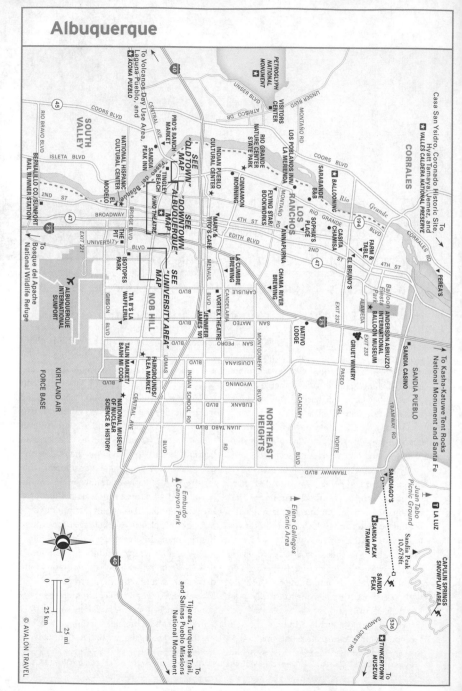

© AVALON TRAVEL

scenic road through the Manzano Mountains, overlaid with Spanish settlements.

Additionally, there are several ways to head north to Santa Fe (or simply make a loop). The most direct is I-25, which cuts through dramatic rolling hills; take a short detour to Kasha-Katuwe Tent Rocks National Monument, where pointed white rocks tower above a narrow canyon. Beginning east of Albuquerque, the historic Turquoise Trail winds along the back side of the Sandias, then through the former mining town of Madrid, resettled as an arts colony, with galleries occupying the cabins built against the black, coal-rich hills.

The most roundabout route north is along the Jemez Mountain Trail, a scenic byway northwest of Albuquerque through the brick-red rocks surrounding Jemez Pueblo, then past natural hot springs. The road runs along the edge of Valles Caldera National Preserve, a pristine valley where the daily number of visitors is carefully limited, so you can enjoy the vistas in solitude.

PLANNING YOUR TIME

Precisely because it's not so full of must-see historic attractions, Albuquerque fares best as the primary focus of a trip, so you have time to enjoy the natural setting, the food, and the people. A possible incentive: Your money will go farther here than it will farther north, especially when it comes to hotels, which offer great value and don't dramatically hike rates for **summer** high season, as is standard in Taos and Santa Fe. Ideally, you would spend a leisurely **four or five days** here, soaking up a little Route 66 neon, enjoying the downtown entertainment, hiking in the Sandias, taking scenic drives, and bicycling along the Rio Grande.

But if you're also planning to visit other parts of the state, it is difficult to recommend more than a **couple of days** in Albuquerque—preferably on the way out, as the city's modern, get-real attitude is best appreciated after you've been in the adobe dreamland of Santa Fe for a bit. Spend a day cruising the neighborhoods along Central Avenue, and for a last dose of open sky, take the tramway up to Sandia Peak

and hike along the Crest Trail. At the end of your trip, you'll be able to handle the elevation with no problem.

In the city proper, most of the year is enjoyable. **Winters** are mild in the low basin around the river, though the Sandias often get heavy snow. As elsewhere in the state, the heat of July and August is usually broken by heavy afternoon rainstorms (though May and June are typically hot and dry). And because Albuquerque is seldom at the top of tourists' lists, there's never a time when it's unpleasantly mobbed.

HISTORY

Albuquerque was established in 1706 as a small farming outpost on the banks of the Rio Grande, where Pueblo Indians had been cultivating crops since 1100, and named after a Spanish duke. Decades later, the Villa de San Felipe de Alburquerque (the first "r" was lost over the years) flourished as a waypoint on the Camino Real trade route.

The city began to transform in 1880, when the railroad arrived, two miles from the main plaza—this sparked the growth of "New Town" (now the downtown business district) and drew tuberculosis patients, who saw the city's crisp air as beneficial. By 1912, these patients made up nearly a quarter of the state's population.

More modernization and growth came from Route 66, which was laid down Central Avenue in the 1930s, and the establishment of Sandia National Labs in 1949, in response to the escalating Cold War. Tourism boomed (and neon signs buzzed on), and new streets were carved into the northeast foothills for lab workers' tract homes. In the 1940s, the population exploded from 35,000 to 100,000; by 1959, 207,000 people lived in Albuquerque.

Growth has been steady ever since, and recent development has been spurred by a growing film industry and other technical innovations. Subdivisions have spread across the West Mesa, and small outlying communities have become suburbs—though portions along the river retain a village feel that's not too far from the city's roots as a farming community three centuries back.

Sights

Most sightseeing destinations are somewhere along Central Avenue (historic Route 66), with a few destinations elsewhere in the greater metro area. To keep your bearings, remember that the mountains run along the east side of the city. Street addresses are followed by the city quadrant (NE, NW, SE, SW); the axes are Central and 1st Street. When locals talk about "the Big I," they mean the relatively central point where I-40 and I-25 intersect.

OLD TOWN

Until the railroad arrived in 1880, Old Town wasn't old—it was the *only* town. The labyrinthine old adobes have been repurposed as souvenir emporiums and galleries; the city's major museums are nearby on Mountain Road. Despite the chile-pepper magnets and cheap cowboy hats, the residential areas surrounding the shady plaza retain a strong Hispano flavor, and the historic Old Town buildings have a certain endearing scruffiness—they're lived-in, not polished.

★ ABQ Trolley Co.

To cruise the major attractions in town and get oriented, put yourself in the hands of the excellent locally owned and operated **ABQ Trolley Co.** (800 Rio Grande Blvd. NW, 505/240-8000, www.abqtrolley.com, Apr.-Oct., $25). Even if you're not normally the

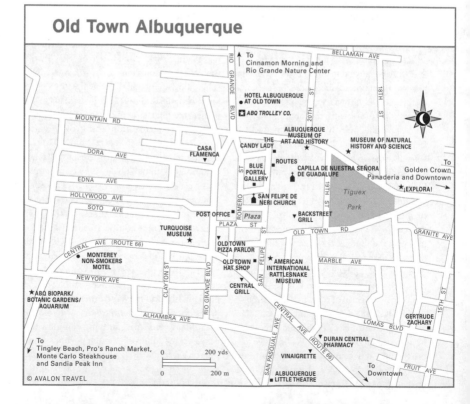

Old Town Albuquerque

Breaking Bad

Walter White and Jesse Pinkman may be gone from television, but their legacy lives on in Albuquerque. The AMC show about a high school chemistry teacher turned meth cook, *Breaking Bad* was originally written for a California setting, but production moved to Albuquerque following tax incentives. It was a happy accident, and unlike other productions shot here anonymously, *Breaking Bad* was explicitly down with the 505.

Dedicated fans should book the monthly "BaD Tour" with the **ABQ Trolley Co.** (800 Rio Grande Blvd. NW, 505/240-8000, www.abqtrolley.com, Apr.-Oct., 3.5 hours, $65)—though its standard route passes a few filming locations as well. The bike rental company **Routes** (404 San Felipe St. NW, 505/933-5667, www.routesrentals.com, $50) offers several "Biking Bad" tours every other Saturday; each route follows a different character.

A few other sights around town include:

- The **Dog House** hot-dog stand, with its exceptionally fine neon sign, is at 1216 Central Avenue Southwest, near Old Town.

- **Los Pollos Hermanos** is actually Twisters, at 4257 Isleta Boulevard Southwest, but the PH logo is painted on the wall outside.

- Walt and Skyler's **A1A Car Wash** is at Menaul and Eubank (9516 Snow Heights Circle NE, for your GPS).

- **The Grove** (600 Central Ave. SE), where Lydia loved her Stevia too well, is a popular café downtown.

As souvenirs of your Albuquerque visit, **Great Face & Body** (123 Broadway SE, 505/404-6670) sells "Bathing Bad" blue bath salts. **The Candy Lady** (424 San Felipe St. NW, 505/243-6239), which cooked the prop "meth" for a few episodes, sells its blue hard candy in zip-top baggies.

bus tour type, you'll find this one special. Not only is it in a goofy faux-adobe open-sided trolley-bus, but the enthusiastic owners give the tours themselves, and their love of the city is clear as they wave at pedestrians and tell stories about onetime Albuquerque resident Bill Gates.

All tours depart from the Hotel Albuquerque at Old Town. The 85-minute standard tour (11am and 1pm Tues.-Sat., 1pm Sun., $25) runs through downtown and some off-the-beaten-track old neighborhoods, passing many TV and movie locations. There's also a periodic *Breaking Bad* tour (3.5 hours, $65) that's hugely popular—book well in advance for this. Or join one of the monthly nighttime theme tours—such as "Albucreepy," a tour of supposedly haunted locations, or a pizza crawl—which draws locals as well. Buy tickets online to guarantee a spot; the tickets also get you discounts around town, so it's good to do this early in your visit.

ABQ BioPark

The kid-friendly **ABQ BioPark** (505/768-2000, www.cabq.gov/biopark, 9am-5pm daily, till 6pm Sat.-Sun. June-Aug.) has three components. On the riverbank just west of Old Town (2601 Central Ave. NW) is a single complex that contains, on one side, an **aquarium,** with a giant shark tank, a creepy tunnel full of eels, and displays on underwater life from the Gulf of Mexico and up the Rio Grande. The other half is **botanic gardens,** including a desert hothouse and a butterfly habitat. The most New Mexico-specific installation, and the most interesting, is the 10-acre **Rio Grande Heritage Farm,** a re-creation of a 1930s operation with heirloom apple orchards and rare types of livestock, such as Percheron horses and Churro sheep, in an idyllic setting near the river.

A few blocks away is the **zoo** (903 10th St. SW), which you can reach from the aquarium via a miniature train. The zoo is not particularly groundbreaking, but there's plenty of space for kids to run around among trumpeting elephants and screeching peacocks. The window into the gorilla nursery is probably the most fascinating exhibit. Tickets for each section (zoo or aquarium/gardens) are $12.50, and a combo ticket for entry at all three, which includes the mini-train ride, is $20.

Between the zoo and aquarium, on the east bank of the river, south of Central, so-called **Tingley Beach** (1800 Tingley Dr. SW, sunrise-sunset, free) is 18 acres of paths and ponds for fishing; you can also rent pedal boats and bicycles here.

Albuquerque Museum of Art and History

The **Albuquerque Museum of Art and History** (2000 Mountain Rd. NW, 505/243-7255, www.cabq.gov/museum, 9am-5pm Tues.-Sun., $4) has a permanent collection ranging from a few choice Taos Society of Artists members to contemporary work by the likes of Nick Abdalla, whose sensual imagery makes Georgia O'Keeffe's flower paintings look positively literal. The history wing covers four centuries, with emphasis on Spanish military trappings, Mexican cowboys, and Albuquerque's early railroad years. Free guided tours run daily around the sculpture garden, or you can join the informative **Old Town walking tour** (11am Tues.-Sun. mid-Mar.-mid-Dec.). The museum has free admission Saturday afternoon (after 2pm) and Sunday morning (9am-1pm), as well as the third Thursday night of the month, when it's open till 8:30pm.

American International Rattlesnake Museum

You'd never guess that a small storefront just off the plaza houses the **American International Rattlesnake Museum** (202 San Felipe St. NW, 505/242-6569, www.rattlesnakes.com, 10am-6pm Mon.-Sat., 1pm-5pm Sun. June-Aug., $5), the largest collection of live snakes in the world. To see the real

Capilla de Nuestra Señora de Guadalupe

critters, you have to wade through an enormous gift shop full of plush snakes, wood snakes, little magnet snakes, and snakes on T-shirts. You'll also see some fuzzy tarantulas and big desert lizards, and the reptile-mad staff are usually showing off some animals outside to help educate the phobic. In the off-season, September-May, weekday hours are 11:30am-5:30pm (weekends are the same).

Capilla de Nuestra Señora de Guadalupe

One of the nifty secrets of Old Town, the tiny adobe **Capilla de Nuestra Señora de Guadalupe** (404 San Felipe St. NW) is tucked off a small side alley. It's dedicated to the first saint of Mexico; her image dominates the wall facing the entrance. The dimly lit room, furnished only with heavy carved seats against the walls, is still in regular use (although, unfortunately, a fire put an end to lit votive candles and required the image of the Virgin be repainted in a more modern style). Despite the building's small scale, it follows the scheme of many traditional New Mexican churches, with a clerestory that allows sunlight to shine down on the altar.

¡Explora!

A 50,000-square-foot complex adjacent to the natural history museum, ¡Explora! (1701 Mountain Rd. NW, 505/224-8300, www.explora.us, 10am-6pm Mon.-Sat., noon-6pm Sun., adults $8, children $4) is dedicated to thrilling—and educating—children. Grown-ups may learn something too. Its colorful geodesic-dome top sets a circuslike tone, and inside, more than 250 interactive exhibits demonstrate the scientific principles behind everything from high-wire balancing to optical illusions. Kids can even build robots using Lego systems, and, since this is the desert, a whole section is dedicated to water.

Museum of Natural History and Science

The **Museum of Natural History and Science** (1801 Mountain Rd. NW, 505/841-2800, www.nmnaturalhistory.org, 9am-5pm daily) is a large exhibit space containing three core attractions: a **planetarium** and observatory; a wide-format **theater** screening the latest vertigo-inducing nature documentaries; and an **exhibit** of Earth's geological history. Admission is $7 to the main exhibit space or the planetarium and $10 for the theater, though there are discounts if you buy tickets to more than one.

The museum section devotes plenty of space to the crowd-pleasers: dinosaurs. New Mexico has been particularly rich soil for paleontologists, and several of the most interesting finds are on display, such as *Coelophysis* and *Pentaceratops*. In addition, the *Startup* exhibit details the early history of the personal computer in Albuquerque and elsewhere. The show was funded by Paul Allen, who founded Microsoft here with Bill Gates, *then* moved to Seattle.

San Felipe de Neri Church

Established in 1706 along with the city itself,

San Felipe de Neri Church (2005 N. Plaza St. NW) was originally built on what would become the west side of the plaza—but it dissolved in a puddle of mud after a strong rainy season in 1792. The replacement structure, on the north side, has fared much better, perhaps because its walls, made of adobe-like *terrones* (sun-dried bricks cut out of sod) are more than five feet thick. As they have for two centuries, local parishioners attend Mass here, which is conducted three times a day, once in Spanish.

Like many religious structures in the area, this church received a late-19th-century makeover from Eurocentric Bishop Jean-Baptiste Lamy of Santa Fe. Under his direction, the place got its wooden folk Gothic spires, as well as new Jesuit priests from Naples, who added such non-Spanish details as the gabled entrance and the widow's walk. The small yet grand interior has brick floors, a baroque gilt altar, and an elaborate pressed-tin ceiling with Moorish geometric patterns. A tiny **museum** (9:30am-5pm Mon.-Sat., free), accessible through the gift shop, contains some historic church furnishings.

Turquoise Museum

The **Turquoise Museum** (2107 Central Ave. NW, 505/247-8650, tours 11am and 1pm Mon.-Sat., $10) is much more substantial than it looks from its strip-mall facade. Exhibits present the geology and history of turquoise, along with legendary trader J. C. Zachary's beautiful specimens from all over the world. But most folks can't help but think how this relates to all the jewelry they plan to buy. So come here to learn the distinction between "natural" and "real" turquoise and otherwise arm yourself for the shopping ahead. Admission is by **guided tour** only (1.5 hours).

DOWNTOWN

Albuquerque's downtown district, along Central Avenue between the train tracks and Marquette Avenue, was once known as bustling New Town, crowded with mule-drawn

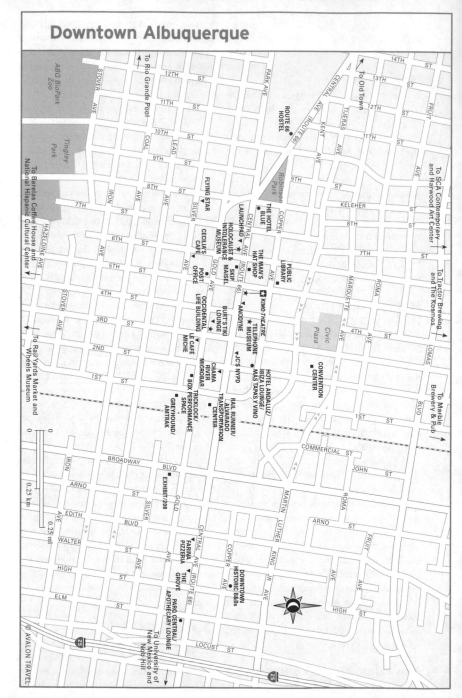

Downtown Albuquerque

505/768-3522 or 505/768-3544, www.cabq.gov/kimo). In 1927, local businessperson and Italian immigrant Carlo Bachechi hired Carl Boller, an architect specializing in movie palaces, to design this marvelously ornate building. Boller was inspired by the local adobe and native culture to create a unique style dubbed Pueblo Deco—a flamboyant treatment of Southwestern motifs, in the same vein as Moorish- and Chinese-look cinemas of the same era. The tripartite stucco facade is encrusted with ceramic tiles and Native American iconography (including a traditional Navajo symbol that had not yet been completely appropriated by the Nazi Party when the KiMo was built).

To get the full effect, take a **self-guided tour** (11am-8pm Wed.-Sat., 11am-3pm Sun.) of the interior to see the cow-skull sconces and murals of pueblo life; enter through the business office just west of the ticket booth.

the Occidental Life Building

Occidental Life Building

On Gold Avenue at 3rd Street, this one-story **Occidental Life Building** is another of Albuquerque's gems, built in 1917 by H. C. Trost, whose work defines downtown El Paso, Texas. With its ornate facade of white ceramic tile, it looks a bit like the Doge's Palace in Venice rendered in marshmallow fluff. After a 1933 fire, the reconstructing architects added even more frills, such as the crenellations along the top. The entire building is surfaced in white terra-cotta; the tiles were made in a factory in Denver, which sprayed the ceramic glaze onto concrete blocks, each individually molded and numbered, and the blocks were then assembled in Albuquerque according to an overall plan. (The building is owned by local-boy-made-good Jared Tarbell, a cofounder of Etsy, the online craft site. Tarbell's toy- and art-manufacturing company, Levitated, is located nearby, on 7th Street.)

Museums

Production value is basic at the storefront **Holocaust and Intolerance Museum** (616 Central Ave. SW, 505/247-0606, 11am-3:30pm

streetcars, bargain hunters, and wheeler-dealers from the East Coast. But in the 1950s and 1960s, shopping plazas in Nob Hill and the Northeast Heights drew business away. By the 1970s, downtown was a wasteland of government office buildings. Thanks to an aggressive urban-renewal scheme initiated in 2000, the neighborhood has regained some of its old vigor, and Central is now a thoroughfare best known for its bars.

By day, you won't see too many specific attractions, but a stroll around reveals an interesting hodgepodge of architectural styles from Albuquerque's most optimistic era. At Central Avenue and 4th Street, two versions of Route 66 intersect. When the original highway was commissioned in 1926, the road from Chicago to the West Coast ran along 4th Street; after 1937, the route was smoothed so that it ran east-west along Central.

★ KiMo Theatre

Albuquerque's most distinctive building is the **KiMo Theatre** (423 Central Ave. NW,

Tues.-Sat., free), but the message is compelling. Displays cover not just World War II, but also the Armenian genocide and actions against Native Americans. The surprisingly detailed three-story **Telephone Museum** (110 4th St. NW, 505/841-2932, 10am-1:30pm Mon., Wed., and Fri., $2) is worth a visit—if you happen to get there in its laughably narrow open time.

The **Wheels Museum** (1100 2nd St. SW, 505/243-6269, www.wheelsmuseum.org, donation) is dedicated to Western transportation, with a special focus on trains—fitting its location in the city rail yard. It displays some great interviews with former workers in the old Santa Fe workshops. The place is still being developed, so at press time did not yet have set hours. But it is reliably open during the **Rail Yards Market** (777 1st St. SW, www.railyardsmarket.org, 9am-3pm Sun. May-Oct.); model-train fans will be well rewarded.

THE UNIVERSITY AND NOB HILL

When it was established in 1889, what's now the state's largest university was only a tiny outpost on the far side of the railroad tracks.

Surrounding the campus, which sprawls for blocks, is the typical scrum of cheap pizza places, bohemian coffeehouses, and dilapidated bungalow rentals. The next neighborhood east along Central is Nob Hill, developed around a shopping plaza in the late 1940s and still showing that decade's distinctive style in marquees and shop facades.

The University of New Mexico

Nearly 25,000 students use the **University of New Mexico** campus, the core of which is bounded by Central Avenue and University Boulevard. The school's oldest buildings are a distinct pueblo-inspired style, commissioned in the early 1900s by college president William George Tight. Trustees later fired Tight in part for his non-Ivy League aesthetics, but the style was in motion. Pueblo Revival pioneer John Gaw Meem carried on the vision through the 1940s, and even with contemporary structures now interspersed among the original halls, it's still a remarkably harmonious vision, uniting the pastoral sanctuary feel of the great East Coast campuses with a minimalist interpretation of native New Mexican forms.

Visitors can park in a complex just inside

the main entrance to the University of New Mexico campus

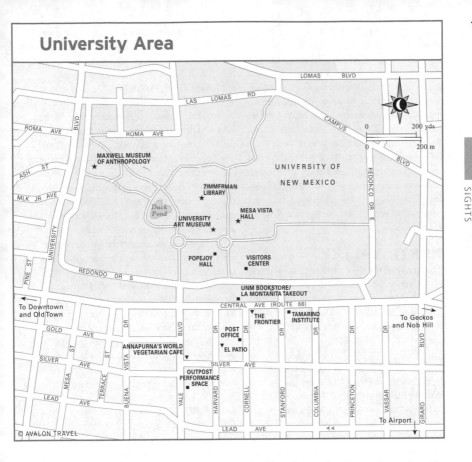

University Area

the UNM campus across from Cornell Street. The info center, where you can pick up a detailed map, is in the southwest corner of the structure. Just across the way, the **University Art Museum** (505/277-4001, www.unmartmuseum.org, 10am-4pm Tues.-Sat., $5 donation) displays treasures from the permanent fine art collection of more than 30,000 pieces from all over the globe.

Wandering around the grounds, you'll see such classic Meem buildings as **Mesa Vista Hall** (now the Student Services Building) and **Zimmerman Library.** Rest up at the bucolic duck pond, then head for the **Maxwell Museum of Anthropology** (off University Blvd., north of M. L. K. Jr. Blvd., 505/277-4405, 10am-4pm Tues.-Sat., free), a Meem building designed as the student union. The museum has a particularly good overview of Southwestern Indian culture and a collection of Native American artifacts from university-sponsored digs all over the state.

Nob Hill

At Girard Street, a neon-trimmed gate marks the start of the **Nob Hill** district, which extends east along Central Avenue about 10 blocks to Washington Boulevard. The area began to grow after 1937, when Route 66 was rejiggered to run along Central. The Nob Hill Shopping Plaza, at Central and Carlisle, signaled the neighborhood's success when it opened as the glitziest shopping district in town a decade later.

The area went through a slump from the 1960s through the mid-1980s, but it's again lined with brightly painted facades and neon signs, making it a lively district where the quirk factor is high—whether you want designer underwear or an antique Mexican mask, you'll find it here. Head off of Central on Monte Vista and keep an eye out for the **Bart Prince House** (3501 Monte Vista Blvd. NE), the home and studio of one of the city's most celebrated contemporary architects, whose favorite forms seem to be spaceships and antennas—it's the residential counterpart to the eccentric businesses that flourish in this area.

NORTH VALLEY

The stretch of the river north of Central is one of Albuquerque's prettier areas, all shaded with cottonwoods and still spotted with patches of farmland. The more scenic route through is Rio Grande Boulevard; the commercial strip is 4th Street.

Indian Pueblo Cultural Center

Just north of I-40 from Old Town, the **Indian Pueblo Cultural Center** (2401 12th St. NW, 505/843-7270, www.indianpueblo.org, 9am-5pm daily, $6) is a must-visit before heading to any of the nearby Indian communities. The horseshoe-shaped building (modeled after the Pueblo Bonito ruins in Chaco Canyon in northwestern New Mexico) houses a large museum that traces the history of the first settlers along the Rio Grande. It depicts the Spanish Conquest as a faintly absurd enterprise and is illustrated with some beautiful artifacts and showcases the best craftwork from each pueblo.

The central plaza hosts **dance performances** (11am and 2pm Apr.-Oct., noon Nov.-Mar.), one of the only places to see them outside of the pueblos themselves. The extensively stocked gift shop is a very good place to buy pottery and jewelry; you can also have a lunch of posole and fry bread at the Pueblo Harvest Café. Don't miss the south wing, which contains a gallery for contemporary

art. At the information desk, check on ceremony schedules and get directions to the various pueblos.

Rio Grande Nature Center State Park

Familiarize yourself with river ecology at the **Rio Grande Nature Center State Park** (2901 Candelaria St. NW, 505/344-7240, www.rgnc.org, 8am-5pm daily, $3/car), in the center of town. You enter the sleek, concrete **visitors center** (10am-5pm daily) through a drainage culvert. Beyond an exhibit on water conservation and river ecology is a comfortable glassed-in "living room," where you can watch birds on the pond from the comfort of a lounge chair, with the outdoor sounds piped in through speakers.

Outside, several **paved trails** run across irrigation channels and along the river, shaded by towering cottonwoods. In the spring and fall, the area draws all manner of migrating birdlife. Borrow binoculars from the staff if you want to scout on your own, or join one of the frequent **nature walks** (including full-moon tours) that take place year-round.

Los Ranchos and Corrales Scenic Byway

For a pretty drive (or bike ride) through these villages that have been all but consumed by greater Albuquerque, head north from Old Town on Rio Grande Boulevard; you first reach **Los Ranchos**, then cross the river at Alameda to Corrales Road and continue up the west bank. These districts remain pockets of pastoral calm where horses gambol and 18th-century acequias water organic herb gardens—a practical melding of old agricultural heritage with modern suburban bliss. The only real sights are in central Corrales, two blocks west of the main road. The folk Gothic **Old San Ysidro Church** (505/897-1513, 1pm-4pm Sat.-Sun. June-Oct.) stands where the center of the village was in 1868, when its bulging adobe piers were first constructed. Every spring, the church gets a fresh coat of mud from the community.

Route 66 Gets a Makeover

the El Vado Motel sign, in better days

Route 66 is one of the biggest repositories of American nostalgia, a little neon ribbon of cool symbolizing the country's economic growth in the 20th century. But the "mother road," on which so many Dust Bowl refugees made their way west and so many beatniks got into their grooves, officially no longer exists. The highway was decommissioned in 1985. You can still follow the brown historic-marker signs from Chicago to Los Angeles, including along Central Avenue.

But the businesses that thrived in the early highway era—especially the numerous 1940s motel courts—have fallen on hard times. As part of Albuquerque's aggressive urban-renewal program, city planners demolished a number of hotels, leaving dead neon signs standing like tombstones amid the rubble. But the city had a change of heart with the 1939 De Anza, on the east edge of Nob Hill, and bought it in 2003 to protect, among other things, beautiful interior murals by American Indian painters. In the meantime, *Burqueños* developed fresh affection for their neon-lit heritage. So when the owner of the El Vado Motel, near Old Town, threatened his vintage property with the wrecking ball, the city bought that too. Plans for redevelopment on both properties are under discussion—at press time, El Vado was slated to become a boutique hotel. Keep an eye on these icons of Route 66 history.

Across the road, **Casa San Ysidro** (973 Old Church Rd., 505/898-3915, www.cabq.gov/museum, $4) was owned by obsessive collectors Alan and Shirley Minge. While they lived in the place, from 1952 to 1997, they heated with firewood and squirreled away New Mexican antiques and craftwork. It is a lovingly preserved monument to a distinct way of life. The Albuquerque Museum gives **tours** (10:30am, noon, and 1:30pm Tues.-Sat. June-Aug.) of the interior with its beautiful brickwork and wood carving; tours are less frequent September-November and February-May (9:30am and 1:30pm Tues.-Fri., 10:30am, noon, and 1:30pm Sat.). You can just turn up, but it's a good idea to call to confirm the times.

ALBUQUERQUE METRO AREA

Beyond Central Avenue, Albuquerque is a haze of houses and shopping centers built during the 1960s and later—decades one local journalist dubbed the city's "Asphalt

Period." A few sights are well worth seeking out, however.

National Hispanic Cultural Center

Just south of downtown (but not quite walking distance), the modern **National Hispanic Cultural Center** (1701 4th St. SW, 505/246-2261, www.nhccnm.org) lauds the cultural contributions of Spanish speakers the world over. It has had a positive influence in the down-at-the-heels district of Barelas (even the McDonald's across the street mimics its architecture), but numerous houses—occupied by Hispanics, no less—were demolished for its construction. One woman refused the buyout, and her two small houses still sit in the parking lot, almost like an exhibit of their own.

The central attraction is the **museum** (10am-5pm Tues.-Sun., $3, free on Sun.), which shows work ranging from the traditional *bultos* and *retablos* by New Mexican craftspeople to contemporary painting, photography, and even furniture by artists from Chile, Cuba, Argentina, and more. If you can, visit on Sunday, when the **torreón** (tower) is open (noon-4pm) to show Frederico Vigil's amazing fresco *Mundos de mestizaje*, a decadelong project depicting the many strands—Arab, Celtic, African—that have contributed to Hispanic culture today.

Adjacent to the museum is the largest Hispanic genealogy library in existence, as well as the giant Roy E. Disney Center for Performing Arts.

National Museum of Nuclear Science & History

The spiffy **National Museum of Nuclear Science & History** (601 Eubank Blvd. SE, 505/245-2137, www.nuclearmuseum.org, 9am-5pm daily, $8) covers everything you wanted to know about the nuclear era, from the development of the weapon on through current energy issues. Exhibits cover the ghastly elements of the atomic bomb, but also wonky tech details (check out the display of decoders, set in suitcases for emergency

National Hispanic Cultural Center

deployment) and pop-culture artifacts, such as "duck and cover" films from the Cold War. Don't miss the beautiful posters by Swiss American artist Erik Nitsche.

★ Sandia Peak Tramway

The longest tramway of its type in the world, the **Sandia Peak Tramway** (505/856-7325, www.sandiapeak.com, $1 parking, $20 round-trip, $12 one-way) whisks passengers 2.7 miles and 4,000 feet up, along a continuous line of Swiss-made cables. The ride from Albuquerque's northeast foothills to the crest takes about 15 minutes. It's a convenient way to get to the ski area in winter, and in summer and fall, you can hike along the ridgeline a few miles to the visitors center. There's a so-so restaurant at the top and a small exhibit about local flora and fauna. The service runs frequently year-round (9am-9pm daily June-Aug., 9am-8pm Wed.-Mon., 5pm-8pm Tues. Sept.-May)—but check the website for periodic maintenance closures in fall and spring.

At the base of the tram, there's a small

Zip up to Sandia Peak on the world's longest tramway.

free museum about skiing in New Mexico, and even from this point, the view across the city is very good. The casual Mexican restaurant here, **Sandiago's** (38 Tramway Rd. NE, 505/856-6692, 11am-8pm daily, $13), is a bit cheesy, but it's still a nice spot for a sunset margarita (one of which, the Doogie, honors

Petroglyph National Monument

Albuquerque actor Neil Patrick Harris, who attended a nearby high school).

★ Petroglyph National Monument

Albuquerque's west side is bordered by **Petroglyph National Monument,** 7,500 acres of black boulders that crawl with some 20,000 carved lizards, birds, and assorted other beasts. Most of the images, which were created by chipping away the blackish surface "varnish" of the volcanic rock to reach the paler stone beneath, are between 400 and 700 years old, while others may date back three millennia. A few more recent examples of rock art include Maltese crosses made by Spanish settlers and initials left by explorers (not to mention a few by idle 20th-century teenagers).

Stop in first at the **visitors center** (Unser Blvd. at Western Tr., 505/899-0205, www.nps.gov/petr, 8am-5pm daily) for park maps, flyers on flora and fauna, and general orientation. From here, you will have to drive to the major trails: **Boca Negra Canyon,** a short paved loop and the only fee area ($1/car on weekdays, $2 on weekends); **Piedras Marcadas Canyon,** a 1.5-mile unpaved loop; and **Rinconada Canyon,** an out-and-back hike (2.2 miles round-trip) that can be tedious going in some spots because the ground is sandy. The clearest, most impressive images can be found here, in the canyon at the end of the trail. Everywhere in the park area, keep an eye out for millipedes, which thrive in this environment; dead, their curled-up shells resemble the spirals carved on the rocks—coincidence?

For the best overview (literally) of this area's geology, head for the back (west) side of the parkland, the **Volcanoes Day Use Area** (9am-5pm daily), where three cinder cones mark Albuquerque's western horizon. Access is via Atrisco Vista Boulevard (exit 149) off I-40; turn right (east) 4.3 miles north of the highway at a dirt road to the parking area.

From this vantage point, you can look down on the lava "fingers" that stretch east to form the crumbled edges of the escarpment where the petroglyphs are found. The fingers were formed when molten rock flowed between sandstone bluffs, which later crumbled away. The volcanoes were last reported emitting steam in 1881, though a group of practical jokers set smoky fires in them in the 1950s, briefly convincing city dwellers of an impending eruption. But the peaks are not entirely dead: Patches of green plants flourish around the steam vents that stud the hillocks, particularly visible on the middle of the three volcanoes.

Anderson Abruzzo Albuquerque International Balloon Museum

Boosters of Albuquerque's hot-air balloon scene—which has been flourishing since the first rally in 1972—include locals Ben Abruzzo, Larry Newman, and Maxie Anderson, who in 1978 made the first Atlantic crossing by balloon in the *Double Eagle II* helium craft. Abruzzo and Anderson also crossed the Pacific and set a long-distance record (5,678 miles) in the *Double Eagle V.*

These pioneers are honored at the so-called **BaMu** (9201 Balloon Museum Dr. NE, 505/768-6020, www.balloonmuseum.com, 9am-5pm Tues.-Sun., $4), in Balloon Fiesta Park just off Alameda Boulevard. The displays are a great mix of historical background, interactive physics lessons, and inspiring footage of record-setting balloon ventures. As long as you don't dwell too long on the zeppelin

---

Albuquerque's Hot-Air History

How did it come to be that one of the most iconic sights in Albuquerque is a 127-foot-tall Mr. Peanut figure floating in front of the Sandias? Albuquerque, it turns out, enjoys the world's most perfect weather for navigating hot-air balloons. A phenomenon called the "Albuquerque Box," created by the steep mountains adjacent to the low river bottom, enables pilots to move at different speeds at different altitudes, and even to backtrack if necessary. Combine that with more than 300 days of sunshine per year, and it's no wonder that now more than 700 balloons—including "special shapes" such as Mr. Peanut—convene each October to show off their colors and compete in precision flying contests.

The city's air currents were discovered to be friendly to balloons for the first time in 1882. That was when an adventurous bartender piloted a hydrogen-filled craft into the sky as part of the New Town's Fourth of July celebrations, much to the delight of the assembled crowd, which had waited almost two days for *The City of Albuquerque,* as the balloon was dubbed, to fill. "Professor" Park Tassell, the showman pilot, went aloft alone and landed successfully; the only mishap was that a ballast sandbag was emptied on a spectator's head.

Then 90 years passed, and in 1972, Albuquerque again drew attention as a place to pursue this gentle sport. This was the year the first balloon fiesta was held, with 13 aircraft participating. The gathering, a rudimentary race, was organized as a publicity stunt for a local radio station's 50th-anniversary celebrations. The spectacle drew 20,000 people, most of whom had never even seen a hot-air balloon before—but within a few short years, the event was internationally renowned, and the **Balloon Fiesta** has been an annual event ever since.

exhibit, complete with salt and pepper cellars from the *Hindenburg,* you may come away inspired by the grace of balloons and wanting to take a ride in one yourself.

Coronado Historic Site

Though named for Spanish explorer Francisco Vásquez de Coronado, who camped on this lush riverside spot during his 1540 search for gold, the **Coronado Historic Site** (485 Kuaua Rd., Bernalillo, 505/867-5351, 8:30am-5pm Wed. Mon., $3) is actually a Native American relic, the partially restored pueblo of Kuaua (Tiwa for "evergreen"), inhabited between 1300 and the early 1600s. The centerpiece is the partially sunken square kiva, its interior walls covered with murals of life-size human figures and animals in ritual poses. What you see are reproductions—the originals have been removed for preservation, and a few are on display in the visitors center.

While not exactly worth its own special trip, the site is a good place to stop on your way up to Jemez, and the setting is pleasant for a picnic. Facing the river and the mountains, with the city hidden from view behind a dense screen of cottonwoods, you get a sense of the lush, calm life along the Rio Grande in the centuries before the Spanish arrived. To reach the monument, exit I-25 in Bernalillo and head west on Highway 550; Kuaua Road is on your right, before the Santa Ana Star casino.

Gruet Winery

The Spanish planted the first vineyards in North America in New Mexico in the 17th century, and the industry persisted until a series of floods finally wiped out the vines by the 1920s. So New Mexico's current wine scene, while strong, is still somewhat young. One of the best wineries, **Gruet** (8400 Pan American Fwy. NE, 505/821-0055, www.gruetwinery.com, 10am-5pm Mon.-Fri., noon-5pm Sat.) began producing its excellent sparkling wines (the Gruet family hails from Champagne) only in 1987; look out especially for its nonvintage sparkling rosé, which is delicious and affordable. The tasting room serves five pours for $7; **tours** of the winery are at 2pm.

Entertainment and Events

NIGHTLIFE

Because Albuquerque doesn't have enough members of any one particular subculture to pack a whole bar, the city's drinking dens can host a remarkable cross section, and even the most chic-appearing places might see an absentminded professor and a veteran Earth Firster propping up the bar next to well-groomed professionals.

That said, the city's main bar and club scene, in a few square blocks of downtown, can feel a bit generic, with free-flowing beer specials for non-choosy students. It ends in a rowdy scene after closing time on weekends, when crowds spill out onto several blocks of Central that are closed to car traffic. So although this area does have a few good bars, you'll find more interesting entertainment elsewhere.

Downtown

The **Hotel Andaluz lobby** (125 2nd St. NW, 505/242-9090) touts itself as "Albuquerque's living room"—Conrad Hilton's original vision for the place—and it's a comfy spot to sip cocktails and nibble Spain-inspired snacks, especially if you reserve one of the private booths ("casbahs") on the weekend, when there's also live tango or salsa and a big crowd of dancers. On the second floor, the indoor-outdoor **Ibiza Lounge** (4pm-11pm Mon.-Thurs., 4pm-1am Fri.-Sat., 11am-4pm Sun.) is a chic scene on weekends. It has a good view of the mountains at sunset, and it's a cooler alternative to the mayhem just over on Central; occasional special events carry cover charges, but usually it's free to enter.

A great spot to watch the Sandia Mountains

turn pink at sunset, the **Apothecary Lounge** (806 Central Ave. SE, 505/242-0040, 3pm-10:30pm Mon.-Thurs., 3pm-1am Fri.-Sun.) is the rooftop bar at the Parq Central hotel in East Downtown. Fitting with the historic atmosphere of the hotel, the bar is good at vintage cocktails, and also has a seasonal drink menu, along with finger food.

The best all-purpose casual bar downtown is the upstairs **Anodyne** (409 Central Ave. NW, 505/244-1820, 4pm-1:30am Mon.-Fri., 7pm-1:30am Sat., 7pm-11:30pm Sun.), a long, wood-floor room filled with pool tables and a younger crowd sprawled on the thrift-store sofas. Choose from more than a hundred beers, and get some quarters to plug in to the good collection of pinball machines. Happy hour is 4pm-8pm Monday to Thursday, and till 9pm on Friday.

To catch touring indie rockers or the local crew about to hit it big, head to the very professional **Launchpad** (618 Central Ave. SW, 505/764-8887, www.launchpadrocks.com). With free live music and a pool table, **Burt's Tiki Lounge** (313 Gold Ave. SW, 505/247-2878, www.burtstikilounge.com, 8:30pm-2am Wed.-Sat.) has a funky feel and an eclectic bill, from British psychedelia to reggae.

The University and Nob Hill

In the Nob Hill shopping plaza, **Gecko's** (3500 Central Ave. SE, 505/262-1848, 11:30am-late Mon.-Fri., noon-late Sat.-Sun.) is a good place for a snack (anything from Thai curry shrimp to chipotle hot wings) and a drink in the sidewalk seats. Sporting its own breezy patio, **O'Niell's** (4310 Central Ave. SE, 505/255-6782, 11am-2pm Mon.-Sat., 11am-midnight Sun.) is a great Irish pub that draws a varied crowd, whether for quiz night or weekend folk bands; the kitchen is open until midnight.

If you're more in the mood for a cozy indoor vibe, head to the cellar wine bar at **Zinc** (3009 Central Ave. NE, 505/254-9462, 5pm-1am Mon.-Sat., 5pm-11pm Sun.), where you can try tasting flights while listening to a jazz trio or watching old movies.

North Valley

A cinder-block bunker in an otherwise unremarkable strip, **Low Spirits** (2823 2nd St. NW, 505/344-9555, www.lowspiritslive.com) nonetheless is one of Albuquerque's better live-music venues, with a mix of country, indie rock, and more, all put together by the same people who run the much-admired

Downtown is Albuquerque's liveliest area at night.

Albuquerque Beer Culture

Burque's beer scene is so lively that the *Journal* has a dedicated "Brews News" beat. There are a number of long-established microbreweries, as well as some newer operations that distribute around the state. These are some of the best spots in town; for more, see the New Mexico Brewers Guild (www.nmbeer.org).

a few of New Mexico's craft beers

- **Il Vicino** (3403 Central Ave. NE, 505/266-7855, 11am-11pm Sun.-Thurs., 11am-midnight Fri.-Sat.): Locals think of this Nob Hill spot primarily as a pizza parlor, but it has been brewing its own beer since 1992 and recently expanded to a larger brewing facility, the **Canteen Brewhouse**, at 2381 Aztec Road NE (noon-10pm Sun.-Thurs., noon-midnight Fri.-Sat.).

- **Kellys Brew Pub** (3222 Central Ave. SE, 505/262-2739, 8am-10:30pm Sun.-Thurs., 8am-midnight Fri.-Sat.): Another long-established Nob Hill brewery, set in an old car showroom. Great outdoor seating.

- **Marble Pub** (111 Marble Ave. NW, 505/243-2739, noon-midnight Mon.-Sat., noon-10:30pm Sun.): Adjacent to the Marble Brewery, which is one of the best newer breweries. Pleasantly out of the downtown fray, with a dog-friendly outdoor area with eclectic bands.

- **Tractor Brewing:** This popular place has two locations: its brewery, in the industrial area north of downtown (1800 4th St. NW, 505/243-6/52, 3pm-late Mon.-Thurs, 1pm late Fri.-Sun.), and a bar in Nob Hill (118 Tulane St. SE, 505/433-5654, 3pm-midnight Mon.-Wed., 3pm-2am Thurs., 1pm-2am Fri.-Sat., 1pm-midnight Sun.). Both have low-fi live music.

- **La Cumbre Brewing** (3313 Girard Blvd. NE, 505/872-0225): In a fairly isolated industrial area, with only the occasional food truck for sustenance, but locals love this beer.

- **Chama River Microbar** (106 2nd St. SW, 505/842-8329, 4pm-midnight daily): A small outpost (no food) downtown, handy for tastings. If you like it, head to the brewery itself (4939 Pan American Fwy. NE, 505/342-1800, 11am-10pm Sun.-Thurs., 11am-11pm Fri.-Sat.), a slick place with a full steakhouse menu.

Launchpad downtown. Cover is usually about $10, but beers can be had for $2.

THE ARTS

Albuquerque has the liveliest theater scene in the Southwest, with some 30 troupes in action. The old reliables are the black box **Vortex Theatre** (2900 Carlisle Blvd. NE, 505/247-8600, www.vortexabq.org), running since 1976 (though in a new location as of 2014), and the more standard repertory **Albuquerque Little Theatre** (224 San Pasquale St. SW, 505/242-4750, www.albuquerquelittletheatre.org), founded in 1930 and performing in a 500-seat WPA-era building. Up in the North Valley, the **Adobe Theater** (9813 4th St. NW, www.adobetheater.org) has been running in some form since 1957; it often mounts plays by local playwrights.

The 70-seat **Cell Theatre** (700 1st St. NW, www.liveatthecell.com) is home to the Fusion Theatre Company, all professional union actors. It often runs recent Broadway dramas.

A more avant-garde group is the two-decade-old **Tricklock** (110 Gold Ave. SW, 505/254-8393, www.tricklock.com), which develops physically oriented shows at its "performance laboratory" downtown. It also hosts an international theater festival (in Jan. and Feb.). The neighboring **Box Performance Space** (114 Gold Ave. SW, 505/404-1578, www.theboxabq.com) hosts various improv groups and satirical comedians; the well-known absurdist comedy duo The Pajama Men often perform here when they're back home.

Also see what **Blackout Theatre** (www.blackouttheatre.com) is up to—it doesn't have its own space, but it mounts interesting shows in interesting places: improv Dickens, for instance, or an interactive zombie apocalypse in a parking lot. Other groups of note: **Duke City Repertory Theatre** (www.dukecityrep.com) and **Mother Road Theatre Company** (www.motherroad.org).

CINEMA

Century 14 Downtown (100 Central Ave. SW, 505/243-9555, www.cinemark.com) devotes most of its screens to blockbusters, while the latest indie and art films are shown at **The Guild** (3405 Central Ave. NE, 505/255-1848, www.guildcinema.com), a snug single screen in Nob Hill.

LIVE MUSIC

Albuquerque's arts scene graces a number of excellent stages. The most beautiful is the city-owned **KiMo Theatre** (423 Central Ave. NW, 505/768-3544, www.cabq.gov/kimo), often hosting locally written plays and dance, as well as the occasional musical performance and film screening.

Bigger classical and folkloric acts visit the **Roy E. Disney Center for Performing Arts** at the National Hispanic Cultural Center (1701 4th St. SW, 505/724-4771, www.nhccnm.org), a modernized Mesoamerican pyramid that contains three venues, the largest of which is a 691-seat proscenium theater. This is the place to catch a performance by visiting or local flamenco artists—with the National Institute of Flamenco headquarters in Albuquerque, there's often someone performing.

UNM's **Popejoy Hall** (UNM campus, 505/277-3824, www.popejoyhall.com) hosts the New Mexico Symphony Orchestra

(which also plays at the Rio Grande Zoo in the summer).

A more intimate classical event is **Chatter Sunday** (505/234-4611, www.chatterabq.org, 10:30am Sun., $15). Originally known as Church of Beethoven, this chamber-music show aims to offer all the community and quiet of church, with none of the religious overtones. It takes place at the funky coffeehouse **The Kosmos** (1715 5th St. NW), part of a larger warehouse-turned-art-studios complex. The "service" lasts about an hour, with two musical performances, interspersed with a poem and a few minutes of silent contemplation. It's all fueled by free espresso.

Flamenco enthusiasts should check the schedule at **Casa Flamenca** (401 Rio Grande Blvd. NW, 505/247-0622, www.casaflamenca.org) in Old Town. The dance school in an old adobe house hosts a monthly *tablao,* in which local teachers and visiting experts perform.

For rock concerts, the biggest concert venue in town is **Isleta Amphitheater** (5601 University Blvd. SE, www.isletaamphitheater.net), with space for some 12,000 people. The

Pueblo Deco style at the KiMo Theatre

next step down is one of the Albuquerque-area casinos, the ritziest of which is **Sandia Casino** (I-25 at Tramway, 800/526-9366, www.sandiacasino.com), which has a 4,000-seat outdoor amphitheater. **Isleta Casino** (11000 Broadway SE, 505/724-3800, www.isleta.com), not to be confused with the amphitheater, has a smaller indoor venue, as does Laguna Pueblo's **Route 66 Casino** (14500 Central Ave. SW, 866/352-7866, www.rt66casino.com).

Also see what's on at **El Rey Theater** (620 Central Ave. SW, 505/510-2582, www.elrey theater.com) and **Sunshine Theater** (120 Central Ave. SW, 505/764-0249, www.sunshinetheaterlive.com)—both converted movie houses, they have excellent sightlines. **Outpost Performance Space** (210 Yale Blvd. SE, 505/268-0044, www.outpostspace.org) books very good world music and dance acts.

FESTIVALS AND EVENTS

The city's biggest annual event is the **Albuquerque International Balloon Fiesta** (505/821-1000, www.balloonfiesta.

preparing for the dawn mass ascension at the Balloon Fiesta

com), nine days in October dedicated to New Mexico's official state aircraft, with more than 700 hot-air balloons of all colors, shapes, and sizes gathering at a dedicated park on the north side of town, west of I-25. During the fiesta, the city is packed with "airheads," who claim this is the best gathering of its kind in the world. If you go, don't miss an early-morning mass ascension, when the balloons glow against the dark sky, then lift silently into the air in a great wave. Parking can be a nightmare—take the park-and-ride bus, or ride a bike (valet parking available!).

In April is the equally colorful **Gathering of Nations Powwow** (505/836-2810, www.gatheringofnations.com), the largest tribal get-together in the United States, with more than 3,000 dancers and singers in full regalia from over 500 tribes crowding the floor of the University Arena. Miss Indian World earns her crown by showing off traditional talents such as spearfishing or storytelling.

Labor Day weekend is dedicated to the casual **New Mexico Wine Festival** (505/867-3311, www.newmexicowinefestival.com), in Bernalillo. It's well attended by a wide swath of *Burqueños,* and the Rail Runner train runs on a special schedule, sparing stress on designated drivers.

Just after Labor Day, the state's agricultural roots get their due at the **New Mexico State Fair** (www.exponm.com), two weeks of fried foods and prizewinning livestock. It's the usual mix of midway craziness and exhibition barns, along with really excellent rodeos, which often end with shows by country music legends.

All that Americana is countered by **Globalquerque** (www.globalquerque.com), an intense two-day world-music fest that runs in mid-September. It draws top-notch pop and traditional performers from the Middle East, Africa, and Asia. Concerts take place at the National Hispanic Cultural Center.

Around November 2, don't miss the **Marigold Parade** (505/363-1326, www. muertosymarigolds.org), celebrating the Mexican Day of the Dead and general South

Ceremonial Dances

This is an approximate schedule for dances at Albuquerque-area pueblos. Pueblo feast days are always on the same date every year, but seasonal dances (especially Easter and other spring rituals) can vary. Confirm details and start times—usually afternoon, but sometimes following an evening or midnight Mass—with **the Indian Pueblo Cultural Center** (505/843-7270, www.indianpueblo.org) before setting out.

- **January 1** - Jemez: Los Matachines
- **January 6** - Most pueblos: various dances
- **February 2** - San Felipe: various dances for Candlemas (Día de la Candelaria)
- **March 19** - Laguna: Feast of San José
- **Easter** - Most pueblos: various dances
- **May 1** - San Felipe: Feast of San Felipe
- **June 13** - Sandia: Feast of San Antonio
- **June 29** - Santa Ana: Feast of San Pedro
- **July 14** - Cochiti: Feast of San Bonaventura
- **July 26** - Santa Ana: Feast of Santa Ana
- **August 10** - Jemez: Pueblo Independence Day and Fair
- **August 2** - Jemez: Feast of Santa Persingula
- **August 15** - Zia: Feast of the Assumption of Our Blessed Mother
- **September 4** - Isleta: Feast of Saint Augustine
- **September 8** - Isleta (Encinal): Feast of the Nativity of the Blessed Virgin
- **September 17-19** - Laguna: Feast of San José
- **November 12** - Jemez: Feast of San Diego
- **December 12** - Jemez: Los Matachines
- **December 24** - San Felipe: various dances

Valley pride. The parade is a procession of skeletons, cars bedecked in flowers, and a little civil-rights activism.

For the **winter holidays**, the city is bedecked with luminarias (paper-bag lanterns), especially in Old Town and the Country Club neighborhood just to the south. The Albuquerque Botanic Garden (www.abq.gov/biopark) is decked out with holiday lights and model trains for much of December, and ABQ Ride, the city bus service, offers a bus tour around the prettiest neighborhoods on Christmas Eve.

The rest of the year, look out for specialist get-togethers, such as the **National Fiery Foods Show** (www.fieryfoodsshow.com) in March, where capsaicin fanatics try out hot new products; the **Mariachi Spectacular** (www.mariachispectacular.com) in early July; and the weeklong **Festival Flamenco Internacional** (www.nationalinstituteofflamenco.org) in June, the largest event of its kind in the United States, with performances and workshops sponsored by the National Institute of Flamenco, which has its conservatory here.

Shopping

Old Town and the environs are where you can pick up traditional American Indian jewelry and pottery for very reasonable prices, while Nob Hill is the commercial center of Albuquerque's counterculture, with body-piercing studios adjacent to comic book shops next to herbal apothecaries.

OLD TOWN

The galleries and gift shops around the plaza can blur together after just a little bit of browsing, but the **Blue Portal Gallery** (2107 Church St. NW, 505/243-6005, 10am-4:30pm Mon.-Sat., 1pm-4pm Sun.) is a nice change, with well-priced and often very refined arts and crafts, from quilts to woodwork, by Albuquerque's senior citizens. And the **street vendors** set up on the east side of the plaza are all artisans selling their own work, at fair prices.

Just outside of Old Town's historic zone, the **Gertrude Zachary** showroom (1501 Lomas Blvd. NW, 505/247-4442, www. gertrudezachary.com, 9:30am-6pm Mon.-Sat., 10am-5pm Sun.) is the place to go for contemporary turquoise-and-silver jewelry.

If you arrived in Albuquerque unprepared for the sun, **Old Town Hat Shop** (205-C San Felipe St. NW, 505/242-4019, 10am-5pm daily) can set you right, with one of the better selections of hats in the city, for both women and men, in styles ranging from full-on cowboy to proper city slicker.

DOWNTOWN

An emporium of American Indian goods, **Skip Maisel's Indian Jewelry & Crafts** (510 Central Ave. SW, 505/242-6526, 9am-5:30pm Mon.-Sat.) feels like a relic from downtown's heyday. Whether you want a warbonnet, a turquoise-studded watch, or deerskin moccasins, it's all here in a vast, overstocked shop with kindly salespeople. Don't miss the beautiful murals above the display windows and in the foyer; they were painted in the 1930s by local Indian artists such as Awa Tsireh, whose work

The Rail Yards Market takes place in Albuquerque's old railroad workshops.

The Albuquerque Art Scene

When it comes to art, the Duke City may not have the buzz or the wealth that's concentrated farther north in Santa Fe, but it does have DIY energy, refreshing diversity, and a long history, thanks to the highly respected fine arts program at the University of New Mexico. On the first Friday of every month, the citywide **Artscrawl** (www.artscrawlabq.org) keeps galleries and shops open late in Nob Hill, Old Town, and downtown. The rest of the time, check out these arts spaces and galleries:

- **Exhibit/208** (208 Broadway SE, www.exhibit208.com, 10am-4pm Thurs.-Sat.): Work by full-time artists, some well-known in the state. Openings are usually the second Friday evening of the month.

- **516 Arts** (516 Central Ave. SW, 505/242-1445, www.516arts.org, noon-5pm Tues.-Sat.): Polished downtown space with numerous international artists.

- **Harwood Art Center** (1114 7th St., 505/242-6367, www.harwoodartcenter.org, 9am-5pm Mon.-Thurs., 9am-4pm Fri.): Classes, exhibits, and special events, all with a strong community connection.

- **Mariposa Gallery** (3500 Central Ave. SE, 505/268-6828, 11am-6pm Mon.-Sat., noon-5pm Sun.): In Nob Hill, long established (since 1974) and eclectic, with jewelry, fiber art, and other crafts.

- **Matrix Fine Art** (3812 Central Ave. SE, 505/268-8952, 10am-4pm Tues., 10am-6pm Wed.-Sun.): In east Nob Hill, showing only New Mexico artists, usually figurative.

- **Richard Levy Gallery** (514 Central Ave. SW, 505/766-9888, 11am-4pm Tues.-Sat.): Ed Ruscha or John Baldessari alongside emerging artists.

- **SCA Contemporary** (524 Haines St. NW, 505/228-3749, www.scacontemporary.com, noon-5pm Thurs.-Fri.): 6,000 square feet in a vast warehouse, devoted to conceptual and experimental work; slated to move to 816 Tijeras Ave NW in late 2015.

- **Tamarind Institute** (2500 Central Ave. SE, 505/277-3901, tamarind.unm.edu, 9am-5pm Mon.-Fri.): Long-established and nationally renowned lithography center; gallery on the second floor shows expert prints.

- **Tortuga Gallery** (901 Edith Blvd. SE, 505/369-1648, www.tortugagallery.org, hours vary): Music, poetry, and more, with a super-grassroots vibe.

hangs in the New Mexico Museum of Art in Santa Fe.

Another throwback is **The Man's Hat Shop** (511 Central Ave. NW, 505/247-9605, 9:30am-5:30pm Mon.-Fri., 9:30am-5pm Sat.), just across the street. It stocks just what it promises, from homburgs to ten-gallons.

Set in the old Santa Fe workshops south of downtown, **Rail Yards Market** (777 1st St. SW, www.railyardsmarket.org, 9am-3pm Sun. May-Oct.) is a festive gathering of arts and crafts, produce, snacks, and live music. With a lot of creative Albuquerque-pride T-shirts for sale, it makes a good place to shop for offbeat souvenirs—and it's a great chance to see inside the positively majestic old buildings where locomotives for the Santa Fe line were built from the ground up.

THE UNIVERSITY AND NOB HILL

Start your stroll on the west end of the Nob Hill district, near Girard. **Masks y Más** (3106 Central Ave. SE, 505/256-4183, 11am-6pm Mon.-Thurs., 11am-7pm Fri., noon-5pm Sun.) deals in all things bizarre, most with a south-of-the-border flavor; here's where to get the outfit for your Mexican-wrestler alter ego.

The A Store (3339 Central Ave. NE, 505/266-2222, 10am-6pm Mon.-Sat., noon-5pm Sun.) specializes in home furnishings for the Southwestern hipster, such as flower-print Mexican tablecloth fabric and handmade candles. The jewelry here, much of it by local designers, is very good too. Across the street, tasteful **Hey Jhonny** (3418 Central Ave. SE, 505/256-9244, 10am-6:30pm Mon.-Sat., 11am-6pm Sun.) stocks gorgeous sushi sets, hip handbags, and travel guides only to the coolest destinations.

Nob Hill's hip businesses expand a little farther east every year—now "upper Nob Hill" extends east of Carlisle. You can keep strolling this way for highlights such as the **Absolutely Neon** (3903 Central Ave. NE, 505/265-6366, 11am-6pm Mon.-Sat.) gallery of new and vintage signs. Farther on are a whole slew of **antiques marts**, comparable to those in Los Ranchos.

NORTH VALLEY

For excellent craft work, head to the shop at the **Indian Pueblo Cultural Center** (2401 12th St. NW, 505/843-7270, www.indianpueblo.org, 9am-5:30pm daily); not only are prices reasonable, but the staff is happy to explain the work that goes into various pieces.

The gorgeous **Los Poblanos Farm Shop** (4803 Rio Grande Blvd. NW, 505/938-2192, 9am-5pm daily) sells soaps, bath salts, and lotion scented with the organic lavender grown in the adjacent field. It also stocks an excellently curated selection of garden gear, books, kitchen supplies, and locally made snacks.

Along 4th Street between Montaño and Ortega in Los Ranchos is a strip of shops collectively called the **Antique Mile.** There are about a dozen huge stores and converted houses crammed with jewelry, vintage clothing, furniture, and architectural salvage.

ALBUQUERQUE METRO AREA

Every Saturday and Sunday, Albuquerque's **flea market** (505/315-7661, $5 parking) takes place at the fairgrounds (enter at Gate 1, on Central just west of Louisiana). It's an interesting outlet where you can pick up anything from new cowboy boots to loose nuggets of turquoise; socks and beef jerky are also well represented. Stop off at one of the myriad food stands for a snack—refreshing *aguas frescas* (fruit juices, in flavors such as watermelon and tamarind) and Indian fry bread are the most popular. It allegedly starts at 7am, but most vendors get rolling around 9am and go till a little after 4pm

Sports and Recreation

With trails running through several distinct ecosystems, Albuquerque gives outdoorsy types plenty to do. Late summer (after rains have started and fire danger is passed) and fall are the best times to head to the higher elevations on the Sandia Mountains. Once the cooler weather sets in, the scrub-covered foothills and the bare, rocky West Mesa are more hospitable. The valley along the Rio Grande, running through the center of the city, is remarkably pleasant year-round: mild in winter and cool and shady in summer. As everywhere in the desert, always pack extra layers of clothing and plenty of water before you set out, and don't go charging up Sandia Peak (10,678 feet above sea level) your first day off the plane.

★ BALLOONING

You don't have to be in town for the Balloon Fiesta to go up, up, and away. Take advantage of Albuquerque's near-flawless weather to take a hot-air balloon ride almost any morning of the year. A trip is admittedly an investment (and you have to wake up before dawn), but the sensation is unlike any other sort of ride, as it's slow and almost completely silent. One of the best established operations is **Rainbow Ryders** (505/823-1111, www.rainbowryders.com, $195 pp). Typically, you're up in the balloon for an hour or so, depending on wind conditions, and you get a champagne toast when you're back on solid ground.

BIKING

Albuquerque maintains a great network of paved trails in the city, and the mountains and foothills have challenging dirt tracks. The most visitor-friendly bike store in town is **Routes** (404 San Felipe St. NW, 505/933-5667, 8am-7pm Mon.-Fri., 7am-7pm Sat.-Sun. Mar.-Oct., 9am-6pm Mon.-Fri., 8am-6pm Sat.-Sun. Nov.-Feb., $15/hour, $35/day), which rents city cruisers, mountain bikes, and more at its handy location in Old Town; pickup and drop-off from hotels is free. It also runs fun daylong **bike tours,** and rents snowshoes in the winter.

City Cycling

Recreational cyclists need head no farther than the river, where the **Paseo del Bosque,** a 16-mile-long, completely flat biking and jogging path, runs through the Rio Grande Valley State Park. The northern starting point is at **Alameda/Rio Grande Open Space** (7am-9pm daily Apr.-Oct., 7am-7pm daily Nov.-Mar.) on Alameda Boulevard. You can also reach the trail through the **Rio Grande Nature Center** (www.rgnc.org, 8am-5pm daily, $3/car), at the end of Candelaria, and at several other major intersections along the way. For details on this and other bike trails in Albuquerque, download a map from the city's bike info page (www.cabq.gov/bike), or pick up a free copy at bike shops around town.

Corrales, in the far North Valley, is also good for an afternoon bike ride: The speed limit on the main street is low, and you can dip into smaller side streets and bike along the acequias. The excellent **Stevie's Happy Bikes** (4585 Corrales Rd., 505/897-7900, 10am-6pm Tues.-Sat.) rents comfy cruisers ($25/day) and even tandems ($35/day) and can advise on the best routes on and around the river. You could bike along the road one direction, perhaps stopping at the church and Casa San Ysidro, and then loop back on the

Routes rents bicycles and runs tours.

riverfront path, an extension of the Paseo del Bosque. In about four hours, you can make a leisurely loop down to Los Poblanos farms and open space and get back up to Corrales.

Mountain Biking

Mountain bikers can take the Sandia Peak Tramway to the **ski area,** then rent wheels to explore the 30 miles of wooded trails. Bikes aren't allowed on the tram, though, so if you have your own ride, you can drive around the east side of the mountain.

Also on the east side of the mountains, a whole network of trails lead off Highway 337 (south of I-25), through **Otero Canyon** and other routes through the juniper-studded Manzanos.

Or stay in the city and explore the foothills. Locals built a small but fun BMX terrain park at **Embudo Canyon;** park at the end of Indian School Road. For a longer cruise, head for the **foothills trails,** a web of dirt tracks all along the edge of the Northeast Heights. **Trail no. 365,** which runs for about

15 miles north-south from near the tramway down to near I-40, is the best run. You can start at either end, or go to the midpoint, at Elena Gallegos Open Space, off the north end of Tramway Boulevard at the end of Simms Park Road. Elena Gallegos in particular is very popular, so go on a weekday if you can, and always look out for hikers and other bikers. Aside from the occasional sandy or rocky patch, none of the route is technical or steep. More complex trails run off to the east; pick up a map at the entrance booth at Elena Gallegos.

Road Biking

A popular tour is up to **Sandia Peak** via the Crest Road on the east side—you can park and ride from any point, but cyclists typically start somewhere along Highway 14 north of I-40, then ride up Highway 536, which winds 13.5 miles along increasingly steep switchbacks to the crest. The **New Mexico Touring Society** (www.nmts.org) lists descriptions of other routes and organizes group rides.

HIKING

Between the West Mesa and the East Mountains, Albuquerque offers a range of day hikes. The least strenuous is the *bosque* (the wooded area along the Rio Grande), where level paths lead through groves of cottonwoods, willows, and olive trees. The **Rio**

Grande Nature Center State Park (2901 Candelaria St. NW, 505/344-7240, www.rgnc. org, 8am-5pm daily, $3/car) is the best starting point for any walk around the area.

On the east side, the easiest approach to the mountains is to take the tram to the peak or drive up the east face of the mountain via scenic byway Highway 536, aka the Crest Road, to the Sandia Crest Visitor Center ($3/car). The 1.6-mile **Crest Trail** links the two points (tram and visitors center), with possible smaller loops in between. The views are fantastic, and the river-stone Kiwanis Cabin, a Civilian Conservation Corps project on a cliff edge, makes a nice picnic destination about halfway along.

In the fall, a hike in **Fourth of July Canyon**, in the Manzano Mountains east of the city, is a wonderful place to see the leaves changing color.

For a little elevation gain, head to the Sandia foothills, ideal in the winter but a little hot in the summertime. The best access is at **Elena Gallegos Picnic Area** (7am-9pm daily Apr.-Oct., 7am-7pm daily Nov.-Mar., $1 weekdays, $2 weekends), east of Tramway Boulevard and north of Academy, at the end of Simms Park Road.

The foothills are also the starting point for the popular but tough **La Luz Trail,** a 7.5-mile ascent to the Sandia Crest Visitor Center. The trail has a 12 percent grade at certain points,

Birding on the Peak

In the dead of winter, **Sandia Peak** does not seem hospitable to life in any form, much less flocks of delicate-looking birds the size of your fist, fluffing around cheerfully in the frigid air. But that's precisely what you'll see if you visit right after a big snowfall. These are rosy finches, a contrary, cold-loving variety (sometimes called "refrigerator birds") that migrate from as far north as the Arctic tundra to the higher elevations of New Mexico, which must seem relatively tropical by comparison.

What's special about Sandia is that it draws all three species of **rosy finch,** which in turn draws dedicated birders looking to add the finches to their life lists, and it's one of the few places to see them that's close to a city and accessible by car. So if you see the finches—they're midsize brown or black birds with pink bellies, rumps, and wings—you'll probably also spy some human finch fans. But they might not have time to talk, as it's not unheard-of for the most obsessive birders—those on their "big year," out to spot as many species as possible in precisely 365 days—to fly in to Albuquerque, drive to the crest, eyeball the finches, and drive right back to the airport again.

The Crest Trail runs along the Sandia Mountains above Albuquerque.

and passes through four climate zones (pack lots of layers) as you climb 3,200 vertical feet. Near the top, you can take a spur that leads north to the Sandia Crest observation point or continue on the main trail south to the ski area and the Sandia Peak Tramway, which you can take back down the mountain. Ideally you'd have someone pick you up at the bottom, because the 2.5-mile trail from the tram back to the trailhead has no shade. (You might be tempted to take the tram up and hike down, but the steep descent can be deadly to toes and knees.) La Luz trailhead ($3/car) is at the far north end of Tramway Boulevard just before the road turns west.

SPAS

Betty's Bath & Day Spa (1835 Candelaria Rd. NW, 505/341-3456, www.bettysbath.com) is the place to get pampered, whether with a massage and a facial or with an extended dip in one of two outdoor communal hot tubs. One is co-ed and the other for women only; both have access to dry saunas and cold plunges—a bargain at just $12. Private reservations are available most evenings.

Closer to downtown, **Albuquerque Baths** (1218 Broadway NE, 505/243-3721, www.abq-baths.com) has similar facilities, though only one communal tub, which is solar-heated; the sauna is done in Finnish cedar. The reasonable rates ($15/two hours) include the use of robes and sandals, and massages are available too.

SPECTATOR SPORTS

Minor-league baseball thrives in Albuquerque, apparently all because of some clever name: The so-so Dukes petered out a while back, but a fresh franchise, under the name of the **Albuquerque Isotopes,** has been drawing crowds since 2003. It's hard to judge whether the appeal is the cool **Isotopes Park** (1601 Avenida Cesar Chavez NE, 505/924-2255, www.albuquerquebaseball.com), the whoopee-cushion theme nights, or just the name, drawn from an episode of *The Simpsons*. Regardless, a summer night under the ballpark lights is undeniably pleasant; it helps that you can usually get good seats for $15.

Albuquerqueans also go crazy for UNM Lobos **basketball,** packing the raucous University Arena, aka **"The Pit"** (Avenida Cesar Chavez at University Blvd., 505/925-5626, www.golobos.com).

Root for the home team at Isotopes Park.

SWIMMING

Beat the heat at the **Rio Grande Pool** (1410 Iron Ave. SW, 505/848-1397, noon-5pm daily June-mid-Aug., $2.25), one of Albuquerque's nicest places to take a dip; the outdoor 25-meter pool is shaded by giant cottonwoods.

WINTER SPORTS

Sandia Peak Ski Area (505/242-9052, www.sandiapeak.com, $50 full-day lift ticket) is open from mid-December through mid-March, though it often takes till about February for a good base to build up. The 10 main trails, serviced by four lifts, are not dramatic, but they are good and long. The area is open daily in the holiday season, then

Wednesday through Sunday for the rest of the winter.

Sandia Peak also has plenty of opportunities for cross-country skiing. Groomed trails start from **Capulin Springs Snow Play Area** (9:30am-3:30pm Fri.-Sun. in winter, $3/car), where there are also big hills for tubing and sledding. Look for the parking nine miles up Highway 536 to the crest. Farther up on the mountain, **10K Trail** is usually groomed for skiers, as is a service road heading south to the upper tramway terminal; the latter is wide and relatively level, good for beginners. For trail conditions, call or visit Sandia **ranger station** (505/281-3304) on Highway 337 in Tijeras.

Accommodations

Because Albuquerque isn't quite a tourist mecca, its hotel offerings have languished a bit, but the scene has improved in recent years. There are still plenty of grungy places, but the good ones are exceptional values. Whether on the low or high end, you'll pay

substantially less here than you would in Santa Fe for similar amenities. The only time you'll need to book in advance is early October, during Balloon Fiesta (when prices are usually a bit higher).

UNDER $100

Funky and affordable, the **Route 66 Hostel** (1012 Central Ave. SW, 505/247-1813, www.rt66hostel.com) is in a century-old house midway between downtown and Old Town and has been offering bargain accommodations since 1978; it's clean despite years of budget travelers traipsing through. Upstairs, along creaky wood hallways, are private rooms ($25-35) with various configurations. Downstairs and in the cool basement area are single-sex dorms ($20 pp). Guests have run of the kitchen, and there's a laundry and room to lounge. The most useful city bus lines run right out front. There have been complaints of staff not being on hand for early or late check-ins—be sure to call and confirm before you arrive.

If you're on a budget but have your own car, you can also stay on the east side of the Sandias, about a half-hour drive from the city. The **Cedar Crest Inn** (12231 Hwy. 14, 505/281-4117) is peaceful, with an orchard out back, and very inexpensive lodging, including a dorm option ($20 pp). The dorm area is well kept, though it's screened from the big, shared kitchen only by a curtain. Upstairs are three private rooms ($50-80). Just up the highway on the west side, the **Turquoise Trail Campground** (22 Calvary Rd., 505/281-2005, www.turquoisetrailcampground.com) has tree-shaded spots for tents ($17.50) as well as two small cabins ($36; no water) and one large one with a bathroom and kitchenette ($58), along with showers and laundry facilities.

Central Avenue is strewn with motels, many built in Route 66's heyday. Almost all of them are unsavory, except for ★ **Monterey Non-Smokers Motel** (2402 Central Ave. SW, 505/243-3554, www.nonsmokersmotel.com, $58 s, $70 d), which is as practical as its name implies. The place doesn't really capitalize on 1950s kitsch—it just offers meticulously clean, good-value rooms with no extra frills or flair. One large family suite has two beds and a foldout sofa. The outdoor pool is a treat, the laundry facilities are a bonus, and the location near Old Town is very convenient.

A fully renovated motel on the west side, just over the river from Old Town, ★ **Sandia Peak Inn** (4614 Central Ave. SW, 505/831-5036, www.sandiapeakinnmotel.com, $60 s, $70 d) is named not for its proximity to the mountain, but its view of it. It's certainly the best value in this category, offering large, spotless rooms, all with bathtubs, fridges, microwaves, and huge TVs. Breakfast is included in the rate, and the proprietors are positively sunny. There's a small indoor pool and free wireless Internet throughout.

The Hotel Blue (717 Central Ave. NW, 877/878-4868, www.thehotelblue.com, $69 s, $79 d) offers great value downtown. The rooms in this '60s block are a slightly odd mix of cheesy motel decor (gold quilted bedspreads) and bachelor-pad flair (a gas "fireplace"), and the windows don't open. But the Tempur-Pedic beds are undeniably comfortable, and the low rates include breakfast, parking, and a shuttle to the airport. There's also a decent-size outdoor pool, open in summers, and the downtown farmers market is in the park right out front. Request a room on the northeast side for a mountain view.

On the north side of town, **Nativo Lodge** (6000 Pan American Fwy. NE, 505/798-4300, www.nativolodge.com, $74 d) is in a less convenient location (though it is good for the Balloon Fiesta, an early start to Santa Fe, or a cheap off-airport rental car pickup, as a Hertz office is in walking distance). But the price is great for this level of comfort and style, with plush pillow-top beds and some rooms designed by local American Indian artists. Definitely request a room in the back, so you're not overlooking I-25.

$100-150

On a narrow road in the rural-feeling Los Ranchos district, **Casita Chamisa** (850 Chamisal Rd. NW, 505/897-4644, www.casitachamisa.com, $105 d) is very informal, and even a little bit worn, but really feels like staying at the home of a friend (who happens to have a swimming pool and an orchard). The rambling 150-year-old adobe compound is the sort of place that could exist only in New Mexico: It sits on an old acequia, amid the remnants of a Pueblo community established seven centuries ago. The site was partially excavated by the owner's late wife, an archaeologist.

Another decent option in Los Ranchos, **Sarabande B&B** (5637 Rio Grande Blvd. NW, 505/933-1760, www.sarabandebnb.com, $109 s) has six rooms in three configurations. They can be a bit jammed with Southwestern tchotchkes, but the owners here are very thoughtful and the breakfasts are good. A small lap pool takes up the backyard.

The heart of **Cinnamon Morning** (2700 Rio Grande Blvd. NW, 505/345-3541, www. cinnamonmorning.com, $129 s), in the North Valley about a mile north of Old Town, is its lavish outdoor kitchen, with a huge round dining table and a fireplace to encourage lounging on nippier nights. Rooms are simply furnished, with minimalist Southwestern detail—choose from three smaller rooms in the main house, each with a private bath, or, across the garden, a two-bedroom guesthouse and a casita with a private patio and a kitchenette.

The exceptionally tasteful ★ **Downtown Historic Bed & Breakfasts of Albuquerque** (207 High St. NE, 505/842-0223, www.albuquerquebedandbreakfasts. com, $139 s) occupies two neighboring old houses on the east side of downtown, walking distance to good restaurants on Central in the EDo (East Downtown) stretch. Heritage House has more of a Victorian feel, while Spy House has a sparer, 1940s look—but both are nicely clutter-free. Two outbuildings are more private suites.

Locally owned **Hotel Albuquerque at Old Town** (800 Rio Grande Blvd. NW, 505/843-6300, www.hotelabq.com, $149 d) is a good backup in this category. Sporting a chic Spanish colonial style, the lobby is lovely and the brick-red-and-beige rooms are relatively spacious. There's a big swimming pool too. Opt for the north side (generally, even-numbered rooms) for a view of the mountains.

$150-200

A beautiful relic of early 20th-century travel, ★ **Hotel Andaluz** (125 2nd St. NW, 505/242-9090, www.hotelandaluz.com, $159 d) was first opened in 1939 by New Mexico-raised hotelier Conrad Hilton. It received a massive renovation in 2009, keeping all the old wood and murals but updating the core to be fully environmentally friendly, from solar hot-water heaters to a composting program. The neutral-palette rooms are soothing and well designed, with a little Moorish flair in the curvy door outlines. The place is worth a visit for the lobby alone; check out the exhibits from local museums on the second-floor mezzanine.

Set in the original AT&SF railroad hospital and sporting a storied past, the stylishly renovated **Parq Central** (806 Central Ave. SE, 505/242-0040, www.hotelparqcentral. com, $159 d), opened in late 2010. It makes a nice alternative to the Andaluz if you prefer your history in paler shades. The rooms are a bit smaller but feel light and airy thanks to big windows and gray and white furnishings, with retro chrome fixtures and honeycomb tiles in the bath. The hospital vibe is largely eradicated, though whimsical vitrines in the halls conjure old-time medical treatments, and the rooftop bar sports a gurney. Perks include free parking, decent continental breakfast, and airport shuttle.

At Albuquerque's nicest place to stay, you don't actually feel like you're anywhere near the city. ★ **Los Poblanos Historic Inn** (4803 Rio Grande Blvd. NW, 505/344-9297, www.lospoblanos.com, $180 d) sits on 25 acres, the largest remaining plot of land in the city, and the rooms are tucked in various corners of a sprawling rancho built in the 1930s by John Gaw Meem and beautifully maintained and preserved—even the huge old kitchen ranges are still in place, as are murals by Taos artist Gustave Baumann and frescoes by Peter Hurd. In the main house, the guest rooms are set around a central patio and retain their old wood floors and heavy viga ceilings. Newer, larger rooms have been added

Los Poblanos Historic Inn was built by noted architect John Gaw Meem.

and fit in flawlessly—Meem rooms have a very light Southwest touch, while the Farm suites have a whitewashed rustic aesthetic, accented by prints and fabrics by modernist designer Alexander Girard, of the folk-art museum in Santa Fe. (A new block of rooms was being added as this book was going to press.) There's also a saltwater pool and a gym, as well as extensive gardens and organic lavender. Included breakfast is exceptional (you get eggs from the farm), as is dinner at the restaurant, La Merienda.

North of the city, on Santa Ana Pueblo land, **Hyatt Regency Tamaya** (1300 Tuyuna Tr., Santa Ana Pueblo, 505/867-1234, www. hyattregencytamaya.com, $199 d) is a pretty resort. Rooms aren't always maintained as well as they could be, but even the standard ones are quite large, with either terraces or balconies. Three swimming pools and a full spa offer relaxation; the more active can play golf or tennis, take an archery class, or attend an evening storytelling program with a pueblo member.

Food

Albuquerque has a few dress-up establishments, but the real spirit of the city's cuisine is in its lower-rent spots where dedicated owners follow their individual visions. A lot of the most traditional New Mexican places are open only for breakfast and lunch, so plan accordingly. Prices given are those of the average entrée.

OLD TOWN

Aside from the couple recommended here, the restaurants in the blocks immediately adjacent to the Old Town plaza are expensive and only so-so; better to walk another block or two for real New Mexican flavor, or drive a short way west on Central.

Cafés

Inside the Albuquerque Museum, **Slate Street Café** (2000 Mountain Rd. NW, 505/243-2220, 10am-2:30pm Tues.-Fri. and Sun., 10am-4pm Sat., $8) is great for coffee and cupcakes, as well as more substantial breakfast and lunch, like a chipotle-spiked meat-loaf sandwich. (Its larger, original location is at 515 Slate Avenue NW.)

A 10-minute walk from Old Town, **Golden Crown Panaderia** (1103 Mountain Rd. NW, 505/243-2424, 7am-8pm Tues.-Sat., 10am-8pm Sun., $4-9) is a real neighborhood hangout that's so much more than a bakery. Famous for its green-chile bread and *bizcochitos* (the anise-laced state cookie), it also does pizza with blue-corn or green-chile crust, to take away or to eat at the picnic tables out back. And you'll want a side salad just to watch them assemble it straight from the hydroponic garden that consumes a lot of the space behind the counter. Wash it down with a coffee milk shake.

American

Built on the bones of an old fast-food joint, **Central Grill** (2056 Central Ave. SW, 505/554-1424, 6:30am-4pm Mon.-Thurs., 6:30am-8pm Fri., 8am-8pm Sat., $7) still does quick food, but with a fresher, more homemade feel. Like a good diner should, it serves breakfast all day, and real maple syrup is an option. Its daily special plate is usually a fantastic deal, with a main like barbecue chicken plus sides and a drink for $9 or so.

Fresh and Local

Founded in Santa Fe, **Vinaigrette** (1828 Central Ave. SW, 505/842-5507, 11am-9pm daily, $13) is a posh-sounding "salad bistro" that is more substantial than it sounds—and it's a welcome spot of healthy eating around Old Town.

Italian

It's not necessarily a destination from elsewhere in the city, but **Old Town Pizza Parlor** (108 Rio Grande Blvd. NW, 505/999-1949, 11am-9pm Mon.-Sat., 11am-8pm Sun., $9) is an unpretentious, kid-friendly place to eat in the relative wasteland of Old Town, with generously topped pizzas, ultra-creamy pastas, and creative "white nachos." The back patio is a bonus.

Mexican

In a shady Old Town courtyard, **Backstreet Grill** (1919 Old Town Rd. NW, 505/842-5434, 11am-9pm Sun.-Thurs., 11am-10pm Fri.-Sat., $12) is a great place to rest your tourist feet and enjoy a New Mexican craft beer, and maybe a bowl of guacamole. For a full meal, though, you're better off elsewhere.

The big-box facade of **Pro's Ranch Market** (4201 Central Ave. NW, 505/831-8739, 7am-11pm daily, $5) hardly hints at the wonders inside. If you haven't been in one of these (it's an Arizona-based chain), step inside for a bonus travel experience, straight to Mexico. The shelves are lined with Bimbo bread and other south-of-the-border essentials, but the real action is in the food court, past the cash registers and to the left, where there's a dazzling array of quesadillas, *sincronizadas*, tamales, and more, with a separate station for fresh fruit juices.

New Mexican

Don't waste a meal on restaurants at the Old Town plaza. Instead, walk a couple of blocks to ★ **Duran Central Pharmacy** (1815 Central Ave. NW, 505/247-4141, 9am-6:30pm Mon.-Fri., 9am-2pm Sat., $9), an old-fashioned lunch counter hidden behind the magazine rack in this big fluorescent-lit drugstore. Regulars pack this place at lunch for all the New Mexican staples: huevos rancheros, green-chile stew, and big enchilada plates. Cash only.

Steak

Don't be put off by the brown, windowless cinderblock facade, with a package-liquor store in the front. **Monte Carlo Steakhouse**

(3916 Central Ave. SW, 505/831-2444, 11am-10pm Mon.-Thurs, 11am-11pm Fri.-Sat., $18) is a fantastic time machine, lined with vintage Naugahyde booths and serving good, hearty food: the prime-rib special Thursday through Saturday, a softball-size green-chile cheeseburger, or marinated pork kebab, all with delicious hand-cut fries. Greek ownership means you get a tangy feta dressing on your salad and baklava for dessert. And even though there's a full bar, you're still welcome to buy wine from the package store up front and have it with your dinner, for a nominal markup.

DOWNTOWN

With so many bars in this area, there's little room left for food, beyond a couple of solid cafés.

Cafés

A branch of **Flying Star** (723 Silver Ave. SW, 505/244-8099, 7am-10pm daily, $10) occupies a hiply restored 1950 John Gaw Meem bank building.

Past the railroad tracks in EDo (East Downtown), **The Grove** (600 Central Ave. SE, 505/248-9800, 7am-4pm Tues.-Sat., 8am-3pm Sun., $12) complements its local-organic menu with big front windows facing Central and a screened-in patio. The chalkboard menu features creative salads (spinach, orange slices, and dates is one combo) as well as sandwiches and cupcakes; breakfast, with farm-fresh eggs and homemade English muffins, is served all day. It's a notch above Flying Star in price, but you're paying for the especially high-quality ingredients.

French

Not that you came to New Mexico to eat *escargots provençal*, but **Le Café Miche** (228 Gold Ave. SW, 505/314-1111, 11am-5pm Mon.-Tues., 11am-9pm Wed.-Sat., $16) is a cozy institution that's been serving unpretentious French food for decades. Its "three-course Thursday" is a steal at $35, and any night of the week, you're likely to be greeted with a glass of cold

vermouth and a nibble of pâté—a fine antidote to green-chile burnout.

Fresh and Local

There are a number of **farmers markets** throughout the city; one of the largest is downtown at Robinson Park on Central Avenue at 8th Street (7am-noon Sat. May-Aug., 8am-1pm Sept.-Nov.). For other markets around the city, visit www.farmersmarketsnm.org.

Italian

A popular hangout for urban pioneers in the EDo neighborhood, ★ **Farina Pizzeria** (510 Central Ave. SE, 505/243-0130, 11am-9pm Mon., 11am-10pm Tues.-Fri., noon-10pm Sat., 5pm-9pm Sun., $14) has exposed brick walls and a casual vibe. The pies come out of the wood-fired oven suitably crisp-chewy and topped with seasonal veggies. Make sure you get a cup of the gorgonzola-crème fraîche-chive dip for your crusts—it's the upscale version of the ranch dressing that's more commonly offered. There's usually a pasta special as well.

If you're on the go, you can grab a slice at **JC's New York Pizza Department** (215 Central Ave. NW, 505/766-6973, 11am-10pm Sun.-Wed, 11am-midnight Thurs., 11am-2:30am Fri.-Sat., $6), which specializes in thin-crust pies named after the five boroughs (Da Bronx: pepperoni and mozzarella).

New Mexican

Even though it's in the middle of Albuquerque's main business district, ★ **Cecilia's Café** (230 6th St. SW, 505/243-7070, 7am-2pm daily, $8) feels more like a living room than a restaurant. Maybe it's the woodstove in the corner—as well as the personal attention from Cecilia and her daughters and the food that's clearly made with care. The rich, dark red chile really shines here.

Spanish

Chef James Campbell Caruso made his name in Santa Fe as a maestro of Spanish cuisine. His Albuquerque outpost, **Más Tapas y Vino**

Cecilia's is a taste of home in downtown Albuquerque.

(125 2nd St. NW, 505/923-9080, 7am-2pm and 5:30pm-9:30pm Sun.-Thurs., 7am-2pm and 5pm-10pm Fri.-Sat., $12 tapas, $28 mains), in the Hotel Andaluz, shows off many of his best dishes, but it's not quite as chummy as his other restaurants. But if you're not also visiting Santa Fe and want a creative bite of Iberian goodness (grilled artichokes, or *jamón* with poached pears), consider this a possible special-occasion meal. It also has happy hour from 4pm to 6pm daily.

THE UNIVERSITY AND NOB HILL

Thanks to the large student population, this area has some great and varied spots to grab a cheap bite, but Nob Hill has some upscale options too.

Cafés

Look for the UFO: **Satellite Coffee** (3513 Central Ave. NE, 505/256-0345, 6am-8pm daily, $3) is Albuquerque's answer to Starbucks: organic brew, assorted pastries,

comfy chairs. This is the original, and most convenient for visitors; there are several more around town.

The same team owns the more full-service **Flying Star Café** (3416 Central Ave. SE, 505/255-6633, 6:30am-10:30pm Mon.-Thurs., 6:30am-midnight Fri.-Sat., $11), across the street. You'll likely be mesmerized by the pastry case, packed with triple-ginger cookies, lemon-blueberry cheesecake, and fat éclairs. But try to look up to appreciate the range on the menu boards: Asian noodles, hot and cold sandwiches, mac-and-cheese, and enchiladas. The food isn't always quite as great as it looks, but with speedy service and locations all over town, it's a handy place to zip in or to lounge around (wireless Internet access is free).

Just a few blocks from the university, **Annapurna's World Vegetarian Café** (2201 Silver Ave. SE, 505/262-2424, 7am-9pm Mon.-Fri., 8am-9pm Sat., 10am-8pm Sun., $9) is a vegetarian's delight, serving a menu that's compatible with Ayurvedic dietary recommendations, with giant masala dosas (rice-flour crepes) as well as less strictly Indian dishes such as cardamom pancakes with maple syrup.

Pick up goods for a picnic at **La Montañita Co-op** (3500 Central Ave. SE, 505/265-4631, 7am-10pm Mon.-Sat., 8am-10pm Sun.), where quinoa salads and stuffed grape leaves are all the rage; look in the dairy section for "sampler" pieces of locally made cheese. There's a snacks-only operation in the **UNM Bookstore** (2301 Central Ave. NE, 505/277-9586, 7am-6pm Mon.-Fri., 10am-4pm Sat.), across from the Frontier

The outpost of Tia Betty Blue's, **Tia B's La Waffleria** (3710 Campus Blvd. NE, 505/492-2007, 7am-2pm Mon.-Fri., 8am-2pm Sat.-Sun., $7) still had some logistical kinks to work out at press time, but should be a good addition to the area. Really, what's not to love about a place built on sweet and savory waffles, plus New Mexican chile?

Asian

The food at **Street Food Asia** (3422 Central

Ave. SE, 505/260-0088, 11am-10pm Sun.-Thurs., 11am-11pm Fri.-Sat., $13) may not be as mind-blowing as it is in Asia, but there's something about its interior, with various cooking stations and lots of plastic, that does conjure a Bangkok mall food court. You can order noodles and other staples prepared in Thai, Vietnamese, Malaysian, and other styles. Two pluses: the authentic shaved-ice-and-bean dessert you often get for free and its late hours.

Latin American

Guava Tree Café (118 Richmond Dr. SE, 505/990-2599, 11am-4pm Mon.-Thurs., 11am-9pm Fri.-Sat., 11am-3pm Sun., $8) is a cheerful place serving succulent cubano sandwiches, as well as pan-Central-American treats like arepas, plus tropical fruit juices. It's very vegetarian-friendly, and the daily set lunch ($12.75) is good for bigger appetites.

New Mexican

You haven't been to Albuquerque unless you've been to ★ **The Frontier** (2400 Central Ave. SE, 505/266-0550, 5am-1am daily, $6), across from UNM. Everyone in the city passes through its doors at some point in their lives, so all you have to do is pick a seat in one of the five Western-themed rooms (Hmm, under the big portrait of John Wayne? Or maybe one of the smaller ones?) and watch the characters file in. You'll want some food, of course: a green-chile-smothered breakfast burrito filled with crispy hash browns, or a grilled hamburger, or one of the signature cinnamon rolls, a deadly amalgam of flour, sugar, and some addictive drug that compels you to eat them despite the hydrogenated goo they're swimming in. If you feel a little unhealthy, you can always get some fresh orange juice and restore your balance by vegging out in front of the mesmerizing tortilla machine.

Near the university, **El Patio** (142 Harvard Dr. SE, 505/268-4245, 11am-9pm Sun.-Thurs., 11am-9:30pm Fri.-Sat., $9) is the kind of old-reliable place that ex-locals get misty-eyed about after they've moved away. The green-chile-and-chicken enchiladas are high on many citywide favorite lists. It doesn't hurt that the setting, in an old bungalow with a shady outdoor space, feels like an extension of someone's home kitchen. The menu is more vegetarian-friendly than most New Mexican joints.

NORTH VALLEY

Cafés

There are two branches of **Flying Star** up this way: one in Los Ranchos (4026 Rio Grande Blvd. NW, 505/344-6714, 6:30am-10pm Mon.-Sat., 7am-9:30pm Sun., $11) and another in Corrales (10700 Corrales Rd., 505/938-4717, 505/938-4717, 6:30am-10pm Sun.-Thurs., 6:30am-11pm Fri.-Sat., $11). **La Montañita Co-op** (2400 Rio Grande Blvd. NW, 505/242-8800, 7am-10pm daily) also has a branch here, good for picnic goodies.

Fresh and Local

On a barren stretch of North 4th Street, where neighboring businesses are feed stores and car washes, ★ **Sophia's Place** (6313 4th St. NW, 505/345-3935, 7am-9pm Mon.-Fri., 7am-9pm Sat., 9am-2pm Sun., $9) is the sort of bohemian café that serves farm-fresh eggs but doesn't brag about it. Get those eggs on a breakfast sandwich, which you're really ordering for the side of highly addictive red-chile-dusted home fries. Lunch and dinner bring goodies like duck enchiladas with tomatillo sauce.

The restaurant at Los Poblanos Historic Inn, ★ **La Merienda** (4803 Rio Grande Blvd. NW, 505/344-9297, 6pm-9pm Wed.-Sat., $26), serves flawless food, a bit Mediterranean in style, but undeniably New Mexican in ingredients like heirloom beans. The short menu changes each night, based on produce. Book well ahead—hotel guests get priority, so tables fill up fast.

If you can't get a table at La Merienda, the next best option is **Farm & Table** (8917 4th St. NW, 505/503-7124, 5pm-9pm Wed.-Thurs., 5pm-10pm Fri., 9am-2pm and 5pm-10pm Sat., 9am-2pm Sun., $30), which has a similar sensibility. Some diners have reported uneven meals and staff, but the setting is bucolic. Plus, the place is kid-friendly, with a big sandbox and plenty of toys within sight of some outdoor tables.

Thanks to its proximity to many fields, the Los Ranchos **farmers market** (6718 Rio Grande Blvd. NW, 7am-noon Sat. May-Aug., 8am-noon Sat. Sept.-Nov., 10am noon second Sat. of the month Dec.-Apr.) is one of the better ones in the city, and one of the few that operates year-round.

Indian

Vegetarians can seek out a branch of **Annapurna's** (5939 4th St. NW, 505/254-2424, 8am-8pm Mon.-Sat., 10am-8pm Sun., $9).

New Mexican

For New Mexican food with a heavier American Indian influence, hit the **Pueblo Harvest Café** (2401 12th St. NW, 505/724-3510, 8am-8:30pm Mon.-Thurs., 8am-9pm Fri.-Sat., 8am-4pm Sun., $10), at the Indian Pueblo Cultural Center. The menu has standard burgers and fries, but specialties such as mutton stew with a side of *horno* bread and a green-chile-and-lamb sandwich are rich and earthy and hard to find elsewhere. Breakfast is also good, with blue-corn mush topped with *carne adovada,* and apple-raisin "Indian toast." The "Rez Breakfast," with Spam on the side, may be a treat for some. There's live music Friday and Saturday evenings, as well as Sunday around noon.

Experts agree: ★ **Mary & Tito's Café** (2711 4th St. NW, 505/344-6266, 9am-6pm Mon.-Thurs., 9am-8pm Fri.-Sat., $7) is the place to go for *carne adovada,* the dish of tender pork braised in red chile, particularly good in what they call a Mexican turnover (a stuffed sopaipilla). The meat is flavorful enough to stand alone, but the fruity, bright red-chile sauce, flecked with seeds, is so good you'll want to put it on everything. This place is such a local icon, seemingly untouched since the 1980s (ah, lovely dusty rose vinyl!), it won a James Beard America's Classics award. Sadly, both Mary and Tito have passed on now, leaving the place ripe for a decline in standards; so far, though, it seems to be holding strong.

Out in Corrales, **Perea's Restaurant & Tijuana Bar** (4590 Corrales Rd., 505/898-2442, 11am-2pm Mon.-Sat., $7) is open only for lunch, but it's worth scheduling around if you know you'll be out this way. Everything's home-cooked, from Frito pie to *carne adovada.*

Join the clean plate club at Perea's Restaurant & Tijuana Bar.

A branch of a long-established family spot in Cuba, northwest of Albuquerque, **El Bruno's** (8806 4th St. NW, Cuba, 505/897-0444, 11am-9pm Mon.-Wed., 11am-10pm Thurs.-Sat., 10am-9pm Sun., $12) gets its share of a tradition that's been going on since the mid-1970s. Every year, a team of women sits out behind the Cuba restaurant, for weeks, and roasts and peels literally tons of chiles for freezing. Everything's good, but the dreamiest is Hazel's Green Chile, fresh in the fall—a big bowl of green, with nothing more than a few flecks of pork.

ALBUQUERQUE METRO AREA

Great places to eat are scattered all over the city, often in unlikely looking strip malls. These places are worth making a trip for, or will provide a pick-me-up when you're far afield.

Asian

Can't decide what kind of food you're craving? Cruise the aisles of **Talin Market World Food Fare** (88 Louisiana Blvd. SE, 505/268-0206, 8:30am-8pm Mon.-Sat., 9am-7pm Sun.), a megamarket near the fairgrounds that's stocked with items from Bombay to the United Kingdom. Its Asian stock is the largest, though, and you can get a variety of hot Laotian, Korean, and Filipino lunch items from the small cafeteria section in one corner and sweets such as pumpkin custard from the bakery. There's also a bubble-tea joint next door, and the parking lot draws a few food trucks.

Just across the parking lot from Talin is the excellent Vietnamese cafe **Banh Mi Coda** (230-C Louisiana Blvd. SE, 505/232-0085, 9am-7pm Mon.-Sat., $5), which specializes in the baguette sandwiches (try the peppery meatball) and also serves chewy-sweet coconut waffles and other treats.

New Mexican

Cruise down by the rail yards south of downtown to find **El Modelo** (1715 2nd St. SW, 505/242-1843, 7am-7pm daily, $7), a local go-to for a hangover-curing *chicharrón* burrito, chile-smothered spare ribs, or tamales for the whole family—you can order a single tamale or a whole platter of food. Because it's really a front for a tortilla factory, the flour tortillas are also particularly tender. If the weather's nice, grab a seat at a picnic table outside and watch the freight trains go by.

Just two blocks from the National Hispanic Cultural Center, popular **Barelas Coffee House** (1502 4th St. SW, 505/843-7577, 7:30am-3pm Mon.-Fri., 7:30am-2:30pm Sat., $7) is potentially confusing to the first-timer: The attraction is not coffee, but chile—especially the red, which infuses hearty, timeless New Mexican standards like posole, *chicharrones*, and *menudo*. The restaurant occupies several storefronts, and even then there's often a line out the door at lunch. But it's worth the wait—this is timeless food.

A New Mexican diner with a little rockabilly flair, **Tia Betty Blue's** (1248 San Mateo Blvd. SE, 505/268-1955, 7am-2pm Mon.-Fri., 8am-2pm Sat.-Sun., $7) is a welcome addition in a previously unhip part of town. (Actually, "unhip" is generous—back in the day, this strip south of Central was known as the War Zone; it's fine now, and very diverse.) It's also a nice return to authentically hot chile. There are great bluecorn waffles, and excellent *carne adovada*, plus veg and gluten-free options, and about a million kinds of soda.

Fine Dining

File under Best High-End Meal in a Strip Mall. The work of a long-respected (and James Beard-honored) chef, ★ **Jennifer James 101** (4615 Menaul Blvd. NE, 505/884-3860, www.jenniferjames101.com, 5pm-9pm Tues.-Sat., $26) is a serene and confident place serving a mix of seasonal ingredients that sound plain on paper but deliver intense flavor: lamb with rhubarb chutney, for instance, or a pasta with fiddlehead ferns and mushrooms. On Thursdays, there's a three-course $25 meal. Check the website for other special events. All diners must reserve ahead.

Outside Albuquerque

Within 45 minutes of the city are some great natural attractions. To the west, on land that looks like a movie backdrop, lies Acoma, an ancient pueblo that seems to have grown out of the tall mesa on which it's built. Southeast of town, a winding road through the mountains brings you past the ruined Salinas Pueblo Missions, an intriguing bit of early Conquest history. To the east is the start of one of three routes to Santa Fe, the Turquoise Trail, which leads through some vestiges of New Mexico's mining past. An equally scenic route north is the more circuitous Jemez Mountain Trail, past red rocks and hot springs. Or you can zip directly up the interstate, where you'll pass the windswept region known as Tent Rocks.

WEST TO ACOMA

I-40 climbs the West Mesa out of Albuquerque and heads dead straight across a plateau lined with flat mesas—archetypal Southwest scenery. Ancient Acoma Pueblo is built on top of one of these mesas, an amazing place to visit and meet the people whose ancestors have lived here for nearly a thousand years.

Laguna Pueblo

About 18 miles west of Albuquerque, I-40 crosses the border onto the 45 square miles of **Laguna Pueblo** (505/552-6654, www.lagunapueblo.org), on which 7,000 Keresan-speaking Ka-waikah (Lake People) live in six villages. From the highway, the only impression you get of Laguna is its Dancing Eagle Casino, but if you have time, get off at exit 114 to visit the **San José Mission Church.** Established in 1699 when the Laguna people requested a priest (unlike any other pueblo), it stands out for its stark white stucco coating, but this is a relatively recent addition, following a 19th-century renovation. It was mudded and whitewashed every year until the 1950s, when the boom in uranium mining in the area left no time for this maintenance; it's now sealed with stucco.

Inside, between a packed-earth floor and a finely wrought wood ceiling, the late-18th-century altar screen commands the room. It's the work of the so-called Laguna Santero, an unidentified painter who made the innovation of placing icons inside a crowded field of

view over the valley around Acoma Pueblo

Outside Albuquerque

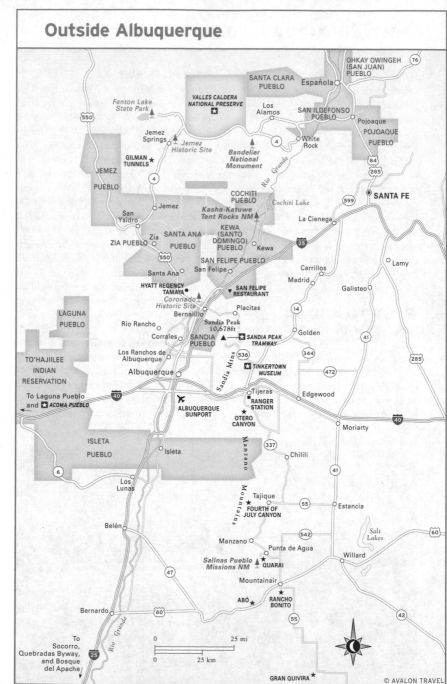

OHKAY OWINGEH (SAN JUAN) PUEBLO
76

SANTA CLARA PUEBLO
Española

VALLES CALDERA NATIONAL PRESERVE
Los Alamos
SAN ILDEFONSO PUEBLO
Pojoaque
POJOAQUE PUEBLO

Fenton Lake State Park
550
Jemez Springs
Jemez Historic Site
White Rock
4
84
285

GILMAN TUNNELS
Bandelier National Monument
Rio Grande

JEMEZ PUEBLO
4
599
SANTA FE

COCHITI PUEBLO
Cochiti Lake

Jemez
Kasha-Katuwe Tent Rocks NM
La Cienega

San Ysidro
Zia
SANTA ANA PUEBLO
KEWA (SANTO DOMINGO) PUEBLO
Kewa
25
Lamy

ZIA PUEBLO
550
SAN FELIPE PUEBLO
Cerrillos
Madrid
Galisteo

Santa Ana
San Felipe

HYATT REGENCY TAMAYA
Coronado Historic Site
SAN FELIPE RESTAURANT
Placitas
14

LAGUNA PUEBLO
Rio Rancho
Bernalillo
Sandia Peak 10,678ft
Golden
41

Corrales
SANDIA PUEBLO
536
SANDIA PEAK TRAMWAY
344
285

Los Ranchos de Albuquerque
TINKERTOWN MUSEUM
472

TO'HAJIILEE INDIAN RESERVATION
Albuquerque
Sandia Mtns

To Laguna Pueblo and ACOMA PUEBLO
40
Tijeras
RANGER STATION
Edgewood
40

ALBUQUERQUE SUNPORT
OTERO CANYON
Moriarty

ISLETA PUEBLO
Isleta
337
Chililí
41

6
Los Lunas
Manzano Mountains

Belén
Tajique
FOURTH OF JULY CANYON
55
Estancia

Salt Lakes
60

Manzano
542
Punta de Agua
Willard

47
Salinas Pueblo Missions NM
QUARAI

Mountainair

ABÓ
RANCHO BONITO

Bernardo
60
42

To Socorro, Quebradas Byway, and Bosque del Apache
25
Rio Grande

0   25 mi
0   25 km

GRAN QUIVIRA

© AVALON TRAVEL

decorative borders and carved and painted columns, creating a work of explosively colorful folk art that was copied elsewhere in the region in subsequent decades.

If you're lucky, **Alfred Pino,** a local artist and informal guide, will be hanging around the church and offer you a personal tour and explanation of the symbols on the altar and the painted elk hides on the walls, in exchange for a tip and donation to the church. The doors are usually open 9am to 3pm weekdays (after a 7am morning Mass), but the church can be open later and on weekends if Alfred's around.

Each of the six villages of Laguna celebrates its own feast day, and then the whole pueblo turns out at the church September 17-19 for the Feast of San José, one of the bigger pueblo events in the Albuquerque area.

★ ACOMA PUEBLO

On the road to Acoma, you may feel as though you've crossed through a pass into a Southwestern Shangri-la, for none of this great basin is visible from the highway. Down in the valley, the route runs directly toward a flat-topped rock that juts up like a tooth.

Atop the rock is the original **Acoma Pueblo,** the village known as **Sky City.** The community covers about 70 acres and is built largely of pale, sun-bleached adobe, as it has been since at least 1100. Only a hundred or so people live on the mesa top year-round, given the hardships of no running water or electricity. But many families maintain homes here, and the place is thronged on September 2, when the pueblo members gather for the **Feast of San Esteban.** The rest of the 2,800 Acoma (People of the White Rock, in their native Keresan) live on the valley floor, which is used primarily as ranchland.

Visiting Sky City

All visitors must stop at the **Sky City Cultural Center and Haak'u Museum** (Indian Rte. 23, 800/747-0181, www.aco-maskycity.org, 9am-5pm daily Mar.-mid-Nov., 9am-5pm Fri.-Sun. mid-Nov.-Feb.) on the main road, which houses a café and shop stocked with local crafts, along with beautiful rotating exhibits on Acoma art and tradition. From here, you must join a guided tour ($23), which transports groups by bus to the village. The road to the top is the one concession to modernity; previously, all goods had to be hauled up the near-vertical cliff faces. The tour lasts about an hour and a half, after which visitors may return by bus or climb down one of the old trails, using hand- and footholds dug into the rock centuries ago. In summer, tours start at 9:30am and depart every 45 minutes or so, with the last one going at 3:30pm. In the winter, the first tour begins at 10:15am, and they go about hourly until 3pm. Definitely call ahead to check that the tours are running and verify times, as the pueblo closes to visitors periodically.

The centerpiece of the village is the **Church of San Esteban del Rey,** one of the most iconic of the Spanish missions in New Mexico. Built between 1629 and 1640, the graceful, simple structure has been inspiring New Mexican architects ever since. Its interior is, like many New Mexican pueblo churches, spare and simple, the white walls painted with rainbows and corn.

As much as it represents the pinnacle of Hispano-Indian architecture in the 17th century, the church is also a symbol of the brutality of Spanish colonialism, as it rose in the typical way: forced labor. The men of Acoma felled and carried the tree trunks for the ceiling beams from the forest on Mount Taylor, more than 25 miles across the valley, and up the cliff face to the village.

Acoma is well known for its pottery, easily distinguished by the fine black lines that sweep around the curves of the creamy-white vessel. On the best works, the lines are so fine and densely painted, they shimmer almost like a moiré. The clay particular to this area can be worked so thin that the finest pots will hum or ring when tapped. Throughout the village, you have opportunities to buy pieces. Given the constraints of the tour, this can feel slightly pressured, but in many cases, you have the privilege of buying work directly from the artisan who created it.

Accommodations and Food

The cultural center contains the **Y'aak'a Café** (9am-4pm daily Mar.-mid-Nov., Fri.-Sun. only mid-Nov.-Feb., $8), which serves earthy local dishes like lamb stew, tamales, and corn roasted in a traditional *horno* oven—as well as Starbucks coffee. Acoma Pueblo operates the small-scale **Sky City Casino & Hotel** (888/759-2489, www.skycity.com, $99 d), also at exit 102. Its rooms are perfectly clean and functional, and there's a little pool.

Getting There

Take exit 102 off I-40 (about 55 miles west of downtown Albuquerque), and follow signs south to Sky City—this drive, along Indian Service Route 38, is the best signposted and offers the most dramatic views of the valley around Acoma. Allow about 1.5 hours for the drive out, and an additional 2 hours for the tour. Leaving Acoma, to avoid backtracking, you can take Indian Service Route 23, from behind the cultural center, northeast back to I-40.

SALINAS PUEBLO MISSIONS NATIONAL MONUMENT

The **Salinas Pueblo Missions** are a trio of ruined pueblos (Quarai, Gran Quivira, and Abó) southeast of Albuquerque, on the plains on the far side of the Manzano Mountains. The ruined mission churches, built by the pueblo residents under pressure from Franciscan brothers in the early years of the Conquest, stand up stark and beautiful amid the other ruined buildings. The drive here also passes one of the area's most beautiful fall hiking spots, a few very old Hispano villages, and the little town of Mountainair.

Allow the better part of a day for a leisurely drive. The whole loop route, starting and ending in Albuquerque, is about 200 miles, and straight driving time is about four hours. From Albuquerque, take I-40 east to exit 179,

to the village of Tijeras (Scissors, for the way the canyons meet here), established in the 1850s. Turn south on Highway 337.

Fourth of July Canyon

After you pass through the Spanish land grant of Chililí, Highway 337 runs into Highway 55—make a right and head to Tajique, then turn onto Forest Road 55 to reach **Fourth of July Canyon.** The area in the foothills of the Manzanos, seven miles down the dirt road, is a destination in late September and early October, when the red maples and oak trees turn every shade of pink, crimson, and orange imaginable. (Surprisingly, the place got its name not for this fireworks-like show of colors, but for the date an Anglo explorer happened across it in 1906.) The canyon is also pretty in late summer, when the rains bring wildflowers. You can explore on the short **Spring Loop Trail** or **Crimson Maple Trail,** or really get into the woods on **Fourth of July Trail** (no. 173), which wanders into the canyon 1.8 miles and connects with **Albuquerque Trail** (no. 78) to form a loop.

Technically, Forest Road 55 continues on to rejoin Highway 55 farther south, but after the Fourth of July campground, the road is not always maintained and can be very rough going. It's wiser to backtrack rather than carry on, especially if you're in a rental car.

Quarai

The first ruins you reach are those at **Quarai** (505/847-2290, www.nps.gov/sapu, 9am-6pm daily June-Aug., 9am-5pm Sept.-May, free), a pueblo inhabited from the 14th to the 17th century. Like the other two Salinas pueblos, Quarai was a hardscrabble place with no natural source of water and very little food, though it did act as a trading outpost for salt, brought from small salt lakes (*salinas*) farther east. When the Franciscans arrived, they put more than the usual strain on this community. The 400 or so Tiwa speakers nonetheless were pressed to build a grand sandstone-and-adobe mission, the most impressive of the ones at these pueblos.

The priests also found themselves at odds with the Spanish governors, who helped protect them but undermined their conversion work by encouraging ceremonial dances. At the same time, raids by Apaches increased because any crop surplus no longer went to them in trade, but to the Spanish. *And* there were terrible famines between 1663 and 1670. No wonder, then, the place was abandoned even before the Pueblo Revolt of 1680. Only the mission has been excavated; the surrounding hillocks are all pueblo structures.

Mountainair

Highway 55 meets U.S. 60 in the village of **Mountainair**, once known as the Pinto Bean Capital of the World. It's less booming now, but you can still pick up a pound of local beans at the grocery store on the main road.

You'll find the **Salinas Pueblo Missions Visitors Center** (505/847-2585, www.nps.gov/sapu, 8am-5pm daily) on U.S. 60 west of the intersection—though it offers not much more information than what's available at the small but detailed museums at each site. The **Mountainair ranger station** (505/847-2990, 8am-noon and 12:30pm-4:30pm Mon.-Fri.) is here as well; coming from the north, follow signs west off Highway 55, before you reach the U.S. 60 intersection.

Mountainair is also home to the weird architectural treasure that is the **Shaffer Hotel** (103 Main St., 505/847-2888, www.shaffer-hotel.com), a 1923 Pueblo Deco confection with a folk-art twist, built by one Clem "Pop" Shaffer, who had a way with cast concrete—look for his name in the wall enclosing the little garden. (Similar stonework of his can also be spotted in the garden at Los Poblanos in Albuquerque.) In terms of decoration, the real draw is the hotel **restaurant** (6am-9pm Mon.-Sat., 6am-8pm Sun., $8). While you're eating your homemade pie or your chile burger, take a long look at the ceiling, Shaffer's masterpiece of carved and painted turtles, snakes, and other critters. As for the hotel itself, it was renovated and deep-cleaned in 2014, and the tidy rooms are furnished with Pop Shaffer's own antique furniture. Ones with an outside bath are a bargain at $50; private-bath rooms start at $70.

And another food option: bustling **Alpine Alley** (210 N. Summit Ave., 505/847-2478, 6am-2pm Mon.-Fri., 8am-2pm Sat., $8), just north of the main intersection on Highway 55. This café is the town living room, serving good baked treats, soups, and creative sandwiches and drinks to a crew of regulars, many of whom have inspired the menu's concoctions.

Gran Quivira

South from Mountainair 26 miles lies Gran Quivira—a bit of a drive, and you'll have to backtrack, but on the way, about one mile south of town, you'll pass another Pop Shaffer creation, **Rancho Bonito,** his actual home. As it's private property, you can't go poking around, but from the road you can see a bit of the little log cabin painted in black, red, white, and blue. (If you happen to be in Mountainair in May for its art tour, the house is open then.)

Where Highway 55 makes a sharp turn east, **Gran Quivira** (505/847-2770, www.nps.gov/sapu, 9am-6pm daily June-Aug., 9am-5pm Sept.-May, free) looks different from the other two Salinas pueblos because it is built of gray San Andres limestone slab and finished with plaster that was painted with symbols. It's the largest of three, with an estimated population between 1,500 and 2,000. The array of feathers and pottery styles found here indicate the community was devoted to trade. Like the people of Abó, the residents spoke Tompiro, and the Spanish dubbed them Los Rayados, for the striped decorations they wore on their faces. They appear to have outwardly accepted the Franciscan mission after the first sermon was preached here in 1627. But they took their own religion literally underground, building hidden kivas underneath the residential structures even as they toiled on two successive missions ordered by the Catholics. Nonetheless, the place was deserted by 1671, after more than a third of the population had starved to death.

Rancho Bonito, Pop Shaffer's home south of Mountainair

Abó

From Gran Quivira, drive back the way you came and turn west on U.S. 60 in Mountainair to reach **Abó** (505/847-2400, www.nps.gov/ sapu, 9am-6pm daily June-Aug., 9am-5pm Sept.-May, free), nine miles on. This was the first pueblo the Franciscans visited, in 1622; the mission here, constructed over more than 60 years, shows details such as old wood stairs leading to the choir loft. (The Franciscans were so dedicated to re-creating the Catholic church experience here in the desert that they brought in portable pipe organs and trained their converts to sing.)

Abó is also notable for the placement of its kiva, right in the center of the *convento* (the compound adjoining the mission) and apparently dating from the same period. This suggests that the local populace came to some agreement with the priests, though no archaeologist or historian has been able to find proof of this. The excellent condition of all of these ruins is due in part to the efforts of the family that owned the land from the mid-19th century. One member, Federico Sisneros, is buried near the mission, at his request.

the ruins at Abó

From Abó, continue west through the mountain pass, then down into the long, flat Rio Grande Valley on U.S. 60. It runs straight into I-25 at Bernardo, but if you're heading back to Albuquerque, you can take Highway 47 northwest to Belén, about 25 miles closer to the city.

THE TURQUOISE TRAIL

This scenic back route to Santa Fe, along the east side of the Sandias and up across high plateaus, revisits New Mexico's mining history as it passes through a series of ghost towns. From Albuquerque, it's about 70 miles and can be driven straight through in just an hour and a half.

Take I-40 east from Albuquerque to exit 175. For hiking maps of the area, bear right to go into the village of Tijeras and the **Sandia ranger station** (11776 Hwy. 337, 505/281-3304), and to gas up if you need it—it's one of the last stops until close to Santa Fe. Go left to continue directly to the junction with Highway 14, the beginning of the Turquoise Trail.

East Mountains

The four-lane road heads north through alternating communities of old Spanish land grants and modern subdivisions collectively referred to as the East Mountains. Despite a few strip malls, the area still has a distinct identity from the city; one hub of mountain culture is **Burger Boy** (12023 Hwy. 14, 505/281-3949, 8am-7pm Mon. and Wed.-Sat., 8am-5pm Sun., $8), which does a mean green-chile cheeseburger, plus a range of breakfast and lunch specials. Don't miss the paintings, inside and out, of founding owner Green Chili Bill, by Ross Ward. If you definitely need fresh vegetables (aside from chile), keep going up the road to the **Greenside Cafe** (12165 Hwy. 14, 505/286-2684, 8am-8pm daily, $8), another area hangout that has a broader menu with interesting international specials (peanut stew, bratwurst, and more).

Another two miles along is a left turn to the **Museum of Archaeology and Material**

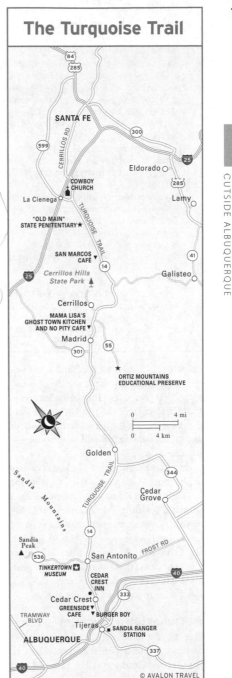

The Turquoise Trail

© AVALON TRAVEL

A Little Farther: Bosque del Apache

Birders may went to take the drive to the **Bosque del Apache National Wildlife Refuge,** 57,000 acres of wetlands along the river where some 15,000 giant sandhill cranes fly in during November, and hundreds of other migratory species winter over. It's a straight shot south on I-25, a little less than 100 miles. (To continue from Abó, head west on U.S. 60 to the interstate.) The **visitors center** (575/835-1828, www.friendsofthebosque.org, 7:30am-4pm Mon.-Fri., 8am-4:30pm Sat.-Sun.) hands out bird lists and maps; a **loop drive** ($5/car) through the wetlands opens one hour before sunrise and closes an hour after dark.

San Antonio, the nearest town, is notable for its green-chile cheeseburgers, especially at the legendary **Owl Bar & Café** (U.S. 380, 575/835-9946, 8am-9pm Mon.-Sat., $6), untouched by time—though rival **Buckhorn Burgers** (U.S. 380, 575/835-4423, 11am-7:50pm Mon.-Fri., 11am-2:45pm Sat., $6), just across the street, is solid too.

You can stay overnight—either in San Antonio at **Casa Blanca B&B** (13 Montoya St., 575/835-3027, www.casablancabedandbreakfast.com, $90 d), or just north on I-25 in **Socorro,** at **America's Best Value Inn** (1009 N. California St., 575/835-0276, $57 d), which has a few chips in its furniture but is otherwise well kept up. Recommended dining here includes brewpub **Socorro Springs** (1012 N. California St., 575/838-0650, 11am-10pm daily, $12), all-night diner **El Camino** (707 N. California St., 575/835-1180, 24 hours, $6), **M Mountain Coffeehouse** (110 Manzanares St., 575/838-0809, 7am-8pm daily), just off the plaza, and, on the plaza, the old-style **Capitol Bar** (575/835-1193, noon-2am Mon.-Sat., noon-midnight Sun.).

To vary the drive back, take the **Quebradas Backcountry Byway,** a 24-mile dirt road that runs in a jagged arc from U.S. 380 up to I-25 north of Socorro, cutting through arroyos and rainbow-striped hills. It adds about two hours to the drive. From the Owl, head east on U.S. 380 for just over 10 miles; then turn north on County Road A-129, the beginning of the byway.

Culture (22 Calvary Rd., 505/281-2005), a private collection of artifacts from the area and beyond, set next to the office of the Turquoise Trail Campground. Unfortunately, as of 2014 it was closed due to financial concerns, but the owners thought it would be temporary—call ahead.

Six miles up, you come to a large triangle intersection—to the left is Highway 536, the so-called **Crest Road** up to Sandia Peak, a beautiful winding drive through steadily thinning forests until you reach the exposed top of the mountain, more than 10,000 feet above sea level and more than 5,500 feet above the center of Albuquerque. At the peak is the Sandia Crest Visitor Center ($3/car), and the 1.6-mile Crest Trail along the rim.

★ Tinkertown Museum

Even if you don't drive to Sandia Peak, do head 1.5 miles up the Crest Road to **Tinkertown Museum** (121 Sandia Crest Rd., 505/281-5233, www.tinkertown.com, 9am-6pm daily Apr.-Oct., $3.50), a temple to efficient use of downtime. Ross Ward, an artist, a certified circus-model builder, and a sign painter who learned his trade doing banners for carnivals, was also a master whittler and creative engineer who built, over 40 years, thousands of miniature figures and dioramas out of wood, clay, and found objects. Some of the scenes are even animated with tiny pulleys and levers: A man with a cleaver chases chickens in a circle; circus performers soar; the blacksmith's bellows huff and puff.

Much of the building is Ward's creation as well—undulating walls made of bottles and studded with odd collectibles, for instance. The museum, like an amoeba, even seems to have taken over a neighbor's 35-foot wooden boat. Ward died in 2002; his family keeps up the museum, and even though it's no longer growing as it used to, it remains a remarkable piece of pure American folk art.

were squatted by hippies willing to live where indoor plumbing was barely available.

Over the decades, Madrid slowly revived. Portable toilets are still more common than flush models, but the arts scene has flourished, and a real sense of community pervades the main street, which is lined with galleries and pretty painted bungalows. In 2006, the village was the setting for the John Travolta film *Wild Hogs,* and the set-piece café built for the production (now a souvenir shop) has become a minor pilgrimage site for bikers.

You can learn more about Madrid's history at the **Old Coal Town Museum** (2846 Hwy. 14, 505/473-0743, www.themineshafttavern. com, 11am-4:30pm Sat.-Sun., $5), where you can wander among sinister-looking machine parts and old locomotives. You'll feel the "ghost" in "ghost town" here.

ACCOMMODATIONS AND FOOD

The **Mine Shaft Tavern** (2846 Hwy. 14, 505/473-0743, www.themineshafttavern. com, 11:30am-7:30pm Sun.-Thurs., 11:30am-9pm Fri.-Sat) is a vibrant remnant of Madrid's company-town days where you can belly up to a 40-foot-long pine-pole bar. Above it are murals by local artist Ross Ward, who built the Tinkertown Museum in Sandia Park. "It is better to drink than to work," reads the Latin inscription interwoven among the mural panels, and certainly everyone in the bar, from long-distance bikers to gallery-hoppers, is living by those encouraging words. It serves solidly satisfying "New Mexico roadhouse cuisine."

For morning coffee and local gossip, hit **Java Junction** (2855 Hwy. 14, 505/438-2772, www.java-junction.com, 7:30am-close daily), which also rents a **guest room** ($129 d).

For more substance, head straight to ★ **Mama Lisa's Ghost Town Kitchen** (Hwy. 14, 505/471-5769, $10). When it's open (seemingly not on a regular basis, but chances are better in the summer, 10am-3pm or so), it's a true treat, a cozy place with an all-over-the-map menu: bison enchiladas,

Folk artist Ross Ward built Tinkertown Museum from wood scraps and bottles.

Golden

Back on Highway 14, continue north through rolling hills and ever-broader sky. After 15 miles, you reach the all-but-gone town of **Golden**, site of the first gold strike west of the Mississippi, in 1825. All that's left now is a handful of homes, an attractive adobe church, and **Henderson Store** (10am-3:30pm Tues.-Sat.), open since 1918. It's largely given over to Indian jewelry and pottery, and antique trinkets line the upper shelves. One other small attraction: the house across the road, bedecked with thousands of colored bottles.

Madrid

Thirteen miles beyond Golden, and about midway along the drive, **Madrid** (pronounced MAD-rid) is a ghost town back from the dead. Built by the Albuquerque & Cerrillos Coal Co. in 1906, it once housed 4,000 people, but by the end of World War II, when natural gas became the norm, it was deserted. By the late 1970s, a few of the swaybacked wood houses

Madrid's Mine Shaft Tavern is a classic old Western bar.

gluten-free pizza, lemon butter cake, and hibiscus mint tea, which you can enjoy out on the tree-shaded front patio. At the very least, get a cookie. When it's closed, all you can do is press your face against the window and dream.

The Hollar (Hwy. 14, 575/471-4821, 11am-9pm daily May-Sept., 11am-7pm Mon.-Wed., 11am-9pm Thurs.-Sun. Oct.-Apr., $9) does Southern standards like po'boys and fried okra. The green tomatoes and goat cheese are both local—and there's a special menu for dogs.

an exceptional salad at Mama Lisa's Ghost Town Kitchen in Madrid

Ortiz Mountains Educational Preserve

The 1,350-acre **Ortiz Mountains Educational Preserve**, managed by the Santa Fe Botanical Garden (505/471-9103, www.santafebotanicalgarden.org), is open by guided tour ($5) only on the weekends. The walks ($5 donation) usually last a few hours, winding through the piñon scrub for viewing local plants and discussing mining history in the area. The reserve is about six miles down County Road 55.

Cerrillos

The source of turquoise that has been traced to Chaco Canyon, Spain, and Chichén Itzá in Mexico's Yucatán Peninsula, **Cerrillos** hasn't been gallerified the way Madrid, its neighbor down the road, has. There's a combo **petting zoo-trading post** with some llamas and goats, plus turquoise nuggets and taxidermied jackalopes. And there's barely one bar, **Mary's,** filled with cats and serving primarily as the package liquor store. The tough-as-nails Mary, now approaching her 11th decade, is a local legend, but these days, her younger family is in charge. Your only drinking options are whiskey shots and not-very-cold beer, which contributes to the aura of ghostly authenticity.

If you want to do something besides wave to the Amtrak train in the afternoon, you can go horseback riding with the **Broken Saddle Riding Co.** (505/424-7774, www.brokensaddle.com, $85 for two hours) or hiking in **Cerrillos Hills State Park** (head north across the railroad tracks, www.nmparks.com, $5/car), more than 1,000 acres of rolling hills and narrow canyons that are also good for mountain biking. A visitors center is in the village, but open only 2pm-4pm daily.

The Home Stretch

After ascending from the canyons around Cerrillos onto a high plateau (look out for pronghorn), you're on the home stretch to Santa Fe—but you'll pass one more dining option, the **San Marcos Café** (3877 Hwy. 14, 505/471-9298, 8:30am-6pm Mon.-Fri., 8:30am-5pm Sat., 8:30am-2pm Sun., $9),

which shares space with a working feed store where chickens and the occasional peacock scratch in the yard. Hearty meals are served in a country-style dining room (complete with potbellied stove); breakfast is especially delicious, with great cinnamon buns, homemade chicken sausage, and a variety of egg dishes.

Five miles farther, off the west side of the road is the **"Old Main" State Penitentiary** (4337 Hwy. 14, www.corrections.state.nm.us), site of a vicious riot in 1980 that is still counted as one of the worst in American history. The state corrections department offers surprisingly detailed and thought-provoking **tours** ($15) of the old facility on Saturdays in summer and early fall.

A possible Sunday-morning diversion is the nearby **Cowboy Church of Santa Fe County** (4525 Hwy. 14, 505/982-9162, www.cowboychurchofsantafe.org), which holds a music-filled service at 10:30am, under the direction of Trail Boss Doc Timmons. It is just north of the intersection with Highway 599.

If you're heading into central Santa Fe, look for the on-ramp to I-25 (signs point to Las Vegas), then go north to the Old Santa Fe Trail exit. This is faster and prettier than

the "Old Main" State Penitentiary

continuing straight in on Highway 14, which turns into Cerrillos Road, a particularly slow and unscenic route to the plaza.

THE JEMEZ MOUNTAIN TRAIL

Beginning just northwest of Albuquerque, the **Jemez** (HAY-mez) **Mountain Trail** is a beautiful drive through Jemez Indian Reservation, the Santa Fe National Forest, and the Valles Caldera National Preserve. It's the least direct way of getting to Santa Fe—from Albuquerque, it covers about 140 miles, and you wind up near Los Alamos and must backtrack a bit south to reach the city. But anyone in search of natural beauty will want to set aside a full day for the trip, or plan an overnight in Jemez Springs, especially in the fall, when the aspen leaves turn gold against the red rocks.

The drive begins on U.S. 550, northwest out of the satellite town of Bernalillo, just west of I-25. (Stop here for gas, if necessary—stations are few on this route.) At the village of San Ysidro, bear right onto Highway 4, which forms the major part of the route north.

Jemez Pueblo

This community of some 1,800 tribal members was settled in the late 13th century, and Highway 4 runs through the middle of the 89,000 acres it still maintains. Before the Spanish arrived, the Hemish (literally, "the people," and which the Spanish spelled *Jemez*) had established more than 10 large villages in the area. **Jemez Pueblo** is quite conservative and closed to outsiders except for holidays. Because Jemez absorbed members of Pecos Pueblo in 1838, it celebrates two feast days, San Diego (November 12) and San Persingula (August 2), as well as Pueblo Independence Day (August 10), commemorating the Pueblo Revolt of 1680. It's also the only remaining pueblo where residents speak the Towa language, the rarest of the related New Mexico languages (Tewa and Tiwa are the other two).

The pueblo operates the **Walatowa Visitor Center** (575/834-7235, www.

jemezpueblo.com, 8am-5pm daily Apr.-Dec., 10am-4pm Wed.-Sun. Jan.-Mar.), about five miles north of San Ysidro. You might miss it if you're gawking off the east side of the road at the vivid red sandstone cliffs at the mouth of the **San Diego Canyon.** From April till October, another, tastier distraction is the Indian fry bread and enchiladas sold by roadside vendors. The center has exhibits about the local geology and the people of Jemez and doubles as a ranger station, dispensing maps and advice on outdoor recreation farther up the road. You can take a one-mile guided hike ($5) up into the red rocks; it's a good idea to call ahead and arrange a time.

Gilman Tunnels

Blasted in the 1920s for a spur of a logging railroad, the two narrow **Gilman Tunnels** over scenic Highway 485 make a good excuse to drive up this narrow road and through a dramatic canyon. Look for the turn left (west) off Highway 4, a couple of miles after the Walatowa Visitor Center, after mile marker 9; the tunnels are about five miles along. After the tunnels, the road turns to dirt and heads into the national forest. (Sturdy vehicles can make a big loop around via Fenton Lake, rejoining Highway 4 north of Jemez Springs.)

Jemez Springs

A funky old resort town and an old-school blend of hippie-Hispano-Pueblo New Mexico, **Jemez Springs** is a handful of little clapboard buildings tucked in the narrow valley along the road. As the most convenient place to indulge in the area's springs, which have inspired tales of miraculous healing since the 1870s, the town makes for a nice afternoon pause or an overnight getaway. **Giggling Springs** (Hwy. 4, 575/829-9175, www.gigglingsprings.com, 11am-sunset Wed.-Sun., $18/one hour, 30/two hours, $60/day) has a spring-fed pool enclosed in an attractively landscaped flagstone area right near the Jemez River; reserve ahead, as occupancy is capped at 10. The **Jemez Springs Bath House** (Hwy. 4, 575/829-3303, www.jemezsprings.

Gilman Tunnels, off the Jemez Mountain Trail

with a few more amenities, is the **Laughing Lizard Inn** (Hwy. 4, 575/829-3108, www.the-laughinglizard.com, $70 d); its four simple but pretty rooms, plus one suite, open onto a long porch. Just across the street, **Jemez Mountain Inn** (Hwy. 4, 575/829-3926, www.jemezmtninn.com, $95 d) is slightly plusher, and its rooms a bit quieter, as they're back from the road. Hot springs are easy walking distance.

Next door to the Laughing Lizard, **Highway 4 Coffee** (17478 Hwy. 4, 575/829-4655, 7:30am-3pm Mon.-Wed., 7:30am-4pm Thurs., Fri., and Sun., 7:30am-7:30pm Sat., $6) has pastries and hearty homemade lunches. For dinner, the only place open all the time is **Los Ojos Restaurant & Saloon** (17596 Hwy. 4, 575/829-3547, 11am-midnight Mon.-Fri., 8am-midnight Sat.-Sun., $10), where horseshoes double as window grills, tree trunks act as bar stools, and the atmosphere hasn't changed in decades. Burgers are the way to go. The kitchen shuts around 9pm, and bar closing time can come earlier if business is slow, so call ahead in the evenings. Across the street, **Jemez Stage Stop Café** (17607 Hwy. 4, 575/829-3829, 8am-3pm and 5pm-9pm Mon. and Fri., 8am-3pm Tues.-Thurs., 8am-5pm Sat.-Sun., $9) has homemade chile and posole, music Thursday through Monday, and a couple of goats in a pen, adjacent to the porch, to entertain the kids. Fifteen minutes up the road, the **Ridgeback Café** (38710 Hwy. 126, 575/829-3322, 8am-8pm Tues.-Sun., $10) has a bit more variety at night, with elk burgers, enchiladas, and more; in winter, it's also closed Tuesday.

Jemez Historic Site
Just north of Jemez Springs, you pass the **Jemez Historic Site** (Hwy. 4, 575/829-3530, 8:30am-5pm Wed.-Sun., $3), a set of ruins where ancestors of the present Jemez people settled more than 700 years ago and apparently lived until 1694 or so, when De Vargas returned after the Pueblo Revolt. The old pueblo, named Giusewa, has almost entirely dissolved; as at the Salinas

org, 10am-7pm daily, $18/hour), in one of the original historic buildings, is operated by the village. (The source is in a gazebo next door—check out the mineral buildup!) Here, the springs have been diverted into eight concrete soaking tubs—a bit austere, but with a cool historic vibe. Reserve ahead here too; massages and other spa treatments are available. The most natural springs (expect some algae) are on the riverside at the **Bodhi Manda Zen Center** (Hwy. 4, 575/829-3854, www.bmzc.org, $10 donation); payment is cash only, on the honor system.

If you're planning to explore the wilderness and missed the Walatowa Visitor Center at Jemez Pueblo, you can stop at the **Jemez Ranger District office** (Hwy. 4, 575/829-3535, 8am-4:30pm Mon.-Fri.) for info; it's on the north edge of town.

ACCOMMODATIONS AND FOOD
The **Bodhi Manda Zen Center** (Hwy. 4, 575/829-3854, www.bmzc.org) rents barebones rooms ($50 pp) and offers vegetarian meals to guests. Another bargain place to stay,

Pueblo Missions south of Albuquerque, the attraction is the Franciscan convent and church. Built starting around 1620, it has been partially reconstructed, enough to show how the architecture—a floor that sloped up to the altar, a unique octagonal bell tower—created maximum awe in the local populace. If you pay $5 admission, you can also visit Coronado State Monument, on the north edge of Albuquerque, on the same or next day.

A couple of curves in the highway past the monument, you reach the rocks of **Soda Dam** off the right side of the road. The pale, bulbous mineral accretions that have developed around this spring resemble nothing so much as the top of a root beer float, with a waterfall crashing through the middle. You can't really get in the water here, but it's a good photo op.

Hot Springs

Outside Jemez Springs, you pass two other opportunities to take a hot bath. Five miles north, where the red rocks of the canyon have given way to steely-gray stone and Battleship Rock looms above the road, is the start of the East Fork Trail (no. 137)—there's a dedicated parking lot just north of the picnic area. From here, the hike up the trail to **McCauley Warm Springs** is a bit more than two miles, mostly uphill; follow the trail until it meets a small stream flowing down from your left (north), then walk up the creek about a quarter mile to the spring, which has been diverted so it flows into a series of pools, only 85°F at most points. (You can also reach the springs from the other direction along East Fork Trail, parking at Jemez Falls, farther north on Highway 4; from here, the hike is downhill—but of course a slog back up.)

More accessible are **Spence Hot Springs,** about two miles north of Battleship Rock, between mile markers 24 and 25. Look for a loop parking area on the east side of the road (if it's full, there is another lot a short way north along the highway). The half-mile trail down to the river is wide and well tended, but then it's a bit more strenuous heading up the steep

Soda Dam is formed by mineral buildup.

hillside to two sets of 100°F pools with milky-blue mineral water.

Hiking

Several trails run through the Jemez, but damage from the 2011 Las Conchas Fire has made some less scenic. Portions of **East Fork Trail** (no. 137) are still quite nice, however. The route runs between Battleship Rock (on the southwest end) and Las Conchas (on the northeast), crossing Highway 4 at a convenient midpoint. If you head south from the highway parking area (about 3 miles after a hairpin turn southeast), you reach Jemez Falls after 1 mile, then gradually descend to Battleship Rock, in about 6 miles, passing McCauley Springs on the way. Heading north from the highway is fine too, following a stream through a pine forest, though near the end of 4.5 miles, you approach the burned area.

Fenton Lake State Park

If you turn left (north) onto Highway 126, you eventually wind up a dirt road to **Fenton Lake State Park** (575/829-3630, www.nmparks.com, $5/car), popular with birders for its migration-season action and with anglers for its trout-stocked waters. Film buffs also make their way here—the lake was the shooting location for Nicolas Roeg's 1976 sci-fi film, *The Man Who Fell to Earth,* starring David Bowie as an alien.

★ Valles Caldera National Preserve

Spreading out for 89,000 acres to the north of Highway 4, **Valles Caldera National Preserve** (866/382-5537, www.vallescaldera.gov) is a series of vast green valleys, rimmed by the edges of a volcano that collapsed into a huge bowl millennia ago. At the center is rounded Redondo Peak (11,254 feet). The park was a private ranch, which the U.S. government purchased in 2000. It's managed with the goal of making the area financially self-sustaining, independent of government funds. To this end, fees can be high, and on weekends, you should make reservations ahead, as there are limits on how many people can enter the park each day. The reward is a hike through untouched land, where you will see herds of elk grazing and eagles winging across the huge dome of the sky.

The easiest way to get a glimpse is at the **Valle Grande Staging Area** (turn between mile markers 39 and 40), where two short interpretive trails lead through the grasslands; both are free. Numerous longer hikes ($10 pp) are also possible, either from the staging area or farther out in the backcountry, accessible by shuttle.

Two other free trails, accessible year-round, run from directly off Highway 4. They cut through area burned in the 2011 Las Conchas wildfire, so the trees are still a bit haggard; you should also avoid the trails during or after rainstorms, due to a high risk of flash floods. **Coyote Call** is the first trail you reach, after mile marker 41; it's a three-mile loop that takes about two hours to hike. **Valle Grande** (two miles) is around mile marker 43, but shows a bit more fire damage.

A full roster of guided activities is available too, in winter and summer: group day hikes, full-moon snowshoeing and sleigh rides, overnight winter yurt camping, tracking classes, horseback riding, and more.

Past Valles Caldera, Highway 4 leads to Bandelier National Monument in about 20 miles. If you're carrying on to Santa Fe, it's another hour's drive (about 40 miles). Continue on Highway 4 through the town of White Rock and join Highway 502. This leads to U.S. 285, which then goes south to the capital.

THE INTERSTATE TO SANTA FE

The most direct route north from Albuquerque to Santa Fe is along I-25, a drive of about 60 miles and just one hour without stops. The road, which passes through the broad

The Interstate to Santa Fe

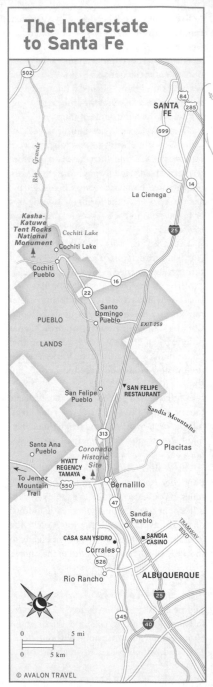

valley between the Sandia and Jemez mountain ranges, is not as scenic as the more meandering routes, but it does cross wide swaths of the undeveloped pueblo lands of Sandia, San Felipe, and Kewa (formerly Santo Domingo).

Kasha-Katuwe Tent Rocks National Monument

A slight detour takes you to **Kasha-Katuwe Tent Rocks National Monument** (Forest Rd. 266, 7am-7pm daily mid-Mar.-Oct., 8am-5pm daily Nov.-mid-Mar., $5/car), one of the region's most striking natural phenomena. The wind-whittled clusters of volcanic pumice and tuff do indeed resemble enormous tepees, some up to 90 feet tall. To reach the area, leave I-25 at exit 259 and head northwest toward Cochiti Pueblo on Highway 22. After about 15 miles, turn south in front of Cochiti Dam. In less than two miles, in the middle of the pueblo, turn right on Indian Service Route 92.

Kasha-Katuwe Tent Rocks National Monument

From the monument parking area, you have the choice of two short trails: An easy, relatively flat loop runs up to the base of the rocks, passing a small cave, while a longer option runs 1.5 miles into a narrow canyon where the rock towers loom up dramatically on either side. The latter trail is level at first, but the last stretch is steep and requires a little clambering. Even if you just want to take a quick peek and don't intend to hike, don't come too late in the day: The gates (close to the junction with Highway 22) are shut one hour before official closing time.

Nearby **Cochiti Lake** (reached by continuing along Highway 22 past the dam) is a popular summer destination for boaters, though it's not particularly scenic.

Food

At exit 252, hop off for a meal at the ★ **San Felipe Restaurant** (26 Hagen Rd., 505/867-4706, 6am-9pm daily, $8), alongside a gas station and past a short hall of dinging slot machines. Its broad diner-ish menu of spaghetti and meatballs as well as New Mexican favorites is superlative, especially pueblo dishes like posole with extra-thick tortillas. The crowd is just as diverse: pueblo residents, day-trippers, long-haul truckers.

Information and Services

TOURIST INFORMATION

The **Albuquerque Convention and Visitors Bureau** (800/284-2282, www.visitalbuquerque.org) offers the most detailed information on the city, maintaining a kiosk on the Old Town plaza in the summer and a desk at the airport near the baggage claim (9:30am-8pm daily). The **City of Albuquerque** website (www.cabq.gov) is very well organized, with all the essentials about city-run attractions and services.

Books and Maps

In the North Valley, **Bookworks** (4022 Rio Grande Blvd. NW, 505/344-8139, 9am-9pm Mon.-Sat., 9am-7pm Sun.) has a large stock of New Mexico-related work as well as plenty of other titles, all recommended with the personal care of the staff.

The **University of New Mexico Bookstore** (2301 Central Ave. NE, 505/277-5451, 8am-6pm Mon.-Fri., 11am-4pm Sat.) maintains a good stock of travel titles and maps, along with state history tomes and the like. In summer, it closes an hour earlier on weekdays.

Local Media

The *Albuquerque Journal* (www.abqjournal.com) publishes cultural-events listings in the Friday entertainment supplement. On Wednesdays, pick up the new issue of the free weekly *Alibi* (www.alibi.com), which will give you a hipper, more critical outlook on city goings-on, from art openings to city council debates. The glossy monthly *ABQ The Magazine* (www.abqthemag.com) explores cultural topics, while the free *Local Flavor* (www.localflavormagazine.com) covers food topics.

Radio

KUNM (89.9 FM) is the university's radio station, delivering eclectic music, news from NPR and PRI, and local-interest shows, such as *Singing Wire,* where you'll hear traditional Native American music as well as pop anthems like Keith Secola's oft-requested "NDN Kars" and the Black Lodge Singers chanting the Mighty Mouse theme song.

KANW (89.1 FM) is a project of Albuquerque Public Schools, with an emphasis on New Mexican music, particularly mariachi and other music in Spanish. It also hosts a Saturday-night old-time country show, and the most popular NPR programs.

SERVICES

Banks

Banks are plentiful, and grocery stores and pharmacies increasingly have ATMs inside. Downtown, look for **New Mexico Bank & Trust** (320 Gold Ave. SW, 505/830-8100, 9am-4pm Mon.-Thurs., 9am-5pm Fri.). In Nob Hill, **Wells Fargo** (3022 Central Ave. SE, 505/255-4372, 9am-5pm Mon.-Thurs., 9am-6pm Fri., 9am-1pm Sat.) is on Central at Dartmouth. Both have 24-hour ATMs.

Post Offices

Most convenient for visitors are the **Old Town Plaza Station** (303 Romero St. NW, 505/242-5927, 11am-4pm Mon.-Fri., noon-3pm Sat.), **Downtown Station** (201 5th St. SW, 505/346-1256, 9am-4:30pm Mon.-Fri.), and an office near **UNM** (115 Cornell Dr. SE, 505/346-0923, 8am-5pm Mon.-Fri.).

Internet

City-maintained **wireless hotspots** are listed at www.cabq.gov/wifi; many businesses around town also provide service.

Getting There and Around

AIR

Albuquerque International Sunport (ABQ, 505/244-7700, www.cabq.gov/airport) is a pleasant single-terminal airport served by all major U.S. airlines. It's on the south side of the city, just east of I-25, about four miles from downtown. It has free wireless Internet access throughout. Near bag claim is an info desk maintained by the convention and visitors bureau.

Transit from the airport includes **bus Route 50** ($1), which runs to the Alvarado Transportation Center downtown every half hour 7am-8pm, and on Saturdays every hour and 10 minutes 9:45am-6:50pm; there is no Sunday service. The ride takes about 25 minutes.

Less frequent, but free, the **Airport Connection shuttle** (aka city bus Route 250) runs weekdays only (9:10am, 4:01pm, 5:09pm, and 6:10pm) to the downtown Alvarado Transportation Center (Central and 2nd St.). The schedule is timed to meet the Rail Runner train to Santa Fe, departing about 30 minutes later. Another free weekday bus (Route 222) runs to the Bernalillo Rail Runner stop, though this is less convenient for visitors. Verify online at www.riometro.org, as the train schedule can change.

TRAIN

Amtrak (800/872-7245, www.amtrak.com) runs the *Southwest Chief* through Albuquerque. It arrives daily in the afternoon from Chicago and Los Angeles. The depot shares space with the Greyhound terminal, downtown on 1st Street, south of Central Avenue and the Alvarado Transportation Center.

The **Rail Runner** (866/795-7245, www.riometro.org) connects downtown Santa Fe with Albuquerque and continues as far south as Belén. The main stop in Albuquerque is downtown, at the Alvarado Transportation Center, at Central and 1st Street. If the not-so-frequent schedule fits yours, it's fantastic service to or from Santa Fe, but within Albuquerque, the system doesn't go anywhere visitors typically go. If you ride, keep your ticket—you get a free transfer from the train to any city bus.

BUS

Greyhound (800/231-2222, www.greyhound.com) runs buses from all major points east, west, north, and south, though departures are not frequent. The bus station (320 1st St. SW, 505/243-4435) is downtown, just south of Central Avenue. Cheaper *and* nicer are the bus services that cater to Mexicans traveling across the Southwest and into Mexico, though they offer service only to Las Cruces and Denver; **El Paso-Los Angeles Limousine Express** (2901 Pan American Fwy. NE, 505/247-8036, www.eplalimo.com) is the biggest operator, running since 1966.

With the city bus system, **ABQ Ride** (505/243-7433, www.cabq.gov/transit), it's possible to reach all of the major sights along Central Avenue, but you can't get to the Sandia Peak Tramway or anywhere in the East Mountains. The most tourist-friendly bus line is Route 66 (of course), the one that runs along Central Avenue, linking Old Town, downtown, and Nob Hill; service runs until a bit past 1am on summer weekends. The double-length red **Rapid Ride** buses (Route 766) follow the same route but stop at only the most popular stops. The fare for all buses, regardless of trip length, is $1 (coins or bills, no change given); passes are available for one ($2), two ($4), and three ($6)

days and can be purchased on the bus. The D-Ride bus is a free loop-route bus around downtown.

CAR

From Santa Fe, Albuquerque is 60 miles (one hour) south on I-25; from Las Cruces, it is 225 miles (a little more than three hours) north on I-25. From Denver, the drive takes about 6.5 hours (445 miles); Phoenix is about the same distance west on I-40.

All the major car-rental companies are in a single complex adjacent to the airport, connected by shuttle bus. **Hertz** and **Enterprise** offer service at the Amtrak depot (really just a refund for the cab ride to the airport offices). Hertz's two other city locations are usually less expensive because you bypass the airport service fee; if you're renting for more than a week, the savings can offset the cab fare.

BIKE

Albuquerque's **bike-route system** (www.cabq.gov/bike) is reasonably well developed, the terrain is flat, and the sun is usually shining. Rent bikes from **Routes** (404 San Felipe St. NW, 505/933-5667, www.routesrentals.com, 8am-7pm Mon.-Fri., 7am-7pm Sat.-Sun. Mar.-Oct., 9am-6pm Mon.-Fri., 8am-6pm Sat.-Sun. Nov.-Feb., $15/hour, $35/day).

Background

The Landscape

Sharp peaks, windswept cliffs, deep gorges—everything about northern New Mexico's landscape is dramatic, and the scenery can change at any bend in the road. The altitude ranges from around 6,500 feet in Albuquerque to more than 13,000 at Wheeler Peak north of Taos. So even if the scenery doesn't make you gasp for breath, the thin air might.

GEOGRAPHY AND GEOLOGY

Much of New Mexico's landscape is the product of volcanic activity that ceased (at least for now) around the year AD 500. The main mountain ranges, which form part of the **Continental Divide**, are relatively young, pushed up in the Eocene era between 55 million and 34 million years ago, when shock waves from the collision of the North American plate and the Farallon plate caused the continent to heave.

Just a few million years later, the **Rio Grande Rift**—one of the biggest rift valleys in the world—formed, as eras' and eras' worth of accumulated rock was pulled apart by shifting faults, leaving the perfect path for the Rio Grande when it began to flow about three million years ago. The water carved deep canyons, such as the 800-foot-deep gorge west of Taos. These canyons are perfect slices of geologic time, layers of limestone, sandstone, clay, and lava neatly stacked up.

Just 1.2 million years back, a volcano's violent eruption and subsequent collapse created the huge **Valles Caldera,** and the jagged edges of the crater have barely softened in the intervening time. A tangible benefit of the state's volcanic activity is the numerous hot springs, especially in the young Jemez Mountains (15 million years old).

Beneath all this is evidence of a stabler time. For some four billion years, the land was completely underwater, then spent hundreds of millions of years supporting prehistoric sealife—hence the marine fossils found at the top of the Sandia Mountains, 10,000 feet above the current sea level. Dinosaurs, too, flourished for a time. One of the first, the nimble meat-eater *Coelophysis,* lived during the Triassic period around Abiquiu, but all of them were apparently killed at once, perhaps by a flash flood. Another product of the dinosaur age (specifically, the Jurassic) was the lurid red, pink, and orange sandstone. It began as a vast desert, then petrified into the very symbol of the American Southwest, and is visible around Abiquiu as well as Jemez Pueblo.

CLIMATE

For the most part, altitude determines the climate in New Mexico, where river-bottom central Albuquerque can be crisp and cloudless while Sandia Peak, 20 miles away and almost 5,000 feet up, is caught in a blinding snowstorm. (Yes, it snows plenty in New Mexico.) Nowhere, though, is it a particularly gentle climate; expect sudden changes in weather and temperature extremes.

At the lower elevations, winter is cold—days usually between 40°F and 55°F—but rarely cloudy, with a few snowstorms that never add up to as much moisture as people hope. Come spring, which starts in late April or May, the number of wildflowers that dot the hills is a direct reflection of the previous winter's precipitation. The higher the elevation, the later the spring: At 8,500 feet, snow could still be on the ground in May. Little rain falls in May and June, typically the hottest and

---

Previous: the Sandia Mountains; Indian paintbrush

windiest months of the year, with temperatures climbing into the 90s—though it can still drop to the 50s at night.

By early or mid-July, the so-called monsoon season brings heavy, refreshing downpours and thunderstorms every afternoon for a couple of months. If you're out hiking in this season, steer clear of narrow canyons and arroyos during and after rains, as they can fill with powerful, deadly flash floods in a matter of minutes. Summer nights are rarely too warm.

September, October, and November are again dry, with the temperature dipping lower each month. Snow can often start falling in late October or November, although in recent years, overall winter precipitation has been quite low, so it takes months for a good base layer to build up at the ski areas.

ENVIRONMENTAL ISSUES

For thousands of years, New Mexicans have faced a water shortage. In prehistoric times,

farming in the river valley was relatively easy, if subject to flooding. But at higher elevations, mountain streams had to be channeled into irrigation ditches. This system was perfected by Spanish settlers, who called their ditches acequias, a word they'd learned from the Arabs (*al-saqiya*), who used the system to cultivate the Iberian Peninsula.

Today, as an ever-growing population demands more amenities, traditional ways of managing water have given way to more complex legal wranglings and outright hostility (*"No chinguen con nuestra agua"*—don't f—k with our water—reads a license plate on some farmers' trucks in northern New Mexico). Some 49 billion gallons are pumped out of the middle Rio Grande aquifer every year, and only a portion of that is replenished through mountain runoff. Albuquerque started using filtered river water in late 2008. "Smart growth" gets lip service in city council meetings, although construction continues apace on Albuquerque's arid West Mesa. Neo-homesteaders are installing cisterns to catch

Yes, it snows in New Mexico!

rain, as well as systems to reuse gray water, but these features are still far from standard.

Years of relative drought have made tinderboxes of the forests. To name just the largest recent incident, in a few weeks in the summer of 2011, several wildfires swept across large swaths of forest. The Las Conchas Fire, near Los Alamos, burned more than 150,000 acres, the largest fire in New Mexico history by far. And it happened on the same terrain that had burned just a decade before.

Visitors to New Mexico can help by following local environmental policies—complying with campfire bans in the wilderness, for instance, and keeping showers short. Golfers may want to consider curtailing their play here. New courses are springing up in every new casino resort and high-end residential development, despite the fact that they're intense draws on the water table.

trees damaged by wildfire in Valles Caldera

Plants and Animals

Just as humans have managed to eke a life out of northern New Mexico, so have plants and animals—and a rather large variety of them. The state supports the fourth most diverse array of wildlife in the country.

PLANTS

Although much of the plant growth in New Mexico is nominally evergreen, the landscape skews toward brown, until you get up to the wetter alpine elevations.

Vegetation Zones

New Mexico's **Upper Sonoran** zone, covering the areas between 4,500 and 7,000 feet, is the largest vegetation zone in the state and includes most of Albuquerque and Santa Fe, where the Sandia and Sangre de Cristo foothills are covered with juniper and piñon trees. The **Transition** zone, from 7,000 feet to 8,500 feet, sees a few more stately trees, such as ponderosa pine, and the state's more colorful wildflowers: orange Indian paintbrush,

bright red penstemon, purple lupine. Above 8,500 feet, the **Mixed Conifer** zone harbors that sort of tree, along with clusters of aspens. The **Subalpine** zone, starting at 9,500 feet, is home to Engelmann spruce and bristlecone pine, while 11,500 feet marks the tree line in most places and the beginning of the **Alpine** zone, where almost no greenery survives.

Trees and Grasses

Trees are the clearest marker of elevation. In low areas—such as on Albuquerque's West Mesa—you'll see few trees, only some of the desert-adapted plants that are more prevalent in the southern part of the state but not in the northern: assorted cacti, such as the common **cane cholla;** the spiky **yucca** plant, which produces towering stalks of blooms in May; and the humble **tumbleweed.** Along the Rio Grande and the Pecos River, thirsty **cottonwoods** provide dense shade; the biggest trees, with their gnarled, branching trunks, are centuries old. In spring, their cotton fills

Leave No Trace

So as not to upset the rather precarious environmental balance in much of New Mexico, you should internalize the ethic of "leave no trace"—even on a short stroll. Let the phrase first guide your trip in the **planning** stages, when you equip yourself with good maps and GPS tools or a compass, to avoid relying on rock cairns or blazes. Backpackers should repackage food and other items to minimize the waste to pack out. And everyone should try to keep group size under six people; pets should not go in wild areas.

On the trail, resist the urge to cut across switchbacks. Stick to the center of the trail, even if it has been widened by others trying to avoid mud. Be quiet, to avoid disturbing wildlife and other hikers. Leave what you find, whether plants, rocks, or potsherds.

Camp only where others have, in durable areas, at least 200 feet from water sources; dig cat holes 200 feet away too. Pack out your toilet paper and other personal waste, and scatter dishwater and toothpaste. Safeguard food in "bear bags" hung at least 15 feet off the ground. Campfires are typically banned in New Mexico—please honor this policy, and keep a close eye on camp stoves. Pack out all cigarette butts.

Day hikers should also maintain a strict policy regarding litter. Tossing an orange peel, apple core, or other biodegradable item along the trail may not cause an environmental disaster, but it reminds other hikers that humans have been there and intrudes on the natural solitude of New Mexico's wilderness.

For more information, contact **Leave No Trace** (https://lnt.org).

the air—hell for the allergic, but the source of a distinctive spicy fragrance—and in fall, their leaves turn pure yellow. Willow and olive are also common.

Everywhere in the foothills grows **piñon** (also spelled "pinyon"), the official state tree that's a slow-growing, drought-resistant scrub evolved to endure the New Mexican climate. When burned, its wood produces the scent of a New Mexico winter night, and its cones yield tasty nuts. Alongside piñon is **shaggy-bark juniper,** identifiable by its loose strips of bark, sprays of soft needles, and branches that look twisted by the wind. In season, it's studded with purple-gray berries—another treat for foraging humans and animals alike. At ground level in the foothills, also look for clumps of sagebrush and bear grass, which blooms in huge, creamy tufts at the ends of stalks up to six feet tall.

Up in the mountains, the trees are a bit taller—here you'll find the towering **ponderosa** pine, tall trees with thick, almost crusty chunks of reddish-black bark; the crevices smell distinctly of vanilla. At slightly higher elevations, dense stands of **aspens** provide a rare spot of fall color in the evergreen forests. The combination of their golden leaves and white bark creates a particularly magical glow, especially in the mountains near Santa Fe. The highest mountain areas are home to a number of dense-needled hardy pines, such as blue-green **Engelmann spruce, corkbark fir, bristlecone pines,** and **subalpine fir,** with its sleek, rounded pinecones. Hike your way up to stands of these, which are tall but with sparse branches, and you'll know you're close to the peak.

ANIMALS

As with plants, what you see depends on whether you're down in the desert or up on the mountain slopes. And you'll have to look carefully, because a lot of the animals that have survived here this long are the sort that have blended in with their surroundings—which means there are a lot of brown critters.

Mammals

In the open, low-elevation areas on Albuquerque's fringes (and sometimes in the occasional vacant urban lot), look for **prairie**

Spiky yucca have lush blooms.

rivers in Taos Pueblo starting in 2008—after their absence from the whole state for some 55 years. The small aquatic mammals seem to be flourishing and can now be spotted in the Rio Grande and tributaries, from the Colorado border to Cochiti Dam.

Black bears crash around the forests, though their name is misleading—at any given time, they can be brown, cinnamon-red, or even nearly blond. (Smokey Bear, the mascot of the National Forest Service, was from New Mexico, a cub rescued from a forest fire in the southern town of Capitan.) Drought has driven the omnivorous beasts into suburban trash cans to forage, with tragic results for both people and the animals. Campers are strongly urged to pack food in bear-proof canisters.

And then there's the elusive **jackalope,** a jackrabbit sporting elaborate antlers. Alas, it seems now to appear only on postcards, although you may occasionally see a taxidermied head in a curio shop.

Birds

New Mexico's state bird is the rather impressive **roadrunner:** It grows up to two feet long, nests in the ground, feeds on insects and even rattlesnakes, and has feet specially adapted to racing on sandy ground. It can be spotted at lower desert elevations, such as Coronado State Monument, north of Albuquerque. Blue-and-black **Steller's jays** and raucous all-blue **piñon jays** are common in the foothills and farther up in the mountains, where you can also see **bluebirds, black-masked mountain chickadees,** and **Clark's nutcrackers,** which hoard great stashes of piñon nuts for winter. Also look around for **woodpeckers,** including the three-toed variety, which lives at higher elevations. On the highest peaks are **white-tailed ptarmigans,** which blend in with their snowy environment. But you can't miss the yellow-and-red **Western tanager,** a vivid shot of tropical delight in the Transition zone forests.

In late summer, keep an eye out for tiny, red-throated **rufous hummingbirds** on

dogs, which live in huge underground warrens. When you're camping, the first creatures you'll meet are **squirrels** and **chipmunks**—at higher elevations, look out for Abert's squirrel, with its tufted ears and extra-fluffy tail. Long-haunched, clever, and highly adaptable, **coyotes** roam the lower elevations and are not shy about nosing around backyards; they make a barking yelp at night.

On the plains just south of Santa Fe, you may see **pronghorns** (often called pronghorn antelope, though they are not related to true antelope) springing through the grasses, while long-eared **mule deer** flourish in mountain forests, such as the Pecos Wilderness. Herds of **elk** live in the high valleys; Rocky Mountain elk are common, thanks to an aggressive reintroduction effort in the early 20th century to make up for overhunting. A group of the largest variety, Roosevelt elk, whose fanlike antlers are the stuff of dreams for trophy hunters, roams in Valles Caldera. **Bighorn sheep** live in the mountains around Taos.

Taos is also a hot spot for **North American river otters,** which were reintroduced in the their way to Mexico for the winter, along with hundreds of other birds that use the center of the state as a migratory corridor. The Sandia Mountains and are on the flight path for **red-tailed hawks, eagles,** and other raptors, especially numerous in the springtime.

With more than 450 species spotted in New Mexico, this list is only scraping the surface. If you're a dedicated birder, first contact the **Randall Davey Audubon Center** in Santa Fe, which leads bird walks, or the **Rio Grande Nature Center** in Albuquerque. **Bosque del Apache National Wildlife Refuge,** south of Albuquerque, is a must in the winter when thousands of **sandhill cranes**—and even the occasional rare **whooping crane**—rest in the wetlands. Jim West of **WingsWest Birding** (800/583-6928, www.wingswestnm.com) is a reputable guide who has been leading groups around New Mexico since 1996.

Fish

Trout is the major endemic fish, found in the cold waters of the Rio Grande as well as the Chama River, the Pecos River, and the Rio Chiquito and Rio Pueblo around Taos. The cutthroat is particularly beloved in New Mexico—the only variety of trout originally found on the eastern side of the Continental Divide. (The more aggressive rainbow and brown trout are interlopers.) The Rio Grande cutthroat, the official state fish, is now quite uncommon. Another local fish in jeopardy is the **Rio Grande silvery minnow,** listed as endangered since 1994. The last of the Rio Grande's five native fish, it's in such a dire state that biologists have scooped them out of the water individually during dry spells and

taken them to the Albuquerque aquarium for safekeeping.

Reptiles

One can't step foot in the desert without thinking of **rattlesnakes,** and New Mexico has plenty of them, usually hidden away under rocks and brush, but very occasionally sunning themselves in full view. The predominant species in the Rio Grande Valley, the **Western diamondback,** can grow to be seven feet long. Although its venom is relatively weak, it has an impressive striking distance of almost three feet. Around Taos and Santa Fe, the main species is the **prairie rattlesnake,** which is only four feet long at most, and the threatened **New Mexico ridgenose** is only about two feet long.

More benign cold-blooded critters include **lizards,** such as the **short-horned lizard** (aka horny toad), a miniature dinosaur, in effect, about as big as your palm. Look for it in the desert and the scrubby foothills.

Insects and Arachnids

Because it's so dry, New Mexico isn't teeming with bugs. The ones that are there, however, can be off-putting, particularly if you chance upon the springtime **tarantula migration,** usually in May around Albuquerque. It's not a true seasonal relocation, just the time when males come out of their dens to prowl for mates. The fist-size spiders move hundreds at a time, and occasionally back roads are closed to let them pass. If you'll be camping in the desert in the spring, ask the ranger's office about the status. Though they're big and hairy, they're not venomous.

History

The historical and cultural continuity in New Mexico is remarkable. The state has been transformed from ice-age hunting ground to home of the atom bomb, but many people claim roots that stretch back hundreds, even thousands, of years.

ANCIENT AND ARCHAIC CIVILIZATION

New Mexico was one of the first places to harbor humans after the end of the last **ice age**. Archaeological findings indicate that some 12,000 years ago, people were hunting mastodons and other big game across the state. Mammoth bones, arrowheads, and the remains of campfires have been found in the Sandia Mountains east of Albuquerque; Folsom, in northeastern New Mexico; and Clovis, in the south. Sometime between 8000 and 5000 BC, these bands of hunters formed a small temporary settlement just north of Albuquerque, but it was not enough to stave off the decline of that ancient culture, as climatic shifts caused the big game to die off. Nomadic hunter-gatherers, seeking out smaller animals as well as seeds and nuts, did better in the new land, and by 1000 BC, they had established communities built around clusters of pit houses—sunken, log-covered rooms dug into the earth.

Along with this new form of shelter came an equally important advance in food: Mexican people gave corn kernels (maize) and lessons in agriculture to their neighbors, the **Mogollon,** who occupied southern New Mexico and Arizona. By AD 400, the Mogollon had begun growing squash and beans as well and had established concentrated communities all around the southern Rio Grande basin. This culture, dubbed the Basketmakers by archaeologists, also developed its own pottery, another skill learned from the indigenous people of Mexico. So

when the Mogollon made contact with the Ancestral Puebloans (also known as the Anasazi) in the northern part of the state, they had plenty to share.

THE PUEBLOS

The year 700 marks the beginning of what archaeologists call the **Pueblo I** phase, when disparate groups began to form larger communities in the upland areas on either side of the northern Rio Grande. Pit houses were still in use, but aboveground buildings of clay and sticks were erected alongside them. Increasingly, the pit houses were sacred spaces, chambers in which religious ceremonies were carried out; these are now known as kivas and are still an integral part of pueblo life.

The **Pueblo II** era begins in 850 and is distinguished by the rise of Pueblo Bonito in Chaco Canyon, northwest of Santa Fe, into a full-scale city and perhaps capital of a small state. It was home to an estimated 1,500 people ruled by a religious elite. But Chaco abruptly began to crumble around 1150, perhaps due to drought, famine, or warfare. This shift marked the **Pueblo III** period, when the people who were to become today's Puebloans began building their easily defended cliff dwellings—most famously in the Four Corners area, at Mesa Verde in present-day Colorado, but also farther south, on the Pajarito Plateau in what's now Bandelier National Monument, and in Puyé, on Santa Clara Pueblo land. A drought at the end of the 13th century cleared out the Four Corners at the start of the **Pueblo IV** era, provoking the population to consolidate along the Rio Grande in clusters of sometimes more than a thousand interconnected rooms. These communities dotted the riverbank, drawing their sustenance both from the river water and from the mountains behind them.

Were the Anasazi Cannibals?

The popular conception of the Ancestral Puebloans (previously known as the Anasazi) has been of a peaceful, egalitarian society based on agriculture. But a theory advanced by physical anthropologist Christy Turner suggests the Pueblo Indians might be better off disavowing their ancestors. In his 1999 book *Man Corn: Cannibalism and Violence in the Prehistoric American Southwest,* Turner proposed that the Anasazi culture was a violent one obsessed with ritual consumption of human flesh. Granted, the cannibalism could have been introduced by a Mexican culture, perhaps the Toltecs, and used against the Anasazi as a means of terrorizing them. In any case, his theory proposed an answer to a nagging question: What about all those piles of mangled human bones and fire-blackened skulls found at Chaco Canyon, Mesa Verde, and other Ancestral Puebloan sites?

Many of Turner's colleagues were skeptical, if not downright shocked, and Pueblo Indians were, and still are, outraged at the accusations about their people. Turner and other archaeologists were banned from excavations in Mesa Verde. In the years since Turner published *Man Corn,* however, evidence to support his theory seems to have grown. For instance, other researchers found coprolites (preserved human feces) that tested positive for human proteins. Whether or not cannibalism was a regular part of Ancestral Puebloan life, the evidence Turner uncovered does create a bleak and violent picture of life in what today appear to be peaceful valleys and canyons.

THE SPANISH ARRIVE

These settlements were what the Spanish explorer **Francisco Vásquez de Coronado** and his crew saw when they first ventured into the area in 1540. Their Spanish word for the villages, *pueblos,* stuck and is still the name for both the places and the people who live in them. Coronado wasn't impressed, however, because the pueblos were made out of mud, not gold as he had been hoping. So after two years and a couple of skirmishes with the natives, the team turned around and headed back to Mexico City.

It took another 50 years for the Spanish to muster more interest in the area. This time, in 1598, **Don Juan de Oñate** led a small group of Spanish families to settle on the banks of the Rio Grande, at a place they called San Gabriel, near Ohkay Owingeh (which they called San Juan Pueblo). About a decade later, the settlers moved away from their American Indian neighbors, to the new village of Santa Fe. The territory's third governor, Don Pedro de Peralta, made it the official capital of the territory of Nuevo México, which in those days stretched far into what is now Colorado and Arizona.

This time the colonists, mostly farmers, were motivated not so much by hopes of striking it rich but simply of making a living. Moreover, they were inspired by Catholic

Don Juan de Oñate was one of the early Spanish governors.

zeal, and Franciscan missionaries accompanied them to promote the faith among the Puebloans. It was partly these missionaries and their ruthless oppression of the native religion that drove the Indians to organize the **Pueblo Revolt** of 1680. The Franciscans' "conversion" strategy involved public executions of the pueblos' medicine men, among other violent assaults on local traditions. But the Spanish colonists were no help either. In their desperation to squeeze wealth out of the hard land, they exploited the only resource they had, the slave labor of the Indians, who were either conscripts or stolen from their families. (The Indians did their share of poaching from Spanish families too, creating a violent sort of cultural exchange program.)

The leader of the Pueblo Revolt was a man named Popé (also spelled Po'pay), from San Juan Pueblo. Using Taos Pueblo as his base, he traveled to the other communities, secretly meeting with leaders to plan a united insurrection. Historians theorize he may have used Spanish to communicate with other Puebloans who did not speak his native Tewa, and he distributed among the conspirators lengths of knotted rope with which to count down the days to the insurrection. Although the Spanish captured a few of the rope-bearing messengers (Isleta Pueblo may never have gotten the message, which could explain its being the only pueblo not to participate), they could not avert the bloodshed. The Puebloan warriors killed families and missionaries, burned crops, and toppled churches. Santa Fe was besieged, and its population of more than 1,000 finally evacuated in a pitiful retreat.

The Spanish stayed away for 12 years, but finally a new governor, **Diego de Vargas**, took it upon himself to reclaim the land the Spanish had settled. He managed to talk many pueblos into peaceful surrender, meeting resistance only in Taos and Santa Fe, where a two-day fight was required to oust the Indians from the Palace of the Governors; in Taos, violence ground on for an additional four years. The Spanish strategy in the post-revolt era was softer, with more compromise between the Franciscans and their intended flock, and a fair amount of cultural and economic exchange. The threat of raiding Comanche, Apache, and Navajo also forced both sides to cooperate. Banding together for defense, they were finally able to drive the Comanche away, culminating in a 1778 battle with Chief Cuerno Verde (Green Horn). The decisive victory is celebrated in the ritual dance called Los Comanches, still performed in small villages by Hispanos and Puebloans alike.

The other bonding force was trade. The Spanish maintained the **Camino Real de Tierra Adentro** (Royal Road of the Interior), which linked Santa Fe with central Mexico—the route follows roughly the line carved by I-25 today. Caravans came through only every year or two, but the profit from furs, pottery, textiles, and other local goods was enough to keep both cultures afloat, if utterly dependent on the Spanish government.

Diego de Vargas reclaimed the city of Santa Fe following the Pueblo Revolt.

1643 — DE VARGAS — 1704

MEXICAN INDEPENDENCE AND THE FIRST ANGLOS

Spain carefully guarded all of its trade routes in the New World, even in a relatively unprofitable territory like Nuevo México. The only outside trade permitted was through the Comancheros, a ragtag band who traded with Comanche and other Plains Indians, working well into what would later be Oklahoma and even up to North Dakota. The Spanish governor encouraged them because their tight relationship with the Comanche helped protect New Mexico and Texas against intruders.

Interlopers were not welcome. Only a few enterprising fur trappers, lone mountain men in search of beaver pelts, slipped in. Spy-explorer **Zebulon Pike** and his crew were captured (perhaps intentionally, so Pike could get more inside information) and detained in Santa Fe for a spell in 1807. But in 1821, Mexico declared independence from Spain, liberating the territory of Nuevo México along with it. One of the first acts of the new government was to open the borders to trade. Initially just a trickle of curious traders came down the rough track from St. Louis, Missouri, but soon a flood of commerce flowed along the increasingly rutted and broad **Santa Fe Trail,** making the territory's capital city a meeting place between Mexicans and Americans swapping furs, gold, cloth, and more.

THE MEXICAN-AMERICAN WAR AND AFTER

Pike's expedition gave the U.S. government new details about the locations of Spanish forts. Just as important, Pike, who returned not long after Lewis and Clark completed their march across the Louisiana Purchase, helped fuel the country's expansionist fervor. In the next few decades, **"manifest destiny"** became the phrase on every American's lips, and the government was eyeing the Southwest. It annexed Texas in 1845, but New Mexico, with its small population and meager resources, didn't figure heavily in the short-lived war that followed. The Mexican governor surrendered peacefully to General Stephen Kearny when he arrived in Santa Fe in 1846. In Taos, the transition was not accepted so readily, as Hispano business leaders and Taos Pueblo Indians instigated a brief but violent uprising, in which the first American governor, Charles Bent, was beheaded.

During the **Civil War,** New Mexico was in the way of a Texan Confederate strategy to secure the Southwest, but the rebels were thwarted in 1862 at the Battle of Glorieta Pass. The territory stayed in the hands of the Union until the end of the war, and people were more concerned with the local, increasingly brutal skirmishes caused by the arrival in Santa Fe of Bishop Jean-Baptiste Lamy, a tyrannical—or at least very out-of-touch—Frenchman who tried to impose a European vision of the Catholic Church on a populace that had been beyond centralized control for centuries.

Even more significant to New Mexico's development was the arrival of the **railroad** in 1880, as it was laid through Raton Pass, near Santa Fe, and close to Albuquerque. Virtually overnight, strange goods and even stranger people came pouring into one of the remoter frontier outposts of the United States. Anglo influence was suddenly everywhere, in the form of new architecture (red brick was an Eastern affectation) and new business. Albuquerque, almost directly on the new railway tracks, boomed, while Santa Fe's fortunes slumped and Taos all but withered away, having peaked back in the late days of the Camino Real.

But while wheeler-dealers were setting up shop in central New Mexico, some more intrepid souls were poking around in the less-connected areas farther north. These tourists were artists who valued New Mexico not for its commercial potential but for its dramatic landscapes and exotic populace who seemed untouched by American ways. From the early 20th century on, Santa Fe and Taos were cultivated as art colonies, a function they still fulfill today.

FROM STATEHOOD TO WORLD WAR II

Based on its burgeoning economy, New Mexico became the 47th state in the union in 1912, effectively marking the end of the frontier period, a phase of violence, uncertainty, and isolation that lasted about 300 years, longer here than anywhere else in the United States. In addition to the painters and writers flocking to the new state, another group of migrants arrived: tuberculosis patients. Soon the state was known as a health retreat, and countless people did stints in its dry air to treat their ailing lungs.

One of these patients was J. Robert Oppenheimer, whose mild case of TB got him packed off to a camp near Pecos for a year after high school. He loved northern New Mexico and got to know some of its more hidden pockets. So when the U.S. Army asked him if he had an idea where it should establish a secret base for the **Manhattan Project,** he knew just the place: a little camp high on a plateau above Santa Fe, named Los Alamos. This was the birthplace of the atomic bomb, a weird, close-knit community of the country's greatest scientific minds (and biggest egos), working in utter secrecy. Only after the bomb was tested at White Sands and Fat Man and Little Boy were dropped over Japan was the mysterious camp's mission revealed.

CONTEMPORARY HISTORY

The A-bomb ushered New Mexico into the modern era. Not only was it world-changing technology, but it also boosted the local economy. High-paying support staff jobs at Los Alamos and Kirtland Air Force Base in Albuquerque helped pull some of the population out of subsistence farming and into a life that involved cars and electricity. But even

so, the character of the state remained conservative and closed, so when the 1960s rolled around and New Mexico's empty space looked like the promised land to hippies, the culture clash was fierce. Staunch Catholic farmers took potshots at their naked, hallucinogen-ingesting neighbors who fantasized about getting back to the land but had no clue how to do it. After a decade or so, though, only the hardiest of the commune-dwellers were left, and they'd mellowed a bit, while the locals had come to appreciate at least their enthusiasm. Even if the communes didn't last, hippie culture has proven remarkably persistent—even today, distinctly straight Hispanos can be heard saying things like, "I was tripping out on that band, man," and the state still welcomes Rainbow Gatherings, would-be Buddhists, and alternative healers.

The end of the 20th century saw unprecedented growth in both Albuquerque and Santa Fe. As usual, Albuquerque got the practical-minded development, such as the Intel chip-manufacturing plant and the services headquarters for Gap Inc., while Santa Fe was almost felled by its own artsiness, turned inside-out during a few frenzied years in the early 1990s when movie stars and other moneyed types bought up prime real estate. In just a matter of months, rents went up tenfold and houses started selling for more than $1 million. Santa Fe has yet to work out the imbalance between its creative forces, which did save the city from utter decline, and economic ones, though it implemented a living-wage law in 2009.

Meanwhile, Taos has grown slowly but steadily, as have the pueblos, thanks to the legalization of gambling on their lands, but all of these communities still have an air of old New Mexico, where the frontier flavor and solitude can still be felt.

Government and Economy

New Mexico doesn't look so good on paper—in national rankings of income, education, and more, it often ranks 49th or 50th. "New Mexico is a third-world country," is a common quip, at least among an older generation that's seen a long lifetime of nepotism and incompetence. But these issues have also inspired a good deal of activist sentiment, and politics are lively as the economy has begun to slip out of some of its old restrictive patterns.

GOVERNMENT

New Mexico's political scene is as diverse as its population, though the cities tend to vote Democrat. In 2008, the state went squarely for Obama, after he rallied Hispanics with the slogan "Obamanos!" Then-governor Bill Richardson was tapped as a potential cabinet member, but then withdrew after insinuations of corruption. He stepped aside in 2010 for Republican Susana Martinez, New Mexico's first woman governor. (The election would've been historic either way: Her opponent was also a woman.) Reacting to post-crash economic woes, Martinez rapidly swung policies to the right. That swing continued in the 2012 presidential election, as counties skewed extremely red or blue; former governor and Libertarian Gary Johnson took 3.5 percent of the vote, his highest stake in the nation.

New Mexico is notable for its high Hispanic representation in every level of government, including the state legislature, which is 44 percent Hispanic. This nearly matches the state Hispanic population of about 47 percent (as of 2012), and it has helped keep the immigration debate at a relatively polite pitch—unlike in neighboring Arizona, where the Hispanic population is underrepresented in the government.

Each American Indian pueblo (as well as Navajo, Zuni, and Apache lands elsewhere in the state) acts as a sovereign nation, with its own laws, tax regulations, police forces, and government. Indians vote in U.S. and state elections, but in the pueblos, most domestic issues are decided by a tribal governor, a war chief, and a few other officials elected by a consensus of men in the kiva.

ECONOMY

In 2011, 21.5 percent of the population was living below the poverty level, compared with the national average of 15.9 percent. It's also near the bottom in the number of high school and college graduates per capita. Statistics in the pueblos and reservations are even grimmer, with up to 50 percent unemployment in some areas—though this is changing due to casino-fueled development.

The 2008 recession hit the state hard, but its overall unemployment rate has been lower than the national average, in part because Albuquerque continues to be a **manufacturing** center for computer chips, mattresses, specialty running shoes, and more. And the city where Microsoft was founded (then Bill Gates and Paul Allen moved back to Seattle to be close to their families) does foster **technology** development, as a range of tech specialists cater to Sandia National Labs. **Aerospace** manufacturing parks are growing outside Albuquerque. At press time, private spaceflights were on the brink of departure from Spaceport America near Truth or Consequences, south of Albuquerque.

Outside the cities, significant profits from coal, copper, oil, and natural gas—most in the southern part of the state, as well as in the northwest—keep the economy afloat. That's the big money, but the **agricultural** sector, from dairy cows in the south to apple orchards along the Rio Grande to beef jerky from the numerous cattle ranches, contributes a decent amount to the pot. And Santa Fe's **arts** sector shouldn't be overlooked—galleries post sales of $200 million every year, though they're criticized for sending much of that money right back to artists who live and work out of state. Thanks to tax rebates, the **film industry,** nicknamed "Tamalewood," has flourished. Albuquerque Studios is one of the largest production facilities in the country.

Even if the economic situation isn't ideal, it's nothing New Mexicans aren't used to—low income has been the norm for so long that a large segment of the population is, if not content with, at least adapted to eking out a living from very little (the median family income is only around $44,800, compared with the U.S. median of $53,000). In this respect, the state hasn't lost its frontier spirit at all.

Local Culture

New Mexico's 1.8 million people have typically been described as a tricultural mix of Indians, Spanish, and Anglos. That self-image has begun to expand as residents have delved deeper into history and seen that the story involves a few more threads.

DEMOGRAPHY

The labels of Indian, Spanish, and Anglo are used uniquely in New Mexico. First, **Indian:** This is still a common term, as "Native American" never fully caught on. You'll see "American Indian" in formal situations, but even the "American" part is a bit laughable, considering "America" wasn't so named until Christopher Columbus made his voyage west. "Indian" refers to a number of different peoples who do not share a common culture or language: Navajo on the west side of the state, Jicarilla and Mescalero Apache, and the Puebloans of the Rio Grande and west as far as Acoma and Zuni. "Pueblo" refers not to a particular tribe, but to a larger group of people who speak four distinct languages but are banded together by a common way of living. Typically, people will identify themselves by their particular tribe: Santa Clara, for instance, or Taos. With about 10.2 percent of the population claiming American Indian ancestry (nearly 10 times the national average, and second only to Alaska), traditions are still strong. Though of course they've changed, as neon-dyed feathers trim kids' ceremonial headdresses and wealth from casinos funds new housing projects.

Spanish really means that: the people, primarily in northern New Mexico, whose ancestors were Spaniards, rather than the mestizos of Mexico. For many families, it's a point of pride similar to that of *Mayflower* descendants. Over the years, particularly during the 20th century, a steady influx of Mexican immigrants blurred racial distinctions a bit, but it also reinforced the use of Spanish as a daily language and inspired pride in the culture's music and other folkways. In some circles, the word **Hispano** is used to label New Mexico's distinct culture with centuries-old Iberian roots, which includes the **Basques,** who came here both during the conquest (Don Juan de Oñate, the first Spanish governor, was Basque) and in the early 20th century as sheepherders. The discovery of families of **crypto-Jews** (Spanish Jews who nominally converted to Catholicism but fled here to avoid the Inquisition) has added another fascinating layer to the Spanish story, along with the knowledge that many of the first Spanish explorers likely had Arab blood as well.

Anglo is the most imprecise term, as it can mean anyone who's not Spanish or Indian. Originally used to talk about traders of European descent who came to hunt and sell furs and trade on the Santa Fe Trail, it still refers to people who can't trace their roots back to the conquistadors or farther. If you're a Vietnamese immigrant, a Tibetan refugee, or an African American whose family settled a farm here after the Civil War, you could be Anglo—though nowadays, it's usually said in jest. (As of 2012, about 39.8 percent of the population was non-Hispanic

Caucasian; Asians were only 1.6 percent, and African Americans made up 2.4 percent.) But all Anglo culture is shot through with Spanish and Indian influence, whether among the organic garlic farmers from California who rely on their acequias for water or the New Age seekers who do sweat-lodge rituals.

Even with a liberal application of "Anglo," the tricultural arrangement is limiting, as it doesn't assign a place to contemporary immigrants from Mexico and other Latin American countries, and their numbers are growing steadily. It also doesn't acknowledge the strong Mexican American **Chicano** culture that's shared across the Southwest, from Los Angeles through Texas. The U.S. census form lumps both newer arrivals and old Spanish under "Hispanic"—a category (distinct from race) that made up 47 percent of the population in 2012, the highest in the country.

RELIGION

Four hundred years after the arrival of the Franciscan missionaries, New Mexico is still a heavily **Catholic** state—even KFC offers a Friday-night fish fry during Lent. But the relative isolation of the territory produced some variances that have disturbed the Vatican. In both Indian and Spanish churches, the pageantry of medieval Christianity is preserved. Las Posadas, the reenactment of Mary and Joseph's search for lodging in Bethlehem, is a festive torch-lit tradition every December, and during the annual Holy Week pilgrimage to Chimayó, devoted groups stage the stations of the cross, complete with 100-pound wood beams and lots of fake blood.

The Pueblo Indians play on church-as-theater too: During Christmas Eve Mass, for instance, the service may come to an abrupt end as the priest is hustled off the pulpit by face-painted clowns making way for the parade of ceremonial dancers down the aisle. In both cultures, the Mexican Virgin of Guadalupe is highly revered, and a number of saints are honored as intercessors for all manner of dilemmas, from failing crops to false imprisonment.

Eastern religions have a noticeable presence in New Mexico as well, and even a bit of political clout. A community of primarily American-born converts to **Sikhism** in Española, for example, is a major donor to both parties. Santa Fe is home to a substantial number of **Buddhists,** both American converts and native Tibetan refugees who have relocated to this different mountainous land. Stupas can be found up and down the Rio Grande.

LANGUAGE

English is the predominant language, but **Spanish** is very commonly used—about 30 percent of the population speaks it regularly. Spanish-speakers in northern New Mexico were for centuries only the old Hispano families, communicating in a variant of Castilian with a distinct vocabulary that developed in isolation. This "Quixotic" dialect changed little until the early 1900s, when immigrants arrived from Mexico and elsewhere in Latin America. For much of the 20th century, English was the only permissible classroom language, although many school districts required Spanish as a foreign language. Since the 1990s, education policy has shifted to include bilingual classrooms.

Additionally, you'll occasionally hear Indians speaking their respective languages. Of the four main Pueblo tongues, **Tewa, Tiwa,** and **Towa** are part of the Tanoan family of languages (Kiowa, spoken by Plains Indians, is the fourth member). They are related but mutually unintelligible, roughly equivalent to, say, French, Spanish, and Italian. Tewa is the most widely spoken, used in all of the pueblos just north of Santa Fe: Ohkay Owingeh, San Ildefonso, Santa Clara, Pojoaque, Tesuque, and Nambé. Four pueblos speak Tiwa—Taos and Picurís share one dialect, while Isleta and Sandia, in an odd pocket near Albuquerque, speak a different dialect. Towa is now spoken only at Jemez Pueblo.

Keresan (spoken in Laguna, Acoma, Cochiti, Kewa, San Felipe, Santa Ana, and Zia) is what linguists call an "isolate." Like Basque,

New Mexico's Penitentes

the Penitente *morada* in Truchas

Most Hispano villages in northern New Mexico have a modest one-story building called a *morada*—the meeting place of **Los Hermanos Penitentes** (The Penitent Brothers), a lay Catholic fraternity with deep roots in medieval Spain and a history that has often put it at odds with the church.

The Penitentes developed in New Mexico in the early colonial era and were at the height of their influence during the so-called Secular Period (1790-1850), when the Franciscans had been pushed out by church leaders in Mexico but no new priests were sent to the territory. Members of the brotherhood cared for the ill, conducted funerals, and settled petty disputes and even elections. They maintained the spiritual and political welfare of their villages when there were no priests or central government to do so.

The Penitentes are best known for their intense religious rituals, which are rumored to still include self-flagellation, bloodletting, and mock crucifixion—activities that took place in public processions for centuries but were driven underground in the late 19th century following official church condemnation. The secrecy, along with sensational journalism by visitors from the East Coast, fueled gruesome rumors. For their crucifixion reenactments, it was said Penitentes used real nails, and the man drawn by lot to be the *Cristo* had a good chance of dying—though no eyewitness ever recorded the practice on paper. One well-documented ritual involves pulling *la carretera del muerte,* an oxcart filled with rocks and a wooden figure of Doña Sebastiana, Lady Death. Morbid imagery bred morbid curiosity: Photos in a *Harper's* magazine story from the early 1900s show Anglos looking on agog as Penitentes clad in white pants and black hoods whip themselves.

In 1947, after years of concerted lobbying (but not an official renunciation of its rituals), the Penitentes were again accepted into the fold of the Catholic Church. The *hermanos mayores* (head brothers) from all of the *moradas* convene annually in Santa Fe, and the group, which has an estimated 3,000 members, functions as a political and public-service club.

The rituals do continue, most visibly during Holy Week, when the group's devotion to the physical suffering of the human Jesus is at its keenest. The Penitentes reenact the stations of the cross and the crucifixion, and although ketchup is more prevalent than real blood and statues often stand in for the major players, the scenes are solemn and affectingly tragic. On some days during Holy Week, the *morada* is open to non-Penitentes—a rare chance for outsiders to see the meeting place of this secretive group.

it is not connected to neighboring languages, nor to any other language. Additionally, each Keresan-speaking pueblo has developed its own dialect, so immediately adjacent communities can understand each other, but those farthest apart cannot.

One interesting characteristic of the Pueblo languages is that they have remained relatively pure. Tewa vocabulary, for instance, is still less than 5 percent loan words, despite centuries of Spanish and English influence. This is probably due to the way speakers have long been forced to compartmentalize, using Tewa for conversation at home and switching to English or Spanish for business and trade. For centuries, the Franciscan priests, then the U.S. government, attempted to stamp out Native American languages. Following the Civil War, Puebloan children were moved forcibly to boarding schools, where they were given Anglo names and permitted to speak only English, a policy that continued for decades.

Only in 1990, with the passage of the **Native American Languages Act,** were American Indian languages officially permitted in government-funded schools—indeed, they are now recognized as a unique element of this country's culture and encouraged. In Taos, where the Tiwa language is a ritual secret that outsiders are not permitted to learn, one public school has Tiwa classes for younger students, open only to tribe members and taught by approved teachers; as an added measure against the language being recorded, the classroom has no chalkboard. Less-formal instruction within the pueblos as well as on the Navajo Nation has also helped the Indian languages enjoy a renaissance.

The Arts

New Mexico is a hotbed of creativity, from Santa Fe's edgy contemporary art scene to traditional Spanish folk artists working in remote villages, using the same tools their great-grandfathers did. Here's what to look out for in the more traditional arenas of pottery, weaving, jewelry, and wood carving.

POTTERY

New Mexico's pottery tradition thrives, drawing on millennia of craftsmanship. About 2,000 years ago, the **Mogollon** people in the southern part of the state began making simple pots of brown coiled clay. A thousand years later, the craft had developed into the beautiful black-on-white symmetry of the **Mimbres** people. Later, each of the pueblos developed its own style.

By the 20th century, some traditions had died out, but almost all felt some kind of renaissance following the work of San Ildefonso potter **María Martinez** in the first half of the 20th century. Along with her husband, Julian, Martinez revived a long-lost style of lustrous black pottery with subtle matte decoration. The elegant pieces, which looked at once innovative and traditional, inspired Anglo collectors (who saw the couple's work at the 1934 Chicago World's Fair, among other places) as well as local potters. Today, many artists make their livings with clay.

The various tribal styles are distinguished by their base clay, the "slip" (the clay-and-water finish), and their shape. Taos and Picurís pueblos, for instance, are surrounded by beds of micaceous clay, which lends pots a subtle glitter. (It also helps them withstand heat well; they're renowned for cooking beans.) Acoma specializes in intricate black designs painted on thin white clay. Pottery from Ohkay Owingeh (formerly San Juan) is typically reddish-brown with incised symbols. And Santa Clara developed the "wedding jar," a double-neck design with a handle. If a particular style catches your eye in city galleries, then you can visit the specific pueblo, where you may be able to buy directly from the artisan and perhaps see where the piece was made.

Luminarias or *Farolitos?*

The cultural differences between Santa Fe and Albuquerque don't apply just to the number of art galleries per square block and whether you eat posole or rice with your enchiladas. Every Christmas, a debate rears its head: What do you call a paper bag with a bit of sand in the bottom and a votive candle inside? These traditional holiday decorations, which line driveways and flat adobe rooftops in the last weeks of December, are commonly known as luminarias in Albuquerque and most towns to the south, and as *farolitos* in Santa Fe and all the villages to the north.

To complicate matters, another holiday tradition in Santa Fe and other northern towns is to light small bonfires of piñon logs in front of houses. And Santa Feans call these little stacks of wood ... luminarias. *Farolitos*, they argue, are literally "little lanterns," an accurate description of the glowing paper bags—and under this logic, the use of the term *farolito* has spread a bit in Albuquerque, at least among people who weren't raised saying luminaria from birth.

But *Burqueños* have Webster's on their side; the dictionary concurs that luminarias are paper-bag lanterns and notes the tradition comes from Mexico, where the bags are often colored and pricked with holes. Because this author's loyalties are to Albuquerque, the argument is settled, at least in these pages: Luminaria it is.

TEXTILES

After pottery, **weaving** is probably the state's most widespread craft. Historically, Indian and Spanish weaving styles were separate, but they have merged over the centuries to create some patterns and styles unique to the Rio Grande Valley. The first Spanish explorers marveled at the Navajo cotton blankets, woven in whole panels on wide looms; Spaniards had been working with narrow looms and stitching two panels together. Spanish weavers introduced the hardy Churro sheep, with its rough wool that was good for hand-spinning, as well as new dyes, such as indigo (although the blue-tinted rugs are often called **Moki** rugs, using a Navajo word).

In the early 1800s, in an attempt to make a better product for trade, the Spanish government sent Mexican artists north to work with local weavers. Out of this meeting came the distinctive **Saltillo** styles (named for the region the Mexican teachers came from), such as the running-leaf pattern, which Rio Grande weavers alternated with solid-color stripes. In the 1880s, New Mexican artisans first saw quilts from the eastern United States, and they adapted the eight-pointed star to their wool rugs. Another popular motif from the 19th century is a zigzag pattern that resembles lightning.

One item that shows up in antiques shops is the **Chimayó blanket,** an invention of the tourist age in the early 20th century, when Anglo traders encouraged local Hispano weavers to make an affordable souvenir to sell to visitors looking for "Indian" blankets. They're handsome, single-width rugs with a strong central motif, perhaps the iconic Southwestern-look rug.

Also look for *colcha* work, a Spanish style in which a loose-weave rug is decorated with wool embroidery. It was revived in the 1930s by Mormons, and you will occasionally see beautiful examples from this period in collectors' shops. Contemporary weaving can draw on any and all of these innovations and is practiced just as often by a young Anglo as a Hispano grandmother. A strong small-batch wool industry in New Mexico helps the scene tremendously—expect to see vivid color-block contemporary pieces alongside the most traditional patterns.

JEWELRY

Despite a long native tradition, the familiar forms of jewelry seen today date only from the mid-19th century, when the Navajo of western New Mexico pioneered silversmithing and taught it to the Pueblo Indians. The most iconic piece of Southwestern jewelry, a signature Navajo design, is the turquoise-and-silver **squash-blossom necklace,** a large crescent pendant decorated with flowerlike silver beads. Actually derived from Spanish pomegranate decorations, rather than native plant imagery, it's seen in every Santa Fe jewelry store.

Look also for shell-shaped **concha belts** (also spelled "concho"), silver "shells" linked together or strung on a leather belt, and the San Felipe specialty, *heishi,* tiny disks made of shell and threaded to make a rope-like strand. The Zuni carve small animal **fetishes**—bears, birds, and more—often strung on necklaces with heishi. In addition to turquoise, opals are a popular decorative stone, along with brick-red coral, lapis lazuli, and black jet and marble. Whatever you buy, the gallery or artisan should supply you with a written receipt of its components—which stones, the grade of silver, and so forth.

Turquoise

Although New Mexico's turquoise is all mined out, the stone is still an essential part of local jewelry-making; most of it is imported from

mines in China. It is available in shades from lime-green to pure sky-blue, and much of it has been subjected to various processes to make it stabler and more versatile, which affects the price.

Rare gem-grade turquoise is the top of the line—a high-quality piece with complex spiderwebbing from now-empty mines like Lander or Lone Mountain can cost $350 per carat. "Gem-grade" applies only to **natural stones** (those that have not been chemically treated in any way) and is based on the piece's luster, hardness, and matrix, the term for the web of dark veins running through it, which you should be able to feel in any natural turquoise, regardless of grade. Highest-quality stones from still-functioning mines in China or Tibet will cost significantly less ($10-20 per carat) but will be of the same quality as some premium American stones. Slightly less splendid natural stones are graded jewelry-quality, high-quality, or investment-quality—but they are not quite hard enough to guarantee they will not change color over decades. They cost $2-5 per carat. For any natural stone, the seller must provide you with a written certificate of its status.

Because good natural turquoise is increasingly difficult to come by and turquoise is

raw turquoise for sale at a flea market

such an unreliable stone, various treatments are a common and acceptable way of making a great deal of the stuff usable. **Treated turquoise** refers to any stone that has added resins, waxes, or other foreign elements. A certain proprietary treatment, **enhanced turquoise,** also called "Zachary process turquoise," is usually applied to medium-grade or higher stones.

Turquoise that has been **stabilized,** or submerged in epoxy resin to harden it and deepen the color, makes up the bulk of the market. Because it's less expensive, it allows for a little waste in the carving process, and good quality stabilized turquoise is often found in expensive jewelry with elaborate inlay. Average-quality stabilized stone, the next grade down, is used by perhaps 70 percent of American Indian artisans—it can stand up to being carved and is very well priced. Though it ranks relatively low in the range of turquoise available, it produces an attractive piece of jewelry—perhaps not with the elaborate spiderwebbing of a rare piece, but with an overall good color and luster.

Below this are low-quality stabilized stones that have been artificially colored (often called "color shot," or, more confusing, "color stabilized"). **"Synthetic"** stones are actually real turquoise—small chunks mixed with a binding powder of ground turquoise or pyrite, then pressed into shapes and cut. The result is surprisingly attractive, with natural spiderwebbing, but it should be clearly labeled as synthetic. And of course there is the turquoise that isn't at all—plastic stuff that can be quite convincing.

Aside from the synthetic stuff, don't worry too much about getting "bad" or "cheap" turquoise—because each stone is different, the more important thing is to find a piece that's attractive to you and is priced to reflect its quality. Just remember that the words "genuine," "authentic," or "pure" have no real meaning—only "natural" is legally defined. Likewise, the phrase **"authentic Indian handmade"** is a legal one—any variation on this wording (such as "Indian crafted") is likely some kind of ruse. Shopping in New Mexico provides many opportunities to buy direct from the artisan—under the portal at the Palace of the Governors in Santa Fe, for instance. Otherwise, just avoid shopping in too-good-to-be-true stores that are perpetually "going out of business" or "in liquidation."

WOOD AND TINWORK

When Spanish colonists arrived in New Mexico, they had few resources, little money, and only the most basic tools. A group of settlers would typically include one carpenter, whose skills helped fill everyone's houses with heavy wood **furniture** (still made today). But the carpenter also helped the group to worship—for chief among the wood-carvers was (and is) the *santero* or *santera,* who carves images of saints. These so-called **santos** can be either flat (*retablos*) or three-dimensional (*bultos*) and are typically painted in lively colors, though some outstanding work has been produced in plain, unpainted wood.

Santo styles have shown remarkable continuity over the centuries. The most notable break from tradition was by Patrocinio Barela, whose WPA-sponsored work in the 1930s was almost fluid, utilizing the natural curves and grains of the wood. His sons and grandsons practice the art today. For centuries, the piousness of the *santero* was valued at least as much as his skill in carving, though many contemporary carvers do their work for a large market of avid collectors. One popular figure is San Isidro, patron saint of farmers, from 12th-century Spain.

Look also for **straw marquetry,** another product of hard times in the colonial period, in which tiny fibers of "poor man's gold" replaced precious metals as inlay to make elaborate geometric designs on dark wood. Tinwork is another ubiquitous craft, found in inexpensive votive-candle holders as well as elaborately punched and engraved mirror frames and chandeliers.

Essentials

Transportation

GETTING THERE

Air

Albuquerque International Sunport (ABQ; 505/244-7700, www.cabq.gov/airport) is the main access point to the region. It's served by all major U.S. air carriers, including Southwest Airlines and JetBlue. Fares fluctuate on the same schedule as the rest of the country, with higher rates in summer and over holidays; in the winter, it's wise to choose a connection through a more temperate hub, such as Dallas (American) or Salt Lake City (Delta).

Small **Santa Fe Municipal Airport** (SAF; 121 Aviation Dr.; 505/955-2900), west of the city, receives direct flights from Dallas and Los Angeles with American Eagle, and from Denver with United.

Train

Amtrak (800/872-7245, www.amtrak.com) runs the *Southwest Chief* daily between Chicago and Los Angeles, stopping in **Lamy** (18 miles from Santa Fe) and **Albuquerque.**

Arriving in Albuquerque, you're in the middle of downtown, in a depot shared with Greyhound. There are lockers here (occasionally full), and city buses are available just up the block. Lamy (the stop nearest Santa Fe) is no more than a depot—though it is a dramatic and wild-feeling place to get off the train. Amtrak provides an awkwardly timed shuttle service to Santa Fe hotels (passengers arriving on eastbound trains must wait for passengers from the westbound train, an hour later). From Chicago, Amtrak pads its schedule heavily between Lamy and Albuquerque—so if the train is running behind, you'll be late arriving in Lamy but generally will still get to Albuquerque on schedule.

Bus

Greyhound (800/231-2222, www.greyhound.com) connects New Mexico with adjacent states and Mexico. Routes run roughly along I-40 and I-25, with little service to outlying areas. If you're coming from elsewhere in the Southwest, you may want to investigate **El Paso-Los Angeles Limousine Express** (915/532-4061 in El Paso, 626/442-1945 in Los Angeles, 505/247-8036 in Albuquerque, www.eplalimo.com), a long-established operator that originally served the Mexican immigrant population—it connects Denver and Albuquerque.

Car

Conveniently, northern New Mexico is crisscrossed by interstates: **I-40** runs east-west, and **I-25** cuts roughly down the center, north-south. Denver, Colorado, to Santa Fe is 450 miles, about a 6-hour drive; add another hour to reach Albuquerque. El Paso, Texas, to Albuquerque is 275 miles, about 4 hours. Coming from Flagstaff, Arizona, Albuquerque is 325 miles along I-40, about 4.5 hours; from Amarillo, Texas, it's just slightly less distance in the other direction.

Southwest road-trippers often combine New Mexico with southwestern Colorado, in which case **U.S. 550** makes a good route south from Durango, and **U.S. 84** runs from Pagosa Springs. From Tucson, Arizona, a nice route into New Mexico is to cut north off I-10 at Lordsburg, following Highway 90 to Silver City and winding through the mountains northeast to reach I-25 to Albuquerque.

GETTING AROUND

This book covers a relatively small area—about 200 miles from north to south. Within

Albuquerque and Santa Fe, you can often get around by walking, biking, or public transport, but count on having a car for at least a portion of your trip.

If you're visiting just Albuquerque or Santa Fe, you can get around on foot and public transport—easily in Santa Fe, and with a little planning in Albuquerque. A commuter rail line links the two cities, with handy stops in each downtown area. Parking in downtown Santa Fe can be expensive and difficult, so it's best to rent a car only for day trips out of the city. Taos, however, has only minimal bus service, so a car will make things much easier.

Bus

Between Santa Fe and Taos (and communities around and in between, including the pueblos), the **North Central Regional Transit District** (866/206-0754, www.ncrtd.org) offers commuter bus service. It's not very frequent, but it's free, and it covers a lot of area, making it an option for the hard-core no-car traveler.

Train

The **Rail Runner** (866/795-7245, www.riometro.org) commuter train connects Albuquerque and Santa Fe, with convenient downtown stations in both cities, making a car-free visit quite feasible, or even a day trip. (It also runs south to Belén.) The route passes through odd pockets of Albuquerque and stunning, untouched pueblo lands. Tickets are based on a zone system; the 90-minute ride between downtown Albuquerque and Santa Fe costs $9, or $10 for a day pass. Kids: Listen for the "meep-meep!" warning as the doors close!

Car

Driving New Mexico's scenic byways is definitely one of the pleasures of traveling here. On the other hand, parking in Santa Fe can be unpleasant, or at least expensive—and you can get around the center of town very easily on foot. So, ideally, you would rent a car only for the days you plan to go out of the city. Central Taos is small, but sights are spread out on the fringes, and only the most dedicated can manage without a car. In Albuquerque, you can live without a car for a few days, but it requires planning and rules out a few of the sights. All of the major car-rental chains are at Albuquerque's airport, in a single building; see the respective city chapters for other rental companies and offices.

All but a few roads are passable year-round. You won't need four-wheel drive, but be prepared in winter for ice and snow anywhere other than central Albuquerque. Plan on an hour's drive from Albuquerque to Santa Fe via I-25, and an hour and a half from Santa Fe to Taos via the low road.

Bike

With beautiful vistas, often deserted roads, and a strong community of both road cyclists and mountain bikers, northern New Mexico can be a great place to get around on two wheels, as long as it's not your main form of transport. Whether you'll be riding your own bike or renting one here, always pack a patch kit, and consider installing tire liners. Goathead thorns and broken glass are particular scourges of the highway shoulder.

Central Albuquerque and Santa Fe are both manageable by bicycle, with separate lanes in many cases. Taos is less accommodating, and traffic on the main road through town can be unpleasantly heavy and fast. But both the Rail Runner and the Taos Express bus service accommodate bicycles, so it's possible to take your wheels with you from town to town.

Accommodations and Food

ACCOMMODATIONS

Throughout the book, distinctive choices (along with many exceptionally comfortable bed-and-breakfasts, lodges, and small hotels) are emphasized over chain options as much as possible. But just because the chains are not listed doesn't mean they're not available.

The prices listed are the official high-season rack rates—that is, what you'd pay if you just walked in off the street, with no discounts; tax is not included. Most often, the numbers are the least expensive room for one person in one bed (a single, abbreviated *s*) and two people in two beds (a double, abbreviated *d*). **High season** is usually June-August. **Ski season** is January-March, so prices in Taos and Santa Fe don't completely bottom out—but they are still much cheaper than summer.

Religious Retreats

Christ in the Desert Monastery

One quirk of northern New Mexico is that the area harbors an exceptionally high number of religious retreats of all stripes, set in some of the most scenic, quiet areas. Most of them welcome guests, with no religious strings attached. Facilities are usually basic but comfortable, and rates (suggested donations, officially) are very reasonable, especially for solo travelers, and often include meals. Look for the following properties:

- **Bodhi Manda Zen Center:** Buddhist retreat in Jemez Springs (page 193)
- **Quaker Meeting House:** A single charming guesthouse, in Santa Fe (page 38)
- **Benedictine Monastery:** Not just for men, in the town of Pecos (page 69)
- **Ghost Ranch:** A large Presbyterian retreat in Abiquiu, the most secular-feeling of the bunch (page 86)
- **Christ in the Desert Monastery:** Very remote, outside Abiquiu (page 86)

Expect higher rates in the week following Christmas and during special events, such as Indian Market in Santa Fe and Balloon Fiesta in Albuquerque, but overall you will be able to secure lower rates than those listed simply by looking online or calling the hotel directly.

Note that while many hotels tout their swimming pools, they are often forced to leave them empty due to water restrictions imposed during droughts. If you've booked at a hotel specifically for the pool, call to check the status before your trip, so you don't wind up paying a premium for a service you can't use. Santa Fe is the strictest area in the state, and it also limits hotels to changing towels and bed linens only every four days during your visit.

FOOD

New Mexicans love their food so much, they have been known to enshrine it on lottery tickets, with scratch cards named Chile Cash, Chips and Salsa, and Sopaipilla Dough (promising "lots of honey and plenty of money"). The state cuisine is a distinctive culinary tradition that shouldn't be confused with Tex-Mex, Californian Mex, or south-of-the-border Mexican—even though most locals will say they're going out for "Mexican" when they mean they want a bowl of purely *New* Mexican green-chile stew. (But if you're eating mole or ceviche, that's "*Mexican* Mexican," and you can get more of it the farther south you drive.) New Mexican cuisine doesn't typically do bean-and-meat chili, certainly not mango-flavored anything, and only rarely guacamole—you can get it, but avocados are expensive here.

All Chile, All the Time

The cuisine's distinguishing element is the **New Mexico chile pepper.** The best-known variety is the Hatch chile, named for the southern New Mexican town that's the center of the industry. In the north, Chimayó is another big chile-producing town, with its own heirloom strain, usually picked red.

When the chile is picked green, it is roasted and peeled, then used whole to make chiles rellenos (stuffed with cheese and fried in batter) or cut into chunks and cooked in sauces or used as the base of a meaty green-chile stew. Green chile is a popular pizza topping (great with pepperoni or ham), and the **green-chile cheeseburger** is a top choice everywhere. Also look out for **breakfast burritos,** big flour tortillas filled with scrambled eggs, hash browns, and some kind of meat—bacon, crumbled sausage, or sometimes Mexican chorizo, a spicy pork sausage. Some places sell them as to-go food, wrapped in foil with green chile added to the mix. At a sit-down restaurant, they're smothered in either red or green chile.

When the New Mexico chile is left to ripen, then dried in the sun, it turns turn dark red and leathery. These dry red chiles are stored whole, in long chains called *ristras*, or ground into flakes (*chile caribe*) or finer powder to be the base of a sauce or marinade. The heartiest red-chile dish is *carne adovada*, chunks of pork shoulder stewed with pure red sauce.

Most other items—enchiladas, burritos, and eggs (huevos rancheros), to name a few—can be ordered with either variety of chile, so a standard question in restaurants is "Red or green?" You can have both, splitting the plate half-and-half, a style most people call "Christmas," though old-timers still call it "Mexican flag."

The chile is often coupled with the traditional Native American triad of **corn, squash,** and **beans.** The beans are typically brown, meaty pintos, served whole in a stew or mashed up and "refried" (not actually fried twice—the term is a mistranslation of Spanish *refrito,* which means "really fried"). Corn takes the form of tortillas as well as hulled kernels of hominy, called posole here and often cooked into a stew with chile, oregano, and meat. Ground corn paste (masa) is whipped with lard (or Crisco, if you're "healthy") and wrapped around a meaty filling, then tied in a corn husk and steamed to make a **tamale.** Squash comes in a common side dish called *calabacitas,* sautéed with onions and a touch of green chile.

Red-Chile Sauce

Use only freshly ground New Mexico red chile for this sauce—not the "chile powder" sold in most grocery stores. The sauce will keep in the refrigerator for a month, and you can use it to top eggs or steaks, or devote the whole batch to a tray of enchiladas. (If you're doing the latter, you'll want to keep the sauce relatively runny, so you can easily coat the tortillas with sauce before filling them.) The flavor is best if it is prepared ahead and left to sit overnight.

Yield: 2 cups

½ c. New Mexico red chile powder
½ tsp. ground cumin (optional)
1 tsp. ground coriander (optional)
2 Tbsp. all-purpose flour

2 Tbsp. lard (or vegetable oil)
2 or 3 cloves garlic, crushed or minced
2 c. chicken stock or water
1 tsp. dried oregano (optional)

Measure the chile, cumin, coriander, and flour into a heavy-bottomed saucepan and place over medium-high heat. Stir continuously until the spices are just fragrant and the flour has darkened slightly. Remove the chile-flour mix to a small bowl. Heat the lard or oil in the pan, and add the garlic and stir until fragrant. Then stir the chile-flour mix into the oil-garlic mixture—you will have a very coarse paste. Stirring constantly, slowly add half of the stock or water. Continue stirring, and the mixture will thicken and become velvety. Add the remaining stock or water and the oregano, mix well, turn heat to low, and let sauce simmer for about 20 minutes, until it is somewhat reduced and thickened to your liking. If the mixture becomes too thick, simply add more water.

Spanish settlers brought lamb, which finds its way into tacos and stews.

Sopaipillas are another New Mexican specialty. They're palm-sized pillows of deep-fried dough, used to mop up chile and beans during the main meal, then slathered with honey for dessert. (In a disturbing trend, some restaurants are switching to a honey-flavored corn syrup, because it's cheaper and doesn't crystallize—if you encounter this, complain at top volume.) At the pueblos, sopaipillas are replaced by **fry**

green chile

bread, a round of deep-fried dough served with honey or filled with ground meat, cheese, and lettuce to make an "Indian taco." Pueblo cooks also make more use of the domed adobe horno, or "outside oven," a baking tool brought by the Spanish (and first developed by the Arabs).

Bizcochitos, little anise-laced cookies, are the state's official sweet treat. Wash it all down with a **margarita,** which purists insist should involve only lime, tequila, and triple sec and be served on the rocks in a salt-rimmed glass. (Restaurants with only a beer-and-wine license often offer an agave-wine margarita—okay flavor, but pretty weak.)

How to Take the Heat

When your server plunks down a heavy white ceramic plate covered in chile and melted cheese, the words "this plate is very hot" cover only half of the story. Every year the harvest varies a bit, and the chile can be mild or so spicy as to blister lips and produce a dizzying (and addictive) endorphin rush. Locals look back on particularly incendiary seasons with that mixture of awe, fear, and longing that junkies reserve for their best scores. In general, green chile tends to be hotter than red, but it's best to ask your server what to expect—some restaurants specialize in one or the other.

You can protect yourself against chile-induced burns by ordering a side of sour cream with your enchiladas or burrito—although be warned that this is seen as a "Texan" affectation and may be derided by your fellow diners. Locals usually just reach for a **sopaipilla,** the starch from which can absorb some of the chile oils. Don't gulp down water, which only spreads the searing oils around your mouth. Beer is a marginal improvement, and margaritas are at least distracting.

Fine Dining and Wine

While there are plenty of time-warp diners and mom-and-pop hole-in-the-wall joints in New Mexico, dining can also be very sophisticated, keeping pace with the national trend toward local and organic produce. This movement hasn't been such a huge leap here: Many small family farms didn't have to "go organic," because they were never very industrialized in the first place. At white-tablecloth places, Southwestern fusion is still common, with chile working its way into foie gras appetizers and even high-concept desserts.

The fine dining scene is enhanced by a burgeoning wine industry, initiated by Spanish settlers in the 17th century but enjoying a resurgence since the 1980s. Gruet Winery in Albuquerque is the best-known New Mexico producer, especially for its excellent sparkling wine. This makes for a nice little perk of New Mexico dining: You can get inexpensive bubbly by the glass almost everywhere. The **New Mexico Wine Growers Association** (www.nmwine.com) has information on more wineries, and you can read more about the high-end and organic food scene in *Local Flavor* (www.localflavormagazine.com), a monthly tabloid, and the quarterly *Edible Santa Fe* (www.ediblesantafe.com).

Vegetarian Food

New Mexican food isn't meat-centric, but vegetarians will have to be vigilant, as many chile dishes are traditionally made with beef or chicken stock as well as lard for flavoring. The closer you get to Texas, the more likely it is that red chile sauce will contain bits of meat. Decades of hippie influence, though, have resulted in many menus stating clearly whether the chile is meatless. Some restaurants have an unreconstructed 1970s worldview, with alfalfa sprouts and squash casseroles galore.

Travel Tips

WHAT TO PACK

The contents of your suitcase will be determined largely by the time of year, but be prepared for a **wide range of temperatures**—with a variety of layers—whenever you visit. Many people wrongly assume that New Mexico's desert setting means heat all day, all year round. In fact, due to the altitude, you may encounter severe cold. Winter temperatures can dip well below freezing even in the relatively low elevations of central Albuquerque, though it sees little snow. If you think you'll attend pueblo ceremonial dances during the winter, pack mittens, long underwear, double-thick wool socks, and a hat with earflaps—there will be a lot of standing around outside.

Spring is mud season—if you hike or head to rural areas during this time, save a clean pair of shoes for around town. Summers are hot by day (July's average temperature is 92°F), but as soon as the sun dips below the horizon, the temperature can drop up to 30°F, especially outside of city centers; always keep a sweater on hand. Brief afternoon "monsoons" in July and August sometimes warrant an umbrella or rain slicker. In the strong sun, you'll be more comfortable if you cover up, in long-sleeve, light-colored shirts and pants in silk or cotton. In fact, you should guard against the sun any time of year, as the thin atmosphere at this altitude means you'll burn more quickly than you're used to. You should never be without **sunglasses,** heavy-duty **sunscreen,** and a **brimmed hat.**

As for style, anything goes. If you'll be hobnobbing with Santa Fe's upper echelon, you might want to pack something dressy—the local formalwear for men is clean jeans, shined cowboy boots, and a bolo tie. Otherwise, though, New Mexicans are very casual. But note that when visiting churches

and pueblos, it's respectful to not show excessive skin—women should avoid obvious cleavage and super-short skirts.

TOURIST INFORMATION

For pre-trip inspiration, the New Mexico Tourism Board publishes the monthly **New Mexico** magazine (www.nmmagazine.com), which does an excellent job covering both mainstream attractions and more obscure corners of the state.

If you plan to do a lot of hiking, you can order detailed topographical maps from the **National Forest Service** office in New Mexico (505/842-3292) or from the Bureau of Land Management's **Public Lands Information Center** (www.publiclands.org). Santa Fe's **Travel Bug** (839 Paseo de Peralta, 505/992-0418, 7:30am-5:30pm Mon.-Sat., 11am-4pm Sun.) bookstore also stocks maps.

Telephone and Internet

Albuquerque and Santa Fe use the area code 505, while Taos numbers (and most of the rest of the state) start with 575.

For mobile phone reception, the corridor between Albuquerque and Santa Fe is fine, but in rural areas, phones on the GSM network (AT&T, T-Mobile) get very poor or no reception. Data service is equally spotty. If you'll be spending a lot of time outside of the city or counting on your phone for emergencies, you might consider a CDMA phone (Verizon is best).

Internet access is widespread, though DSL and other high-speed service is still not necessarily the norm, and thick adobe walls can be a hindrance for wireless signals. Rural areas still rely on satellite Internet, which can be poor in bad weather. In the cities, cafés often have hotspots, and the city of Albuquerque even maintains a few free ones in public spaces, such as the Old Town plaza.

TIME ZONE

New Mexico is in the **mountain time** zone, one hour ahead of the West Coast of the United States and two hours behind the East Coast. It's -7 GMT during the winter and -6 GMT in summer, when daylight saving time is followed statewide.

CONDUCT AND CUSTOMS

New Mexico is a part of the United States, but it can sometimes feel quite foreign, particularly in the high mountain Spanish villages and in the Indian pueblos. Regardless, basic courtesy rules, and in smaller communities, modest dress are appreciated, especially at the older Catholic churches.

Some Pueblo Indians find loud voices, direct eye contact, and firm handshakes off-putting and, by the same token, may not express themselves in the forthright way a lot of visitors are used to. Similarly, a subdued reaction doesn't necessarily mean a lack of enthusiasm.

New Mexico is not a wealthy state, and the gap between rich and poor can be wide. In general, people don't appreciate conspicuous displays of wealth, and it's doubly rude to flash cash, fancy gadgets, and jewelry in tiny villages and pueblos (and public cell-phone use is still considered tacky most places). Be thoughtful when taking photos, particularly of people's homes—always ask permission, and consider that some of the more "scenic" elements of New Mexico are also the products of poverty, which some people may not be proud to have captured on film.

You can help the local economy by favoring New Mexican-owned businesses, rather than chain operations, and buying directly from artisans wherever possible. In these situations, don't get too bent on bargaining—the item you're buying represents not just raw materials and hours of work, but a person's particular talent, skill, and heritage; insisting on an extra-low price belittles not just the item, but the artisan as well.

Pueblo Etiquette

When visiting pueblos, remember that you are not at a tourist attraction—you are walking around someone's neighborhood. So peeking in windows and wandering off the suggested route isn't polite. If you want to take photos, you'll usually need a camera permit, for an additional fee. Always ask permission before taking photos of people, and ask parents, rather than children, for their consent. Virtually all pueblos ban alcohol.

Some pueblos are more welcoming than others. San Ildefonso, for instance, is open year-round, whereas Jemez is completely closed, except for some feast days. So it's flawed logic to seek out the less-visited places or go in the off times in order to have a less "touristy" experience. In fact, the most rewarding time to visit *is* on a big feast day—you may not be the only tourist there, but you have a better chance of being invited into a local's home.

CLASSES AND VOLUNTEERING

From afternoon cooking workshops to intensives on adobe building techniques, the opportunities to learn in northern New Mexico are broad.

General Education

Look first into the art, music, and outdoors programs at **Ghost Ranch** (877/804-4678, www.ghostranch.org), the beautiful property in Abiquiu. Santa Fe and Albuquerque are both home to renowned alternative healing, herbal medicine, and massage schools, more than can be listed here; visit **Natural Healers** (www.naturalhealers.com) for a list.

Arts and Crafts

Taos in particular is a hotbed for art classes. **Fechin Art Workshops** (575/751-0647, www.fechin.com) are five-day live-in retreats that have been running for more than two decades; they are now based in Taos Ski

Valley. The equally long-established **Taos Art School** (575/758-0350) focuses on landscape techniques, in six-day painting or photo workshops that include hiking and rafting options.

For crafts, Taos is also the place to be: **Weaving Southwest** (575/758-0433, www. weavingsouthwest.com) gives three-day workshops on Navajo frame looms; **Taos School of Metalsmithing and Lapidary Design** (575/758-0207, www.taosjewelryschool.com) covers a range of jewelry-making topics, starting with half-day sessions.

In Albuquerque, **Casa Flamenca** (505/247-0622, www.casaflamenca.org) offers classes in flamenco dance and classical Spanish guitar.

Cooking

Santa Fe School of Cooking (125 N. Guadalupe St., 505/983-4511, www.santafeschoolofcooking.com) offers day classes in contemporary Southwestern cuisine, as well as traditional Native American cooking and New Mexican standards; nice farmers market trips and restaurant walking tours are offered too.

In Dixon, **Comida de Campos** (505/852-0017, www.comidadecampos.com) offers classes on cooking in a traditional outdoor *horno,* and occasionally on clay-pot cooking, all in a beautiful farm setting.

Permaculture and Alternative Construction

In Albuquerque, **The Old School** (www. abqoldschool.com) teaches skills such as canning, quilting, and building solar phone chargers. If you're interested in New Mexico's solar architecture movement, you can take a three-day **Earthship Seminar** (575/751-0462, www.earthship.org), a crash course in building the off-the-grid rammed-earth houses that are springing up around Taos. The Earthship Biotecture organization also accepts volunteers. For more on local building styles, look into the intensive semester-long classes in adobe construction at **Northern New Mexico College** (575/581-4115, www. nnmc.edu).

FOREIGN TRAVELERS

As for any destination in the United States, check before departure whether you'll need a **visa** to enter; most European nationals do not need one.

New Mexico uses the **United States dollar**, and currency exchange is available at most banks as well as in better hotels, though the rates in the latter case will not be as good. For the best rates and convenience, withdraw cash from your home account through **automatic teller machines** (ATMs); check first, though, what fee your home bank and the ATM's bank will charge you for the transaction, including any fee for a foreign-currency transaction.

Tipping is similar to elsewhere in the country: 15 percent to cab drivers, and 15-20 percent on restaurant bills. For larger groups, often restaurants will add 18 percent or so to the bill; this is suggested, and you may refuse it or write in a lower amount if service was poor. Add $1 or so per drink when ordered at the bar; $1 or $2 to staff who handle your luggage in hotels; and $3-5 per day to housekeeping in hotels—envelopes are often left in rooms for this purpose. **Bargaining** is usually acceptable only if you're dealing directly with an artisan, and even then, it is often politely deflected. But it doesn't hurt to ask, nicely, if the quoted price is the best possible one.

Electricity is 120 volts, with a two-prong, flat-head plug, the same as Canada and Mexico.

ACCESS FOR TRAVELERS WITH DISABILITIES

Wheelchair access can be frustrating in some historic properties and on the narrower sidewalks of Santa Fe and Taos, but in most other respects, travelers with disabilities should find no more problems in New Mexico than elsewhere in the United States. Public buses are wheelchair-accessible, an increasing number of hotels have ADA-compliant rooms, and you can even get out in nature a bit on paved trails such as the Santa Fe Canyon Preserve loop and the Paseo del Bosque in Albuquerque.

If you'll be visiting a number of wilderness areas, consider the National Park Service's **Access Pass** (888/467-2757, www.nps.gov), a free lifetime pass that grants admission for the pass-holder and three adults to all national parks, national forests, and the like, as well as discounts on interpretive services, camping fees, fishing licenses, and more. Apply in person at any federally managed park or wilderness area; you must show medical documentation of blindness or permanent disability.

TRAVELING WITH CHILDREN

Though the specific prices are not listed in this guide, admission at major attractions is almost always lower for children than for adults. Your little ones will be welcome in most environments, the only exceptions being a few of the more formal restaurants in Santa Fe and Albuquerque. Kids are sure to be fascinated by ceremonial dances at the pueblos, but be prepared with distractions, because long waits are the norm. Prep children with information about American Indian culture, and brief them on the basic etiquette at dances, which applies to them as well. Kids will also enjoy river rafting (relaxing "floats" along placid sections of the Rio Grande and Rio Chama are good for younger ones). For skiing, Taos Ski Valley has a very strong program of classes for youngsters.

SENIOR TRAVELERS

Senior discounts are available at most museums and other attractions. If you'll be visiting

a number of wilderness areas, look into a **Senior Pass** ($10), a lifetime pass for people 62 and older that grants free admission for the pass-holder and three additional adults to national parks, National Forest Service lands, and many other areas, as well as a 50 percent discount on activities such as camping and boat-launching. The pass can be purchased only in person at any federally managed wilderness area; for more information, contact the **National Park Service** (888/467-2757, www.nps.gov).

Road Scholar (800/454-5768, www.road-scholar.org) runs more than 20 reasonably priced group trips in northern New Mexico, from a five-day general introduction to Santa Fe history to longer tours focusing on the legacy of Georgia O'Keeffe, for instance, or Tony Hillerman's landscape.

GAY AND LESBIAN TRAVELERS

Gay marriage was legalized in New Mexico in late 2013, but Santa Fe has been one of the major gay capitals in the United States for decades, second only to San Francisco in the per-capita rates of same-sex coupledom. There are no designated "gay-borhoods" (unless you count RainbowVision Santa Fe, a retirement community) or even particular bar scenes—instead, gay men and lesbian women are well integrated throughout town, running businesses and serving on the city council. The city's Pride parade is usually in late June, and preceded by several big events.

Albuquerque also has a decent gay scene, especially if you want to go clubbing, which is not an option in quieter Santa Fe. One big event is the annual **Zia Regional Rodeo,** sponsored by the **New Mexico Gay Rodeo Association** (505/720-3749, www.nmgra.org). It takes place every July, with all the standard rodeo events, plus goat dressing and a wild drag race.

Health and Safety

Visitors to New Mexico face several unique health concerns. First and foremost are the environmental hazards of **dehydration, sunburn,** and **altitude sickness.** The desert climate, glaring sun, and thinner atmosphere conspire to fry your skin and drain you of all moisture. (On the plus side, sweat evaporates immediately.) Apply SPF 30 sunscreen daily, even in winter, and try to drink at least a liter of water a day, whether you feel thirsty or not. (Request water in restaurants—it's usually brought only on demand, to cut down on waste.) By the time you start feeling thirsty, you're already seriously dehydrated and at risk of further bad effects: headaches, nausea, and dizziness, all of which can become full-blown, life-threatening **heatstroke** if left untreated. It doesn't even take serious exertion—just lack of water and very hot sun—to develop heatstroke, so if you're feeling at all woozy or cranky (another common symptom), head for shade and sip a Gatorade or similar electrolyte-replacement drink.

Staying hydrated also staves off the effects of the high elevation, to which most visitors will not be acclimated. The mildest reaction to being 7,000 feet or more above sea level is lethargy or light-headedness—you will probably sleep long and soundly on your first night in New Mexico. Some people do have more severe reactions, such as a piercing headache or intense nausea, especially if they engage in strenuous physical activity. Unfortunately, there's no good way to judge how your body will react, so give yourself a few days to adjust, with a light schedule and plenty of time to sleep.

More obscure hazards include **West Nile virus** (wear a DEET-based insect repellent if you're down along the river in the summer); **hantavirus,** an extremely rare pulmonary ailment transmitted by rodents; and the even rarer **bubonic plague** (aka The Black Death), the very same disease that killed millions of Europeans in the Middle Ages. Luckily, only a case or two of the plague crops up every year, and it's easily treated if diagnosed early. **Lyme disease** is almost as rare, as deer ticks do not flourish in the mountains.

If you'll be spending a lot of time hiking or camping, take precautions against **giardiasis** and other waterborne ailments by boiling your water or treating it with iodine or a SteriPen (www.steripen.com), as even the clearest mountain waterways may have been tainted by cows upstream. **Snake bites** are also a hazard in the wild, so wear boots that cover your ankles, stay on trails, and keep your hands and feet out of odd holes and cracks between rocks. Only the Western diamondback rattlesnake is aggressive when disturbed; other snakes typically will not bite if you simply back away quietly.

General **outdoor safety rules** apply: Don't hike by yourself, always register with the ranger station when heading out overnight, and let friends know where you're going and when you'll be back. Pack a good topographical map and a compass or GPS device; people manage to get lost even when hiking in the foothills, and if you're at all dehydrated or dizzy from the altitude, any disorientation can be magnified to a disastrous degree. Also pack layers of clothing, and be prepared for cold snaps and snow at higher elevations, even in the summer.

CRIME AND DRUGS

Recreational drug use is not uncommon in New Mexico—generally in a relatively benign form, with marijuana fairly widespread. (Former governor and Republican presidential candidate Gary Johnson, though no longer a user himself, has been a strenuous advocate for its legalization.) But as in much of the rural United States, crystal methamphetamine is an epidemic, and some villages in northern New Mexico have also been devastated by heroin use, with overdose deaths at a rate several hundred times higher than the national average. None of this affects travelers, except that petty theft, especially in isolated areas such as trailheads, can be an issue; always lock your car doors, and secure any valuables in the trunk. Don't leave anything enticing in view.

Drinking and driving is unfortunately still common, especially in rural areas; be particularly alert when driving at night. A distressing number of crosses along the roadside (*descansos*) mark the sites of fatal car accidents, many of which had alcohol involved.

A *descanso* marks a dangerous spot in the road.

Resources

Glossary

abierto: Spanish for "open"

acequia: irrigation ditch, specifically one regulated by the traditional Spanish method, maintained by a *mayordomo,* or "ditch boss," who oversees how much water each shareholder receives

adobe: building material of sun-dried bricks made of a mix of mud, sand, clay, and straw

arroyo: stream or dry gully where mountain runoff occasionally flows

asado: stew (usually pork) with red-chile sauce

atrio: churchyard between the boundary wall and the church entrance, usually used as a cemetery

bizcochito: anise-laced shortbread, traditionally made with lard

bosque: Spanish for "forest," specifically the cottonwoods and trees along a river

bulto: three-dimensional wood carving, typically of a saint

caldera: basin or crater formed by a collapsed volcano

canal: water drain from a flat roof; pl. *canales*

carne adovada: pork chunks marinated in red chile, then braised; meatier and dryer than *asado*

cerrado: Spanish for "closed"

chicharrón: fried pork skin, usually with a layer of meat still attached

chile: not to be confused with Texas chili, Cincinnati chili, or any other American concoction; refers to the fruit of the chile plant itself, eaten green (picked unripe and then roasted) or red (ripened and dried)

colcha: style of blanket, in which loom-woven wool is embellished with long strands of wool embroidery

concha belt: belt made of stamped, carved silver medallions; "concha" is Spanish for "shell"; also concho

convento: residential compound adjoining a mission church

enchilada: corn tortilla dipped in chile sauce, filled with cheese or meat, and topped with more chile; can be served either rolled or flat (stacked in layers)

farolito: in Santa Fe and Taos, a luminaria

GCCB: common abbreviation for green-chile cheeseburger

genízaro: during Spanish colonial times, a detribalized Indian (usually due to having been taken as a slave) who lived with Spaniards and followed Catholic tradition

heishi: fine disk-shaped beads carved from shells

horno: traditional dome-shaped adobe oven

jerga: Spanish-style wool blanket or rug, loosely woven and barely decorated, meant for daily use

kachina: ancestral spirit of the Pueblo people as well as the carved figurine representing the spirit; also spelled "katsina"

kiva: sacred ceremonial space in a pueblo, at least partially underground and entered by a hole in the ceiling

latillas: thin saplings cut and laid across vigas to make a solid ceiling

lowrider: elaborately painted and customized car with hydraulic lifts

luminaria: in Albuquerque, lantern made of a sand-filled paper bag with a votive candle set inside; in Santa Fe and Taos, refers to small bonfires lit during the Christmas season

menudo: tripe soup, said to be good for curing a hangover

morada: meeting space of the Penitente brotherhood

nicho: small niche in an adobe wall, usually meant to hold a santo

Penitente: member of a long-established Catholic brotherhood in northern New Mexico

petroglyph: rock carving

pictograph: painting on a rock surface

piñon: any of several fragrant varieties of pine tree that grow in New Mexico

portal: the covered sidewalk area in front of a traditional adobe structure; pl. *portales*

posole: stew of hulled corn (hominy), pork, and a little chile, either green or red

pueblo: Spanish for "village," referring to the various communities of American Indians settled in the Rio Grande Valley, as well as the larger land area owned by the community (preferable to the term "reservation"); also, capitalized, the people themselves, though they speak several different languages

rajas: rough-hewn slats laid over vigas to form a ceiling; also, strips of roasted chile

ramada: simple structure built of four sapling posts and topped with additional saplings laid flat to form a shade structure and a place to hang things to dry

reredos: altar screen, usually elaborately painted or carved with various portraits of Christ and the saints

retablo: flat portrait of a saint, painted or carved in low relief, usually on wood

ristra: string of dried red chiles

santero/santera: craftsperson who produces santos

santo: portrait of a saint, either flat (a *retablo*) or three-dimensional (a *bulto*)

sipapu: hole in the floor of a kiva, signifying the passage to the spirit world

sopaipilla: square of puffed fried dough, served with the main meal for wiping up sauces and with honey for dessert

tamale: corn husk filled with masa (hominy paste) and a dab of meat, vegetables, or cheese, then steamed; usually made in large quantities for holidays

terrón: building material of bricks cut out of sod and dried in the sun, similar to adobe, but less common

Tewa: language spoken by the majority of Pueblo Indians; others in the Rio Grande Valley speak Tiwa, Towa, and Keresan

torreón: round defensive tower built in Spanish colonial times

vato: cool Chicano, usually driving a lowrider

viga: ceiling beam made of a single tree trunk

zaguán: long central hallway

Suggested Reading

ART AND CULTURE

Clark, Willard. *Remembering Santa Fe.* Layton, UT: Gibbs Smith, 2004. A small hardback edition of selections from the Boston artist who stopped off in Santa Fe in 1928. He stayed to learn printmaking and produce this series of etchings depicting city life.

Gandert, Miguel. *Nuevo México Profundo: Rituals of an Indo-Hispanic Homeland.* Santa Fe: Museum of New Mexico Press, 2000. Like Enrique Lamadrid's work, but with a slightly broader scope. There's an attempt at scholarly analysis in the text, but it's really about the 130 beautiful photographs.

Lamadrid, Enrique. *Hermanitos Comanchitos: Indo-Hispano Rituals of Captivity and Redemption.* Albuquerque: University of New Mexico Press, 2003. Fascinating documentation, in descriptive prose and rich black-and-white photos, of the traditional Spanish dances of northern New Mexico, such as Los Comanches and Los Matachines.

Lummis, Charles F. *A Tramp Across the Continent*. Lincoln: University of Nebraska Press, 1982. In 1884, fledgling journalist Lummis decided to walk from Cincinnati to his new job in Los Angeles; this book chronicles his trip. The sections on New Mexico shine, and Lummis was so entranced that he later moved to the territory. He was the first to write stories about the Penitente brotherhood in the national press.

Padilla, Carmella, and Juan Estevan Arellano. *Low 'n Slow: Lowriding in New Mexico*. Santa Fe: Museum of New Mexico Press, 1999. Lovingly lurid color photographs by Jack Parsons are the centerpiece of this book, which pays tribute to New Mexico's Latino car culture—an art form that has even landed a lowrider from Chimayó in the Smithsonian.

Parhad, Elisa. *New Mexico: A Guide for the Eyes*. Los Angeles: EyeMuse Books, 2009. Informative short essays on the distinctive things you see in New Mexico and then wonder what the backstory is: concha belts, beat-up pickup trucks, blue sky. The richly illustrated book makes good pre-trip reading or a souvenir when you return.

Price, Roberta. *Across the Great Divide: A Photo Chronicle of the Counterculture*. Albuquerque: University of New Mexico Press, 2010. Documentary photographer Price "went native" with a Colorado commune in the 1960s and visited several groups in New Mexico. She also wrote the narrative *Huerfano: A Memoir of Life in the Counterculture* (Amherst: University of Massachusetts Press, 2004).

Price, V. B. *Albuquerque: A City at the End of the World*. Albuquerque: University of New Mexico Press, 2003. Journalist and poet Price writes a travel guide to New Mexico's biggest metropolis but disguises it as a discourse on urban theory, recommending his favorite spots in the context of the city's unique position and growth processes. Black-and-white photographs by Kirk Gittings highlight the stark landscape.

Robinson, Roxana. *Georgia O'Keeffe: A Life*. Lebanon, NH: University Press of New England, 1998. A strong and intimate biography, focusing on the celebrated painter's role as a protofeminist and her difficult relationships.

FOOD

Feucht, Andrea. *Food Lovers' Guide to Santa Fe, Albuquerque & Taos*. Guilford, CT: Globe Pequot, 2012. A good companion for adventurous eaters, with especially good coverage of Albuquerque's more obscure ethnic restaurants. The author maintains an update website (www.foodloversnm.com).

Frank, Lois Ellen. *Foods of the Southwest Indian Nations*. Berkeley, CA: Ten Speed Press, 2002. Beautiful photographs are a highlight of this thorough documentation of a little-covered cuisine. They help make an ancient culinary tradition accessible and modern without subjecting it to a heavy-handed fusion treatment. For good reason, it earned a James Beard Award.

Kagel, Katharine. *Cooking with Café Pasqual's: Recipes from Santa Fe's Renowned Corner Cafe*. Berkeley, CA: Ten Speed Press, 2006. Re-create your best meals from the legendary restaurant that set the standard for Santa Fe fusion cooking. Chef Kagel is a charming contrarian too, which makes for great reading.

HISTORY

Childs, Craig. *House of Rain: Tracking a Vanished Civilization Across the American Southwest.* New York: Little, Brown, 2007. The story of the Ancestral Puebloans (Anasazi), as told by a curious naturalist, becomes less a solution to an archaeological puzzle than a meditation of why we romanticize "lost" civilizations. His more recent book, *Finders Keepers: A Tale of Archaeological Plunder and Possession* (Little, Brown, 2010), takes the drama to the academy, with tales of scholarly intrigue.

Held, E. B. *A Spy's Guide to Santa Fe and Albuquerque.* Albuquerque: University of New Mexico Press, 2011. A former CIA agent reveals nefarious Cold War intrigue—fascinating details, if not so grippingly told.

Hordes, Stanley. *To the End of the Earth: A History of the Crypto-Jews of New Mexico.* New York: Columbia University Press, 2008. An exhaustive but intriguing account of the Jewish families who fled the Inquisition and lived in the Southwest as Catholic converts. The communities, some still practicing distinctly Jewish rituals, came to light only a few decades ago.

Horgan, Paul. *Great River.* Middletown, CT: Wesleyan University Press, 1991. Two enormous tomes (*Vol. 1: The Indians and Spain* and *Vol. 2: Mexico and the United States*) won the Pulitzer Prize for history. They're packed with drama, on a base of meticulous analysis of primary sources.

Martinez, Esther. *My Life in San Juan Pueblo.* Champaign: University of Illinois Press, 2004. Born in 1912, Martinez has a lot of stories to tell. This free-flowing book incorporates her memories with larger pueblo folklore, and a CD with recordings of some of her stories is included.

Poling-Kempes, Lesley. *Valley of Shining Stone: The Story of Abiquiu.* Tucson: University of Arizona Press, 1997. Georgia O'Keeffe fans will like the personal stories of those in her circle in the 1930s, while historians will appreciate the detailed, linear second half of the book, about the transformation of this remote valley into an artists' haven.

Sides, Hampton. *Blood and Thunder: An Epic of the American West.* New York: Doubleday, 2006. Working from the story of Kit Carson and the campaign against the Navajo, including the Long Walk, Sides tells the gripping story of the entire American West. He's an excellent storyteller, and the 480 pages flow by in a rush of land grabs, battles on horseback, and brutality on all sides.

Simmons, Marc. *New Mexico: An Interpretive History.* Albuquerque: University of New Mexico Press, 1988. The state's historian laureate presents an easy, concise overview of the major historical events. Also look into his more specialized titles, such as *The Last Conquistador: Juan de Oñate and the Settling of the Far Southwest* (Norman: University of Oklahoma Press, 1993).

Smith, Mike. *Towns of the Sandia Mountains.* Charleston, SC: Arcadia, 2006. This slim volume of vintage photographs and juicy stories in extended captions is about a very specific region, but it could tell the story of much of New Mexico in its shift to modernity.

Usner, Donald J. *Sabino's Map: Life in Chimayó's Old Plaza.* Santa Fe: Museum of New Mexico Press, 1995. A balanced and gracefully written history of the author's hometown, illustrated with fond photos of all the craggy-faced characters involved. Usner's follow-up, *Benigna's Chimayo: Cuentos from the Old Plaza* (Santa Fe: Museum of New Mexico Press, 2001) relates his grandmother's story of the village and her trove of folktales.

LITERATURE AND MEMOIR

Anaya, Rudolfo. *Bless Me, Ultima*. New York: Warner, 1994. Anaya's story of a young boy coming of age in New Mexico in the 1940s is beautifully told. The book, first published in 1973, launched Anaya into his role as Chicano literary hero; his later books, such as *Alburquerque* (1992), are not quite so touching, but they have a lot of historical and ethnic detail.

Blume, Judy. *Tiger Eyes*. New York: Delacorte, 2010. A young girl with family troubles relocates to Los Alamos, giving a great teen's-eye view on the landscape of New Mexico.

Goodman, Tanya Ward. *Leaving Tinkertown*. Albuquerque: University of New Mexico Press, 2013. A poignant memoir of growing up in the wondrous folk-art assemblage outside Albuquerque. The author's father, Ross Ward, died of early-onset Alzheimer's disease, and this book logs that medical tale, unflinchingly, alongside the larger-than-life artist's own story.

Hillerman, Tony. *Skinwalkers*. New York: HarperTorch, 1990. Hillerman's breakout detective novel, set on the Navajo Nation, weaves a fascinating amount of lore into the plot—which comes in handy when Tribal Affairs police Joe Leaphorn and Jim Chee investigate homicides. Hillerman spun Leaphorn and Chee into a successful franchise, and all of the books show the same cultural depth.

Pillsbury, Dorothy. *Roots in Adobe*. Santa Fe: Lightning Tree Press, 1983. Pillsbury's charming stories capture the strangeness and warmth of Santa Fe culture in the 1940s. The author tells hilarious stories of settling into her little home and the characters she meets.

Quade, Kirstin Valdez. *Night at the Fiestas*. New York: W. W. Norton, 2015. Quade, who grew up in New Mexico, sets many of the short stories in this collection there, in tiny Hispano towns, amid the most intense belief and ritual. A great mix of cultural detail and poignant characters.

Silko, Leslie Marmon. *Ceremony*. New York: Penguin, 1988. Silko's classic novel about the impact of the atomic bomb on Native Americans' worldview (and that of all Americans) is brutal, beautiful, and bleak.

NATURE AND THE ENVIRONMENT

Coltrin, Mike. *Sandia Mountain Hiking Guide*. Albuquerque: University of New Mexico Press, 2005. A print version of Coltrin's meticulously maintained website (www.sandiahiking.com), with thorough trail descriptions, GPS coordinates, and a foldout map of the east and west slopes of the mountain.

Julyan, Robert, and Mary Stuever, eds. *Field Guide to the Sandia Mountains*. Albuquerque: University of New Mexico Press, 2005. A thorough guide illustrated with color photographs, detailing birds, animals, plants, even insects of the Sandias. Most of it applies to the Santa Fe area too.

Kricher, John. *A Field Guide to Rocky Mountain and Southwest Forests*. New York: Houghton Mifflin Harcourt, 2003. A Peterson Field Guide, covering both flora and fauna: trees, birds, mammals, you name it. It's illustrated with both color photos and drawings. It's not encyclopedic, but it's a great basic reference. Peterson guides are also available for narrower categories such as reptiles and amphibians or butterflies.

McFarland, Casey, and S. David Scott. *Bird Feathers: A Guide to North American Species*. Mechanicsburg, PA: Stackpole Books, 2010. While not New Mexico-specific, it is the only guide of its kind, and its authors grew up in the state and know the birdlife well. Great for serious birders and curious hikers, with detailed photographs.

Nichols, John. *On the Mesa.* Layton, Utah: Gibbs Smith, 2005. Best known for his comic novel *The Milagro Beanfield War*, Nichols here writes some visionary nonfiction about traditional life and the environment near his home in Taos.

Price, V. B. *The Orphaned Land: New Mexico's Environment Since the Manhattan Project.* Albuquerque: University of New Mexico Press, 2011. Journalist Price examines New Mexico's droughts and other trials—in the same vein as Reisner's *Cadillac Desert.*

Reisner, Marc. *Cadillac Desert: The American West and Its Disappearing Water.* New York: Penguin, 1993. Not specifically about New Mexico, but an excellent analysis of the Southwest's water shortage and how the U.S. government's dam-building projects exacerbated it. Apocalyptic, sarcastic, and totally compelling.

Sibley, David Allen. *The Sibley Field Guide to Birds of Western North America.* New York: Knopf, 2003. The New Mexican birder's book of choice, with 810 species listed, about 4,600 color illustrations, and a handy compact format. Generally beats out Peterson's otherwise respectable series.

Tekiela, Stan. *Birds of New Mexico: Field Guide.* Cambridge, MN: Adventure Publications, 2003. A great book for beginning birders or curious visitors, with 140 of the state's most common species listed, many illustrated with photographs.

Internet Resources

TRAVEL INFORMATION

Albuquerque Convention and Visitors Bureau
www.visitalbuquerque.org
The official intro to the city and surrounding areas, with events listings as well as hotel-booking services.

Fiber Arts Trails
www.nmfiberarts.org
A guide to the wool-loving state via the work of ranchers and artisans, both traditional and modern. The North Central route covers Albuquerque, Santa Fe, and Taos.

Hiking in the Sandia Mountains
www.sandiahiking.com
Mike Coltrin hiked every trail in the Sandias over the course of a year, covering about 250 miles. He detailed each hike, complete with GPS references, here.

New Mexico Board of Tourism
www.newmexico.org
The best of the official sites, this one has thorough maps, suggested itineraries, and background info like weather. Includes the Green Chile Cheeseburger Trail and the Breakfast Burrito Byway, as well as routes based on Hollywood filming locations, among other suggested itineraries.

Public Lands Information Center
www.publiclands.org
Buy USGS, Forest Service, and other topographical maps online from the Bureau of Land Management's well-organized website. Good stock of nature guides and other travel books too.

Santa Fe Convention and Visitors Bureau
www.santafe.org
Near-exhaustive listings of tourist attractions and services on this slickly produced site.

Santa Fe Creative
www.santafecreativetourism.org
The Santa Fe Arts Commission's listings of arts classes, workshops, and other special events in this creative hub.

Taos Vacation Guide
www.taos.org
A thorough directory and events listings.

Visit Los Alamos
www.visitlosalamos.org
Colorful and helpfully arranged with suggestions based on the time you have available.

NEWS AND CULTURE

Albuquerque Journal
www.abqjournal.com
The state's largest newspaper is available free online after answering survey questions.

Alibi
www.alibi.com
This free weekly has been cracking wise since 1992, taking a critical look at politics and culture. Its annual "Best of Burque" guide is usually reliable.

Chasing Santa Fe
www.chasingsantafe.blogspot.com
The glamorous Santa Fe lifestyle, lovingly documented: local chefs, new shops, and fashion spotting.

Duke City Fix
www.dukecityfix.com
This Albuquerque-centric discussion forum covers everything from politics to gossip about the restaurant scene.

New Mexico Magazine
www.nmmagazine.com
Not everything from the print edition of the excellent state magazine is online, but it's rounded out with video, a dedicated food blog, and a general travel guide.

New Mexico Politics with Joe Monahan
www.joemonahan.com
Analyst Monahan's obsessive, snarky blog charts the circus that is state politics.

Santa Fe New Mexican
www.santafenewmexican.com
Santa Fe's main newspaper. The gossip column *El Mitote* documents celebs in Santa Fe, and the Roundhouse Roundup does roughly the same—but with politicians.

Santa Fe Reporter
www.sfreporter.com
Santa Fe's free weekly is politically sharp and often funny. Get opinionated reviews and news analysis here.

Smithsonian Folkways
www.folkways.si.edu
Prep for your road trip at this enormous online music archive, which has a number of traditional treasures from the state, including the excellent *Music of New Mexico: Hispanic Traditions* and *New Mexico: Native American Traditions*.

Taos News
www.taosnews.com
The town paper is a weekly, but its website has daily updates and an events calendar.

Index

List of Maps

Photo Credits

Acknowledgments

Thanks first and foremost to the readers of previous editions who have taken the time to write with tips, corrections, and compliments. It is always encouraging to know the book is in such good hands.

I'm also grateful to Richard Todd, Jesse Wood, Casey McFarland, and Shannon at the Monte Carlo, for recommendations and good shared meals, and to Beverly McFarland for a home base.

Finally, thanks to the team at Avalon Travel—especially Sabrina Young, Kat Bennett, and Elizabeth Jang—for making the book read smoothly and look fantastic.

...and *hasta la vista!*

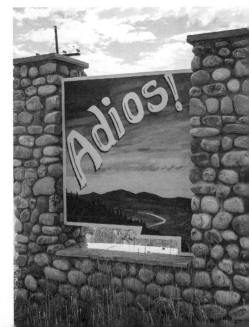

MAP SYMBOLS

▦ Expressway	○ City/Town	✕ Airport	⚲ Golf Course
▬ Primary Road	◉ State Capital	✗ Airfield	🅿 Parking Area
▭ Secondary Road	◉ National Capital	▲ Mountain	▰ Archaeological Site
▭ ▭ Unpaved Road	★ Point of Interest	✚ Unique Natural Feature	⌂ Church
▬ Feature Trail	• Accommodation		⛽ Gas Station
- - - Other Trail	▼ Restaurant/Bar	🌿 Waterfall	⬭ Glacier
⋯ Ferry	▲ Park	⬭ Mangrove
▦ Pedestrian Walkway	■ Other Location	🏕 Trailhead	⬭ Reef
▥ Stairs	⋀ Campground	⛷ Skiing Area	▱ Swamp

CONVERSION TABLES

$°C = (°F - 32) / 1.8$

$°F = (°C \times 1.8) + 32$

1 inch = 2.54 centimeters (cm)
1 foot = 0.304 meters (m)
1 yard = 0.914 meters
1 mile = 1.6093 kilometers (km)
1 km = 0.6214 miles
1 fathom = 1.8288 m
1 chain = 20.1168 m
1 furlong = 201.168 m
1 acre = 0.4047 hectares
1 sq km = 100 hectares
1 sq mile = 2.59 square km
1 ounce = 28.35 grams
1 pound = 0.4536 kilograms
1 short ton = 0.90718 metric ton
1 short ton = 2,000 pounds
1 long ton = 1.016 metric tons
1 long ton = 2,240 pounds
1 metric ton = 1,000 kilograms
1 quart = 0.94635 liters
1 US gallon = 3.7854 liters
1 Imperial gallon = 4.5459 liters
1 nautical mile = 1.852 km

DA 5/15 V

MOON SANTA FE, TAOS & ALBUQUERQUE
Avalon Travel
a member of the Perseus Books Group
1700 Fourth Street
Berkeley, CA 94710, USA
www.moon.com

Editor: Sabrina Young
Series Manager: Kathryn Ettinger
Copy Editor: Ashley Benning
Production and Graphics Coordinators:
  Kathryn Osgood, Elizabeth Jang
Cover Design: Faceout Studios, Charles Brock
Moon Logo: Tim McGrath
Map Editor: Kat Bennett
Cartographers: Brian Shotwell, Stephanie Poulain
Proofreader: Jamie Leigh Real
Indexer: Greg Jewett

ISBN-13: 978-1-63121-021-1
ISSN: 1557-7163

Printing History
1st Edition — 2006
4th Edition — May 2015
5 4 3 2 1

Text © 2015 by Zora O'Neill
Maps © 2015 by Avalon Travel.
All rights reserved.

KEEPING CURRENT

If you have a favorite gem you'd like to see included in the next edition, or see anything that needs updating, clarification, or correction, please drop us a line. Send your comments via email to feedback@moon.com, or use the address above.